Acknowledgements

There are many parallels between the socio-cultural status of minority languages in Europe which are worth investigating. As part of its programme *Which languages for Europe?*, the European Cultural Foundation (an international non-profit, non-governmental organization established in Amsterdam), together with Babylon (Tilburg University) and the Fryske Akademy (Leeuwarden) organized a seminar to bring together researchers and policy makers on both regional and immigrant minority languages. This book is the outcome of that seminar, organized in Oegstgeest, the Netherlands, from 28-30 January, 2000. The seminar was the first time experts representing such a broad spectrum of interest were brought together. The aim was to reflect upon a more integrated approach to research on minority languages and upon policy making on their behalf. The similarities and differences between the different language groups as well as between the different nation-states in which they live were brought to the fore. The spread, status and vitality of both regional and immigrant minority languages were compared from the perspectives of demography, sociolinguistics and education. This book comes at a time that language policy is becoming an increasingly important topic in the public debate on European integration. At the initiative of the Council of Europe and the European Union, the year 2001 has been designated as the European Year of Languages.

We want to thank the European Cultural Foundation for its interest and support in establishing a platform to exchange experiences and ideas in this domain at an international level. The European Cultural Foundation takes a special interest in language issues because of its commitment to supporting cultural diversity and intercultural dialogue. The cultural aspect of European integration has for a long time remained in the background and it is therefore all the more important to now give it a more prominent place in the current debate. The organization of the seminar in Oegstgeest and the publication of this volume would not have been possible without the financial support of the European Cultural Foundation, the Dutch Ministry of Education, Culture and Sciences, and Globus, Institute for Globalization and Sustainable Development at Tilburg University.

Special and personal thanks go to Nicki Bos (European Cultural Foundation, Amsterdam) and Carine Zebedee (Babylon, Tilburg University) for their professional commitment and support in the processes of preparing and organizing the seminar and preparing and editing this volume respectively. We hope that the book will serve as an extension of the seminar in stimulating both research and policies on both regional and immigrant minority languages, because they are such an important part of Europe's multicultural heritage and future.

Guus Extra
Durk Gorter

MULTILINGUAL MATTERS 118
Series Editor: John Edwards

44 0533076 4

 University of

The Other Languages of Europe

Demographic, Sociolinguistic and Educational Perspectives

Edited by
Guus Extra and Durk Gorter

EUROPEAN CULTURAL FOUNDATION

FONDATION
EUROPÉENNE DE LA
CULTURE

MULTILINGUAL MATTERS LTD
Clevedon • Buffalo • Toronto • Sydney

Library of Congress Cataloging in Publication Data
The Other Languages of Europe: Demographic, Sociolinguistic and
Educational Perspectives/Edited by Guus Extra and Durk Gorter.
Multilingual Matters.
Includes bibliographical references and index.
1. Linguistic minorities–Europe. 2. Europe–Languages. I. Extra, Guus.
II. Gorter, D. (Durk). III. Multilingual Matters (Series).
P119.315.O87 2001
408'.6'93094–dc21   00-063823

British Library Cataloguing in Publication Data
A catalogue entry for this book is available from the British Library.

ISBN 1-85359-510-1 (hbk)
ISBN 1-85359-509-8 (pbk)

Multilingual Matters Ltd
UK: Frankfurt Lodge, Clevedon Hall, Victoria Road, Clevedon BS21 7HH.
USA: UTP, 2250 Military Road, Tonawanda, NY 14150, USA.
Canada: UTP, 5201 Dufferin Street, North York, Ontario M3H 5T8, Canada.
Australia: P.O. Box 586, Artarmon, NSW, Australia.

Printed and bound in Great Britain by the Cromwell Press Ltd.

Contents

Part III   Outlook from abroad

Appendices

Preface

Which languages for Europe? This question is still a long way from being answered. Some prefer to ask the question in a singular form as they already have an easy answer to hand which favours Euro-English. Others, and they are the majority, reject this answer. Europe is becoming more and more complex as are the solutions to its problems.

The debate deepens. It revolves around an epicentre, the power of languages. There are plenty of examples in daily life in Europe. Let me mention just a few: a national delegation that sits down at the negotiating table only if its language is recognized as an official language of communication; a representative of a South-Eastern European country who remains silent because he is insufficiently able to express himself in English, whilst another dominates all the discussions thanks to his mother tongue which is... English; a salesman who reports that the enthusiasm of Dutchmen for foreign languages is based on their desire to sell and to stay one step ahead of their business partners; a young lady, representative of an association of Turkish youngsters, who realizes her luck at having access to two cultures and two languages which she feels makes her superior to 'monoculturals' and 'monolinguals'.

The Age of Enlightment discovered the unifying power of language in terms of *state is language*. The following centuries propagated its identifying power in terms of *nation is language*. At the turn of the century, what will be its power in the new multicultural Europe? Will it differentiate or discriminate? Or shall we succeed in bringing out a new motto in terms of *Europe is languages*?

No text on cultural policy leaves out the fundamental principle of respect for cultural diversity. And diversity of cultures by implication means diversity of languages. Whoever rejects a language, denies a culture and vice versa. This implication is barely recognized, so it seems, and cultural policies do not take it into account. The European Union supports regional minority languages but not immigrant minority languages. Is recognition of cultural diversity limited by this attitude?

The debate also widens. In the European Union, the debate on languages will open itself to two new elements. The first element is enlargement. By integrating just six countries - Cyprus, the Czech

Republic, Estonia, Hungary, Poland and Slovenia - new majority and minority languages will enter the Union. The second element is the development of our cities as centres of multiculturalism where immigrant languages will flourish in all their diversity. Mutual understanding and communication will become an important factor of social solidarity here.

Should not linguistic policies at the local, national and European level be urgently reviewed against this background?

Rüdiger Stephan
Secretary-General of the European Cultural Foundation

Comparative perspectives on regional and immigrant minority languages in multicultural Europe

GUUS EXTRA
DURK GORTER

In this introductory chapter we will address the three perspectives referred to in the subtitle of this Volume, i.e. demographic, sociolinguistic and educational perspectives on the *other* languages of Europe, in terms of both regional and immigrant minority languages. Apart from these three perspectives, we will open this chapter with a discussion of the rationale of this Volume and the semantics of our field of interest. The chapter will be concluded with an outline of the contents of the Volume.

Rationale and semantics

Europe has a rich diversity of languages. This fact is usually illustrated by reference to the eleven official languages of the European Union (henceforward EU). However, there are many more languages spoken by the inhabitants of Europe. Examples of such languages are Welsh and Basque, or Arabic and Turkish. These languages are usually referred to as 'minority languages', even when in Europe as a whole there is not one majority language because all languages are spoken by a numerical minority. The title of the present Volume brings to mind, of course, the well-known study of the Linguistic Minorities Project from the mid-eighties: *The Other Languages of England*. In that study, the following explanation was given of its title: 'The other languages of England are all those languages apart from English that are ignored in public, official activities in England' (LMP 1985: xiv). We extend this title in grateful memory to this *opus magnum*. In our case the 'other' languages of Europe are all those languages apart from the eleven official languages that are ignored in public and official activities of the EU. An important issue which remains is how to refer to the different categories of languages we are dealing with. There is no easy or final solution. In the end, we have opted in this chapter for 'regional minority languages' and 'immigrant minority languages', henceforward referred to as RM and IM languages respectively.

RM and IM languages have much in common, much more than is usually thought. On their sociolinguistic, educational and political agenda's we find issues such as their actual spread, their domestic and public vitality, the processes and determinants of language maintenance versus language shift towards majority languages, the relationship between language, ethnicity and identity, and the status of minority languages in schools, in particular in the compulsory stages of primary and secondary education. Our subtitle thus refers to the three dimensions (demographic, sociolinguistic and educational perspectives) which we have drawn into comparison. First of all, it is important to know about the size of the groups, vis-a-vis the total population. We are dealing with languages that have - taken together- a substantial number of mother tongue speakers. Statistics about these languages, however, are scarce, and where such statistics are available they are based upon different criteria for counting numbers of speakers (see below). In the second place, we want to find out more about the sociolinguistic status of different language groups. The way they are treated by society differs from language to language and from state to state. Some of them have obtained extended legal protection and language policies, whereas for others there are no legal arrangements at all, not even the bare recognition of their existence (as is the case for Romani in a number of states). Finally, we focus on education as the social institution which is very important for the continued existence of these languages. Whether and how these languages are taught in schools differs widely within and between the nation-states of Europe. Various bilingual or multilingual models have been developed over the past decades and applied with more or less success. Discovering the differences and similarities in educational opportunities is an important part of the exercise of confronting the different minority languages.

The origin of most RM languages as *minority* languages lies in the 19th century, when, during the processes of state-formation in Europe, they found themselves excluded from the state level, in particular from general education. RM languages missed the boat, so to speak, and did not become official languages of the nation-states which were then established. Centralizing tendencies and an ideology of 'one language - one state' have threatened the continued existence of RM languages. The greatest threat to RM languages, however, is lack of intergenerational transmission. When parents give up speaking the ancestral language to their children it becomes almost impossible to reverse the ensuing language shift. In addition to parents, education can be a major factor in the maintenance and promotion of a minority language. For most RM languages some kind of educational provisions have been established in an attempt at reversing ongoing language shift. Only in the last few decades some of these RM languages have become relatively well protected in legal terms, as well as by affirmative educational policies and programmes, both at the level of various nation-states and at the level of the EU. In practice, however, such provisions still leave much to be desired.

Over the centuries there have always been speakers of IM languages in Europe, but they have only recently emerged as community languages spoken on a wide scale in North-Western Europe, due to intensified processes of immigration and minorization. Turkish and Arabic are good examples of so-called 'non-European' languages that are spoken and learned by millions of inhabitants of the member states of the EU. Although IM languages are often conceived and transmitted as core values by IM language groups, they are much less protected than RM languages by affirmative action and legal measures in e.g. education. In fact, the learning and certainly the teaching of IM languages are often seen by speakers of dominant languages and by policy makers as obstacles to integration. At the European level, guidelines and directives regarding IM languages are rather scant and outdated.

Despite the possibilities and challenges of comparing the status of RM and IM languages, amazingly few connections have been made in the sociolinguistic, educational and political domain. The Linguistic Minorities Project, which was restricted to England and did not cover all of Britain, made an observation which still applies to the situation today: 'The Project has been struck by how little contact there still is between researchers and practitioners working in bilingual areas and school systems, even between England and Wales. Many of the newer minorities in England could benefit from the Welsh experience and expertise' (LMP, 1985: 12). In our opinion, little has improved over the past fifteen years, and contacts between researchers and policy makers working with different types of minority groups are still scarce. Integral publications which focus on both types of minority languages are rare; an exception is the work by Alladina and Edwards (1991), although RM and IM languages are dealt with in two separate and unrelated volumes. Overall, we see disjointed research paradigms and circles of researchers which have very little or no contact, although they could learn a lot from each other.

Against this background, the objective of this Volume is to compare the status of RM and IM languages in Europe from the three already mentioned perspectives. As yet, we are lacking a common referential framework for the languages under discussion. As all of these RM and IM languages are spoken by different language communities and not at state-wide levels, it may seem logical to refer to them as community languages, thus contrasting them with the official languages of nation-states. However, the designation 'community languages' as title of this Volume would at least lead to surface confusion because it is already in use to refer to the official languages of the EU. In that sense the designation 'community languages' is occupied territory. From an inventory of the different terms in use (see also throughout this Volume) we learn that there are no standardized designations. Table 1 gives a non-exhaustive overview of the nomenclature of the field. As is clear from Table 1, the utilized terminology is variable and in flux.

Imagine a European citizen who has never been abroad and travels to San Francisco for the first time in life, walks around downtown for a week, gets an impression of the Chinese community and food, happens to be invited for dinner by a Chinese family, and asks the host at the dinner table: 'How many foreigners live in San Francisco?', in this way referring to the many Asian, Latin and other non-Anglo Americans (s)he has seen during that week. Now, two things might happen: if the guest's English is poor, the Chinese host might leave this European reference to ethnocultural diversity unnoticed and go on with the conversation; if the guest's English is good, however, the Chinese host might interrupt the dinner and charge his guest with discrimination.

In the European public discourse on IM groups, two major character-istics emerge (see also Extra & Verhoeven, 1998): IM groups are often referred to as *foreigners* (*étrangers, Ausländer*) and as being in need of *integration*. First of all, it is common practice to refer to IM groups in terms of *non-national* residents and to their languages in terms of *non-territorial, non-regional, non-indigenous* or *non-European* languages. The call for integration is in sharp contrast with the language of exclusion. This conceptual exclusion rather than inclusion in the European public discourse derives from a restrictive interpretation of the notions of citizenship and nationality. From a historical point of view, such notions are commonly shaped by a constitutional *ius sanguinis* (law of the blood)

Table 1 Nomenclature of the field

Reference to IM groups • non-national residents • foreigners, étrangers, Ausländer • (im)migrants • new Xmen (e.g. new Dutchmen) • ethnic/cultural/ethnocultural minorities • linguistic minorities • allochthones, allophones • non-English speaking (NES) residents (in particular in the USA) • anderstaligen (Dutch: those who speak other languages) *
Reference to RM and IM languages • community languages (cf. in Europe vs. Australia) • anchestral/heritage languages • national/historical/regional/indigenous minority languages vs. • non-territorial/non-regional/non-indigenous/non-European minority lang. • autochthonous vs. allochthonous minority languages • lesser used/less widely used/les widely taught languages ** • stateless/diaspora languages (in particular used for Romani) • languages other than English (LOTE: common concept in Australia)
Reference to RM and IM language teaching • community language teaching (CLT) • mother tongue teaching (MTT) • home language instruction (HLI) • regional minority language instruction (RMLI) vs. • immigrant minority language instruction (IMLI) • enseignement des langues et cultures d'origine (ELCO: in French elementary schools) • enseignement des langues vivantes (ELV: in French secondary schools) • Muttersprachlicher Unterricht (MSU) • Herkunftssprachlicher Unterricht (HSU)

*   Cf. also the Dutch concept of *andersdenkenden* (those who think differently) for reference to non-Christians.
**   The concept of lesser used languages has been adopted at the European Union level; the European Bureau for Lesser Used Languages (EBLUL), established in Brussels and Dublin, speaks and acts on behalf of 'the autochthonous regional and minority' languages of the EU'.

in terms of which nationality derives from parental origins, in contrast to *ius solis* (law of the ground) in terms of which nationality derives from the country of birth. When European emigrants left their continent in the past and colonized countries abroad, they legitimized their claim to citizenship by spelling out *ius solis* in the constitutions of these countries of settlement. Good examples of this strategy can be found in English-dominant immigration countries like the USA, Canada, Australia and South Africa. In establishing the constitutions of these (sub)continents, no consultation took place with native inhabitants, such as Indians, Inuit, Aboriginals and Zulus respectively. At home, however, Europeans predominantly upheld *ius sanguinis* in their constitutions and/or perceptions of nationality and citizenship, in spite of the growing numbers of IM groups who strive for an equal status as citizens in a new multicultural European context.

A second major characteristic of the European public discourse on IM groups is the focus on *integration*. This notion is both popular and vague, and it may actually refer to a whole spectrum of underlying concepts that vary over space and time (cf. Kruyt and Niessen, 1997 for a comparative study of the notion of integration in five EU countries since the early seventies). The extremes of the spectrum range from assimilation to multiculturalism. The concept of assimilation is based on the premise that cultural differences between IM groups and established majority groups should and will disappear over time in a society which is proclaimed to be culturally homogeneous. On the other side of the spectrum, the concept of multiculturalism is based on the premise that such differences are an asset to a pluralist society which actually promotes cultural diversity in terms of new resources and opportunities. While the concept of assimilation focuses on unilateral tasks of *newcomers*, the concept of multiculturalism focuses on multilateral tasks for *all* inhabitants in demographically changing societies (cf. Cohn Bendit & Schmid, 1992). In practice, established majority groups often make strong demands on IM groups for integration in terms of assimilation and are commonly very reluctant to promote or even accept the notion of cultural diversity as a determining characteristic of an increasingly multicultural environment.

It is interesting to compare the underlying assumptions of *integration* in the European public discourse on IM groups at the national level with assumptions at the level of cross-national cooperation and legislation. In the latter context, European politicians are eager to stress the importance of a proper balance between the loss and maintenance of 'national' norms and values. A prime concern in the public debate on such norms and values is cultural and linguistic diversity, mainly in terms of the national languages of the EU. However, both national languages and RM are often referred to as core values of cultural identity. It is a paradoxical phenomenon that in the same public discourse IM languages and cultures are commonly conceived as sources of problems and deficits and as obstacles to integration, while national languages and cultures in an expanding EU are regarded as sources of enrichment and as prerequisites for integration.

The public discourse on integration of IM groups in terms of assimilation vs. multiculturalism can also be noticed in the domain of education. Due to a growing influx of IM pupils, schools are faced with the challenge of adapting their curricula to this trend. The pattern of modification may be inspired by a strong and unilateral emphasis on learning (in) the language of the majority of society, given its significance for success in school and on the labour market, or by the awareness that the response to emerging multicultural school populations can not be reduced to monolingual education programming (cf. Gogolin, 1994). In the former case, the focus will be on learning (in) the national language as a second language only, in the latter case on offering more languages in the school curriculum. In particular in the domain of education, there is a wide conceptual gap between the discourse on RM and IM languages, as will be outlined later in this chapter.

Demographic perspectives

In this section we focus on the definition and identification of minority groups in terms of four widely but differentially used criteria, i.e. nationality, birth-country, selfcategorization (or ethnicity) and (home) language use. Derived from this overview, we will present some basic data on RM groups and IM groups in EU countries respectively.

Definition and identification of minority groups

Collecting reliable information about the number and spread of RM and IM population groups in EU countries is no easy enterprise. What is, however, more interesting than presented numbers or estimates of particular groups, are the *criteria* for such numbers or estimates. Throughout the EU it is common practice to present data on RM groups on the basis of (home) language and/or ethnicity and to present data on IM groups on the basis of nationality and/or country of birth. However, convergence between these criteria for the two groups appears over time, due to the increasing period of migration and minorization of IM groups in EU countries. Due to their prolonged/permanent stay, there is strong erosion in the utilization of nationality or birth-country statistics.

Given the decreasing significance of nationality and birth-country criteria, collecting reliable information about the composition of IM groups in EU countries is one of the most challenging tasks facing demographers. Complementary or alternative criteria have been suggested in various countries with a longer immigration history, and, for this reason, a history of collecting census data on multicultural population groups. In English-dominant countries such as the USA, Canada and Australia, census questions have been phrased in terms of self-categorization or ethnicity ('To which ethnic group do you consider yourself to belong?') and home language use. In Table 2, the four criteria mentioned are discussed in terms of their major advantages and disadvantages (see also Broeder & Extra, 1998: 4). As Table 2 makes clear, there is no single royal road to a solution of the identification problem. Different criteria may complement and strengthen each other. Given the decreasing significance of nationality and birth-country criteria in the European context, the combined criterion of self-categorization and home language use is a potentially promising long-term alternative. As a result, convergence will emerge between the utilized criteria for the definition and identification of IM and RM groups in increasingly multicultural societies.

Regional minority groups in EU countries

We will try to give an approximation of the distribution of different RM language groups in the EU. Of course, here too, we are faced with much diversity in the quality of the data. In some states, there are fairly accurate figures because a language question has been included in the census several times; in other cases, we only have rough estimates by insiders to the language group (usually language activists who want to boost the figures) or by outsiders (e.g. state officials who quite often want to downplay the number of speakers).

We will use a simple typology and distinguish between five categories of RM languages within the EU. For each language we will give an estimate of the number of speakers (see also Gorter, 1996). Some figures given are adequate and recent estimates based upon census or survey research. However, many other figures are, due to the lack of other data, derived from informed estimates by experts and take the average of such subjective estimates (these are commonly referred to as 'disputed numbers'). Also, some languages would perhaps not be included

Table 2 Criteria for the definition and identification of population groups in a multicultural society (P/F/M = person/father/mother)

Criterion	Advantages	Disadvantages
Nationality (NAT) (P/F/M)	• objective • relatively easy to establish	• (intergenerational) erosion through naturalization or double NAT • NAT not always indicative of ethnicity/identity • some (e.g. ex-colonial) groups have NAT of immigration country
Birth-country (BC) (P/F/M)	• objective • relatively easy to establish	• intergenerational erosion through births in immigration country • BC not always indicative of ethnicity/identity • invariable/deterministic: does not take account of dynamics in society (in contrast to all other criteria)
Self-categorization (SC)	• touches the heart of the matter • emancipatory: SC takes account of person's own conception of ethnicity/identity	• subjective by definition: also determined by language/ethnicity of interviewer and by the spirit of times • multiple SC possible • historically charged, especially by World War II experiences
Home language (HL)	• HL is most significant criterion of ethnicity in communication processes • HL data are cornerstones of government policy in areas such as public information or education	• complex criterion: who speaks what language to whom and when? • language not always core value of ethnicity/identity • useless in one-person households

according to certain criteria; others might be split up further (e.g. for some outsiders, Frisian in the Netherlands and North Frisian and Saterfrisian in Germany are considered as one language) or again others be taken together as one group (e.g. outsiders would not distinguish between Catalan in Valencia, the Balearic islands and Catalonia). Limburgian has been perceived as a dialect of Dutch until 1998 when it was recognized by the government of the Netherlands as a regional language in terms of the European Charter for Regional or Minority languages; in Belgium, where the same variety is spoken, the government has so far not followed this step. The figures given are based upon Breatnach (1998), Euromosaic (1996), Istituto della Enciclopedia Italiana (1986), Siguan (1990) and Tjeerdsma (1998).

1   The first category concerns unique RM languages. They are defined by the fact that they are spoken in one part of only one EU member state. The languages in this category are the following ones:
    • France: Breton (300,000), Corsican (160,000);
    • Germany: North Frisian (8000) Saterfrisian (2000) and Sorbian (60,000) ;
    • Italy: Friulan (550,000), Ladin (35,000) and Sardinian (1,000,000);
    • the Netherlands: Frisian (450,000);
    • Portugal: Mirandes (15,000);
    • Spain: Galician (2,300,000), Aragonese (30,000), Asturian (450,000);
    • Great Britain: Scottish Gaelic (67,000), Scots (1,500,000), Ulster Scots (100,000), Welsh (500,000) and Cornish (200);

2   The second category concerns those RM languages that are spoken in more than one member state of the EU. This category may include the following languages:
    • Basque in Spain (Basque Autonomous Community 515,000, Navarre 50,000) and in France (70,000);
    • Catalan in Spain (Catalonia 4 million, Balearic Islands 428,000, Valencia 1.9 million and Aragon 48,000), in France (102,000) and in Italy (20,000);
    • Occitan in Spain (4000), in France (3,500,000) and in Italy (50,000);
    • Sami in Sweden (18,000) and in Finland (3000, spread over dialects: North, Inari and Solt);
    • Low-Saxon in the Netherlands (1.8 million) and Low-German (8-10 million) in Germany;
    • Limburgian in the Netherlands (1 million) and in Belgium.

3   Languages which are a minority language in one member state, but the dominant official language in another, neighbouring state (the latter not necessarily being a member state of the EU). There are quite a few of them and the linguistic relationship between the dominated and dominant language differs from case to case. Some of these languages might perhaps also be considered as examples of category 1. Multiple cases are Albanian in Italy (100,000) and Greece (80,000); Croatian in Italy (2000) and Austria (25,000); German in France (975,000), Italy (280,000), Belgium (69,000) and Denmark (20,000); Slovenian in Austria (17,000) and Italy (75,000). Single cases are Swedish (296,000) in Finland and Finnish (305,000) in Sweden, French (including Franco-Provencal: 115,000) in Italy and Walloon in Belgium (600,000, including Champenois, Lorraine and Picard), although Walloon seems difficult to categorize; it is referred to in category 2 and not 1 because its relationship to French seems so close (cf. Franco-Provencal). Furthermore there is Berber (25,000) and Portuguese (3600) in Spain; Dutch (80,000) in France; Danish (50,000) in Germany; Greek (11,000) in Italy; Magyar (Hungarian) (14,000), Czech (8000) and Slovak (1000) in Austria; Turkish (100,000), Macedonian (75,000), Aromanian (also called Vlach: 50,000), Pomak (from Bulgarian: 27,000) in Greece (although there is no or very little recognition of these languages by the state).

4   Two languages have a special status because they are official state languages but not official working languages of the EU. These are Luxemburgish (359,000), also spoken in France (35,000), and Irish (1.5 million speakers have some ability, 353,000 use it everyday), also spoken in Great Britain (in Northern Ireland by 142,000 speakers who have some knowledge, of whom perhaps 15,000 use it regularly).

5   Finally there are non-territorial minority languages, which will be found in smaller or larger numbers in almost all member-states; the most prominent ones are Romani (see Bakker in this Volume for numbers in all European states) and Yiddish (see e.g. Huss in this Volume for Sweden).

Our typology refers mainly to the geographic dimension of state boundaries and partially to legal status. In that sense the typology has its inherent difficulties. The distinctions may be gradual or some language groups may not fit in nicely (e.g. Slovenian, Croatian or Czech). Of course, other typologies are possible (e.g. Edwards, 1991: 215; Euro-mosaic, 1996). Our aim is to present a typology here for the purpose of making the diversity of contexts visible (see also Gorter *et al.*, 1990).

Demographic size has some importance in order to better understand the sociolinguistic status of languages. Included in the latter are factors such as use in the family, legal status and protection by government, provisions in the media and in cultural life, development of a written standard, economic prosperity of the community, attitudes to language(s), and level of organized activities. The demographic and sociolinguistic status are related strongly with the educational status of these languages. Educational provisions in turn influence the numerical development and social status of RM languages.

Immigrant minority groups in EU countries

As a consequence of socio-economically or politically determined processes of migration, the traditional patterns of language variation across Western Europe have changed considerably over the past several decades (cf. Extra & Verhoeven, 1998). The first pattern of migration started in the sixties and early seventies, and it was mainly economically motivated. In the case of Mediterranean groups, migration initially involved contract workers who expected - and were expected - to stay for a limited period of time. As the period of their stay gradually became longer, this pattern of economic migration was followed by a second pattern of social migration as their families joined them. Subsequently, a second generation was born in the immigrant countries, while their parents often remained uncertain or ambivalent about whether to stay or to return to the country of origin. These demographic shifts over time have also been accompanied by shifts of designation for the groups under consideration - 'migrant workers,' 'immigrant families,' and 'ethnic minorities,' respectively (see also Table 1).

As a result, many industrialized Western European countries have a growing number of immigrant populations which differ widely, both from a cultural and from a linguistic point of view, from the mainstream indigenous population. In spite of more stringent immigration policies in most EU countries, the prognosis is that immigrant populations will continue to grow as a consequence of the increasing number of political refugees, the opening of the internal European borders, and political and economic developments in Central and Eastern Europe and in other regions of the world. It has been estimated that in the year 2000 about one third of the population under the age of 35 in urbanized Western Europe had an immigration background.

Within the various EU countries, four major immigrant groups can be distinguished: people from Mediterranean EU countries, from Mediterranean non-EU countries, from former colonial countries, and political refugees (cf. Extra & Verhoeven, 1993a; 1993b). Comparative information on population figures in EU member states can be obtained from the Statistical Office of the EU in Luxembourg (EuroStat). An overall decrease of the indigenous population has been observed in all EU countries over the last decade; at the same time, there has been an increase in the immigration figures. Although free movement of migrants between EU member states is legally permitted and promoted, most immigrants in EU countries originate from non-EU countries. According to EuroStat (1996), in January 1993, the EU had a population of 368 million, 4.8% of whom (almost 18 million people) were not citizens of the country in which they lived. The increase in the non-national population since 1985 is mainly due to an influx of non-EU nationals, whose numbers rose from 9 to 12 million between 1985 and 1992. The largest numbers of immigrants have been observed in France, Germany and Great Britain.

For various reasons, however, reliable demographic information on immigrant groups in EU countries is difficult to obtain. For some groups or countries, no updated information is available or no such data have ever been collected at all. Moreover, official statistics only reflect immigrant groups with legal resident status. Another source of disparity is the different data collection systems being used, ranging from nation-wide census data to more or less representative surveys. Most importantly, however, the most widely used criteria for immigrant status - nationality and/or country of birth - have become less valid over time because of an increasing trend toward naturalization and births within the countries of residence. In addition, most residents from former colonies already have the nationality of their country of immigration.

There are large differences among EU countries as regards the size and composition of IM groups. Owing to labour market mechanisms, such groups are found mainly in the northern industrialized EU countries, whereas their presence in Mediterranean countries like Greece, Italy, Portugal, and Spain is as yet rather limited. Mediterranean groups immigrate mainly to France or Germany. Portuguese, Spanish and Maghreb residents concentrate in France, whereas Italian, Greek, former Yugoslavian and Turkish residents concentrate in Germany. The largest immigrant groups in EU countries are Turkish and Maghreb residents;

the latter originate from Morocco, Algeria or Tunisia. Table 3 gives official numbers of their size in twelve EU countries in January 1994.

Table 3   Official numbers of inhabitants of Maghreb and Turkish origin in twelve EU countries, January 1994, based on the nationality criterion (EuroStat, 1997)

EU countries	*Maghreb countries*			*Total Maghreb*	*Turkey*
	Morocco	*Algeria*	*Tunisia*		
Belgium	145,363	10,177	6,048	161,588	88,302
Denmark	3,180	368	404	3,952	34,658
Germany	82,803	23,082	28,060	133,945	1,918,395
Greece	333	180	314	827	3,066
Spain	61,303	3,259	378	64,940	301
France	572,652	614,207	206,336	1,393,165	197,712
Italy	77,180	3,177	35,318	115,675	3,656
The Netherlands	164,567	905	2,415	167,887	202,618
Portugal	221	53	28	302	65
Finland	560	208	142	910	995
Sweden	1,533	599	1,152	3,284	23,649
Great Britain	3,000	2,000	2,000	7,000	41,000
Total	1,112,695	658,215	282,595	2,053,505	2,514,417

According to EuroStat (1997) and based on the conservative nationality criterion, in 1993 the largest Turkish and Maghreb communities could be found in Germany (almost 2 million) and France (almost 1.4 million), respectively.

Within the EU, the Netherlands is in second place as the country of immigration for Turkish and Moroccan residents. Table 4 gives an overview of population groups in the Netherlands on January 1, 1996, based on the combined birth-country criterion (birth country of person and/or mother and/or father) *versus* the nationality criterion, and derived from CBS statistics (CBS, 1997).

Table 4 shows strong criterion effects of birth-country *versus* nationality. All IM groups are in fact strongly underrepresented in nationality-based statistics. However, the combined birth-country criterion does not solve the identification problem either. The use of this criterion leads to non-identification in at least the following cases:

- An increasing group of third and further generations (cf. the Moluccan and Chinese communities in the Netherlands; see Van der Avoird *et al.* in this Volume).
- Different ethnocultural groups from the same country of origin (cf. Turks *versus* Kurds from Turkey).
- The same ethnocultural group from different countries of origin (cf. Chinese from China *versus* Vietnam).
- Ethnocultural groups without territorial status (cf. Roma).

Table 4 Population of the Netherlands (x 1000) based on the combined birth-country criterion (BCPMF) and the nationality criterion on January 1, 1996 (CBS, 1997)

Groups (x1000)	BCPMF	Nationality	Abs. diff.
Dutch	12,872	14,768	1,896
Turks	272	154	118
Moroccans	225	150	75
Surinamese	282	15	267
Antilleans	94	-	94
Greeks	11	5	6
Italians	32	17	15
Former Yugoslavs	56	34	22
Portuguese	13	9	4
Spaniards	29	17	12
Cape Verdians	17	2	15
Tunisians	6	2	4
Other groups	1,585	331	1,254
Total	15,494	15,494	-

Verweij (1997) made a short *tour d'horizon* in four EU countries (i.e. Belgium, Germany, France, Great Britain) and in the USA in order to study criteria utilized in the national population statistics of these countries. In Belgium, Germany and France, such statistics have traditionally been based on the nationality criterion; only in Belgium has additional experience been gained with the combined birth-country criterion of persons, parents, and even grandparents. For various reasons, identification on the basis of the grandparents' birth-country is very problematic: four additional sources of evidence are needed (with multiple types of outcomes) and the chances of non-response are rather high. Verweij (1997) also discussed the experiences with the utilization of ethnic self-categorization in Great Britain and the USA, leaving the home language criterion out of consideration. Given the increasing identification problems with the combined birth-country criterion, Verweij, on the basis of Anglo-Saxon experiences, suggested including the self-categorization criterion in future population statistics as the second-best middle- and long-term alternative in those cases where the combined birth-country criterion would not suffice. Moreover, he proposed carrying out small-scale experimental studies on the validity and social acceptance of the self-categorization criterion, given its subjective and historically charged character, respectively (see also Table 2), before this criterion would be introduced on a nation-wide scale. As early as 1982, the *Australian Institute of Multicultural Affairs* recognized the above-mentioned identification problems for inhabitants of Australia and proposed including questions on birth-country (of person and parents), ethnic origin (based on self-categorization), and home language use in their censuses (see Broeder & Extra, 1998).

As yet, little experience has been gained in EU countries with periodical censuses, or, if such censuses have been held, with questions on ethnicity or (home) language use. It is expected that, as a consequence of ongoing processes of immigration and minorization, EU countries will show a development towards periodical censuses with questions on language and ethnicity. Given the decreasing significance of nationality and birth-country criteria, the combined criterion of ethnocultural self-categorization and home language use would be a potentially promising long-term alternative for obtaining basic information on the multicultural composition of societies. The added value of home language statistics is that they can offer valuable insights into the distribution and vitality of home languages across cultures and can thus raise the awareness of multilingualism. Moreover, data on home language use are indispensable tools for educational policy in the domains of both first and second language instruction.

Sociolinguistic perspectives

In this section we focus on the status of RM and IM languages in terms of declared language rights. For a valuable overview and discussion of existing policy documents on the theme of minority language rights we refer to De Varennes (1997). Here we will only deal with an important selection.

There is a growing international awareness that, irrespective of the fundamental freedoms of the individual as expressed most noteworthy in the *Universal Declaration of Human Rights* adopted by the General Assembly of the United Nations in December 1948, minority groups have rights that should be acknowledged and accommodated as well. As a result, the recognition and protection of minorities has become a significant issue in international law. At the UN World Conference on Human Rights in Vienna in June 1993, a Declaration was adopted which confirmed

> the importance of the promotion and protection of the rights of persons belonging to minorities and the contribution of such promotion and protection to the political and social stability of the State in which such persons live.

It is important to note that diversity is recognized in this Declaration as a prerequisite and not as a threat to social cohesion. A complicated issue is the definition of 'minority' in legal documents. The concept has both quantitative and qualitative dimensions, based on dominated size and dominated status respectively. Dominated status may refer to, e.g. physical, social, cultural, religious, linguistic, economic or legal character-istics of minority groups. Attempts by the UN to reach an acceptable definition, however, have been largely unsuccessful (see Capotorti, 1979). The *UN International Covenant on Civil and Political Rights* (1966) endures as the most significant international law provision on the protection of minorities. Article 27 of the covenant states:

> In those states in which ethnic, religious or linguistic minorities exist, persons belonging to ethnic, religious or linguistic minorities shall not be denied the right, in community with others of their group, to enjoy their own culture, to profess and practice their own religion, or to use their own language.

Article 27 of this Covenant does not contain a definition of minorities, nor does it make any provision for a body to designate them. Nevertheless, it refers to three prominent minority properties in terms of ethnicity, religion or language, and it refers to 'persons', not to 'nationals'.

While Article 27 of the 1966 UN Covenant takes a defensive perspective on minority rights ('shall not be denied'), later UN documents give evidence of more affirmative action. Article 4 of the *UN Declaration of the Rights of Persons Belonging to National or Ethnic, Religious and Linguistic Minorities*, adopted by the General Assembly in December 1992, contains certain modest obligations on states

> to take measures to create favourable conditions to enable persons belonging to minorities to express their characteristics and to develop their culture, to provide them with adequate opportunities to learn their mother tongue or to have instruction in their mother tongue and to enable them to participate fully in the economic progress and development in their country.

Although adopted by the UN General Assembly, this document remains as yet a non-binding Declaration. In contrast to the protection offered to individuals in terms of international human rights (cf. the previously cited Article 27 of the 1966 UN Covenant or Article 4 of the 1992 UN Declaration), minority groups as such appear to be largely ignored.

At the European level, language policy has largely been considered as a domain which should be developed within the national perspectives of the different EU member states. Proposals for a common EU language policy are labouriously achieved and non-committal in character (see Coulmas, 1991 for a historical perspective). The most important declarations, recommendations, or directives on language policy, each of which concepts carry a different charge in the EU jargon, concern the recognition of the status of (in the order mentioned):

- National EU languages.
- Indigenous or RM languages.
- Immigrant or 'non-territorial' minority languages.

The *Treaty of Rome* (1958) confers equal status on all national languages of the EU member states (with the exception of Irish and Luxembourgian) as working languages. On numerous occasions, the EU ministers of education have declared that the EU citizens' knowledge of languages should be promoted (see Baetens Beardsmore, 1993). Each EU member state should promote pupils' proficiency in at least two 'foreign' languages, and at least one of these languages should be the official language of one of the EU states.

Promoting knowledge of RM and/or IM languages has been left out of consideration in these ministerial statements. At the European level many linguistic minorities have nevertheless found in the institutions of the former European Communities (EC) and the present EU a new forum for formulating and defending their right to exist. Although the numbers of both RM and IM groups are often small within the borders of particular nation-states, these numbers become much more substantial at the European level. The EC/EU institution which has shown the most affirmative action is the European Parliament.

The European Parliament accepted various resolutions in 1981, 1987 and 1994, in which the protection and promotion of RM languages was recommended. The first resolution led to the foundation of the _European Bureau for Lesser Used Languages_ in 1982. Meanwhile, the Bureau has member state committees in 13 EU countries and it has recently acquired the status of _Non-Governmental Organization_ (NGO) at the levels of the European Council and the United Nations. Another result of the European Parliament resolutions is the foundation of the European _MERCATOR Network_, aimed at promoting research on the status and use of RM languages.

The Council of Europe, set up in 1949, is a much broader organization than the EU, with 41 member states. Its main role today is to be 'the guardian of democratic security - founded on human rights, democracy and the rule of law'. A bottom-up initiative from its Council for Local and Regional Authorities resulted in the _European Charter for Regional or Minority Languages_, which was opened for signature in November 1992 and came into force in March 1998. In October 2000 it has been ratified by 11 out of 41 Council of Europe member states. The Charter is aimed at the protection and the promotion of 'the historical regional or minority languages of Europe'. Article 1a of the Charter states that the concept of 'regional or minority languages' refers to languages that are

i   traditionally used within a given territory of a State by nationals of that State who form a group numerically smaller than the rest of the State's population; and
ii different from the official language(s) of that State;
    it does not include either dialects of the official language(s) of the State or the languages of migrants.

It should be noted that the concepts of 'regional' and 'minority' languages are not specified in the Charter and that (im)migrant languages are explicitly excluded from the Charter. States are free in their choice of which RM languages to include. Also the degree of protection is not prescribed; thus a state can choose for light or tight policies. The result is a rich variety of different provisions accepted by the various states. At the same time the Charter implies some sort of European standard which most likely will gradually be further developed. Enforcement of the Charter is under control of a committee of experts which every three years examines reports presented by the Parties. The Charter asks for recognition, respect, maintenance, facilitation and promotion of RM languages, in particular in the domains of education, judicial authorities, administrative and public services, media, cultural activities, and socio-economic life (Articles 8-13). Article 8 states a whole set of measures for all stages of education, from pre-school to adult education, which are cited here in full ((R)RML = (relevant) regional or minority language(s)):

1 With regard to education, the Parties undertake, within the territory in which such languages are used, according to the situation of each of these languages, and without prejudice to the teaching of the official language(s) of the State:
   a i   to make available pre-school education in the RRML; or
      ii   to make available a substantial part of pre-school education in the RRML; or
      iii to apply one of the measures provided for under i and ii above at least to those pupils whose families so request and whose number is considered sufficient; or
      iv   if the public authorities have no direct competence in the field of pre-school education, to favour and/or encourage the application of the measures referred to under i to iii above;
   b i   to make available primary education in the RRML; or
      ii   to make available a substantial part of primary education in the RRML; or
      iii to provide, within primary education, for the teaching of the RRML as an integral part of the curriculum; or
      iv   to apply one of the measures provided for under i to iii above at least to those pupils whose families so request and whose number is considered sufficient;

c i to make available secondary education in the RRML; or

ii to make available a substantial part of secondary education in the RRML; or

iii to provide, within secondary education, for the teaching of the RRML as an integral part of the curriculum; or

iv to apply one of the measures provided for under i to iii above at least to those pupils who, or where appropriate whose families, so wish in a number considered sufficient;

d i to make available technical and vocational education in the RRML; or

ii to make available a substantial part of technical and vocational education in the RRML; or

iii to provide, within technical and vocational education, for the teaching of the RRML as an integral part of the curriculum; or

iv to apply one of the measures provided for under i to iii above at least to those pupils who, or where appropriate whose families, so wish in a number considered sufficient;

e i to make available university and other higher education in RML; or

ii to provide facilities for the study of these languages as university and higher education subjects; or

iii if, by reason of the role of the State in relation to higher education institutions, sub-paragraphs i and ii cannot be applied, to encourage and/or allow the provision of university or other forms of higher education in RML or of facilities for the study of these languages as university or higher education subjects;

f i to arrange for the provision of adult and continuing education courses which are taught mainly or wholly in the RML; or

ii to offer such languages as subjects of adult and continuing education; or

iii if the public authorities have no direct competence in the field of adult education, to favour and/or encourage the offering of such languages as subjects of adult and continuing education;

g to make arrangements to ensure the teaching of the history and the culture which is reflected by the RML;

    h   to provide the basic and further training of the teachers required to implement those of paragraphs a to g by the Party;

    i   to set up a supervisory body or bodies responsible for monitoring the measures taken and progress achieved in establishing or developing the teaching of RML and for drawing up periodic reports of their findings, which will be made public.

2   With regard to education and in respect of territories other than those in which the RML are traditionally used, the Parties undertake, if the number of users of a RML justifies it, to allow, encourage or provide teaching in or of the RML at all the appropriate stages of education.

As a parallel activity to the *European Charter for Regional or Minority Languages*, the Council of Europe opened the *Framework Convention for the Protection of National Minorities* for signature in February 1995. This treaty does not focus on language(s). It is more general in its aims and scope, and it has far less specific provisions for protection and promotion of the minorities concerned. Still it also offers a European standard to which states have to adhere. Although in this framework no definition of 'national minorities' is given, it is clear from the document that 'non-national' immigrant groups are again excluded from the considerations. Articles 5 and 6 of the Framework state the following:

Article 5

1   The Parties undertake to promote the conditions necessary for persons belonging to national minorities to maintain and develop their culture, and to preserve the essential elements of their identity, namely their religion, language, traditions and cultural heritage.

2   Without prejudice to measures taken in pursuance of their general integration policy, the Parties shall refrain from policies or practices aimed at assimilation of persons belonging to national minorities against their will and shall protect these persons from any action aimed at such assimilation.

Article 6

1   The Parties shall encourage a spirit of tolerance and intercultural dialogue and take effective measures to promote mutual respect and understanding and co-operation among all persons living on their territory, irrespective of those persons' ethnic, cultural, lin-

guistic or religious identity, in particular in the fields of education, culture and the media.

2 The Parties undertake to take appropriate measures to protect persons who may be subject to threats or acts of discrimination, hostility or violence as a result of their ethnic, cultural, linguistic or religious identity.

Ratification of this framework was more successful than in the case of the European Charter mentioned before. At the end of 2000, 29 out of 41 Council of Europe member states had ratified the framework. It is interesting to note that the Netherlands, being among the first four states to sign the Charter, has not yet signed the Framework Convention. In the preparations for the ratification of the Framework Convention the proposal to the Parliament was to include Frisians as well as IM groups as 'national minorities'; in the latter case, however, only those that are target groups of the Netherlands' formal IM policy.

A final document of the Council of Europe that should be referred to in this context, is *Recommendation 1383 on Linguistic Diversification*, adopted by the Council's Parliamentary Assembly in September 1998. Article 5 states that

there should (...) be more variety in modern language teaching in the Council of Europe member states: this should result in the acquisition not only of English but also of other European and world languages by all European citizens, in parallel with the mastery of their own national and, where appropriate, regional language.

In Article 8i the Assembly also recommends that the Committee of Ministers invite member states

to improve the creation of regional language plans, drawn up in collaboration with elected regional representatives and local authorities, with a view to identifying existing linguistic potential and developing the teaching of the languages concerned, while taking account of the presence of non-native population groups, twinning arrangements, exchanges and the proximity of foreign countries.

While Article 5 is restricted to 'regional' languages, Article 8i recognizes for the first time the relevance of 'non-native' groups in the context of language planning.

Apart from the Council of Europe's efforts, two other initiatives on linguistic rights should be mentioned here as well. A host of institutions and non-governmental organizations signed the *Universal Declaration on Linguistic Rights* in Barcelona, June 1996. This Declaration takes as a starting point language groups instead of states and explicitly includes both RM and IM languages, in contrast to the earlier mentioned *European Charter for Regional or Minority Languages*. Article 1.5 says:

> This Declaration considers as a language group any group of persons sharing the same language which is established in the territorial space of another language community but which does not possess historical antecedents equivalent to those of that community. Examples of such groups are immigrants, refugees, deported persons and members of diasporas.

Articles 4 deals with the issue of integration and assimilation in the following way:

Article 4.1
This Declaration considers that persons who move to and settle in the territory of another language community have the right and the duty to maintain an attitude of integration towards this community. This term is understood to mean an additional socialization of such persons in such a way that they may preserve their original cultural characteristics while sharing with the society in which they have settled sufficient references, values and forms of behaviour to enable them to function socially without greater difficulties than those experienced by members of the host community.

Article 4.2
This Declaration considers, on the other hand, that assimilation, a term which is understood to mean acculturation in the host society, in such a way that the original cultural characteristics are replaced by the references, values and forms of behaviour of the host society, must on no account be forced or induced and can only be the result of an entirely free decision.

Article 5 indirectly criticizes the European Charter's focus on RM languages by stating:

This Declaration is based on the principle that the rights of all language communities are equal and independent of their legal status as official, regional or minority languages. Terms such as regional or minority languages are not used in this Declaration because, though in certain cases the recognition of regional or minority languages can facilitate the exercise of certain rights, these and other modifiers are frequently used to restrict the rights of language communities.

In line with the European Charter, the Universal Declaration defines domains of linguistic rights in terms of public administration and official bodies, education, proper names, media and new technologies, culture and the socio-economic sphere. Another recent and important document on linguistic rights is *The Oslo Recommendations Regarding the Linguistic Rights of National Minorities*, approved by the Organization for Security and Cooperation in Europe (OSCE) in Oslo, February 1998. The focus of this document is on 'persons belonging to national/ethnic groups who constitute the numerical majority in one State but the numerical minority in another (usually neighbouring) State'. The document was designed in the context of many recent tensions surrounding such groups in Central and Eastern Europe. Its *Explanatory Note* contains valuable sources of information on related documents in the domains of (proper) names, religion, community life, media, economic life, administrative authorities and public services, independent national institutions, judicial authorities and deprivation of liberty. In an earlier separate document, referred to as *The Hague Recommendations Regarding the Education Rights of National Minorities* and published in October 1996, the OSCE focuses on educational measures.

As yet, specific documents on the linguistic rights of IM groups in Europe hardly exist. The major document is the *Directive of the Council of the European Communities* (now the EU) *on the schooling of children of migrant workers*, published in Brussels, July 1977. Although this Directive has promoted the legitimization of IM language instruction and occasionally also its legislation in some countries (see Reid & Reich, 1992; Fase, 1994), the Directive was very limited in its ambitions regarding minority language teaching and has become completely outdated.

In the final session of the seminar from which this book is the result, a concept version of the *Declaration of Oegstgeest: Moving away from a monolingual habitus* was presented for discussion by the participants. On the basis of recommendations put forward by the experts in the seminar, a basic list of 12 articles was drafted. The Declaration proposes a set of measures to improve (home) language data-gathering methods and stimulate action programmes in, e.g. education and research, thus improving the status of RM and IM languages across Europe. The idea behind the Declaration was to prepare a readable document that would be useful for decision makers in the development of further policy, whether on the regional, national or European level. The final text of the Declaration was unanimously adopted on 30 January 2000 in Oegstgeest and is presented as an Appendix to this Volume. The Declaration has been distributed to many politicians and decisions makers across Europe. By including it in this Volume we hope to reach an even wider audience.

As mentioned at the beginning of this section, it is important to note that in many of the quoted documents cultural pluralism or diversity is conceived as a prerequisite for, and not a threat to, social cohesion or integration. A plea for reconciling the concepts of diversity and cohesion has recently also been made by the Migration Policy Group (2000), in co-operation with the European Cultural Foundation, on the basis of a comprehensive survey and evaluation of available policy documents and new policy developments and orientations. The Migration Policy Group's report puts 'historic' and 'new' minorities in Europe in an overarching context. Both types of minorities significantly contributed and contribute to Europe's cultural, religious, linguistic and ethnic diversity.

European nation-states are reluctant to recognize and respect this diversity as part of their national, and increasingly European, identity. However, multicultural and multi-ethnic nation-states are a common phenomenon in Europe's distant and recent past. Abroad, diversity due to immigration and minorization, has become part of the national identity and heritage of English-dominant countries such as the USA, Canada, Australia and South Africa. Without losing sight of the enormous diversity between and within 'historic' and 'new' minorities, European nation-states should learn to appreciate and use the contributions of all of them.

Educational perspectives

In this section we discuss the *status quo* of RM and IM languages in European education. Our focus is on primary and/or secondary schools as part of compulsory education and, as in the former section, on EU countries.

Regional minority languages in education

In the European Framework Convention on National Minorities and in the European Charter for Regional or Minority Languages we find a sort of European standard. The groups covered by these treaties are RM languages. The Framework Convention outlines some aims in a very general sense. In that way it forces a standard on the states that become signatories. As far as education is concerned, there is first of all the encouragement 'to foster knowledge of the culture, language and history of the national minorities, also among the majority' (Article 12) as well as 'the recognition of the right to learn the minority language' (Article 14). This means that all citizens have to be informed, through the school curriculum, about the minorities, and also that the members of a minority group have a right to receive at least some minimal teaching of their own language.

The Charter is much more elaborate on the use of language in education. As was outlined before it offers the adhering states the opportunity of choice between different alternatives. Even if one has decided upon the goals of education, what languages are actually used as the target languages within the curriculum can vary from situation to situation. The complexity can be summarized as a typology with four categories: 1) no minority language teaching at all; 2) the minority language as a subject, the dominant language as a medium of instruction; 3) both the minority language and the dominant language as a medium of instruction; and 4) the minority language as a medium of instruction and the dominant language as a subject. The fifth logical possibility, no teaching at all of the dominant language, does not occur.

The number of RM languages for which there is no teaching at all, is decreasing, although in many cases there is only a very small amount of teaching available, confined to pre-primary education only (e.g. Sater-frisian in Germany). What happens most frequently is the pattern denoted in category 2, with the minority language as a subject. The categories 3 and 4 contain fewer language groups, and especially category 4, where it occurs (Basque Country, Wales), is limited to a certain level of the educational system or to certain types of schools (immersion education).

Of greatest importance are, of course, the final outcomes of the teaching of RM languages. Does such teaching lead to increased maintenance or has it encouraged the transition to the dominant language? Very few evaluation studies have been carried out throughout Europe. In the case of transitional education, where a small amount of attention is given to the RM language (for example, one lesson per week only at primary level), this may work as a stimulus for assimilation to the mainstream society. In such cases, the RM language is often defined as a 'learning deficit' which has to be remedied through education. In the case of stronger provisions for RM education, learning the RM language is conceived of as an enrichment and the language is defined as worthy of maintenance and promotion. The outcome of such education is a contribution to cultural pluralism. In principle, all pupils do become bilingual and biliteral. Examples of such well-established RM languages are Catalan, Basque, Welsh and Swedish (in Finland).

Immigrant minority languages in education

We examine the policies of a number of EU countries regarding IM language instruction in both primary and secondary education (see also Broeder & Extra, 1998). The cross-national terminology for this type of instruction is not consistent, as can be derived from designations like *home language instruction, instruction in the native language and culture, instruction in immigrant languages,* or *instruction in ethnic minority languages* (see also Table 1). We will use the acronym IMLI (Immigrant Minority Language Instruction) when referring to this type of instruction in the countries under consideration. The decision to use the designation IMLI is motivated by the inclusion of a broad spectrum of potential target groups. First of all, the status of an IM language as 'native' or home language can change through intergenerational processes of language shift. Moreover, in secondary education, both minority and majority pupils are often *de jure* (although seldom *de facto*) admitted to IMLI (in the Netherlands, e.g. Turkish is a secondary school subject called 'Turkish' rather than 'home language instruction'; see also the concept of *Enseignement des Langues et Cultures d'Origine versus Enseignement des Langues Vivantes* in France).

For various reasons, the development of an educational policy regarding IMLI was, and continues to be, a complex and challenging task. In view of the multicultural composition of many schools, this task involves the organization of multilingual rather than bilingual instruction. Experiences with, and the results of research into, an exclusively bilingual context are therefore only transferable to a limited degree. In addition, there are big differences as to the nature and extent of bilingualism of IM pupils, both within and across different language groups. Moreover, from an intergenerational perspective, these differences tend to increase and shift in the direction of the dominant language of the immigrant country. Furthermore, given the very divergent target groups, it is no easy task to fit IMLI into the rest of the curriculum. In a number of countries, the current policy is ambivalent in the sense that, for some groups, IMLI is an addition to the curriculum, while for others, IMLI replaces a part of the curriculum. Finally, there is the question of feasibility in the case of a relatively modest demand for instruction and of relatively small or widely scattered groups.

The cross-national comparison of the countries in this section is based on secondary analyses of the available data and on oral or written information supplied by key informants. The focus of Broeder and Extra (1998) is on three EU countries with relatively large numbers of IM groups (Germany, France, Great Britain), on two countries which partially share their language of public use (The Netherlands and Flanders/Belgium) and on one of the Scandinavian countries (Sweden). In all the countries involved in this study, there has been an increase in the number of IM pupils who speak a language at home other than or in addition to the dominant school language in primary and secondary education. The schools have responded to this home-school language mismatch by paying more attention to the learning and teaching of the national standard language as a second language. A great deal of energy and money is being spent on developing curricula, attainment targets, teaching materials and tests for second-language education. Instruction in the IM languages stands out in stark contrast to this, as it is much more susceptible to an ideological debate about its legitimacy. While there is consensus about the necessity of investing in second-language education for IM pupils, there is a lack of such support for IMLI. IM languages are commonly considered sources of problems and deficiencies, and they are rarely seen as sources of knowledge and enrichment. Policy makers, headmasters, and teachers of 'regular' subjects often have reservations or are negative towards IMLI. On the other hand, parents of IM pupils, IMLI teachers, and IM organizations often make a case for having IM languages in the school curriculum. These differences in top-down and bottom-up attitudes emerge in all the countries focused upon.

From a historical point of view, most of the countries in the study of Broeder and Extra (1998) show a similar chronological development in their argumentation for IMLI. IMLI was generally introduced into primary education with a view to family remigration. In the seventies, this argumentation was virtually abandoned. Demographic developments showed no substantial sign of families remigrating to their former recruitment countries; instead, a process of generation building and minorization came about. This development resulted in a shift and IMLI became aimed at combatting disadvantages. IMLI had to bridge the gap between the home and school environment and to encourage school achievement in 'regular' subjects. Because such an approach tended to underappreciate ethnocultural dimensions, a number of countries began to emphasize the intrinsic importance of knowledge of IM languages from a cultural, legal, and economic perspective:

- In cultural respects, IMLI can contribute to maintaining and advancing a pluralist society.
- In legal respects, IMLI can meet the internationally recognized right to language development and language maintenance, in correspondence with the fact that many IM groups consider their own language of key value to their cultural identity.
- In economic respects, finally, IM languages and cultures can be an important pool of knowledge in a society that is increasingly internationally oriented.

The historical development of arguments for IMLI in terms of re-migration, combatting deficiencies, and cultural policy is particularly evident in the Netherlands, Germany and Belgium. In France and Great Britain, cultural policy is tied in with the respective national languages French and English to such an extent that IMLI is only tolerated in its margins. In contrast to each of these five countries, cultural-political motives have always taken pride of place in Sweden. It should, however, be noted that cultural-political arguments for IMLI have not led to an educational policy in which the status of IM languages has been substantially advanced in any of the countries involved in this study.

The target groups of IMLI are considered disadvantaged groups in virtually all countries focused upon in Broeder and Extra (1998); only Sweden has an explicit home language criterion rather than a socio-economic status or generation criterion for admission to IMLI. Actual enrolment in IMLI varies widely not only between countries (cf. enrolment figures in the Netherlands *versus* Flanders), but also between groups (cf. the enrolment percentages of Moroccan and Turkish pupils *versus* those of Southern European pupils). Variation in enrolment is determined by a combination of factors, such as the attitudes of IM parents and pupils, and indigenous majority headmasters and teachers, and the geographical distribution of IM groups (which will decide whether or not numerical criteria can be met). As yet, comparative cross-national studies on the actual causes of this differentiated picture are not available.

Table 5 Status of IMLI in European primary and secondary education (Broeder & Extra, 1998: 107)

Immigrant Minority Language Instruction	Primary education	Secondary education
Target groups	• *de iure*: mostly immigrant minority pupils from specific source countries • *de facto*: mostly subset	• *de iure*: mostly all pupils • *de facto*: mostly subset of immigrant minority pupils
Arguments	mostly in terms of a struggle against deficits: • bridging home/school gap • promoting school success in other ('regular') subjects rarely multicultural policy: • promoting cultural pluralism • promoting knowledge of languages in a multicultural and globalizing society	mostly multicultural policy: • promoting cultural pluralism • promoting knowledge of languages
Goals	rarely specified skills to be reached with IMLI	commonly specification of oral and written skills to be reached with IMLI
Evaluation	rarely judgement/report figure for IMLI: 'language' in school report = national standard language	examination and report figure for IMLI: national standard language is explicitly referred to and separately evaluated in school report
Minimal enrolment	relatively high number of pupils: specified per class, school or municipality	relatively low number of pupils: specified per class, school or municipality
Time-table	not perceived as 'regular' education: instead of other subjects or at extra-curricular hours	regular optional subject in regular free time-table space
Funding	• by national, regional or local authorities • by consulates/embassies of source countries	by national, regional or local authorities
Teaching materials	rarely originating from country of settlement, often from abroad/source country	commonly originating from country of settlement

There are remarkable differences in status between IMLI in primary and secondary education in EU countries. A comparison of target groups, arguments, objectives, evaluation, enrolment restrictions, curricular status, funding, and teaching materials shows that IMLI in secondary education has gained a higher status than IMLI in primary education. In primary education, IMLI is generally not part of the 'regular' or 'national' curriculum, and, consequently, it tends to become a negotiable entity in a complex and often opaque interplay of forces by several actors, in contrast with other curricular subjects. These differences are summarized in Table 5.

The higher status of IMLI in secondary education is largely due to the fact that instruction in one or more languages other than the national standard language is a traditional and regular component of the (optional) school curriculum. *Within* secondary education, however, IMLI must compete with languages that, in their turn, have a higher status or a longer tradition. The hierarchy of languages in secondary education is schematically represented in Table 6 in six categories with descending order of status. With regard to category 6, it should be noted that some countries provide instruction and/or exams in non-standard language varieties. In France, for instance, pupils can take part in examinations for several varieties of Arabic and Berber (see Tilmatine, 1997); Dutch schools provide instruction in Moluccan Malay (as an alternative to Indonesian), and Sweden offers Kurdish (as an alternative to Turkish).

Another remarkable fact is that in some countries (particularly France, Belgium and some German federal states), IMLI in primary education is funded by the consulates or embassies of the countries of origin concerned. In these cases, the national government does not interfere in the organization of IMLI, or in the requirements for, and the selection and employment of teachers. A paradoxical consequence of this phenomenon is that the earmarking of IMLI budgets by the above-mentioned consulates or embassies is often safeguarded. National, regional, or local governments often fail to earmark budgets, so that funds meant for IMLI are not infrequently appropriated for other educational purposes.

IMLI may be part of a largely centralized or decentralized educational policy. In the Netherlands, national responsibilities and means are gradually being transferred to the local level. In France, government policy is strongly centrally controlled. Germany has devolved governmental responsibilities chiefly to the federal states with all their mutual differences. Sweden grants far-reaching autonomy to municipal councils

Table 6 Hierarchy of languages in secondary education, in descending order of status (categories 1-6)

	1	2	3	4	5	6
English	+		+			
French		+	+			
German		+	+			
Danish			+			
Dutch			+			
Swedish			+			
Finnish			+		+	
Portuguese			+		+	
Spanish			+		+	
Italian			+		+	
Greek			+		+	
Basque				+		
Frisian				+		
Gaelic				+		
...						
Arabic					+	
Turkish					+	
...						
Berber						+
Kurdish						+
...						

1: Often compulsory subject
2: Often optional subject as 'second foreign language'
3: National languages of EU countries, often supported by positive action programs at the EU level
4: Regional minority languages, often supported by positive action programs in the region and/or at the EU level
5: Immigrant minority languages, often offered to immigrant minority pupils only
6: Rarely offered non-standardized immigrant minority languages

Table 7   Status differences between instruction in Frisian and IMLI in Dutch elementary and secondary education

Parameters	Elementary education		Secondary education	
	Frisian	*IMLI**	*Frisian*	*Turkish/Arabic*
Target groups	compulsory for all pupils (with optional dispensation from provincial authorities at the request of school board)	optional for immigrant pupils, at the request of parents, and available for a municipal set of priority languages	compulsory for all pupils in lower grades, optional subject in higher grades	*de iure*: optional for all pupils / *de facto*: available most commonly as optional subject for immigrant pupils
Arguments	historical development from deficit struggle towards multicultural policy	lower grades 1-4: deficit struggle / higher grades 5-8: multicultural policy	multicultural policy	multicultural policy
Goals	specified skills to be reached at the end of elementary schooling	-	specified oral and written skills to be reached at interim stage and end of secondary schooling	specified oral and written skills to be reached at end of secondary schooling
Evaluation	sometimes judgment/report figure ('language' on report = Dutch)	sometimes unofficial supplement to report with evaluative figure ('language' on report = Dutch)	examination and report figure	examination and report figure

Minimal enrolment	–	municipality and school decide on (inter)school quotum	no minimum required by ministry, sometimes by schools	at least 4 pupils during 2 hours per week
Time-table	historical development from extra-curricular to peripheral curricular status	lower grades: curricular status higher grades: extra-curricular status	lower grades: curricular status higher grades: in 'free space'	in 'free space'
Funding	state through municipality	municipality through lump-sum of state	lower grades: state higher grades: school	state
Teaching materials	'De Taalrotonde'	few and diverse in quality, often from abroad/source-country	'Flotwei Frysk'	'Turks/Arabisch Communicatief'
Language tests	technical reading in Frisian (national test)	Turkish/Arabic (optional national test)	oral/written Frisian (national test + final exam)	oral/written Turkish/Arabic (national tests + final exams)
Teacher training	two teacher training schools (little interest, knowledge of Frisian problematic)	some teacher training schools (little interest, knowledge of Dutch problematic)	one teacher training school (knowledge of Frisian problematic)	two teacher training schools (knowledge of Dutch problematic)

*   On the basis of the present law on IMLI (1998)
**   In a forefront position compared to other IML

in dealing with tasks and means. In Great Britain, there is a mixed system of shared national and local responsibilities (cf. the ministerial guidelines for special target groups *versus* the guidelines of the local educational authorities).

In general, comparative cross-national references to experiences with IMLI in the various EU member states are rare (e.g. Reich, 1991; 1994; Reid & Reich, 1992; Fase, 1994) or they focus on particular language groups (e.g. Tilmatine, 1997; Obdeijn & De Ruiter, 1998). With a view to the demographic development of European states into multicultural societies and the similarities in IMLI issues, more comparative research and cross-national policy initiatives would be desirable.

Derived from the parameters in Table 5 for an outline of status differences between IMLI in primary and secondary education, we expand our comparative perspective in Table 7 by including both RM and IM languages. In this context, our focus is on the Netherlands, in particular on the status of Frisian vs. IM languages in both primary and secondary schools. Table 7 gives an outline of status differences from these comparative perspectives. There are remarkable differences between the *status quo* of Frisian and IMLI at elementary schools on the one hand and remarkable similarities between Frisian and IMLI (in particular Turkish/Arabic) at secondary schools on the other. Elementary school differences emerge in particular on the parameters of target groups, arguments, goals, minimal enrollment and time-table. The historical development of the status of Frisian at elementary schools, in terms of arguments and time-table, has a remarkable longitudinal parallel in the status of IMLI at elementary schools.

Contents of this Volume

The contributors to this book are a mixed group of specialists in the field of RM and IM languages. They have been asked to describe and analyse the status of the language group(s) they were most familiar with in the context of the member state in the EU where the language group(s) reside(s). In the domain of RM languages, the experts usually are concerned with a particular language in a particular region. Their counterparts, specialists with an expertise in the domain of IM languages, originate from the same EU member states but not from one specific region, because IM languages are spread over the various states and are not bound to specific regions. They treat one or more IM languages in one particular state. Also experts from five non-European countries where English functions as a *lingua franca* (Australia, Canada, India, South Africa and the United States) have been invited to contribute because the issue of RM and IM languages is, of course, not unique to Europe. For the purpose of crosscontinental comparison, these authors were asked to share their knowledge of, and experience with, their respective multilingual societies with the European experts along the same three dimensions. These five countries have a much longer history of immigration and minorization and have, therefore, a longer history of collecting large-scale census data on (home) language use and ethnicity. Their experiences in the domains of demography, sociolinguistics and education are insightful and profitable for all of Europe.

This Volume consists of three parts, with a focus on RM languages in Europe, IM languages in Europe, and an outlook from abroad respectively. The contributions come from seven selected member states of the EU, i.e. Austria, Finland, France, the Netherlands, Spain, Sweden and Great Britain. Within these states we had to be selective again. Our overall purpose was to have, in most cases, both representatives of RM and IM languages.

We include countries with a relatively long history of immigration, some of them with a colonial past (Great Britain, Netherlands, France) others without such a history (Germany, Sweden, Finland). This circumstance has had great influence on which groups have immigrated to which countries. For Austria, one RM language is represented (Slovenian, chapter by Busch). The case of Austria is special because most of the older and recent immigration comes from the center of Europe (e.g. from the Czech and Slovak republics, Hungary and Poland). The other special cases are France and Germany where we have a chapter on Arabic (by Caubet) and on Turkish and other IM languages (by Gogolin and Reich) respectively, but none on one of the RM languages. In the case of Great Britain we include as RM languages both Welsh (by Williams) and Scottish Gaelic (by Robertson). They represent two contrasting cases of languages which did go through an interesting development over the last decades, and policies for Welsh and Gaelic have been examples for other RM languages in Europe. IM languages in Great Britain are dealt with in a general overview (by Edwards). Finland and Sweden do contrast because Finland has a well established policy towards Swedish (chapter by Østern), whereas Sweden has more recently 'discovered' its historical minorities, of which Finnish is by far the largest (chapter by Huss). In terms of IM languages it is the other way around, because Sweden (chapter by Boyd) has been considered in the past by some to be a model country for North-Western Europe and Finland has experienced far less immigration (thus no chapter on IM languages in Finland). It is interesting to observe that whereas Spain used to be an emigration country for North-Western Europe in the sixties, it has more recently become an immigration country (in particular for Arabic and/or Berber speaking Moroccans; chapter by Lopez and Mijares). Spain is also an interesting case for regional minorities because it has experienced a rather rapid development of languages policies, among others for Basque (chapter by Cenoz). The Netherlands has a long history of immigration from the former colonies, but also more recent immigration (chapter by Van der Avoird, Broeder and Extra), as well as one well-established regional language, i.e. Frisian (chapter by Gorter, Riemersma and Ytsma). Finally, the category of diaspora languages across Europe is dealt with in a study on Romani (by Bakker).

When we look at the first five cases with an outlook from abroad (Part 3 of this Volume), all five countries have English as a *lingua franca*, but in each case there are differences in its status. The way English functions may explain part of the way minority (and majority) language groups are perceived and treated. In Australia, Canada and the USA (in this Volume with a focus on California), English is unquestionaly the dominant language. From such a position of strength it is possible to grant rights and provisions to minority languages. Even when English is spoken in Canada and the USA by an overwhelming majority, it has one important competitor, i.e. French and Spanish, respectively (chapters by Edwards and Macias). Many other groups are, however, represented in these countries, both older or recent immigrant languages and indigenous languages. Edwards illustrates the difference by the struggle for recognition by the Makah tribe and the influence of the struggle surrounding French in the case of Canada. In Australia there is no clear second status language; probably therefore the catchall phrase *Languages Other Than English* or LOTE could arise in particular there; all other languages are more or less equal (chapter by Clyne and Ozolins). Australia (in particular Victoria State) has rather liberal policies towards multiculturalism and multilingualism. In South Africa and India (chapters by Alexander and Choudhry) the status of English is different from the former three countries, as it is the language of former oppression. There are 11 main language groups (plus other smaller groups) in South Africa, none of which has more than 25% mother tongue speakers. South Africa may evolve towards a situation similar to Australia, without strong domination of English. The ultimate challenge is offered by India. In India, English is a *lingua franca*, but it is the mother tongue of only a tiny minority; other language groups are much stronger. If we think of Europe as having a rich diversity of languages, we only have to remind ourselves of the more than 1650 languages present on the Indian subcontinent, of which 67 are taught in education, in order to realize that Europe may have much more in common with the rest of the world than it is usually inclined to think.

The two concluding chapters deal with the languages of Turkey (by Yağmur) and Morocco (by Saïb). As Table 3 makes clear, former inhabitants of these source countries, and therefore also their children and languages, are well represented in EU countries. Both majority and minority languages of Turkey and Morocco are spoken and more or less intergenerationally transmitted in the EU context of migration and minorization. In particular, the status of Kurdish in Turkey and Berber in Morocco as minority languages shows interesting similarities and differences. The typological distance between Turkish and Kurdish on the one hand and Berber and Arabic on the other is large, while at the same time 'Berber' and 'Kurdish' are cover concepts for different subvarieties which in some cases are hardly or not mutually intelligible. Moreover, Berber and Kurdish are non-codified language varieties, although Kurmanci (a major variety of Kurdish), Tashelhit and Tarifit (two varieties of Berber) have made important steps towards a generally accepted codification.

From a historical point of view, Islam as the unifying determinant of the Ottoman empire has been ideologically substituted by language (=Turkish) since the establishment of Turkey as a republic under the leadership of Kemal Atatürk. In Morocco, such substitution never took place. As a result, the concept of 'one nation - one language' has been imposed much more on the people of Turkey than on the people of Morocco. Nevertheless, both Kurdish and Berber are dominated language varieties in Turkey and Morocco, which have traditionally been denied access to school. In contrast to Kurdish, however, Berber is increasingly being accepted in oral and written mass media. Language policy in both Turkey and Morocco is made in the absence of any reliable recent survey data on (home)language use. Census data on (home) language use have been regularly collected in Turkey until 1985 and published until 1965. In Morocco, only in the latest 1994 census such data have been collected, but they have not been published either.

Both in Turkey and in Western Europe, Kurdish is spoken by a minority of the Turks. Berber is to a much lesser degree a minority language in Morocco than Kurdish is in Turkey, and Berber is frequently spoken as a home language by Moroccans in Western Europe in addition to, or instead of, Arabic. As an addition to Turkish and Arabic, both Kurdish and Berber are accepted as optional elementary and/or secondary school languages in a number of EU countries.

References

Alladina, S. and Edwards, V. (eds) (1991) *Multilingualism in the British Isles* (Vol. 1: The older mother tongues and Europe; Vol. 2: Africa, the Middle East and Asia). London/New York: Longman

Baetens Beardsmore, H. (1993) *European models of bilingual education.* Clevedon: Multilingual Matters.

Breatnach, D. (ed.) (1998) *Mini guide to lesser used languages of the European Union.* Dublin: European Bureau for Lesser Used Languages.

Broeder, P. and Extra, G. (1998) *Language, ethnicity and education: Case studies on immigrant minority groups and immigrant minority languages.* Clevedon: Multilingual Matters.

Capotorti, B. (1979) *Study of the rights of persons belonging to ethnic, religious and linguistic minorities.* New York: United Nations, nr. E.78.XIV.1.

CBS (1997) *Allochtonen in Nederland 1997.* Voorburg/Heerlen: CBS.

Cohn-Bendit, D. and Schmit, Th. (1992) *Heimat Babylon. Das Wagnis der Multikulturellen Demokratie.* Hamburg: Hoffmann & Campe.

Coulmas, F. (1991) *A language policy for the European Community. Prospects and quandaries.* Berlin: Mouton De Gruyter.

De Varennes, F. (1997) *To speak or not to speak: The rights of persons belonging to linguistic minorities.* Working paper prepared for the UN Sub-Committee on the rights of minorities (www.unesco.org/most/ln2pol3.htm).

Edwards, J.A. (1991) Socio-educational issues concerning indigenous minority languages: terminology, geography and status. In J.A. Sikma and D. Gorter (eds) *European lesser used languages in primary education* (pp. 207-226). Ljouwert/Leeuwarden: Mercator Education/Fryske Akademy.

Euromosaic (1996) *The production and reproduction of the minority language groups of the EU.* Luxembourg: Office for Official Publications of the European Communities.

EuroStat (1997) *Migration statistics 1996. Statistical document 3A.* Luxembourg: EuroStat.

Extra, G. and Verhoeven, L. (eds) (1993a) *Community languages in the Netherlands.* Amsterdam: Swets and Zeitlinger.

Extra, G. and Verhoeven, L. (eds) (1993b). *Immigrant languages in Europe.* Clevedon: Multilingual Matters.

Extra, G. and Verhoeven, L. (eds) (1998). *Bilingualism and migration*. Berlin: Mouton De Gruyter.

Fase, W. (1994) *Ethnic divisions in Western European education*. Münster/New York: Waxmann.

Gogolin, I. (1994) *Der monolinguale Habitus der multilingualen Schule*. Münster/New York: Waxmann.

Gorter, D. (1996) *Het Fries als kleine Europese taal*. Amsterdam/Ljouwert: Fryske Akademy.

Gorter, D., Hoekstra, J., Jansma, L. and Ytsma, J. (eds) (1990) *Fourth international conference on minority languages*. (Vol 1: General papers; Vol 2: Western and Eastern European papers). Clevedon: Multilingual Matters.

Instituto della Enciclopedia Italiana (1986) *Linguistic minorities in countries belonging to the European Community*. Luxembourg: Office for Official Publications of the European Communities.

Kruyt, A. and Niessen, J. (1997) Integration. In H. Vermeulen (ed.) *Immigrant policy for a multicultural society. A comparative study of integration, language and religious policy in five Western European countries*. Brussels: Migration Policy Group.

LMP (Linguistic Minorities Project) (1985) *The other languages of England*. London: Routledge and Kegan Paul.

Migration Policy Group (2000) *Diversity and cohesion: New challenges for the integration of immigrants and minorities. Final draft*. In co-operation with the European Cultural Foundation, Amsterdam.

Obdeijn, H. and De Ruiter, J. (eds) (1998) *Le Maroc au coeur de l'Europe. L'Enseignement de la langue arabe aux élèves marocains dans les pays d'accueil*. Leiden: Centre pour l'histoire des migrations.

Reich, H. (1991) Developments in ethnic minority language teaching within the European Community. In K. Jaspaert and S. Kroon (eds) *Ethnic minority languages and education* (pp. 161-174). Amsterdam/Lisse: Swets and Zeitlinger.

Reich, H. (1994) Unterricht der Herkunftssprachen von Migranten in anderen europäischen Einwanderungsländern. In A. Dick (ed.) *Muttersprachlicher Unter-richt. Ein Baustein für die Erziehung zur Mehrsprachigkeit* (pp. 31-46). Wiesbaden: Hessisches Kultusministerium.

Reid, E. and Reich, H. (1992) *Breaking the boundaries. Migrant workers' children in the EC*. Clevedon: Multilingual Matters.

Siguan, M. (1990) *Linguistic Minorities in the European Economic Community: Spain, Portugal, Greece (Summary of the report)*. Luxembourg: Office for Official Publications of the European Communities.

Tilmatine, M. (ed.) (1997) *Enseignment des langues d'origine et immigration nord-africaine en Europe: langue maternelle ou langue d'état?* Paris: INALCO/CEDREA-CRB.

Tjeerdsma, R.T. (1998) *MGO: Mercator Guide to Organizations*. Ljouwert/Leeuwarden: Mercator Education/Fryske Akademy.

Verweij, A. (1997) *Vaststelling van etnische herkomst in Nederland. De BiZa-methode nader bekeken*. Rotterdam: ISEO.

Part I

Regional languages in Europe

Basque in Spain and France

JASONE CENOZ

Basque (*Euskara*) is a unique language in Western Europe for being non-Indo-European. It is a highly inflected language with 16 morphological cases; typologically, it has been defined as ergative and agglutinative (Saltarelli, 1988). The Basque language has been in contact with Latin and Romance languages for centuries and it has been influenced by them mainly at the phonological and lexical levels. The limited use of Basque at the institutional level, the insufficient number of written texts and the spread of the Basque Country North and South of the Pyrenees can explain the existence of six Basque dialects: three in the Northern Basque Country (Lapurtera, Nafarrera Beherea, Zuberera) and three South of the Pyrenees (Bizkaiera, Gipuzkera, Nafarrera). In the last decades, the Academy of the Basque Language (*Euskaltzaindia*) has played a crucial role in the standardization of the Basque language at the oral and written levels. Even though dialectal differences are present, 'unified Basque' (*Euskara batua*) is the variety based on the central dialects of Basque which is widely accepted in the Basque Country. Nowadays, about 80% of the books published in Basque are published in *Batua*. *Batua* is also the variety used for education and official documents. There is an increasing number of grammars and dictionaries in Basque but the standardization of the Basque language is still an open process.

The Basque Country covers an area of approximately 20,742 square kilometres and comprises seven provinces, three belonging to the French *Pyrenees Atlantiques* community (Lapurdi, Nafarroa Beherea, Zuberoa), and four to two autonomous regions in Spain (the Basque Autonomous Community or BAC and Navarre). Nowadays Basque is a minority language within its own territory and the disappearance of Basque from important areas of the Basque Country is a relatively recent phenomenon resulting from the intense contact with Romance languages and immigration. The contact with Romance languages explains the important retreat suffered by Basque in Araba and Navarre in the 18th and 19th centuries (Hualde, Lakarra & Trask, 1995). This contact has increased in the 20th century as a result of industrialization and the development of communications and mass media. The industrialization of the BAC and Navarre attracted an important number of Spanish speaking immigrants in the fifties, sixties and seventies. Furthermore, the 'Spanish only' policy during Franco's dictatorship (1939-1975) had important consequences not only at the institutional and educational levels but also in the private domain.

The political and social changes that have taken place in the last decades of the 20th century in Spain have favoured attempts to maintain and revive the Basque language but the lack of institutional support for Basque in the Northern Basque Country is affecting its maintenance and revival North of the Pyrenees. The Spanish Constitution (1978) declared Spanish the nationwide official language and guaranteed the rights of Spanish speakers to use their language but also raised the possibility of recognizing other languages as co-official in their own territories. Nowadays, Basque has a co-official status in the BAC and the Northern area of Navarre but not in the Northern Basque Country. The differences in legislation have important implications for the resources allocated to the development of Basque and therefore for its maintenance and revival.

Apart from Basque and the Romance languages, English is becoming increasingly important for Basque citizens as a medium of intra-European and international communication. The status of English in the Basque Country is different from that of Basque because English is regarded as a foreign language and it is not used at the community level. The growing interest in learning English has resulted in demands for more English instruction in Basque schools that may implicate a change from bilingual to multilingual education in many Basque schools.

The demographic status of Basque

The total Basque population is approximately three million, 91% being Spanish citizens. The BAC is the most highly populated area with 73% of the total population; 18% live in Navarre and 9% in the Northern Basque Country. The studies conducted by the Basque Government, with the collaboration of the Government of Navarre and the Basque Cultural Institute of the Northern Basque Country (*Euskararen Jarraipena II*, 1997) indicate that 22% of the population is bilingual (Basque-Spanish or Basque-French), and 14.5% passive bilingual. Monolinguals in Basque are only 0.5% of the population and monolinguals in either French or Spanish are 63% of the population. Therefore, with very few exceptions, speaking

Basque equals being bilingual in Basque and a Romance language. In this chapter, speakers who are proficient in Basque will be referred to either as 'Bascophones' or 'bilinguals'.

The distribution of the Basque-speaking population varies considerably from region to region. In the BAC, 24.7% of the population is bilingual and 16.3% passive bilingual; in the Northern Basque Country, 25.7% is bilingual and 9.3% passive bilingual. In Navarre, only 9.4% of the population is bilingual and 9.8% passive bilingual. The proportion of people who are proficient in Basque has increased in the three BAC provinces. In 1991 there were 95,000 bilinguals more than in 1981, mainly because of the educational system (Garmendia, 1994). The percentage of the Basque-speaking population is quite stable in Navarre but the lack of institutional support for Basque is favouring its decline in the Northern Basque Country.

Most Basque speakers are found in the provinces of Gipuzkoa, Nafarroa Beherea and Zuberoa, where the number of Bascophones is relatively high in rural and isolated areas. When towns and cities began to develop in the Southern Basque Country as a result of industrialization, most Spanish speaking newcomers did not learn Basque and Spanish became the main language of communication. Nowadays, San Sebastian (Gipuzkoa) is the only capital city with more than 25% of Bascophones. The use of Basque in the BAC is most common in villages and towns of less than 10,000 inhabitants. In Spanish speaking areas (Araba, South of Navarre) the number of Bascophones, mainly being speakers of Basque as a second language, is higher in bigger towns such as Vitoria-Gasteiz or Pamplona-Iruñea.

The percentages corresponding to the distribution of bilinguals (Basque and Spanish/French) and monolinguals (either Spanish or French) according to age groups are given in Table 1. The data indicate that there are important differences when the three territories are compared. The percentage of Spanish-speaking mono-linguals in the BAC is much lower in the younger generations; the same trend is observed in Navarre even though the differences between the age groups are not as important. The data reveal that there is an increasing number of French-speaking monolinguals among the younger generations in the Northern Basque Country. That threatens the future of Basque in this area where Basque is not recognized as an official language.

Table 1   Distribution of bilinguals and monolinguals in different age groups
(in %)

Territories	16-24	25-34	35-49	50-64	65 plus
BAC					
Bilinguals	33	25	21	21	26
Passive bilinguals	37	27	11	6	5
Monolinguals	30	48	68	73	67
Navarre					
Bilinguals	11	9	9	9	9
Passive bilinguals	12	14	14	5	3
Monolinguals	77	77	77	86	87
Northern BC					
Bilinguals	11	14	27	31	35
Passive bilinguals	13	13	9	9	6
Monolinguals	75	73	64	60	56

The sociolinguistic status of Basque

The demographic status of Basque in the BAC (and to a lesser extent in
Navarre) reflects an increase in the number of Bascophones. The use of
Basque and its limitations have recently been analysed in the General Plan
for the Revitalization of Basque (*Euskara Biziberritzeko Plan Nagusia* or
EBPN, 1999; see also Cenoz & Perales, 1997). This revitalization is mainly
reflected in the educational system as we will see in the next section.
Other areas identified in the EBPN are adult education, family life, sports
and leisure activities, the media, publications, advertising, work and
religion. Nevertheless, the use of Basque in these areas is not widespread
and faces serious limitations. It is common for school children instructed
through the medium of Basque to use Spanish with their friends or for
adults to drop their Basque courses before becoming proficient in the
language. Even though there is a Basque-medium television channel,
together with Basque radios and a Basque newspaper, the presence of
Basque cannot compete with that of other languages in the media or in
advertising. The number of publications in Basque has increased in the
last decades but many of these publications are textbooks. Within the

family, Bascophone parents usually speak Basque to their children in the BAC and Navarre but not so often in the Northern Basque Country. The presence of Basque in sports and leisure activities is also weaker than in education. Another problem identified in the EBPN is the quality of the Basque language and the important influence it receives from Spanish.

Bascophones tend to use Basque in the private domain but they frequently use Spanish in more formal settings (*Euskararen Jarraipena I*, 1995). Bascophones also use Basque more often with children than with other members of the family and they tend to use Basque less often when shopping or working. Most bilinguals (77%) listen to the radio in Basque and 82% of them watch television in Basque.

According to the two sociolinguistic surveys already mentioned, there are three main factors affecting the use of Basque (*Euskararen Jarraipena I*, 1995; *Euskararen Jarraipena II*, 1997). The first is the number of Basco-phones in the subject's social networks. As, with a few exceptions, speaking Basque equals being bilingual, it is necessary for everybody or almost everybody in the subject's social networks to know and use Basque if this language is going to be used for communication. The second factor affecting the use of Basque is also related to language proficiency; it is the relative ease that the subject has to use Basque and Spanish. 65% of the bilinguals find it easier or at least not more difficult to speak Basque than Spanish but 35% of the bilinguals find it easier to speak Spanish, which in most cases is their first language. The third factor affecting the use of Basque is the number of Bascophones in the sociolinguistic area where the subject lives.

Attitudes towards the revitalization of Basque are also indicators of the sociolinguistic status of the language. In *Euskararen Jarraipena II* (1997), 6359 subjects were asked if the use of Basque should be promoted. The percentages corresponding to positive, neutral and negative attitudes are given in Figure 1. The data indicate that most subjects present a positive attitude towards the promotion of the use of Basque; in the BAC and in the Northern Basque Country the percentage of subjects against such promotion is much lower than in Navarre.

In sum, the Basque language has increased its use and prestige in the BAC and in the Northern and mixed areas of Navarre but not in the Northern Basque Country. The weak demographic basis of the Basque language is to some extent counterbalanced by the institutional support it receives in the BAC and in some areas of Navarre. This support has been crucial to stop its decline but there are important challenges for the future regarding the use of the language.

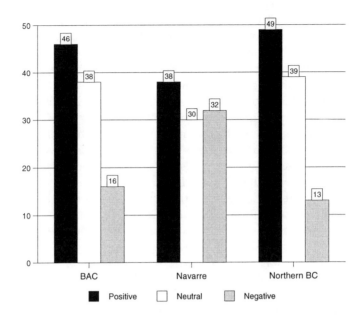

Figure 1 Attitudes towards the promotion of the use of Basque

Bilingual education in the Basque Country

Even though Basque was banned from education during the Franco regime (1939-1975), a number of private Basque-medium schools (or *ikastolak*) were opened in the sixties. These schools were not officially recognized in the beginning, but as the number of students increased they had to be eventually accepted. With the new political situation, in 1979, Basque, along with Spanish, was recognized as an official language in the BAC by the Statute of Autonomy. The law on the Normalization of the Basque Language (1982) made Basque and Spanish compulsory subjects in all schools in the BAC. Three models of language schooling were established: models A, B and D (there is no letter 'C' in Basque). These models differ with respect to the language or languages of instruction used, their linguistic aims and their intended student population.

- *Model A* schools are intended for native speakers of Spanish who choose to be instructed in Spanish. Basque is taught as a second language for three to five hours a week. These schools provide minimal instruction and, thus, minimal proficiency in Basque as a second language.
- *Model B* schools are intended for native speakers of Spanish who want to be bilingual in Basque and Spanish. Both Basque and Spanish are used as languages of instruction for approximately 50% of the school time, although there is considerable variation from school to school (Arzamendi & Genesee, 1997).
- In *Model D* schools, Basque is the language of instruction and Spanish is taught as a subject for three to five hours a week. This model was originally created as a language maintenance programme for native speakers of Basque, but it currently also includes a large number of students with Spanish as their first language. Consequently, Model D schools can be regarded as both total immersion programmes for native Spanish-speaking students and first language maintenance programmes for native Basque speakers.

Parents can choose the model they want for their children, and each model is available in the public and private sectors. Access to all three options is limited in some areas of the country, where there are not enough students interested in a particular model.

When the bilingual models were established, approximately 25% of the students in the BAC attended Basque-medium schools; at present, 79% of elementary school children and 61% of secondary school children have Basque as a language of instruction. The percentages corresponding to enrolment in the three models in elementary and secondary schools in the BAC in the year 1999/2000 are given in Figure 2.

The data indicate that most kindergarten/elementary and secondary school children have Basque as the language of instruction for some or all the subjects both in elementary and secondary schools. The data also indicate that there are more children in Model D in kindergarten and elementary schools than in secondary schools. That means that the percentage corresponding to Model D in secondary schools will increase at the expense of Model A in the near future.

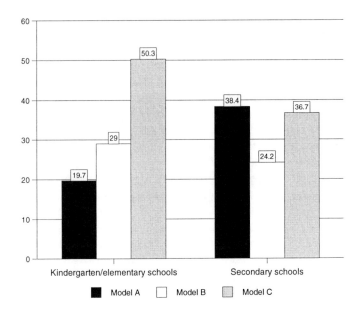

Figure 2 Bilingual education in the BAC

According to the Foral Law of the Basque language (1986), three linguistic areas are distinguished in Navarre: the Bascophone area in the North, the non-Bascophone area in the South and the mixed area which includes the central area of Navarre and its capital city. Foral Decree 159/1988 (1988) establishes that Basque is only compulsory in the Bascophone area where we can find the three educational models of the BAC (A, B and D) but Model B is only chosen by 3% of the elementary school children and 0,1% of the secondary school children. In the mixed and non-Bascophone areas of Navarre there is also a Model G with no Basque at all. In the mixed area there are three models: *A* with Basque as a subject, *D* with Basque as the language of instruction and Spanish as a subject and *G* with no Basque at all. The D model is not offered by the public school system in the non-Bascophone area and there are only a few private Basque-medium schools. The majority of the population lives in the mixed area of Navarre and the Bascophone area is the less populated. The percentages corresponding to the total distribution of the models in elementary and secondary schools in Navarre in the year 1998/1999 are given in Figure 3.

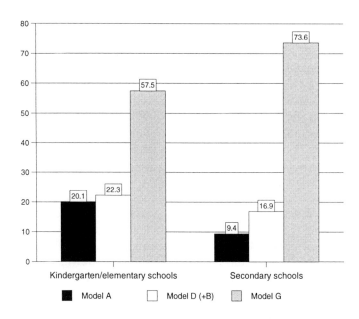

Figure 3 Bilingual education in Navarre (1998/1999)

The data indicate that Model G is the most popular even though there is an important increase of models A and D in kindergarten and primary schools as compared to secondary schools. This increase means that the percentages corresponding to models A and D will increase in secondary schools in the future.

In sum, nowadays instruction through the medium of Basque (models B and D) is increasing both in the BAC and Navarre but there are important differences between these two regions, the presence of Basque in education being more important in the BAC. Within the two regions there are important differences in the distribution of the models according to the sociolinguistic context.

The situation of Basque in education in the Northern Basque Country is weaker than in Navarre or the BAC. The first Basque school (*ikastola*) was opened in 1969 and Basque was introduced into the public educational system in 1983. Nowadays, there are four models which are similar (though not identical) to the A, B, D and G models in Navarre. However, only a small proportion of the population has access to the models in which Basque is a subject or the medium of instruction (Jauréguiberry, 1993). The distribution of the percentages corresponding to the models in kindergarten and primary school is the following: 7% of the school children are in Model A, 15% in Model D or B and 78% in the 'French only' Model G. These percentages are similar to those of Navarre but in the Bascophone area of Navarre 80% of kindergarten and primary school children have Basque as the language of instruction.

Several evaluations of the Basque bilingual programmes have been carried out in the last years and more than 25,000 students have taken part in these evaluations. The evaluations have focused on several areas: proficiency in Basque and Spanish, academic achievement and foreign language skills (see also Cenoz, 1998; Etxeberria, 1999). The results indicate that instruction through Basque (the minority language) is closely related to higher levels of achievement in this language while proficiency in Spanish/French (the majority languages) tends to be unrelated to the language of instruction. It seems likely that since Spanish and French are the majority languages, opportunities for extensive exposure to it outside school compensate for reduced exposure to it in school. Most studies have also found that there are no differences in academic achievement.

Bilingual education and English

Apart from Basque and the Romance languages, the spread of English as a language of international and intra-European communication has also affected education in the Basque Country. As in many other European bilingual communities learning English means learning a third language. It is a process that shares some characteristics with second language acquisition but it is also affected by the outcomes of bilingualism (see also Cenoz & Jessner, 2000).

The increasing need to be proficient in English and the traditional low level of proficiency attained at school in the BAC and Navarre have resulted in different projects to introduce English in kindergarten or to intensify the exposure to English at a later age. A research study on the early introduction of English in kindergarten shows that learning English from age four does not adversely affect the pupils' acquisition of Basque or Spanish or their overall cognitive development (Cenoz, 1997). Research findings on the acquisition of English as a third language in the BAC also indicate that higher levels of bilingualism (Model D) are positively related with higher levels of proficiency in English (Cenoz & Valencia, 1994; Lasagabaster, 1997). These results are compatible with the threshold and interdependence hypotheses proposed by Cummins (1976; 1981), the higher levels of metalinguistic awareness associated with bilingualism and more highly developed learning strategies associated with L3 acquisition (Cenoz & Genesee, 1998). Nevertheless, bilingual and multilingual education are complex educational systems and it is important to conduct further research in order to identify the most efficient formulae of exposure to three (or in some cases four) languages in different sociolinguistic contexts.

In general terms, parents, teachers and school children present a very positive attitude towards the early introduction of English (Cenoz, 1997) but a recent study shows that model D students' attitudes towards Basque are slightly more positive than towards Spanish and English (Cenoz, 1999).

The intensity of the exposure to English and the possibility of using English as the medium of instruction for some school subjects faces some problems. Even though there are special educational programmes for teachers, the number of teachers highly proficient both in Basque and English is still insufficient. Moreover, the different status of Basque and English at the international level also has some implications. There is concern that the gains that Basque has achieved in education after long years of efforts will be threatened by the extended use of English, while others think that more resources should be spent on English than on Basque.

Conclusion

The situation of Basque is different in the Northern and Southern parts of the Basque Country. Basque has stopped its decline in the BAC and Navarre but not in the Northern Basque Country. These differences confirm the crucial role played by institutional support in the revitalization of lesser used languages. Even though the data in the BAC and Northern and mixed areas of Navarre are promising, the future of Basque is still uncertain. A carefully planned linguistic policy involving the community languages and languages of intra-European communication is needed.

References

Arzamendi, J. and Genesee, F. (1997) Reflections on immersion education in the Basque Country. In K. Johnson and M. Swain (eds) *Immersion education: International perspectives* (pp. 151-66). Cambridge: Cambridge University Press.

Cenoz, J. (1997) L'acquisition de la troisième langue: bilinguisme et plurilinguisme au Pays Basque. *AILE* 10, 159-80.

Cenoz, J. (1998) Multilingual education in the Basque Country. In J. Cenoz and F. Genesee (eds) *Beyond bilingualism: Multilingualism and multilingual education.* (pp. 175-191). Clevedon: Multilingual Matters.

Cenoz, J. (1999) *The acquisition of English as a third language at different ages.* Unpublished research report, University of the Basque Country.

Cenoz, J. and Genesee, F. (1998) Psycholinguistic perspectives on multilingualism and multilingual education. In J. Cenoz and F. Genesee (eds) *Beyond bilingualism: Multilingualism and multilingual education* (pp. 16-32). Clevedon: Multilingual Matters.

Cenoz, J. and Jessner, U. (2000) *English in Europe: The acquisition of a third language.* Clevedon: Multilingual Matters.

Cenoz, J. and Perales, J. (1997) Minority language learning in the administration: data from the Basque Country. *Journal of multilingual and multicultural development* 18, 261-270.

Cenoz, J. and Valencia, J. (1994) Additive trilingualism: evidence from the Basque Country. *Applied psycholinguistics* 15, 157-209.

Cummins, J. (1976) The influence of bilingualism on cognitive growth: A synthesis of research findings and explanatory hypotheses. *Working papers on bilingualism* 9, 1-43.

Cummins, J. (1981) The role of primary language development in promoting educational success for language minority children. In California State Department of Education (eds) *Schooling and language minority students: A theoretical framework* (pp. 3-49). Los Angeles: Evaluation, Dissemination and Assessment Centre.

Etxeberria, F. (1999) *Bilingüismo y Educación en el País del Euskara.* Donostia: Erein.

Euskara Biziberritzeko Plan Nagusia/Plan General de Promoción del Uso del Euskara (1999) Vitoria-Gasteiz: Eusko Jaurlaritza.

Euskararen Jarraipena I. La Continuidad del Euskera I. La Continuité de la Langue Basque I. (1995) Vitoria-Gasteiz: Eusko Jaurlaritza.

Euskararen Jarraipena II. La Continuidad del Euskera II. La Continuité de la Langue Basque II. (1997) Vitoria-Gasteiz: Eusko Jaurlaritza.

Garmendia, M.K. (1994) *Eusko Jaurlaritzako hizkuntza politikarako idazkari nagusiaren agerraldia, berak eskatuta, Eusko legebiltzarreko iraskunde eta herrizaingo batzordearen aurrean.* Vitoria-Gasteiz: Eusko Jaurlaritza.

Hualde, J., Lakarra, J. and Trask, R. (eds) 1995, *On the history of the Basque language: Readings in Basque historical linguistics.* Amsterdam: John Benjamins.

Jaureguiberry, F. (1993) *Le Basque à l'ecole maternelle et elémentaire*. Pau: Université de Pau et des Pays de l'Adour.

Lasagabaster, D. (1997) *Creatividad y conciencia metalingüística: Incidencia en el aprendizaje del inglés como L3*. PhD Thesis, University of the Basque Country.

Saltarelli, M. (1988) *Basque*. London: Routledge.

Welsh in Great Britain

COLIN WILLIAMS

Welsh society is characterised by a unilingual majority and a bilingual minority which is gradually benefiting from institutionalised recognition by the state. However, the Welsh language is far from being secure. It faces severe difficulties in being recognised as an essential language even within its own national territory.

Demographic trends and structure

The 20th century has witnessed the collapse of the language as a popular medium of communication in most parts of Wales. In 1901 the census recorded 929,824 of the population as able to speak Welsh and 1,577,141 as able to speak English. Of these 280,905 were Welsh speaking monoglots, 648,919 were bilingual Welsh-English speakers and 928,222 were monoglot English speaking residents. English had become pervasive and advantageous in most spheres of life. Successive inter-censal decline has been the marked feature of census evidence on Welsh-speaking. The peak was 1911, when 977,400 persons were returned as able to speak Welsh, 190,300 of whom were monoglots. The current low (1991) is 590,800 hardly any of whom are adult monoglots. This represents a decline from 43.5% of the population in 1911 to only 18.7% in 1991, a loss of 24.8%. Explanations for this decline focus on the inter-war period when stigmatisation, a collapse in confidence and depression-induced population out-migration encouraged widespread language shift. 1921-1939 was the crisis turning point as a generation was denied the opportunity to learn Welsh. This reflected parental rejection of the language and an unresponsive education system reproducing imperial values and attitudes which deemed that Welsh was irrelevant in a modernising world order. Such convictions have waned since from the fifties the rate of decline has been more moderate, reflecting a reversal in the language's fortunes (see Table 1).

Table 1 Proportion of population speaking Welsh, by county, 1921-1991 (Source: Census, 1981: 50)

	% of all persons speaking Welsh							% of all persons speaking Welsh only					
	1921	1931	1951	1961	1971	1981	1991	1921	1931	1951	1961	1971	1981
Wales	37.1	36.8	28.9	26.0	20.8	18.9	18.7	6.3	4.0	1.7	1.0	1.3	0.8
Counties													
Clwyd	41.7	41.3	30.2	27.3	21.4	18.7	18.2	5.8	3.4	1.3	0.8	1.4	0.8
Dyfed	67.8	69.1	63.3	60.1	52.5	46.3	43.7	15.3	9.6	4.1	2.4	2.4	1.6
Gwent	5.0	4.7	2.8	2.9	1.9	2.5	2.4	0.2	0.1	0.1	0.2	0.1	0.1
Gwynedd	78.7	82.5	74.2	71.4	64.7	61.2	61.0	28.1	22.1	9.1	5.2	4.9	2.6
M. Glamorgan	38.4	37.1	22.8	18.5	10.5	8.4	8.5	2.3	0.8	0.3	0.4	0.8	0.5
Powys	35.1	34.6	29.6	27.8	23.7	20.2	20.2	6.1	3.9	1.6	0.9	1.0	0.9
S. Glamorgan	6.3	6.1	4.7	5.2	5.0	5.8	6.5	0.2	0.1	0.1	0.1	0.4	0.2
W. Glamorgan	41.3	40.5	31.6	27.5	20.3	16.4	15.0	3.6	1.3	0.5	0.5	1.0	0.8

Changes between 1981 and 1991 were minimal while the current bilingual population is stable and likely to grow. The 1991 census reveals significant increases in the 3-15 age group, a consolidation of the 16-44 age group and an expected decline in the older age groups. These trends are likely to be maintained which suggests that the demographic future of Welsh is brighter than at any other time in recent history.

Bilingualism represents a series of social choices for the c.590,800 individuals, who switch language by domain, by interlocutor and by preference as the opportunity allows. The census does not probe deeply into the social context or use of bilingualism. An alternative is the Welsh Office 'Welsh Social Survey' (1993) which contains details of 19,056 households interviewed between September and December 1992. The survey revealed that Welsh speakers represent 21.5% of the total population (see Table 2). Disaggregating the ability factor we find that the highest incidence is in the youngest age range, 3-15, with 32.4% of the population fluent in Welsh. The proportion drops dramatically in the age range of 16-29, at 17.8%, and for the 30-44 age range falls further to 16.7%. For the age range 45-64 the figure rises to 18.7% and reaches 24.2% for those aged 65 and over. Clearly this bodes well for the future, but in- and out-migration, marriage patterns and a host of other reasons preclude any firm prediction that the youngest cohort will necessarily maintain their reasonable levels of fluency into adulthood. We need to know far more about the details of first and second language patterns and in this respect the survey revealed that 55.7% of Welsh speakers considered it to be their mother tongue. They represent 12% of the national population.

The balance between first and second language speakers is a delicate issue. Very often one hears about the need to encourage language reproduction within predominantly Welsh speaking families and communities. However, language production through the education system rather than language reproduction through local community socialisation seems to characterise the younger elements of the population. This is revealed in Table 2, where the school factor is evident for only 27% of the total Welsh speakers in the 3-15 age range considered Welsh their mother tongue. Presumably the remainder consider Welsh fluency to be a school-acquired competence rather than their first, instinctive language of daily life. Each successive age cohort of Table 2 recorded higher proportions of mother-tongue speakers, reaching a peak of 79.3% for the 65 and over group. Older age groups learned Welsh at home within the family and for some linguists this is a significant feature for their use of Welsh is likely to be natural, richer, more idiomatic and colloquial than the rather formal,

Table 2 Welsh by age, 1992 (thousands) (Source: Welsh Office, 1992)

Age category	Sample size	Population base (aged 3 and over)	N of Welsh-speakers	Welsh-speakers as % of population	Mother tongue speakers as % of all Welsh-speakers	Welsh-speakers as % of population, 1991 census
3-15	5,094	486.2	157.4	32.4	27.0	24.3
16-29	4,809	517.0	91.8	17.8	48.9	15.9
30-44	5,741	585.2	97.5	16.7	60.8	14.8
45-65	6,674	664.4	123.7	18.7	70.7	17.4
65+	5,335	498.0	120.4	24.2	79.3	22.6
Total	27,653	2,750.7	590.8	21.5	55.7	18.7

Table 3 Welsh-speakers' current use of Welsh, 1992 (in %) (Source: Welsh Office, 1992)

Welsh ability	Wales	Clwyd	Dyfed	Gwynedd	Powys	W. Glamorgan	G., M. & S. Glamorgan
Rarely	4.5	8.9	1.9	1.3	5.7	6.9	15.3
Occasionally	12.0	21.7	7.4	5.5	17.9	26.8	21.8
Half and half	21.2	28.5	19.6	14.3	25.3	33.6	29.7
Most or all the time	62.3	40.9	71.1	79.0	51.1	32.8	33.1

English-influenced style and patterning of younger Welsh speakers. This raises difficult questions of interpretation, for in terms of vocabulary and domain confidence the quality of Welsh spoken by the youngest group may be superior to that of the eldest group, even if it is less idiomatic. It may also be suggested that for the younger age groups their language loyalty/affiliation may not prove to be as resolute in the future, if Welsh represents for them a predominantly second language: a useful means of communication rather than an automatic first choice language of expression.

The Social Survey also indicates that 368,000 (13.4%) are fluent in Welsh. A further 94,900 (3.5%) described themselves as able to speak quite a lot of Welsh, and 467,300 (17.0%) described themselves as speaking only a small amount of Welsh. Thus 930,200 (33.9%) were able to speak a little Welsh and 462,900 (16.9%) were capable of speaking a considerable amount of Welsh. These figures surpass the census figure of c.590,800 Welsh speakers and offer a rough guide to the potential Welsh-speaking population able to use government services or consumer/audience opportunities. Of those who claimed to be fluent, 80.5% came from families where both parents spoke Welsh, 7.2% from where the mother was fluent, 4.6% from where the father was fluent and 7.7% from families where neither parent was fluent.

Welsh speakers, asked to describe one statement which best re-presented their current use of Welsh (Table 3), reflected interesting county variations, with Gwynedd and Dyfed recording the highest usage of Welsh at 79% and 71.1% respectively. Lower proportions are recorded for Powys and Clwyd at 51.5% and 40.9%, while West Glamorgan and the amalgamated category of the three counties of the south-east record 32.8% and 33.1% respectively. Significantly, whilst only 6.9% of fluent Welsh speakers in West Glamorgan would claim that they rarely use the language, as many as 15.3% in the industrial south-east found little reason or opportunity to use Welsh (Table 3).

Sociolinguistic contexts and language reproduction

The Welsh Language Board's *Strategy for the Welsh Language* (1999) summarises recent achievements as follows:

The Welsh Language Act of 1993, the *Mentrau Iaith*, the spread of bilingual education at primary and secondary level, Welsh as a compulsory subject in the National Curriculum, the vitality of movements such as *Mudiad Ysgolion Meithrin, Urdd Gobaith Cymru,* local and national eisteddfodau, Welsh language schemes, increasing use of bilingualism and business and the economy are just a few of the many examples where language planning has successfully bucked the trend of downward shift. (Welsh Language Board, 1999)

Nevertheless there is still cause for concern because:
- In many families where only one parent can speak Welsh, the children are unable to speak it.
- 40% of children who complete primary education as first language Welsh speakers commence their secondary education as second language Welsh speakers and take their curriculum through the medium of English.
- The Welsh Language Board's commissioned surveys show that more than 40% of Welsh speaking adults lack confidence in using the language, and therefore use it infrequently.
- During adolescence, many bilingual teenagers use the language less frequently as they grow older (though this trend may be reversed in later life).
- Geographically, the Welsh language has tended to decline by a westward movement with many communities lessening in their everyday use of the Welsh language.

Family-household composition

Language survey data suggests that social context, family language transmission and exposure to formal bilingual education are key factors in language reproduction. Yet, community and family are less powerful agents of language reproduction than they were previously. Analysis of family/household composition patterns by Aitchison and Carter (1997) reveal significant and possibly damaging trends. Their analysis of SARs data shows that an extremely high proportion of Welsh speakers are linguistically isolated within their home environments. Table 4 describes a nested hierarchy of four types of households based on the language ability of household members. A basic distinction was drawn by Aitchison and Carter (1997) between Type 1 (i) - those households that have at least one Welsh speaker (defined as 'Welsh speaking house-holds'), and Type 1 (ii) - those that have no Welsh-speakers. 22% of all households belong to the first of these two types, but over half (51%) of the households contain only one Welsh speaker within them and many of these are elderly persons living alone. This does not bode well for the future.

Table 4   Language attributes and household types

Household types	% of households
Type 1 All households	
(i) without Welsh speakers	73.6
(ii) with Welsh speakers	26.4
Type 2 Households with Welsh speakers	
(i) wholly Welsh-speaking	53.6
(ii) partly Welsh-speaking	46.4
Type 3 Household composition and Welsh speech	
a wholly Welsh-speaking	
(i) with children	10.9
(ii) without children	42.7
b partly Welsh-speaking	
(i) with Welsh-speaking children	18.9
(ii) with non-Welsh-speaking children	5.8
(iii) with no children	21.7
Type 4 Household size, composition and Welsh speech	
a wholly Welsh-speaking	
(i) with children	10.9
(ii) single-person households	21.3
(iii) without children	21.5
b partly Welsh-speaking	
(i) with Welsh-speaking children - single speaker	6.2
(ii) with Welsh-speaking children - more than 1 Welsh speaker	12.7
c partly Welsh-speaking, with non-Welsh-speaking children	
(i) single Welsh speaker	4.9
(ii) more than one Welsh speaker	0.9
d partly Welsh-speaking without children	
(i) single Welsh speaker	18.6
(ii) more than one Welsh speaker	3.1

A second distinction is that between households which are wholly or partly Welsh-speaking, Types 2 (i) and 2 (ii). Just over half of Welsh speaking households are wholly Welsh speaking (54%) but they represent only 14% of all households in Wales. Wholly Welsh speaking households can be further sub-divided into those with and those without children (aged 3-17 years) - Types 3a (i) and 3a (ii). Aitchison and Carter (1997) aver that such a pattern is disconcerting for Welsh as the data show that a very high proportion of such households have no children within them; furthermore almost half are single person households (Type 4 (ii)). Similarly of partly Welsh speaking households, nearly two thirds (64%) have just a single Welsh speaker (Types 4a (i), 4b (i) and 4c (i), the majority of whom are in households which have no children. Encouragingly 41% of the households that are partly Welsh speaking have one or more children who are able to speak Welsh. More sobering is the realisation that some 70% of the Welsh speaking households have no Welsh speaking children within them. Welsh households are in the main linguistically fractured and structurally diverse in composition.

The community
Communities of the northern and western heartland seem to be fragmenting irretrievably and if this cultural resource base atrophies what then for the production and reproduction of the identity transmitted through the Welsh language? Strident attempts are being made to counter some of the deleterious tendencies of globalisation and European enlargement. Significant here are three institutional reforms, i.e. *Mentrau Iaith*, language resource centres and linguistic animateurs (Williams, 1999; Williams & Evas, 1998).

Mentrau Iaith
The original *Mentrau Iaith* (language enterprise agencies), dating from 1991-1993, were established in predominantly Welsh-speaking communities. The 18 *Mentrau Iaith* aim to stimulate the development of Welsh within a wide social context as community regeneration movements with a linguistic cutting edge. Prime funding is by the National Assembly through the Welsh Language Board together with some ancillary funding by Local Authorities, which currently totals £310,384 *per annum*. *Mentrau Iaith* offer a significant socio-psychological fillip for Welsh maintenance in contexts which would otherwise lead to fragmentation and they serve as a focus to create a new set of partnerships between the National

Assembly, the Welsh Language Board, local government, statutory public bodies, health trusts and voluntary agencies and private companies.

Mentrau Iaith and their partners are seeking to establish a national framework and core mission, based in part on the recommendations of the Community Language Planning Report (Williams & Evas, 1998) that each *Menter* should:

- Urge and encourage community ownership of the language, together with a transference of responsibility for it back to volunteers and the Menter's community partners.
- By means of social and leisure activities increase the opportunities available for people to use Welsh.
- Work for the promotion of Welsh in the community through co-operation with movements, institutional representatives and other individuals at local and national level.
- Raise the profile of Welsh in business in the local area.
- Promote bilingualism in the workplace.
- Encourage Welsh speakers to use the language and to make use of existing bilingual opportunities.
- To improve the command of fluent speakers.
- To regain uncertain speakers, or those who have lost their Welsh for whatever reason.
- To offer practical assistance to adult learners and pupils who are learning Welsh as a second language.
- To assimilate new speakers to the Welsh-medium community and inform the mother tongue speakers about their needs.
- To lobby training agencies to prepare professional bilingual and language-friendly materials.
- To disseminate information about local Welsh-medium education and training.
- If appropriate, to promote issues which will lead to local economic development.

Additional work is needed on a range of factors which influence the transmission and use of Welsh in the community and regional economy, such as:

- Demographic trends and age/sex differences by language acquisition and maintenance.
- Occupational structures and local economic development.
- Unorthodox social networks, especially in urban contexts.

- Research on the implications of telematic networks and the digital economy.
- A lucid understanding of rural community changes which may be independent of, though contributing to, those conditions which maintain Welsh as a dynamic element in society.
- Consideration of the available methods whereby the linguistic abilities of Welsh speakers could be improved.
- Research on how the *Mentrau* may evolve as agencies in the field of social development.
- Research on how the *Mentrau* may become language centers catering for other languages used within Wales.

Language resource centres

There is also a need for county-level *Mentrau* together with county and national level resource centres, and linguistic *animateurs* as detailed in Williams and Evas (1997). The National Language Resource Centre would act as a language planning support centre and have prime responsibility for the following issues:

- Marketing the economic value of bilingualism to Wales, and to those businesses who are considering locating or investing here, especially within the context of a multilingual European Union.
- Monitoring, supporting and transplanting practical language planning activities together with new theories in this field, by drawing on international precedents.
- Surveying and reviewing materials which facilitate the use of Welsh, especially in relation to software developments in the workplace.
- Creating a central data base of Welsh materials so that individuals can profit from examples of good working practice which may be adapted to various circumstances.
- Preparing guides and materials to assist individuals and voluntary organisations to work in practical terms to promote Welsh in their communities.
- Providing a support help-line which the public could access to gain authoritative advice on the use of Welsh, for example, on how to express complex ideas when the language has to be very precise as in preparing a contract or a legal document.
- Acting as a national and international information centre for translation services and other language-related services.

- Hosting or co-promoting seminars on practical aspects of language planning in Wales and in an international context, drawing on good practice from Canada/Quebec, Catalonia, Ireland and Euskadi.

Linguistic animateurs

An essential means of increasing Welsh-medium services is to create a framework which normalises the application of civil rights incorporated in the Language Act of 1993 and the respective charters on human rights. One of the CLP's principal recommendations is that the Welsh Language Board, government departments, companies and all types of institutions should develop the idea of linguistic *animateurs* - individuals charged with the special responsibility of promoting the use of the language. Linguistic *animateurs* would function at three levels and with varying degrees of financial support and authority: 1) at the local level, selected social workers, nurses, health visitors, mid-wives, could employ more Welsh whilst discharging their responsibilities; 2) within a county or a specific region, *animateurs* could promote Welsh use in hitherto under-used services; and 3) within specific agencies such as the police service, local authorities or health trust, the ambulance and fire services linguistic *animateurs* could help establish a new bilingual framework in order to improve good practice or to prepare the ground for the implementation of work-place language plans by adopting best case examples from other sectors.

Animateurs should be well trained and supported by the Board's expertise and provision of the following:

- An information pack which includes examples of 'good practice' and 'bad practice', worked examples of successful and unsuccessful language planning.
- A comprehensive analysis of the agencies promoting Welsh in the local target area, together with names and addresses of contact personnel to encourage effective networking.
- In-service training at a national level for all linguistic *animateurs* to include international perspectives drawn from respective Language Boards, the European Bureau for Lesser Used Languages and the European Union.

Legislative recognition

It was not until the passing of the Welsh Courts Act of 1942 that the provisions prohibiting the use of Welsh by the Acts of Union 1536-1543 were rescinded. Further legal recognition was given in the Welsh

Language Act of 1967 which offered an initial and inadequate definition of equal validity of English and Welsh in Wales. During the sixties and seventies a number of statutory and non-statutory bodies called for greater state support for the language. One initial response by the Welsh Office was the establishment in 1977 of the short-lived *Cyngor yr Iaith Gymraeg* (The Welsh Language Council). It also led to some limited financial support for Welsh language activities, both in the public arena and in education via specific provisions in two government acts passed during the latter part of the seventies. Under section 26 of The Development of Rural Wales Act 1976, the Welsh Office provided support for Welsh language social activities, most importantly the work of *Mudiad Ysgolion Meithrin* (The Welsh Nursery Schools Movement, founded in 1971), *Eisteddfod Genedlaethol Cymru* (The National Eisteddfod of Wales), *Cyngor Llyfrau Cymraeg* (The Welsh Books Council) and via *Menter a Busnes* (Business and Enterprise), concerned with the promotion of a new spirit of enterprise in rural Welsh speaking communities. The major piece of legislation in the 20th century was the Welsh Language Act, 1993, discussed below.

The media and cultural organisations

The greatest boost to the popular and technical use of Welsh was the inauguration of the television service, *Sianel Pedwar Cymru*, on November 1, 1982. Some 34 out of 145 hours per week are transmitted in Welsh, mainly at peak time. The programmes reach a relatively high percentage of their target audience. S4C is a commissioning rather than a production body, and in consequence has spawned a network of independent film makers, animators, creative designers, writers etcetera who can turn their original Welsh language programmes into English or 'foreign' languages for sale in the international media market place. Cardiff ranks second to London as a UK media-production centre in the UK. Three issues dominate the broadcasting debate viz.:

* Financial self-sufficiency versus subsidy.
* The relaxation of boundaries inside programmes between the use of Welsh and English.
* The multicultural nature of S4C which transmits European soccer and sport, repackaged documentaries, soaps, quizzes and other material all dubbed into Welsh.

In part this is to attract new viewers to the channel and in part it reflects S4C's participation in the European Broadcasting Union and commercial marketing of international television material.

At a voluntary level there is a network of *Eisteddfodau* (competitive cultural festivals) which nurture school-based and community-based performances of Welsh plays, or plays in translation, of musical items, poetry, craft work, art and design and scientific projects. This network starts at the local level and the successful competitors progress through intervening stages to reach the *National Eisteddfod* and the *Urdd National Eisteddfod*. It was the *Eisteddfod* which acted as a vehicle for national culture, setting both the themes and the standards of popular representation of Welshness. More recently the *Urdd* (The Welsh League of Youth) has re-interpreted traditional Welsh mass culture by adding go-karting, tenpin bowling, discos and surfing 'in Welsh'. A second feature is adult learning of Welsh through *Wlpan* and related schemes which are geographically widespread and well subscribed. These often feed Welsh clubs and social centres which may have sport, folk dancing or music as their focus but offer a wider entree into the indigenous culture. Adult learners' children, and those of in-migrants, may attend Language Centres for English only speakers, designed to speed up their integration into the local community. However, there are severe difficulties in reconciling the rights and obligations of indigenous citizens with those of incomers, many of whom are antagonistic or hostile to the requirement that their children learn Welsh or attend a bilingual school. Thus Wales possesses both grass-roots parents movements in favour of extending bilingual education, and a lesser number of well organised groups who oppose such an extension on the grounds that it limits their rights as British citizens.

Language planning and policy measures

The Welsh Language Act (1993) provided a statutory framework for the treatment of English and Welsh on the basis of equality and inaugurated a new era in language planning. Its chief policy instrument is the re-fashioned and strengthened Welsh Language Board, established on December 21, 1993, as a non-departmental statutory organisation. It is funded by a grant from the Welsh Office, which in the year ending March 31, 1998, totalled £5,756,00. It has three main duties:

- Advising organisations which are preparing language schemes on the mechanism of operating the central principle of the Act, that the Welsh and English languages should be treated on a basis of equality.

- Advising those who provide services to the public in Wales on issues relevant to the Welsh language.
- Advising central Government on issues relating to the Welsh language.

The Act details key steps to be taken by the Welsh Language Board and by public sector bodies in the preparation of Welsh language schemes which are designed to treat Welsh and English on the basis of equality. Since 1995 a total of 67 language schemes have been approved including all 22 local authorities. In 1998 notices had been issued to a further 59 bodies to prepare schemes.

The Welsh Language Board's primary goal is to enable the language to become self-sustaining and secure as a medium of communication. It has set itself four priorities:

- To increase the numbers of Welsh-speakers.
- To provide more opportunities to use the language.
- To change the habits of language use and encourage people to take advantage of the opportunities provided.
- To strengthen Welsh as a community language.

The establishment of a National Assembly for Wales in May 1999 signalled a new era in the development of a bilingual society. For the first time ever Wales has its own bilingual, decision-making political body and despite severe criticism in its first year of operation, the Assembly deliberations do impact directly on the lives of citizens including decisions on language policy. These are likely to focus on three important aspects. First, language policy in relation to education and public administration, equal rights and the socialisation of citizens within civil society. This involves, *inter alia*, issues such as interaction with the British state and its unwritten constitution, the European Convention on human rights, European Community language policies, the development of bilingual education, bilingual service provision in local government, health and social services. Secondly, economic policies and regional development initiatives which seek to stabilise predominantly Welsh-speaking communities, to create employment and to promote bilingual working opportunities. Thirdly, consideration of the interests of Welsh language and culture as they are impacted upon by town and country/ structure planning and improvements to the transport system. In addition, the pressing housing, property control and rural service issues highlighted by various bodies including *Jigso and Cymdeithas yr Iaith* should be addressed directly. A fundamental precept of the Assembly's mission should be that its policies on bilingualism should be complemented by the promotion of positive attitudes to Welsh culture and heritage.

A prime issue in the normalisation of Welsh will be the extent to which it can become a cross-cutting medium of governance and administration and not limited to its own Committee for the Welsh language and culture, i.e. not become commodified and separated out as a 'problem area'. A second issue is the degree to which establishing a bilingual Assembly will influence the language-choice behaviour of the public. Critics sympathetic to the promotion of Welsh have observed that local authorities have invested heavily in statutory language schemes which in reality are of little interest to all but a handful of Welsh speakers. It would be regrettable if the Assembly's commitment were not matched by the public's adoption of Welsh as a language of interaction with national government. In turn the Assembly may use its position as an exemplar, a testing ground, an educator and a significant actor to influence behaviour in this regard.

Two other issues of direct importance for education will be the wider exposure of all children in Wales to bilingual instruction and the introduction of new software and terminological data bases which will enable students to shift back and forth between information generated in English and that generated in Welsh.

Education and the structure of bilingual Wales

The school's role in promoting a bilingual society has increased following the reforms of the 1988 Education Act which insisted that Welsh be a core subject in the National Curriculum. A wider range of subjects including Maths and Science, Design and Computing are now capable of being taught through the medium of Welsh. In Higher Education there is a wide range of vocational and non-vocational courses available to full and part-time students, but again it must be emphasised that in such developments the numbers involved within particular courses are small. These trends are significant for they reinforce the value of bilingual skills in society. From 1990-1997 the proportion and number of pupils in formally designated Welsh medium primary and secondary schools had grown very slowly. It is within the dominant, conventional English-medium sector where the greatest impact of educational reforms may be charted

Table 5 Maintained primary schools teaching through the medium of Welsh (number of schools)

Schools having classes where:	1990/91	1993/94	1994/95	1995/96	1996/97
A Welsh is the sole or main medium of instruction	445	460	465	455	499
% of schools	25.9	27.1	27.5	27.1	26.7
B Welsh is used as a medium of teaching for part of the curriculum	–	116	108	106	95
% of schools	–	6.8	6.4	6.3	5.7
(b) Schools having classes of first and second language pupils where some of the teaching is through the medium of Welsh	36	–	–	–	–
% of schools	2.1	–	–	–	–
(c) Schools having classes of second language pupils where some of the teaching is through the medium of Welsh	122	–	–	–	–
% of schools	7.1	–	–	–	–
C Welsh is taught as a second language only	870	1,068	1,091	1,109	1,136
% of schools	50.7	62.9	64.5	66.0	67.6
D No Welsh is taught	244	54	27	11	1
% of schools	14.2	3.2	1.6	0.7	0.1
Total schools	1,718	1,698	1,691	1,681	1,681

and analysed. Table 5 charts the trends in maintained primary schools teaching through the medium of Welsh, 1990-1997. Of the 1718 schools in 1990, designated Welsh-medium schools where Welsh was the sole or main medium of instruction accounted for 25.9% (445) of the total. The number in this category had risen slightly to 26.7%, (449) schools by 1997 and will witness a gradual growth over the next decade.

However, it is in the non-conventional Welsh-medium sector that significant changes have been recorded. In 1990 50.7% (870) of schools had classes where Welsh was taught as a second language only. By 1997 this proportion had risen to 67.6% (1136). Most of the increase was due to the curriculum impact of the 1988 Education Act and the social effects of the Welsh Language Act (1993) which in effect abolished Category D schools (Table 5). Whilst in 1990, 14.2% (244) of primary schools were not obliged to teach any Welsh, by 1997 only one school was exempted from this statutory requirement.

An alternative method of measuring the impact of the reformed curriculum is to analyse changes in the numbers of children able to speak Welsh as a direct result of being exposed to the school influence in addition to any home or parental fluency in Welsh. Over the period 1990-1997, about the same number of children (aged 5-11) (c.14,500) speak Welsh at home. But throughout this period there is a steady increase in the number of children who can speak Welsh fluently but who do not speak it at home, from 15,181 to 21,221. Again, there is a doubling of the numbers who can speak Welsh but are not completely fluent, from 30,753 in 1990 to 67,666 in 1997, and therefore a corresponding drop in the numbers who cannot speak Welsh at all from 155,796 to 124,682.

Alternative evidence of the same structural change may be presented in relation to the organisation of teaching through the medium of Welsh in maintained primary schools, by class distribution and by pupil distribution. There has been a general increase in the range and number of classes taught through the medium of Welsh and a corresponding absolute drop of 4/5 in those classes wherein Welsh is taught, down from 2,455 in 1990 to only 550 in 1997. Similarly there has been a significant growth in the number of pupils in classes where Welsh was the sole or main medium of instruction from 38,404 in 1990 to 50,392 in 1997. Conversely there has been a sharp decline in the numbers of pupils in classes being taught no Welsh from 62,245 in 1990 to 14,553 in 1997.

At the secondary level a similar picture obtains but we may trace the trend over a longer time period 1980-1997. Table 6 reveals that there has been a more structured and linguistically differentiated pattern of school

Table 6 Maintained secondary schools teaching Welsh* (number of schools)

	1980/81	1990/91	1993/94	1995/95	1995/96	1996/97
Schools where Welsh is taught as both a first and second language	82	68	53	48	50	50
% of schools	34.5	29.6	23.3	21.1	21.9	21.8
Schools where Welsh is taught as a first language only	5	11	13	18	17	18
% of schools	2.1	4.8	5.7	7.9	7.5	7.9
Schools where Welsh is taught as a second language only	116	129	153	158	159	161
% of schools	48.7	56.1	67.4	69.6	69.7	70.3
Schools where no Welsh is taught	35	22	8	3	2	0
% of schools	14.7	9.5	3.5	1.3	0.9	0.0
Total	238	230	227	227	228	229

* At January each year. Prior to 1993/94 at September each year. Includes grant maintained schools.

type. The composite school category, where Welsh was taught as both a first and second language has shrunk, while there has been a corresponding increase in the number of schools where Welsh is taught as a first language only, from the five pioneering schools which existed in 1980 to the 18 such schools by 1997. A larger number of secondary schools are now classified as equipped to teach Welsh as a second language from 116 in 1980 to 161 in 1997. As a consequence the final category of schools (N=35) where no Welsh was taught in 1980 has been eliminated from the classification by 1997. Most of these 35 schools were either state-funded Catholic schools or secondary schools located within long-Anglicised areas of Wales, mostly in the border counties abutting England.

Welsh in schools at the end of the 20th Century

What is the current situation as we address the needs of the 21st century? The percentage of primary pupils who can speak Welsh fluently is increasing though the percentage that speaks Welsh as a home language is decreasing. About 2% of pupils assessed as fluent Welsh speakers at the end of their primary education do not study Welsh as a first language when they start in secondary school. In the primary sector, the percentage of pupils assessed in Welsh as a first language in National Curriculum assessments is higher than the percentage fluent in the language. Specific data on pupils and schools is presented successively.

Pupils

- In January 1999, 16% of primary school children were fluent Welsh speakers which included 6.3% who spoke Welsh at home. 13.3% of pupils in year groups 7-11 (compulsory school age) in maintained secondary school were taught Welsh as a first language.
- The percentage of primary school children speaking Welsh fluently increased from 13.1% in 1986/1987 to 16% in 1998/1999. The percentage of primary school children speaking Welsh at home fell over the same period from 7.3% to 6.3% while the percentage speaking Welsh fluently but not as a home language rose from 5.8% to 9.7%.
- 19.8% of primary school pupils are taught in classes where Welsh is used as a medium of teaching to some degree.
- At the end of Key Stage 1 in 1999, 18.2% of pupils were assessed in Welsh although of that age group (7-year-olds), head teachers thought only 16.1% spoke Welsh fluently. On average over the period 1996-

1999 the percentage assessed in Welsh at the end of Key Stage 1 was just over 2% higher than the percentage considered by headteachers to be fluent in the language.

- At the end of Key Stage 2 in 1999, 17.6% of pupils were assessed in Welsh although of that age group (11-year-olds), head teachers thought only 16.2% spoke Welsh fluently. On average over the period 1996-1999 the percentage assessed in Welsh at the end of Key Stage 2 was just over 1% higher than the percentage considered by head-teachers to be fluent in the language.
- At January 1999, 13.3% of secondary school pupils in Years 7 to 11 were taught Welsh as a first language; the percentage has increased virtually every year since 1977/1978 when the comparable figure was 9.3%. By 1999, 14.6% of pupils in Year 7 were being taught Welsh as a first language.
- Each year, around 2% of fluent speakers do not continue to learn Welsh as a first language when they transfer from primary to secondary school. This is apparent by comparison of the percentage of pupils learning Welsh as a first language in their first year in secondary school with the percentage of 11-year-old pupils considered as fluent speakers by primary head teachers in the previous year.
- At January 1999, 13% of pupils in Year 9 studied Welsh as a first language and in the Summer Term of 1998/1999 a similar percentage were assessed in Welsh first language at the end of Key Stage 3.
- At January 1999, 67.8% of secondary school pupils in Years 7 to 11 were taught Welsh as a second language. A major growth has occurred since 1987/1988 when the comparable figure was only 42%.

Schools
- 445 schools, 27% of all primary schools, are mainly Welsh medium schools. A further 82 schools, 5% of the total, use Welsh as a teaching medium to some extent. In the remaining 1133 schools, 68% of all primary schools, Welsh is taught as a second language only.
- The percentage, and number, of primary schools where Welsh is used as a medium to teach only a minority of pupils, or to teach less than half of the curriculum, has been falling in recent years.
- The number of 'Welsh speaking' secondary schools increased from 44 in 1990/1991 to 52 in 1998/1999.

That the position of Welsh medium education has been strengthened is a significant development in its own right and is recorded in much more positive attitudes towards bilingualism and the construction of a bilingual society *per se*. However, beneath this positive trend there remains for many a grumbling doubt as to the real worth of bilingualism, for it is argued that once pupils have left the confines of the school classroom there is little economic and instrumental justification for maintaining fluency in Welsh. Time will tell as to whether this judgement can still be made after the current period of institutional bilingualism has had its full impact.

Outside the educational system many other pillars of Welsh culture are entering a more dynamic phase which also leads to increased language reproduction. Political change at both the domestic and European levels has encouraged the recognition of pluralism in Wales. The language struggle is by no means over. However, attempts to honour the equality of Welsh and English are now taken seriously and both government planning and popular initiative are focussed on seizing the opportunities which are currently available. The keywords describing the formal relationship between English and Welsh speakers are partnership, mutual respect and recognition. The key phrase describing the situation of their relationship with immigrant minority languages in Wales is *terra incognita*, not in the sense that we do not know much about the context of such speakers, but more that we have yet to decide what role such language and their speakers will be encouraged to play within our new public policy initiatives based upon our apparently characteristic features of openness, transparency and citizen diversity.

Policy implications

A pressing need is comparative work on bilingual policy and language equality issues within the UK and Ireland. Future policy could be directed toward instigating research-based answers which sought to:

- Contribute both a theoretical and a practical element to language planning and language policy in the UK, Ireland and within member states of the Council of Europe.
- Assess the character, quality and success of the institutional language policies of the political assemblies in Scotland, Wales and Northern Ireland.
- Investigate the complex nature of bilingual educational and administrative systems in Wales together with regional specific systems in Scotland and Northern Ireland.

- Assess the role of cross-border arrangements for the increased recognition of Irish on the island of Ireland, together with Northern Irish, Gaelic and Ulster Scots links with Scotland. This involves the role of the Irish-British Council in terms of co-operation, and political bargaining at the UK and European level, together with bilingual education, civil rights and group equality issues in Northern Ireland.
- Investigate to what degree the institutionalisation of Celtic languages vis-à-vis the established dominance of English can be a model for the relationship of other lesser used languages world-wide in their relationship with English. Potentially this issue is of global significance if one can transfer several of the lessons to be learned from the survival of the Celtic languages to multilingual contexts as varied as contemporary India, and much of Sub-Saharan Africa, let alone the evolving European political system.
- Gauge the degree to which the information technology and media opportunities developed in connection with the National Assembly of Wales and the Northern Irish Assembly are capable of sustaining a wider range of bilingual practices in public life. It is noteworthy that the development of _Sianel 4 Cymru_, and to a lesser extent the Gaelic medium television service, has created a self-confident and pluralist bilingual workforce which sustains a wide range of media activities. It is possible that both Assemblies will have a similar impact in relation to the information society as it relates to matters of public adminis-tration, education, legal affairs and the voluntary sector.
- Analyse the economic demand for a skilled bilingual workforce in several sectors of the economy; determine to what extent bilingual working practices in Wales offer a model for subsequent parallel developments within a range of multilingual contexts within the English regions, e.g. either in respect of several European languages or selected non-European languages such as Arabic, Urdu, Hindi or variants of Chinese languages of wider communication.
- Investigate what effect will the arrangements for the bilingual servicing of the National Assembly have on the legitimisation of bilingualism as a societal norm.
- Assess how the experiences generated within the National Assembly will impact on the bilingual character of educational and public administrative services, together with the local government and legal system.

- Analyse the extent to which European Union and Council of Europe language initiatives related both to regional and immigrant minority languages are adopted in the various political contexts which comprise the UK and Ireland.

Acknowledgements

The data on recent trends on education is derived from National Assembly of Wales education statistics as compiled by Jones and as reported upon in Jones and Williams (in press).

References

Aitchison, J. and Carter, H. (1997) *Language, family structure and social class, 1991 census data*. Area.

Jones, H. and Williams, C. (in press) The statistical basis of Welsh language planning. In C. Williams (ed.) *Language revitalization: Policy and planning in Wales*. Cardiff: University of Wales Press.

Morris Jones, R. and Ghuman Singh, P. (eds) (1995) *Bilingualism, education and identity*. Cardiff: University of Wales Press.

Welsh Language Board (1999) *A strategy for the Welsh language*. Cardiff: Welsh Language Board.

Welsh Office (1993) *Welsh social survey. The statistical section*. Cardiff: The Welsh Office.

Welsh Office (1998) *Statistics of education and training in Wales: Schools 1998. The statistical section*. Cardiff: The Welsh Office.

Williams, C. (1994) *Called unto liberty*. Clevedon: Multilingual Matters.

Williams, C. (1998) Operating through two languages. In J. Osmond (ed.) *The national assembly agenda* (pp. 101-116). Cardiff: The Institute of Welsh Affairs.

Williams, C. (1999) Legislation and empowerment: A Welsh drama in three acts. *International conference on language legislation*. Dublin: Comhdháil Náisiúnta na Gaeilge.

Williams, C. and Evas, J. (1998) *The community language project*. Cardiff: The Welsh Language Board/Cardiff University.

Gaelic in Scotland

BOYD ROBERTSON

The end of the second millennium has seen major constitutional reform in the United Kingdom with devolution of government from London to Edinburgh, Cardiff and Belfast and the restoration of a parliament in Scotland for the first time since the Union of the Parliaments of England and Scotland in 1707. The new Scottish Parliament, inaugurated in July 1999, has conferred on Scotland a substantial degree of autonomy including legislative and fiscal powers in the fields of education, health, industry, transport, environment, agriculture and fisheries, and the law.

The debate on devolution and the advent of the Parliament revived interest in questions of national identity and focussed attention on distinctive elements of Scottish culture. Language is an intrinsic part of culture and, in Scotland, the Gaelic language has played a fundamental part in the creation of the nation's culture and identity. The very name Scotland derives from the Gaelic-speaking immigrants from Ireland who settled in the western coastal areas from the fourth century AD and many of the badges of Scottish identity, eg tartans, bagpipes, whisky and Mac surnames, have their origins in Gaelic culture.

Demographic status

Gaelic, a close relative of Irish and more distant relative of Welsh, is the longest-established of Scotland's languages but it is spoken by fewer than three in every 200 Scots. A mere 1.4% of the Scottish population of just over 5,000,000 speak this regional language which was once spoken in virtually every part of Scotland and was, for a time at the beginning of the second millennium, the language of the Scottish Crown and Government.

The decline in Gaelic from a national language spoken throughout the country to a minority language confined largely to peripheral areas of the Western seaboard was, in part, due to a conscious effort by central government to subdue the independent-minded and, sometimes, rebellious Highlands and Islands which were the stronghold of the language. Gaelic speakers, at times, suffered outright persecution and deliberate attempts were made to extirpate the language. The status of the language was also eroded by anglicising influences from the south, by centuries of emigration and migration and by discriminatory policies. These factors all contributed to a lack of self-confidence amongst the population and, in some cases, a negative perception of the value of the language amongst Gaelic speakers. The fall in the number of Gaelic speakers is clearly demonstrated by the census figures for the period 1881-1991 shown in Table 1.

Table 1   Censuses 1881-1991

Census	N of Gaelic speakers	% of population	N of Gaelic only speakers	% of population
1881	231,594	6.2	--	--
1891	210,677	5.2	43,738	1.1
1901	202,700	4.5	28,106	0.6
1911	183,998	3.9	18,400	0.4
1921	148,950	3.3	9,829	0.2
1931	129,419	2.8	6,716	0.1
1951	93,269	1.8	2,178	0.04
1961	80,004	1.5	974	0.01
1971	88,415	1.7	477	0.009
1981	82,620	1.6	--	--
1991	65,978	1.4	--	--

The Gaelic-speaking population of Scotland is to be found mostly in the Western Isles and on the western fringes of the Highland mainland but there are also significant pockets of Gaelic speakers in urban centres such as Glasgow, Edinburgh and Inverness. Of the 32 local authority areas in Scotland, only 11 have more than 1000 Gaelic speakers. These authorities are identified in Table 2.

The most strongly Gaelic-speaking communities are to be found in the islands of the Outer Hebrides and Skye, particularly in the more rural areas. 68% of the population of the Outer Hebrides was Gaelic-speaking in 1991 but the Isle of Skye was no longer predominantly Gaelic-speaking, having dropped to 47%.

Table 2   Gaelic speakers (N=1000) in local authority areas

Local authority	N of Gaelic speakers over three years	% of population
Comhairle nan Eilean Siar	19,546	68.42
Highland	14,713	7.49
Glasgow	6,018	1.03
Argyll & Bute	4,880	5.51
Edinburgh	3,089	0.76
Fife	1,477	0.45
Perth & Kinross	1,392	1.17
South Lanarkshire	1,228	0.52
Aberdeen	1,134	0.57
North Lanarkshire	1,069	0.34
East Dunbartonshire	1,017	0.96

An analysis of the age and sex structure of the Gaelic-speaking population shows that the population is skewed towards the older age groups and that women outnumber men by 5%. 25% of Gaelic speakers are aged 65 or over while only 11% are aged 3-15. More than half (52%) of Gaelic speakers are aged 45 or over. The age profile of the Gaelic-speaking population in 1991 makes it clear that the downward spiral is set to continue and can only be arrested by very substantial rises in the numbers of young children speaking Gaelic and a large influx of learners.

Research conducted over the last two decades shows 'sharp inter-generational decline of language abilities and use' (MacKinnon, 1997). In particular, a language maintenance and viability survey conducted in the Western Isles in 1986-88, and a similar survey conducted in 1994-95, as part of the Euromosaic Project, revealed 'substantial slippage' over the nine years interval and also 'an even steeper intergenerational decline between subjects' grandparents and their own children (MacKinnon, 1997). These findings were corroborated by 1991 Census data which showed that in homes in which both parents spoke Gaelic, only 73% of children were Gaelic-speaking. In the comparable situation in Wales, 94% of the children could speak Welsh. In homes in which one parent spoke Gaelic, only 14% of the children spoke the language, a percentage which contrasts sharply with 78% of Welsh-speaking children in the same category. Where the lone parent spoke Gaelic, the transmission rate to children was 38%. The corresponding Welsh figure was 79% (MacKinnon, 1999). A further finding of the Euromosaic survey was that only a very small proportion of the children of Gaelic-speaking respondents speak Gaelic to one another. The implications of these findings for the future of the language are dire. Indeed, MacKinnon warns 'The prospects are of the language rapidly on its way to extinction as a community vernacular within the next couple of decades or so' (MacKinnon, 1997).

Sociolinguistic status

The research surveys referred to above also investigated the extent of use of Gaelic and English in community life. Gaelic was used most extensively in croft work and in prayer meetings and was also used substantially at the post office, social events and in local shopping. Exchanges with friends and neighbours were very strongly Gaelic and the language was also used frequently in exchanges with the local councillor, nurse, minister or priest and child's teacher. The weakest domains for Gaelic were dealings with officialdom and the workplace.

MacKinnon identified factors such as a general English work culture, anglicised administrative centres and a substantial number of monoglot staff as contributing to the dominance of English in the work situation. In the communications media, the survey showed that Gaelic television and radio were popular, print media less so and personal letter-writing was conducted almost entirely in English. The 1994-95 research indicated that religion is not as strongly Gaelic a domain as it was earlier and MacKinnon wondered whether any other domain might replace it as 'a bulwark' for the language (MacKinnon, 1999).

Legal status

Gaelic has no official status within the United Kingdom or within Scotland but the language does have a limited degree of legal protection. The authors of *An Comunn na Gàidhlig* (CNAG) report on the status of the language contend that 'such protection as does exist has been given on a piecemeal basis and is inadequate, given the legitimate needs of the linguistic community and the importance of the language to the continuing development of Scotland's national identity' (*Comunn na Gàidhlig*, 1997).

The Education (Scotland) Act of 1872 which set up a national system of state education made no provision for Gaelic education. After a campaign led by the main Gaelic language body of that period, *An Comunn Gaidhealach*, a clause was added to the 1918 revision of the 1872 Act. This clause has been incorporated in subsequent Acts including the current Education (Scotland) Act of 1980 which places an obligation on education authorities to make provision for 'the teaching of Gaelic in Gaelic-speaking areas'. Both of these terms are ambiguous and offer little support to parents seeking Gaelic-medium education provision for their children.

A much more meaningful item of legislation in respect of Gaelic education was the 1986 Grants for Gaelic Language Education (Scotland) Regulations which made provision for a Scheme of Specific Grants for Gaelic education. This Scheme enables local authorities to bid for 75% funding for new projects and initiatives and it has been a major catalyst for the expansion of Gaelic education in recent years.

The Broadcasting Act of 1990 made significant provision for Gaelic with the creation of a Gaelic Television Committee, *Comataidh Telebhisein Gàidhlig*, to administer a fund called The Gaelic Television Fund. The Broadcasting Act of 1996 extended the Committee's remit to include radio and the Committee's name was changed to the Gaelic Broadcasting Committee, *Comataidh Craolaidh Gàidhlig*.

It is only in the field of local administration that Gaelic enjoys a measure of official status and even that is confined to one local authority area, the Western Isles. A major reorganisation of local government in Scotland in 1974 led to the creation of *Comhairle nan Eilean*, the Western Isles Islands Council. This was a very significant event in that it brought public administration home to the Islands from urban and anglicised East Coast mainland centres in Dingwall and Inverness. One of the first acts of the new Council was the adoption of a bilingual policy. This was quickly followed by a bilingual education policy and a number of other significant initiatives on behalf of the language. After an initial highly pro-active phase in which the bilingual policy was actively applied in Council meetings and business, it has not been as assiduously or widely implemented as was originally envisaged.

In 1996, the leading Gaelic language agency, CNAG, made the issue of official recognition and legal status for the language a top priority and a Working Group was set up to examine the issues involved and to bring forward recommendations regarding the general principles which should inform legislation in respect of the language. The Group's recommendations, published in March 1997, were fully endorsed by an extensive consultation process in the Gaelic community. The deliberations of the Working Group were subsequently translated into a Draft brief for a Gaelic Language Act which was submitted to the First Minister of the Scottish Parliament in June 1999 (*Comunn na Gàidhlig*, 1999).

The Group concluded that 'the only way in which meaningful protection - secure status - can be given to Gaelic is the passage of specific legislation which will impose certain binding standards on politicians and public servants' and they called on the Scottish Parliament to pass a Gaelic Language Act which would establish 'a basic principle of equal validity for Gaelic and English in Scotland, along the lines of the recognition given to Welsh by virtue of the Welsh Language Act 1993'. There has already been progress with some of the proposals relating to the Parliament itself with the appointment of a Gaelic Officer and the use of bilingual signs throughout the parliamentary chambers. Gaelic has also already been used in debates and in committee proceedings of the Parliament. The Group further proposed that a Parliamentary Standing Committee on Gaelic be set up to advise the Minister with responsibility for Gaelic.

The Draft brief recommends that all government and quasi-governmental bodies should be required to develop Gaelic policies and appoint a Gaelic Officer to design and implement policies. In the legal context, it is recommended that 'persons appearing before all courts of general jurisdiction, administrative tribunals and other judicial or quasi-judicial bodies be entitled to both present cases and give evidence through the medium of Gaelic where they so choose' and that any document in Gaelic should have full legal force and validity for all purposes.

Education and broadcasting, non-discrimination and enforcement are the other key areas covered by these proposals. In education, the report argues for statutory provision to be put in place which would place a requirement on local authorities to make Gaelic-medium school education available where reasonable demand exists. Reasonable demand is defined as demand made on behalf of five or more pupils.

The precise nature of the Government's response to the Draft brief for a Gaelic Language Act is not yet known but the Scottish Executive has given a commitment to include legislation on Gaelic in its legislative programme for the next parliamentary session and the Minister for Gaelic announced in June 1999 that working to achieve secure status will be top of the Executive's agenda for Gaelic. The Labour Government has also reversed the previous Government's policy by agreeing to sign the Council of Europe Charter for Regional or Minority Languages.

Media status

Broadcasting

Broadcasting, and television in particular, have been identified by a leading Gaelic broadcaster as one of the main contributors to the decline of the language (MacPherson, 1999). MacPherson claims that the influence of broadcasting on Gaelic has been 'both pervasive and pernicious'. Few would dispute his assertion that 'Broadcasting, with its high-status role in society, disseminates the majority language to the detriment of the minority language. It has not only brought the English language into Gaelic-speaking homes but also anglified values and role models with which people can increasingly be identified, particularly young people'. MacPherson contends that broadcasting can have a positive influence on intergenerational transmission in the minority language in a similar way to the advantages it confers on transmission in majority languages and he argues that broadcasting is a necessity, not an optional extra or a luxury, in terms of language development.

A similar conclusion was reached by a review of Gaelic broadcasting commissioned by CNAG in 1988. The review concluded that the failure to provide an adequate television service contrasted sharply with positive developments in other fields such as education, the arts and local government and regarded a television service as essential for the future viability of the language. A highly professional lobbying campaign conducted by CNAG resulted in the inclusion of two important measures in respect of Gaelic in the 1990 Broadcasting Act. A Gaelic Television Fund was created and a Gaelic Television Committee was set up to administer the Fund and to enable an additional 200 hours of Gaelic programming to be broadcast annually.

The significance of this measure is illustrated by the increase in the hours of Gaelic broadcast on television from 102 in 1988 to 337 in 1998. The Government allocated £9.5 million per annum to the Gaelic Television Fund when it became operational in 1992 and the expectation was that this would rise incrementally annually. This has not happened. The Labour Party made education a key issue in the 1997 Election and, on taking office, increased the Gaelic education budget by £1 million but did so by transferring the money from broadcasting. Under the 1996

Broadcasting Act, radio was brought within the remit of the Committee but no significant additional funding was provided for this redesignated Gaelic Broadcasting Committee.

Gaelic television programmes are not concentrated on one channel as in Wales or Ireland and there is no sense of a coherent service. The scheduling of programmes by the Independent Television companies is a bone of contention between the viewers, the Gaelic Broadcasting Committee and the broadcasters. Very few programmes are shown at peak hours and several are transmitted during the night.

Gaelic radio offers the community a much more comprehensive service than does television. The BBC broadcasts 45 hours of Gaelic programming each week, mainly in two blocks from 7.30 am to 12.00 noon and from 5.00 pm to 7.30 pm on weekdays. Programmes can be received by listeners in most parts of Scotland and have a high penetration in the Gaelic community. Some community stations carry Gaelic programming but there is little Gaelic broadcasting on independent radio.

Printed media
Provision for Gaelic in the print media is much weaker than in the broadcast media. Only one national newspaper features Gaelic on a regular basis while another carries a weekly Gaelic column. Various attempts have been made over the years to establish a Gaelic newspaper but none of these has survived for long. A fresh attempt was made in 1997 with the launch of *An Gaidheal Ur*, a monthly title distributed in a local weekly newspaper.

Gaelic features regularly in the columns of the two main local weekly papers for the Outer Hebrides and Skye and there are regular Gaelic columns in two other local weeklies. Community newspapers, normally published on a monthly basis, include some Gaelic items. The longest-established extant Gaelic publication is a quarterly literary magazine, *Gairm*, founded in 1952.

Publishing
The state of Gaelic publishing can be gauged by the fact that, in a good year, only 45 new titles are published. Around half of these titles are produced for use in schools. Only three Gaelic publishers employ full-time staff. All three outfits run operations on the margins of viability and rely heavily on financial support given by The Gaelic Books Council, *Comhairle nan Leabhraichean*. There are also a number of small publishers

but these tend to be part-time operations, often individual initiatives and cottage industries. The market for Gaelic books is small and unit production costs arising from low print runs are much higher than for similar English language publications. Limited literacy amongst the older generations caused by a lack of schooling in the mother tongue is one of the factors that restricts the potential readership.

The arts

One of the most buoyant sectors of Gaelic activity in recent years has been the arts field and research has shown that Gaelic arts contribute over £10 million annually to the Scottish economy. Gaelic poets, bands and folk singers have won international acclaim in their art forms and have played a significant part in elevating the status of the Gaelic arts at home and abroad. For many years, the main vehicles for the transmission of music and song were *ceilidhs* (concerts) and *mods*. *Mods* are principally competitive music festivals, broadly equivalent to the Welsh *Eisteddfod* and the *Oireachtas* of Ireland. The main showcase for Gaelic culture has traditionally been the *National Mod* held in October each year in a different venue throughout the country. The *Mod* is a major cultural event in the Scottish calendar and incorporates music, song, drama, and linguistic and literary competitions in its week-long programme.

Fresh impetus was given to the Gaelic arts with the setting up, in 1987, of a National Gaelic Arts Project. The Project's remit was to promote and co-ordinate Gaelic arts development and it has given the Gaelic arts greater professionalism and a higher public profile. The audience for Gaelic arts has been considerably expanded through events organised by the National Gaelic Arts Agency (NGAA), as it is now called, and through the incorporation of Gaelic arts within major events such as the annual Edinburgh International Festival and Glasgow's Celtic Connections Festival.

The Arts Agency has done much to develop Gaelic drama including the formation of a touring Gaelic theatre company, *Tosg*. It has also been instrumental in initiating projects such as the *Ceòlas* Summer School in South Uist. *Ceòlas* offers master classes in Gaelic song, fiddle, pipes and dance and is very much a community-based project. Its success was recognised by the 1999 Scottish Tourist Board Thistle Award for cultural tourism.

One of the most successful artistic endeavours in the past two decades has been the *fèisean* movement. *Fèisean* are local community festivals which offer young people tuition in various Gaelic art forms including

Hebridean dancing, step-dancing, Gaelic language, drama, traditional arts and crafts, Gaelic song, the sport of shinty and traditional Highland instruments such as the bagpipe, harp and fiddle. The first *fèis* was held in Barra in 1981 and there are now over 30 such festivals held in different parts of Scotland. A national organisation, *Fèisean nan Gaidheal*, co-ordinates and promotes *fèisean* activity. The typical *fèis* lasts for a week and the more successful *fèisean* have follow-up tuition programmes at various times of the year. Over 3500 young people attend these *fèisean* annually and they provide many youngsters with their first experience of the language and culture. While the *fèisean* have undoubtedly been a great success culturally, the charge is levelled that they have not contributed as strongly to linguistic regeneration except in the few instances where a *fèis* operates entirely through the medium of Gaelic.

One of the main aims of the *fèisean* movement is to give access to the culture and to transmit the traditional arts. This is also the philosophy underlying the Dualchas Project, which is designed to bring together and digitise the archives of folk tradition and song currently held by institutions such as the BBC and The School of Scottish Studies at Edinburgh University.

Socio-economic status

Agriculture, fishing and production of Harris tweed have traditionally been the mainstays of the economy of the Gaelic-speaking areas and tourism has made an increasingly important contribution in the post-war years. These industries are susceptible to the vagaries of the market-place and of the climate and few people gain employment wholly from one sector. Smallholdings, known as *crofts*, are the basic unit of agriculture in the Western Highlands and Islands. The typical *croft* cannot, of itself, offer families the kind of income required today and it is thus very common to find *crofting* families also engaged in fishing, weaving, tourism and other industries and occupations.

Gaelic has traditionally been the main vehicle of communication used by *crofters*, fishermen and weavers and the language has a rich vocabulary associated with each. The more commercial aspects of these industries tend to be conducted in English and tourism, by its very nature, uses the main common denominator. There is no research evidence as yet as to the level of Gaelic usage in the newer industries such as fish-farming, construction, electronics and information and communication technology

(ICT) but each is making a vital contribution in sustaining the economy of Gaelic communities. Indeed, some of these, particularly ICT, are enabling exiled Gaels to return to live and work in their home areas. For instance, a significant and growing number of broadcasting jobs are now located in the Highlands and Islands.

Gaelic language development was, in the past, largely divorced from socio-economic development. That has changed in the last ten to fifteen years and there is now a keener awareness of the inter-relationship between the two. One of the first people to recognise this interdependence was Sir Iain Noble, a merchant banker who acquired a large estate in the Isle of Skye. The estate was in a run-down condition and the local economy was at a low ebb but Noble recognised its potential and saw Gaelic as an engine of regeneration.

Noble set up a bilingual estate company, *Fearann Eilean Iarmain*, which spawned developments in fishing, tourism, knitwear and whisky production and Gaelic became a requirement for employment in the estate's hotel, shop, offices etc. He was also instrumental in establishing a Gaelic College in a derelict barn on his estate. This has now grown into the highly successful *Sabhal Mòr Ostaig* which is one of the main employers in the south of Skye. Taken together, Noble's language-based entrepreneurial initiatives have been the main reason for the rejuvenation of the economy in that part of the island.

The realisation that the language and culture could have economic significance for the Highlands and Islands has gradually set in and both the private and the public sector are now beginning to exploit the potential of markets such as cultural tourism. This manifests itself in, for example, the increasing adoption of Gaelic and bilingual signage and business nomenclature, Gaelic holidays, cultural brochures and courses, and the establishment of artistic, cultural and interpretative centres.

Educational status

Provision is made for Gaelic in all sectors of education. There are two broad strands of provision - Gaelic as a subject of study and Gaelic as a medium of instruction. As previously indicated, the 1872 Act which set up a national system of state schools in Scotland overlooked the needs of Gaelic speakers, including the many who at that time could not speak any other language. When a concession to Gaelic education was wrung from the Government in 1918, the Act specified only the teaching of Gaelic, not teaching in Gaelic. Thus was set in train a system of Gaelic subject teaching which was to prevail for many decades.

Gaelic as subject of study

Most of the formal teaching of the subject took place in secondary school where study of the language and literature led to national certificate examinations in the subject. Even in classes of fluent speakers, most of the teaching was conducted through the medium of English. In 1965, separate courses and examinations were introduced for fluent speakers and learners. Provision for learners of Gaelic was thus brought into line with provision for learners of foreign languages.

Gaelic is offered as a subject in 40 of the 389 secondary schools in Scotland. The vast majority of these are located in the Highlands and Islands and access to learning the language at secondary school is denied to children in Glasgow, Edinburgh, Aberdeen, Dundee and many other parts of the country. Some 700 follow fluent speakers' courses, while around 2200 take learners' courses in Secondary.

Teaching of Gaelic in primary schools has been sporadic and less systematic. Provision for fluent speakers tends to be governed by local circumstances and is often the result of individual initiative. Outwith the Gaelic-speaking areas, tuition in Gaelic for learners has been provided largely by itinerant teachers who were often asked to cover many schools in a geographically widespread area. The amount of contact time with pupils was very limited and varied greatly from school to school. A new approach based on a Modern Languages model in which classroom teachers receive training in the target language to enable them to provide tuition on a regular basis has been introduced by Highland Regional Council.

The bilingual approach

The use of Gaelic as a medium of instruction was not officially sanctioned until 1975 when the newly constituted local authority for the Outer Hebrides, *Comhairle nan Eilean*, launched the Bilingual Education Project. The authority received Government backing for this radical departure from previous practice and the Scottish Office Education Department jointly funded the first two phases of the project. The project sought to build on the home language of the majority of pupils and both Gaelic and English were used as languages of instruction from the beginning of primary school.

There was a favourable parental response to the project in its early years but, by the early eighties, concern was being expressed about the level of fluency in Gaelic being attained by pupils in some schools after several years of bilingual schooling. Parents also voiced dissatisfaction with the progress being made by certain schools in implementing the bilingual model. A similar bilingual scheme was piloted in 1978 in five Skye schools by Highland Regional Council and was eventually extended to all primary schools on the island.

Doubts about the ability of bilingual models to deliver fluency in Gaelic, comparable to that in English, and a growing awareness of the extent of language erosion amongst children brought parents, educationalists and language activists to the realisation that a different approach was required. Developments in other minority language communities were studied and it became apparent that use of the minority language as the medium of education had to be maximised to ensure maintenance and transmission of the language. By this time, a number of Gaelic pre-school playgroups had been set up and had demonstrated the viability of the Gaelic-medium method. Parents were convinced that this was the way forward and that the Gaelic-medium approach should be continued in primary school.

Gaelic-medium education in primary schools

1985 saw the beginning of Gaelic-medium education in the primary sector with the opening of units in schools in Glasgow and Inverness. The success of these units and the rapid growth in playgroups, fostered by a national association, *Comhairle nan Sgoiltean Araich*, fuelled demand for similar units in other areas. The rate of growth has been such that, in session 1999-2000, there were 59 schools and 1835 pupils engaged in Gaelic-medium primary school education. Most schools with Gaelic-medium provision are in the Highlands and Islands but there are several in non-Gaelic-speaking areas such as Aberdeen, Edinburgh and Perth. 25% of primary pupils in the Western Isles receive their education through the medium of Gaelic and English-medium education is the exception in some island schools. *Comhairle nan Eilean Siar* has responded to this situation by designating five of its primary schools as Gaelic schools. Another measure of the advances made in Gaelic-medium education was the opening in September 1999 of the first dedicated Gaelic-medium school in Scotland, in Glasgow.

In virtually all Gaelic-medium classes, there is a mix of fluent speakers and learners. The proportions vary depending on the type of community the school serves. In rural, island schools, many of the pupils come from Gaelic-speaking homes but this is seldom the case in urban, mainland schools. Research shows that parents choose Gaelic-medium education for reasons such as maintenance and development of the mother tongue, restoration to a family of a language that has skipped a generation or two, acquisition of a second language, the perceived advantages of bilingualism and access to Gaelic culture and heritage.

The Gaelic-medium curriculum follows the National Guidelines on Gaelic for the ages 5-14. The Guidelines specify that Gaelic-medium education should aim 'to bring pupils to the stage of broadly equal competence in Gaelic and English, in all skills, by the end of Primary 7'. Research commissioned by the Government concluded that 'pupils receiving Gaelic-medium primary education, whether or not Gaelic was the language of their home, were not being disadvantaged in comparison with children educated in English. In many though not all instances, they out-performed English-medium pupils and, in addition, gained the advantage of having become proficient in two languages'. (Johnstone *et al.*, 1999) The research involved 34 schools and comparisons were made with pupils receiving English-medium education in the same schools, in other schools, in the same authority and nationally. Attainments in English, Gaelic, Maths and Science were studied and analysed and one of the most significant findings was that pupils educated through the medium of Gaelic 'did better than their English-medium counterparts in English'.

Gaelic-medium education in secondary schools

The use of Gaelic as a medium of education in secondary schools was pioneered in 1983 in two schools in Lewis. This pilot project, involving the teaching of social subjects through Gaelic, was an extension of the Council's then primary school bilingual education programme. The pilot was deemed a success and these two schools continued to teach History and Geography in Gaelic.

Development of Gaelic-medium education in other parts of the country resulted from the establishment of primary provision and the need to provide continuity of experience for pupils transferring from primary to secondary. There are now 13 secondary schools which offer some form of Gaelic-medium curriculum. History is the subject most widely available through the medium of Gaelic, while Geography, Personal and Social Education, Mathematics, Science, Home Economics, Technical Education and Art are also taught in Gaelic in one or more of the schools. Candidates may elect to sit Gaelic versions of national Standard Grade Examinations in History, Geography and Maths. It is hoped that other subjects will be added to the examination options as the system develops and that Gaelic versions of Higher examinations will also be made available.

Development facilitation

The development of Gaelic-medium education has been greatly facilitated by the Scheme of Specific Grants for Gaelic education, initiated by the Government in 1986. Under this scheme, local authorities submit proposals to SEED and receive 75% funding for approved projects. Grants are only awarded for new or additional provision and authorities are expected to meet the full costs of developments after three years. The Government has committed £2.6 million funding to the scheme in 1999-2000. Authorities can bid for funding on an individual or collective basis but they are expected to allocate a proportion of total funding to collaborative ventures. An inter-authority network has been formed to help co-ordinate action by local authorities and this has helped to bring about a major improvement in the production of teaching and learning materials. The establishment of a Gaelic National Resource Centre in Lewis in 1999 should also go some way to addressing the resource requirements in particular curricular areas.

One of the factors inhibiting further growth in Gaelic-medium schooling is the shortage of Gaelic-medium teachers. Recruitment drives have helped to reduce the gap between supply and demand but there is still an insufficient number of trained personnel to sustain, let alone expand, the Gaelic-medium service. There is also concern and dis-satisfaction about the training currently provided. Newly-qualified teachers feel inadequately prepared for the additional demands and specialised requirements of the Gaelic-medium classroom. Recommendations in a recent report from the General Teaching Council for Scotland should, if fully implemented and adequately resourced, considerably improve the initial training of Gaelic-medium teachers.

The time children spend in school is only a fraction of the time spent in the home and the community and the contribution of these domains to the education of the child is being recognised and addressed increasingly. Reinforcement of the language beyond the school is regarded as a vital part of the Gaelic-medium strategy, especially for children from non Gaelic-speaking backgrounds, and a nationwide network of Gaelic clubs has been set up by CNAG. Over 1500 children between the ages of five

and twelve attend forty, or so, *Sradagan* clubs. Local authorities throughout Scotland arrange evening classes for parents who wish to learn Gaelic
and want to assist, and keep in step with, the linguistic progress of their
children. The growth of local history societies, *comainn eachdraidh,* which
gather and collate local material and make it available to the general
public and to schools for local studies and projects has contributed to a
strengthening of school and community interaction in recent years.

Pre-school and post-school education
The use of Gaelic as a medium of education has developed to such an
extent that it is now possible, depending on where you live, to be
educated in Gaelic from playgroup to post-graduate level. Around 1800
children take advantage of the parent and toddler groups and playgroups
laid on by the Gaelic Preschool Council and the last two years have seen
a dramatic growth in nursery school provision. This has been stimulated
by a national Government drive to expand nursery education. It is
Government policy that Gaelic nursery units are based in, or closely
associated with, primary school Gaelic-medium classes.

After leaving the school sector, young people can elect to continue
with Gaelic-medium education in the tertiary sector. Indeed, the use of
Gaelic as a medium of instruction is at its most comprehensive in one
further education college. *Sabhal Mòr Ostaig* was founded in 1973 as a
Gaelic College in Sleat in Skye. From modest beginnings as a college
offering short courses in Gaelic language and culture, it has grown into a
fully-fledged college and an integral part of the University of the
Highlands and Islands Project (UHIP). *Sabhal Mòr* today offers national
qualifications and postgraduate courses in Business Studies, Information
Technology, Management, Communications, Broadcasting and the Arts.
All these courses, and others in Gaelic Language and *Gaidhealtachd*
Studies, are delivered and assessed in Gaelic.

Sabhal Mòr is one of 13 colleges and institutions participating in UHIP,
which hopes to win university status for the federal, collegiate institution
by 2004. It is envisaged that UHI will reflect the character and culture of
the region and give Gaelic a higher profile and an enhanced role in higher
education as a specialist subject of study and as a medium of learning and
assessment. Students wishing to study Gaelic at an established university
can choose between Aberdeen, Edinburgh and Glasgow, each of which
has a Celtic Department. These departments offer a range of undergraduate courses in Gaelic and Celtic Studies and students can take an
Honours degree in Celtic or a joint Honours in Celtic and another subject.

Some Celtic Studies classes are taught in Gaelic but the language is not yet deployed as a medium in other subject areas. Provision is made for students wishing to learn the language and Celtic Civilisation classes cater for those with an interest in cultural heritage. Postgraduate study opportunities are also available in the discipline. The University of Strathclyde has, following the merger with Jordanhill College, established Gaelic classes for undergraduates.

Policy development

Impressive though the development of Gaelic-medium education has been over the last 15 years, members of an Education Action Group set up by CNAG found that provision made by local authorities varied considerably in terms of the level of service and of supportive infra-structure. It was felt to be over-dependent on political goodwill and, therefore, vulnerable to political and administrative change.

The Group recommended that a national committee on Gaelic education be established by the Government to advise on all aspects of provision and funding and asked that the language be given the same kind of recognition that is afforded to Welsh in Wales in order to give Gaelic education a secure status. These recommendations were accepted by CNAG and they form key elements of a paper, A National Policy for Gaelic Education, submitted to the Government in 1997. There has been progress on some of the more detailed proposals made in this document but the main recommendations are the subject of ongoing negotiations between CNAG and the Scottish Executive in the wider context of deliberations on legislative action on secure status.

Conclusions

Census figures show that there has been a relentless fall in the number of Gaelic speakers over the past century and an analysis of the age profile of the Gaelic-speaking population suggests that this downward spiral is set to continue for some time yet. Research data on the intergenerational rates of transmission of the language confirms this projection.

Bleak as the prospects might appear from the statistical perspective, there is cautious optimism in the Gaelic community that the long-term decline can be halted and, indeed, reversed. This positive outlook is based on the turnaround in the fortunes of the language in the last 40, or so, years. There has been a distinct improvement in attitudes to the language and culture, in provision made for Gaelic and in the commitment of Gaels to their language.

Negative and hostile attitudes still exist and are voiced periodically in the media but public opinion surveys indicate a broad measure of support for initiatives to support the language. A remarkable renaissance in Gaelic poetry in the middle part of the century was one of the main agents of change in public perception of, and attitude to, the language. This attitudinal shift has led to unprecedented interest in the language and its associated culture.

The flowering of Gaelic poetry did not just impact on the consciousness of non-Gaels. It also had a considerable influence on the mind set of the Gael. The poets instilled in their fellow Gaels a renewed pride in their culture and a greater self-esteem and self-belief and this validation of their culture was reinforced by subsequent events such as the foundation of the Gaelic College in Skye, the adoption of a bilingual policy in the Western Isles and the expansion in Gaelic television. All of this helped to galvanise the Gaelic-speaking community and produced an enhanced level of commitment to the language.

That sense of commitment has been nowhere more apparent than in the education sector where developments have resulted invariably from parental initiatives and grassroots action. The fact that there are now some 3500 children aged 3-15 being educated through the medium of Gaelic testifies to the new-found will and tenacity of Gaelic-speaking parents and activists. But, for all that provision for the language has increased in education, broadcasting, the arts, public administration and the socio-economic sector, the fact remains that 1500 children are required annually to replenish the pool of Gaelic speakers depleted by the demise of older speakers.

There are, however, grounds for optimism within the community itself and in the wider national context. A vital factor in securing the future of the language will be the granting of official recognition by the State. Political support for the language has never been stronger and the reconstituted Scottish Parliament has a splendid opportunity to demonstrate the benefits devolved government can confer in regard to matters of language, culture and heritage.

References

Comunn na Gàidhlig (1997) *Framework for growth - A national policy for Gaelic education*. Inverness: Comunn na Gàidhlig.

Comunn na Gàidhlig (1999) *Inbhe Thèarainte dhan Ghàidhlig; Secure status for Gaelic - Draft brief for a Gaelic Language Act*. Inverness: Comunn na Gàidhlig.

Johnstone, R. *et al*. (1999) *The attainments of pupils receiving Gaelic-medium primary education in Scotland*. Stirling: Scottish Centre for Information on Language Teaching and Research.

MacKinnon, K. (1997) *Gaelic as an endangered language: Problems and prospects*. University of York Workshop on Endangered Languages: Steps in Language Rescue.

MacKinnon, K. (1999) *Gaelic in family, work and community domains: Euromosaic Project 1994-95*. Fifth International Conference on the Languages of Scotland and Ulster.

MacPherson, J. (1999) *The evolution of Gaelic broadcasting in Scotland*. Institut Culturel de Bretagne, Conference Les pays celtiques dans l'Europe du XXIe siècle.

The Scottish Office Education Department (1993) *Curriculum and assessment in Scotland: National Guidelines: Gaelic 5-14*. Edinburgh: HMSO.

Frisian in the Netherlands

DURK GORTER
ALEX RIEMERSMA
JEHANNES YTSMA

The province of Friesland (*Fryslân*) is one of the twelve provinces of the Netherlands. The total population is 618,000 (1998) which is equal to 184 inhabitants per km^2 (cf. the Netherlands: 15.6 million inhabitants; 462 per km^2). The capital is the city of Leeuwarden (*Ljouwert*), which has some 88,000 inhabitants. In this chapter we will focus on the demographic, sociolinguistic, political and educational status of Frisian respectively.

Demographic status

Leeuwarden is one of the eleven 'cities' in Friesland, which obtained city rights during the Middle Ages. Some of these 'cities' are quite small and would be considered small villages by today's standards. Friesland has 31 municipalities. A dense pattern of over 300 villages (many with a population less than 1500) and only a few larger towns is typical for Friesland. The second largest place is Drachten with some 41,000 inhabitants, the tiniest villages may have less than 25 inhabitants. The administrative borders of the province coincide well with the geographic area in which the Frisian language (*Frysk)* is spoken today. Only in a small part of the neighbouring province of Groningen (*Grinslân*), where the language border crosses the administrative border, we also find a few thousand speakers of Frisian (Gorter *et al.*, 1990).

In 1830 the population of Friesland (205,000) comprised almost 8% of the total population of the Netherlands, by 1920 the relative share had declined to 5.6%. By 1950 the absolute number of inhabitants had more than doubled (468,000), but it had further decreased relatively (only 4.6%). Today it is less than 4% of the total population of the Netherlands. The relative decrease is mainly due to a continued departure surplus from Friesland, caused especially by its relatively weak economy. Friesland is traditionally an agricultural area, with relatively little industry. Today the (financial) service sector is quite important. According to age, the young-est group (below 19 years) and the oldest group (over 65 years) are over represented in Friesland compared to the average of the Netherlands. Many young people leave the province to study at a university (mainly Groningen) or to obtain a job in the 'city belt' (*Randstad*) of Amsterdam, The Hague and Rotterdam. In terms of educational level and income the population of Friesland is somewhat below average.

Migration is thus an important factor (Van Langevelde, 1993). During the fiftiess there was massive emigration from Friesland. From 1960 till today the number of people leaving the province every year has remained fairly constant, averaging some 25,000. However, the number of new-comers has fluctuated from just over 20,000 in 1960, going up to a high point of almost 35,000 in 1974, decreasing to 22,000 in 1984 and settling at almost 27,000 in 1997. The outcome has been a surplus of immigrants between 1971 and 1982 and a negative departure balance in most other years. Population growth has come from a surplus of births. There is also internal migration to and from the countryside, where living in towns has become more important. The effect of this relocation of the population on the distribution of Frisian has been substantial. Both processes of migration made language-related differences less distinct.

Sociolinguistic status

The census in the Netherlands has never contained a language question. Therefore, there are no detailed data available on the numbers of Frisian language speakers (nor on Dutch or other languages). From repre-sentative sample surveys among the population of 12 years and older, which were repeatedly carried out in 1967, 1980 and 1994 (Pietersen, 1969; Gorter *et al.*, 1984; Gorter & Jonkman, 1995), we can deduce that today 74% of the population is able to speak Frisian. This figure implies an absolute number of roughly 400,000 speakers of Frisian. From the same survey studies we know that a substantial part of them (19%) must be second language learners, because 55% reports to have learned Frisian as their first language as a child. Currently, just over half of the population usually speaks Frisian at home. Again from these same surveys it is known that approximately 94% of the population can understand Frisian, 65% can read it and only 17% can write the language. What we observe over a timespan of more than 25 years is a slow decline in speaking proficiency and an increase in writing abilities. Yet, overall, the percentages have been relatively stable, as can be derived from Figure 1.

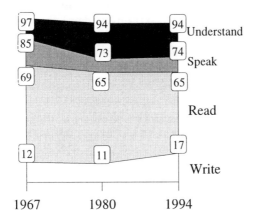

Figure 1 Ability to understand, speak, read and write Frisian (1967-1994)

As a rule, all inhabitants of Friesland are able to speak, read and write Dutch. There is, however, a substantial part of Frisian-speakers who claim to have greater oral fluency in Frisian than in Dutch (about 60%).

In terms of language geography there has been a contrast between the towns and the countryside for at least four centuries. Predominantly during the first part of the 16th century a distinct linguistic system came into being in at least eight towns: the so-called 'city-Frisian' (*Stedfrysk*). This was caused by a change in government (new rulers with immigrant civil servants) and increased trade contacts with the towns in the province of Holland (e.g. Amsterdam) (Jonkman, 1993). City-Frisian is basically a Dutch dialect, although it has strongly been influenced by Frisian, especially in its lexicon and pronunciation.

The emergence of city-Frisian gave rise to a lasting historical contrast between the towns and the countryside. Before World War II we can estimate that over 90% of households in the countryside spoke Frisian and less than 20% of households in towns where city-Frisian was spoken. Both internal and external migration has changed this pattern, but even today the spread of Frisian reflects a contrast between towns and countryside. Frisian still has its strongest base in the countryside. In the villages the figure for Frisian as home language is around 70% and in the towns over 10,000 inhabitants it is about 40% or less.

Some other dialect varieties can be found in Friesland. On three of the four Waddensea islands separate dialects for *Amelânsk*, West- (*Westersk*), Middle- (*Midslânsk*) and East-Terschelling (*Aastersk*) and for *Skiermûntseagersk* are spoken. All five can be thought of as being heavily influenced by both Dutch and Frisian, or, as a sort of mixed language. For all varieties the number of speakers is declining. The municipality of *It Bilt* in the north-western part of the province consists mainly of land reclaimed from the 'Middle-sea' by the beginning of the 16th century. Thereafter the area was settled by farmers from the province of South-Holland. Up until today a separate dialect (*Biltsk*) is in use by a few thousand speakers. At the north-eastern border a dialect is spoken referred to as *Kollumerks*; it has only a limited geographical spread. In two south-eastern munici-palities, i.e. *East-* and *West-Stellingwerf*, a Saxon dialect (*Stellingwerfsk*) is spoken by about one-third of the inhabitants as home language (± 17,000 persons). In recent years efforts aimed at revival of the dialects have gained some popularity. Taken together, the dialect areas mentioned are sometimes referred to as 'non-Frisian speaking' areas, which is only in part correct and mainly based upon historical considerations.

Frisian forms a rather homogeneous speech community, where all dialect varieties are mutually understood with ease. A major dialect is the speech variety of the south-western part which is known as *Súdhoeksk*. It differs from other varieties mainly because it has no breaking, a phonological feature, which makes the pronunciation quite characteristic. Another major dialect variety is spoken in the part of the Wâlden (see above) and is accordingly called *Wâldfrysk*. Finally, the third major variety is *Klaaifrysk*, spoken in the western part, *de Klaaihoeke*. There is another subvariety *Noardklaaifrysk*, in the north; there is some discussion whether it should be referred to as a separate variety, included with *Wâldfrysk* or with *Klaaifrysk*. The standard variety of Frisian is an amalgam of *Wâldfrysk* and mainly *Klaaifrysk* (Tiersma, 1985; Breuker, 1993).

When we look at the distribution of the use of Frisian over different social domains or contexts, we see an uneven pattern. In the domains of the family, the working place and the village community, Frisian holds a relatively strong position, because a majority of the population habitually uses Frisian. In the more formal domains of media, public administration, law and education the use of Frisian has made some inroads during the last decades, but overall it is fairly limited. Survey research has shed some light on the patterns of differential language use. Figure 2 contains a summary of twelve conditions in public life for which respondents (N = 1368) have answered what language they ordinarily use. The conditions can be distinguished according to the degree of formality and familiarity with the interlocutor. A cross-tabulation has been made with language background. Thus those respondents that have learned Frisian as their first language (L1) are distinguished from those who indicated that they could speak Frisian, but that it was not their mother tongue (L2).

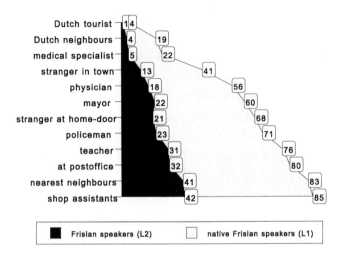

Figure 2 Use of Frisian (in %) as first (L1) and second language (L2) in different types of interactions

At the top of the graph there is very small difference between first and second language speakers of Frisian. In speaking to a Dutch tourist it seems obvious that using Frisian is not done. However, already in the second situation - language use with Dutch neighbours - a degree of difference does occur. Second-language learners barely use Frisian with Dutch-speaking neighbours, whereas first language speakers do so in about one fifth of the cases (19%). A similar pattern occurs for medical specialists; usually they have a Dutch language background and the situation is defined as formal and non-familiar.

In descending this 'mountain graph' the gap between L1 and L2 speakers widens in terms of the percentage that does use Frisian in the selected contexts. At the bottom we find that 85% of Frisian L1-speakers habitually speak Frisian in the shop where they do their daily shopping, whereas only 42% of L2-speakers use Frisian.

In the survey many other questions were asked on language use (Gorter & Jonkman, 1995). Two questions were concerned with language choice. All respondents were asked to situate themselves in a shop in a Frisian town and answer the question of the language they would choose for the interaction with a shop assistant. They were first asked 'What do you speak when you are spoken to in Frisian by the salesperson?', and secondly, its complement: 'When the salesperson speaks Dutch to you?' The results are presented in Figure 3.

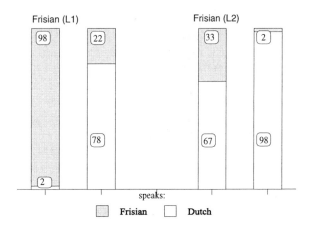

Figure 3   Language choice (in %) according to a Frisian or Dutch speaking salesperson

In the left-hand side of the graph we observe that when a salesperson addresses the respondent in Frisian, almost all Frisian speakers (with Frisian as their first language) will also use Frisian in return (98%). However, when the salesperson speaks Dutch to this same group, 78% of the Frisian speakers accommodates to the shop-assistant and also use Dutch. Only 22% speaks Frisian in case of a Dutch speaking shop-assistant. When we turn to the right-hand part of the figure, we see a totally different outcome. These are the remaining respondents (including 42% who claimed to have speaking ability in Frisian, and learned it as a second language). We observe here that only one third converges to a Frisian speaking salesperson by answering him in Frisian. In the case of a Dutch speaking salesperson, hardly anyone will answer in Frisian. Of course, these results do inform us only about a particular situation of language choice. It is, however, obvious that the language of the interlocutor is a very important factor. Language choice is, so to speak, 'person-bound'. It also turns out to be quite important whether Frisian has been learned as a first or second language. On the basis of such results and taking into consideration the rule that in interaction with strangers Dutch will be the 'unmarked' and safe choice, it will not come as a surprise that many non-Frisian persons make the observation that they hear little Frisian spoken in the capital of Leeuwarden.

There are still other factors involved in language choice. One such factor is language attitude (Gorter & Ytsma, 1988). There is a wide variety of attitudes towards the Frisian language. Frisian speakers seem to be basically positively predisposed toward their own language. They express a certain emotional attachment and there is widespread agreement on the 'beauty' and 'value' of Frisian. At the same time speakers of Frisian can wholeheartedly oppose certain specific measures to promote the use of Frisian, e.g. in the domains of education or public administration.

On the basis of systematic participant observation language attitudes (in terms of emotions and opinions) about Frisian can be placed in four simple categories (Gorter, 1993: 155-165). In the first category we find persons with negative emotions and negative opinions concerning Frisian: e.g. they are against any use of Frisian for official purposes. They will often deny to be 'anti-Frisian', but consider Frisian a language to be used only by Frisian speakers among themselves. There are two categories in between. In one category we find persons who hold the opinion that Frisian is useless for economic purposes or any 'serious' use, although at the same time they feel positively towards maintenance of the 'beautiful' Frisian language. Probably this is the largest group. There is another category, similar to the former, but reverse in terms of opinions and emotions. They will approach Frisian positively as a technical policy problem that has to be solved in a rational way, but they feel little emotional attachment towards the language. There are not many who are outspokenly negative in their emotions but rather neutral. Finally, there is a category with both positive emotions and opinions. This last category comprises a relatively small number of persons. With such contrasting language attitudes, language conflicts are part and parcel of daily life in Friesland, but usually only on a small scale at the level of individual interaction. There is no large-scale social conflict over the use of the language. An exception was the introduction of Frisian place names in 1989, when organized resistance by local businessmen made it difficult to implement the measure.

Outside the province of Friesland people are often hardly aware of the dynamics concerning Frisian. The outside prestige of the language is relatively low, even though it may be held in high regard inside the province of Friesland. Although Frisian-speakers are a quantitative majority in Friesland, Dutch-speakers are the social group that has more chance of its (language) interests and desires being realized and thus exerts more power (Gorter, 1993; Ytsma, Viladot & Giles, 1994). The stable diglossia relationship with Dutch as the exclusive language in formal domains and Frisian as the 'lower' language no longer exists. In the current situation it is less clear when and where what language can be used or has to be used. Frisian is allowed, and its use must be possible, but other mechanisms (such as rules of linguistic etiquette) are now constraining its use. It is clear that older strict 'divisions of functions' between the two languages has given way to new patterns. Dutch enters into and cannot be kept out of the intimate spheres of the home, friends, family and neighbourhood. At the same time Frisian seeks to 'conquer' some of the 'higher' domains of media, public administration and education.

In the media Frisian has only a minimal presence. The two major daily newspapers have a small number of Frisian texts every day (< 3%) and one special Frisian page every week. Local papers generally follow this pattern; here and there some have a bit more. There are a few literary journals, *Trotwaer* and *Hjir* and a two-monthly magazine for education, *De Pompebléden*. There are two special youth magazines, *Sjedêrrr!!!* and *De Holder*, aiming at the age category under 18. From September 1999 there is a general magazine *Frsk*, which is spread door-to-door among all households in Friesland.

The number of hours broadcast by the regional radio station has gone up quite considerably over the last few years, to some 50 hours a week. Frisian television was very modest for many years with less than one hour a week, including school tv. Since 1994 there has been one hour of original tv-programming every day (plus the rerunning of programmes). These programmes are well received and have a relatively high viewing rate. Research conducted in 1998 showed that 58% of the population listened to *Omrop Fryslân* radio and 77% watched Frisian television (Spinhof & Keijzer, 1998). Frisian has only a very modest place in more recent new media developments, such as CD-roms and the Internet.

Political status

Frisian has been officially recognized as the second language of the Netherlands. That formal recognition has, however, only entailed moderate promotion of the language by the state. In a slow process of legal codification certain provisions for the use of Frisian in dealings with the government have been made. As Schmidt (1997) observes 'the Frisian language underwent an important increase in prestige'. He refers to what has happened in Friesland for the legal framework over the last few years. In that framework four parts can be distinguished.

1 The first part is the covenant between the State and the Province. The Province of Friesland began its language policy in the seventies. Because provinces are not an important layer of government in the Netherlands, it was remarkable that the Province of Fryslân tried to establish a formal policy. In 1985 it published an important report with the meaningful title 'From a favour to a right', which was unanimously accepted by the provincial government. At that time the opinion of the State was on the contrary that Frisian was not a right, but only a favour. A little extra could be given, e.g. in terms of provisions for Frisian in schools or a small subsidy for Frisian theatre. The conflicting perspectives between the State and the Province in the eighties led to long and tedious negotiations. Finally, in 1989, there was formal agreement, a covenant, between the Province and the State Government. The covenant includes provisions for media, education, culture and scientific research, as well as for public administration and the use of Frisian in the courts. However, once this agreement between the State and the Province was legally tested on the issue of publishing binding documents in Frisian, it was rejected, within one year, by the highest court of the Netherlands. Thus the language policy for public administration needed a stronger legal base. In 1993 the covenant was renewed and expanded. Since 1998 there have been new negotiations between the State and the Province for an update of the covenant, which will be structured similar to the European Charter (see below).

2 Work started in 1990 to draft a Frisian language law, which was a long process again. That special language act was almost finished, just before it went to parliament, when the State government decided it wanted similar legal arrangements for the Dutch language as well. This resulted in the introduction of some articles on the official use of Dutch in the General Act on Administrative Law, which deals with how public administration in the Netherlands is arranged. As an

exception one article on Frisian was added, which contains the core
from the draft of the language act on Frisian. The general act became
effective in July 1995. Today it is officially possible and cannot be
rejected anymore in the courts to use Frisian in a legal way, in
documents and in speaking.

3   There were similar problems with Frisian in the courts. Frisian was
allowed by a law of 1956 in the court, because there had been some
riot in Friesland in 1951 over the use of Frisian in one particular court
case. The Dutch government in reaction drafted an Act which allowed
some oral use of Frisian, which again had to be approved by the
presiding judge. As a result, in very few cases anyone used Frisian.
The law has now been changed and the new regulations have become
effective in 1997, including the official documents (e.g. birth certificates
and marriage licences) of the municipal Registrars Office which are
always in both languages. This adjusted law on Frisian in the court
also includes many legal provisions on Frisian in written documents.
Frisian can be used in documents as long as the process of the law is
not 'unduly obstructed'. That kind of provision may easily lead to
problems of interpretation. Time will tell what happens in practice and
what jurisprudence will be established. Today one has, in principle,
the full right to speak and write the Frisian language during court
proceedings.

4   Finally, there is the European Charter for minority or regional
languages of the Council of Europe. In the Netherlands the Charter is
perceived as quite important. The Dutch State was among the first to
sign (in 1992) and also to ratify (in 1995) the Charter, which has
become effective on March 1, 1998. But the crucial issue is whether the
position of Frisian will improve. The Charter undoubtedly has a
positive effect in the sense of a symbolic act where the Dutch member
State is binding itself internationally, albeit only to what is a con-
firmation of already existing policy. Implementation of that policy
based upon the obligations the Netherlands has agreed to (48 options),
is of importance. For Frisian the hope of ratification of the Charter is
that in the future additional provisions will be signed. Of course, it
also becomes more difficult to reverse existing provisions. There are,
however, some other developments as well which may influence such
a process. The Dutch government has also decided to place the Low-
Saxon language (or dialect) and the Limburg dialect, as well as
Romani and Yiddish under the working of the Charter. Thus, where
there used to be only one minority language in the Netherlands

(Frisian) there are now according to the European Charter five minority or regional languages. These languages have only obtained formal recognition under part II of the Charter, whereas Frisian was brought under part III. Thus the State only has an obligation towards Frisian and can leave the policy for the other mentioned languages to a mere symbolic deed. Yet, it is unclear what the effect of the Charter will be on the policy towards Frisian.

In conclusion, one can say that there is substantial political agreement that the government has a task to protect and promote the Frisian language. However, the policy plans have by and large a non-committal character and they have hardly been implemented. The power of the taken-for-grantedness of Dutch appears stronger than the formal operationalization of the language policy intentions.

Educational status

Compared with other indigenous language minorities in Europe, bilingual education in Friesland can be placed at an intermediate position (Sikma & Gorter, 1991: 109). The provisions for Frisian appear to be better than for migrant groups in the Netherlands (Extra, 1989). However, notwithstanding a tradition of education in Frisian that goes back to the beginning of this century, Frisian still has a modest place in the educational system.

Pre-primary education

Pre-primary education (2.5-4 years) is not part of compulsory schooling in the Netherlands. Playgroups are mostly privately run, supervised by municipalities, where 'teachers' do not need any formal qualification. There are around 250 playgroups in Friesland in total, catering for some 8000 pre-schoolers.

As a rule, children are free to use their first language in the playgroup. A somewhat outdated study on language aspects of pre-primary education in Friesland revealed that Frisian is hardly used in urban playgroups, whereas rural playgroups are predominantly bilingual (Duipmans, 1984). A recent study put forward that the number of playgroups with relatively many Dutch-speaking children has increased (Boneschansker & Le Rütte, 1999). In contrast, the language background of the teachers has remained fairly stable. Finally, it was found that Dutch was used much more often than Frisian as medium of instruction during group activities. An exception are seven Frisian playgroups, established by the *Stifting Pjutteboartersplak*. This association, founded in 1989, aims at creating a Frisian-speaking environment for young children. Most of the toddlers are Frisian-speaking; those who speak Dutch at home are immersed in Frisian.

Primary education

Frisian has been an obligatory school subject at primary level (4-12 year) since 1980. Frisian is legally obliged as a subject and permitted as a medium of instruction in every grade. Obligatory core objectives have been set for the teaching of the Frisian language. The objectives completely mirror those for the teaching of Dutch. This implies that the educational programmes of the primary schools in the province should aim at full bilingualism for both Frisian and Dutch speaking students. A Frisian language course called *Fryske Taalrotonde* (Frisian Language Rotunda) was published by the Centre for Educational Advice in 1994. This language course can be used from grade 1 (age 4) to grade 8. The course is based on the core objectives set for the teaching of Frisian. At present, over 70% of primary schools in Friesland (n = 500 in total) make use of this language course. A problem with the actual implementation of the *Fryske Taalrotonde* in schools is that two-thirds of the teachers working with the course report not to use the teaching materials on an integral basis (Le Rütte, 1998). In practice, these teachers select certain parts of the course for their lessons. It goes without saying that this is not conducive to a continuous line in the Frisian curriculum. In addition to the *Fryske Taalrotonde*, many primary schools make use of the special Frisian school radio and school television programmes.

A study of the Inspectorate regarding the school year 1988-89 showed that nearly all primary schools spend one lesson (30-45 minutes) on education in Frisian per week, so time expenditure was limited (*Ministerie van O&W*, 1989). The status of Frisian as a medium of instruction was also weak. One fifth (22%) of the primary schools made no use of Frisian as a medium and a majority of the schools used Frisian as medium of instruction for 10 to 30% of the teaching time. Moreover, it appeared that the use of Frisian as a medium decreased according to the proportion of Frisian-speaking students attending the school. In all likelihood, the status of Frisian at primary schools has not improved appreciably since the study of the Inspectorate ten years ago.

Given the unfavourable position of Frisian in Frisian primary schools, it should not come as a surprise that evaluation research conducted in the early nineties has shown poor outcomes in general. As far as Frisian language skills are concerned, the pupils' results with regard to oral and reading comprehension can be considered satisfactory. However, their performance in the areas of basic (technical) reading and spelling is insufficient and remains behind the desired level of speaking and writing (De Jong & Riemersma, 1994: 244). All in all the findings illustrate that there is a considerable gap between the core objectives and achievements of the children. In contrast, students' command of Dutch in terms of oral comprehension, basic technical reading, reading comprehension, spelling and writing ability turns out to be of a respectable level. A comparison of the Frisian data with those of a national study shows that there are no significant negative differences between Frisian-speaking and Dutch-speaking students attending primary schools in Friesland and Dutch students living in the rest of the Netherlands.

An interesting new development in the school year 1997-98 is the establishment by the provincial Centre for Educational Advice (*GCO-Fryslân*) and the *Fryske Akademy* of an experiment with trilingual primary education. The Centre for Educational Advice counsels the schools and develops Frisian learning materials; the *Fryske Akademy* evaluates the project through research. At present, seven experimental schools participate in the project. The aim is to reach full Frisian-Dutch bilingualism among the students and to foster their English language proficiency. The three languages are taught as a subject and used as a medium of instruction as well. In grades 1 to 6, 50% of the teaching time is in Frisian and 50% in Dutch. In grades 7 to 8, the division is 40% Frisian, 40% Dutch and 20% English as a medium. In practice, the latter means that English is used for two afternoon sessions per week as a medium of instruction.

Secondary education

Until 1990, secondary schools could optionally teach Frisian, and Frisian lessons have been offered in some secondary schools up till examination level. The Dutch Parliament agreed in 1991 to compulsory Frisian in the 'basic education' (*basisvorming*), that is, in the first three years of secondary schooling. The 'basic education' came into effect in 1993. Frisian is an additional school subject in the province, where the schools do not receive any supplementary financing for its teaching.

For the teaching of Frisian at secondary level, the language course *Flotwei Frysk* has recently been developed. Moreover, there is a Frisian youth magazine called *Sjedêrrr!!!* which is frequently used by secondary schools. The aforementioned language course has separate, adapted teaching units for non-Frisian speaking students and for students with low learning capacities. Research has shown that a vast majority of teachers at secondary level (82%) use the new language course, often supplemented with other teaching materials (Inspectie van het Onderwijs, 1999). Furthermore, guidelines have been formulated in 1993 and renewed in 1998, which describe the educational goals for teaching Frisian in the 'basic education'. As a whole, the non-obligatory targets for Frisian correspond to the obligatory core-objectives set for the teaching of Dutch.

A survey study conducted in the school year 1997-98 by the Inspectorate evaluated the position of Frisian at secondary level (Inspectie van het Onderwijs, 1999). The study was an evaluation of the first five years in which Frisian was compulsory in 'basic education'. It was concluded that the teaching of Frisian as a subject had developed only weakly. Time spent on the teaching of Frisian was low. Out of 53 secondary schools in total, 43 were teaching Frisian only in grade 1, for one hour per week. In addition, it was found that the quality of Frisian lessons was low in general. Furthermore, the study showed that Frisian was seldom used as a medium of instruction to teach other school subjects. Only 1% of the schools reported using Frisian as medium of instruction on a regular basis, 30% did so incidentally, and the remaining part of the schools (69%) never used Frisian to teach other subjects. Lastly, an interesting finding in the survey was that only 27 students took a final examination in Frisian in 1999. On the basis of the outcomes of the study, the Inspectorate concluded that the current Frisian lessons do not contribute meaningfully to the linguistic and cultural development of the students.

Higher education

Three institutes for higher vocational education are located in the capital Ljouwert/Leeuwarden, the *Christelijke Hogeschool Noord Nederland* (CHN), the *Noordelijke Hogeschool Leeuwarden* (NHL) and the *Van Hall Instituut*. They have a total enrolment of approximately 13,000 students, in many faculties. Recently all three institutes have drafted regulations on language use (Dutch, Frisian, English and other languages). Most faculties formally allow the use of Frisian in oral exams or in writing a thesis. In general, however, Frisian has a limited role as subject or as medium of instruction.

Part of these institutes are two teacher training colleges, which both provide teacher training for the primary level. Frisian as a subject is incorporated into the primary level teacher training programmes. In the first two years of their four-year programme, NHL students are obliged to attend a Frisian course. Afterwards Frisian is optional. At the CHN the students are not obliged to attend Frisian lectures, but all students are invited to obtain a formal certificate, qualifying them to teach Frisian in primary schools. Most students at the NHL and CHN obtain the required certificate, but this does not always imply a satisfactory command of the Frisian. For secondary school teachers, part-time training is provided by the NHL and full-time training by the University of Groningen (in a neighbouring province). However, the number of students is limited.

In Friesland itself there is no university, but Frisian can be studied at three Dutch universities. The universities of Amsterdam and Groningen offer Frisian language and literature as a main subject (MA degree), as well as possibilities for a PhD degree. Frisian is a subsidiary subject at Leiden university. In all three universities the number of students is small. In scientific research Frisian has hardly any place at all, except for the universities and the *Fryske Akademy*. Since its foundation in 1938 the Fryske Akademy has occupied a central place in research on the Frisian language, history and society. Important projects regard lexicography (larger dictionary of the Frisian language), history and social sciences. The latter are mainly concerned with the sociology of language and international comparative research on other European minority languages (Mercator Education).

References

Boneschansker, E. and Le Rütte, M. (1999) *Pjuttepraat. Friestaligheid in peuterspeelzalen en kinderdagverblijven*. Leeuwarden: Fryske Akademy/Economisch Bureau Coulon.

Breuker, P. (1993) *Noarmaspekten fan it hjoeddeiske Frysk*. Groningen: Rijksuniversiteit Groningen.

De Jong. S. and Riemersma, A. (1994) *Taalpeiling yn Fryslân*. Leeuwarden: Fryske Akademy.

Duipmans, D. (1984) *Frisian in playgroup and Kindergarten: a survey of the use of Frisian and Dutch in playgroups and kindergartens in Friesland*. Leeuwarden: Fryske Akademy.

Extra, G. (1989) Ethnic minority languages versus Frisian in Dutch primary schools. *Journal of multilingual and multicultural development* 10 (1), 59-73.

Gorter, D. *et al.* (1984) *Taal yn Fryslân.* Leeuwarden: Fryske Akademy.

Gorter, D., Jansma and Jelsma (1990) *Taal yn it grinsgebiet.* Leeuwarden: Fryske Akademy.

Gorter, D. and Ytsma, J. (1988) Social factors and language attitudes in Friesland. In R. van Hout and U. Knops (eds) *Language attitudes in the Dutch language area* (pp. 59-71). Dordrecht: Foris Publications.

Gorter, D. (1993) *Taal fan klerken en klanten.* Leeuwarden: Fryske Akademy.

Gorter, D. and Jonkman, R. (1995) *Taal yn Fryslân: op 'e nij besjoen.* Leeuwarden: Fryske Akademy.

Inspectie van het Onderwijs (1999) *Fries in de basisvorming. Evaluatie van de eerste vijf jaar.* Den Haag: Ministerie van OC&W.

Jonkman, R.J. (1993) *It Leewarders.* Leeuwarden: Fryske Akademy.

Le Rütte, M. (1998) *Evaluaasje Fryske Taalrotonde.* Leeuwarden: Fryske Akademy.

Ministerie van O&W (1989) *Het onderwijs in het Fries op de basisschool: stand van zaken 1988-1989.* Zoetermeer: Ministerie van O&W.

Pietersen (1969) *De Friezen en hun taal.* Drachten: Laverman.

Schmidt (1997) Die friesische Sprache im Verwaltungsverfahren und vor Gericht-Neuregelungen in den Niederländen zur Förderung einer Minderheitensprache. *Europa ethnica* 1-2 (54), 30-39.

Sikma, J. and Gorter, D. (1991) *European lesser used languages in primary education.* Leeuwarden: Mercator Education/Fryske Akademy.

Spinhof, H. and Keijzer, R. (1998) *NOS Kijk- en luisteronderzoek.* Hilversum: NOS-Dienst Kijk-en Luisteronderzoek.

Tiersma, P. (1985) *Frisian reference grammar.* Dordrecht: Foris/Leeuwarden: Fryske Akademy.

Van Langevelde, A. (1993) Migration and language in Friesland. *Journal of multilingual and multicultural development* 14 (5), 393-409.

Ytsma, J., Villadot, M. and Giles, H. (1994) Ethnolinguistic vitality and ethnic identity: some catalan and Frisian data. *International journal of the sociology of language* 108, 63-78.

Slovenian in Carinthia

BRIGITTA BUSCH

Slovenian is an indigenous language spoken in the southern part of two Austrian provinces, Carinthia and Styria, and has since 1991 been the state language in the neighbouring Republic of Slovenia. This chapter focusses on the demographic, sociolinguistic and educational status of Slovenian in Carinthia. The latter will be dealt with in a longitudional perspective from pre-school to adult education.

Demographic and legal status

In 1951 the first official census was carried out by the Austrian Second Republic. Since then the censuses have consistently asked for current language use and the figures are therefore comparable. In 1951 approximately 42,000 Carinthians indicated that they were Slovenian-speaking. This figure rapidly dropped to a low of 17,000 in 1981. This development seems to have somewhat stabilised between 1981 and 1991 (Ethnic group report, 1996: 17).

In Austria the last census was carried out in 1991 and the next takes place in 2001. According to the last census 15,000 persons in Carinthia (3% of the population) speak Slovenian, but representatives from minority organizations and the Catholic Church estimate that the figure is at least twice as high (Reiterer, 1996: 150). The assumption that there are more Slovenian-speaking Carinthians than according to the census relies partly on a telephone survey carried out in 1990. The extrapolation of this survey permits to estimate that there are about 40,000 people who do speak Slovenian, but also use German on a regular base as an everyday language (*Vertretung der Slowenischen Volksgruppe in Kärtnen*, 1990). A second inquiry undertaken by Catholic priests in the region suggests that as many as 50,000 people understand Slovenian, with 33,000 speaking it on a fairly regular basis (Williams, 1997). The use of administrative population censuses for determining the size of speech communities is problematic. In Austria minority organisations have repeatedly contested the practice of taking the census figures for an absolute measure determining the numerical size of the minority population. Administrative surveys are obligatory procedures carried out by administrative organs and collected by local authorities. Especially in small communities the anonymity thus cannot be guaranteed. As in the past claiming a Slovenian identity in Carinthia could have discriminatory consequences, people might feel susceptible when declaring themselves to be Slovene. Even if - as it is the case in Austria - the question asked in the census is not directly on ethnic affiliation, but rather on current language use, it is in public commonly interpreted in this way. Also in past censuses certain irregularities concerning 'corrections' made by local officials were reported. Another problem is that the census does not allow multiple answers as e.g. German and Slovenian. Therefore in 1991 the Austrian statistical office (ÖSTAT) initially planned to exclude from the survey questions on religious affiliation and language use which do not serve a strictly administrative purpose. But the local governments of Carinthia and Burgenland as well as the Catholic Church objected (Reiterer, 1996: 149).

Until the sixties the Slovene minority was socially and economically a rather homogeneous group settled in a clearly defined area. The percentage of Slovenian-speaking people working in agriculture was considerably higher than that of German speakers and the share of Slovenian speakers with higher education was significantly lower than average. In the past two decades the composition of the Slovenian population has become very heterogeneous and does not differ anymore significantly from that of the German-speaking population. Among the elder generation there still is a relatively higher percentage active in the agricultural sector, and among younger people the educational level is higher than among the majority population (Reiterer, 1996). This change is to a large extent due to the founding of the Federal Secondary School for Slovenes in 1957 and the University of Klagenfurt in the seventies, which enabled the internal development of a significant intellectual start inside the ethnic group.

Due to social changes within the Slovenian-speaking community, there has been a considerable migration towards the regional capital of Klagenfurt, which originally according to Austrian legislation was not considered to be part of the bilingual territory. The Austrian Supreme Court decided in the early nineties that there should also be an opportunity for primary bilingual education in the town of Klagenfurt and thus provided a less restrictive interpretation of area of settlement.

Sociolinguistic status

Slovenian belongs to the southern Slavic language group and has been used in writing since the 16th century (translation of the Bible). Today it is spoken by approximately 2.4 million people living in the Republic Slovenia and in the neighbouring border regions of Austria, Italy and Hungary. Geographical, cultural and historical factors have led to the development of a large number of dialects with pronounced differences at the phonological and lexical level. Sociolinguistic factors have prevented the evolution of a single and common colloquial variety of Slovenian which could be used as a functional means of communication throughout the bilingual area in Carinthia (Lausegger, 1993).

Language shift and construction of identities

Sociolinguistic research shows that language shift from Slovenian to German in Carinthia occurred with surprising speed (*Lage und Perspektiven der Volksgruppen in Österreich*, 1989: 89). Today speakers of Slovenian are probably without exception bilingual, whereas only very few German speakers master Slovenian. The situation has been characterized as 'one-sided, natural, collective Slovenian-German bilingualism' (Lausegger, 1993).

The reasons for this rapid language shift must be seen in the historical and political context. The administrative system of the Austrian monarchy in the 19th century was highly centralistic and when general compulsory school was introduced, German was initially the only medium of instruction. Only later minority languages were allowed and used as auxiliary languages. Historical research describes the situation in the middle of the nineteenth century as polarized. The Slovenian national movement was mainly represented by the clergy and organized as a political party, whereas German national parties were more secularly organized. It seems that political affiliation and social belonging played a more important role in patterns of identification than ethnic affiliation (De Cillia, 1998). When the Austro-Hungarian Monarchy broke apart in 1918, the new border between Austria and the Yugoslav Kingdom was disputed and armed struggles broke out. The disputes were settled with international intervention and in a referendum the border was finally fixed. This gave birth to the myth, propagated from the German national side of the 'Slavic threat in the south' which has for decades influenced the German-Slovenian relationship in Carinthia. During the Hitler regime the Slovenian population was heavily persecuted and deported to concentration camps. The Slovenian language was forbidden, but became at the same time a symbol for resistance. After World War II a more generous policy granting minority rights was adopted under the influence of the Allied Forces, but under German national pressure some of the measures were soon abrogated again. Only in the eighties of the 20th century assimilation pressure diminished with the emergence of social movements that made minority rights one of their concerns.

Language does not only have at the level of *parole* an identity-founding component but also at the level of *langue* in the sense that it can mark the belonging to a particular group for outside purposes and create this feeling for internal purposes. In Carinthia the Slovenian language has such a connotation. Research projects about the discursive construction of the Austrian national identity (Wodak *et al.*, 1996) have shown that also among German-speaking Austrians language has this symbol character to define in- and out-groups. For minority group members this means that what they have to construct is a more or less balanced double identity on the language level. In order to escape from stress, the minority identity is often lived as a private, family or 'weekend' identity. Among younger Slovenian speakers another strategy exists that considers multilingualism to be a life quality or life style, and escapes from identity stress in this way. Therefore they would declare to be bilingual rather than to claim an 'exclusive' identity. It seems that such a strategy has replaced to some extent patterns of assimilation.

For German speakers in Carinthia Slovenian has hardly any relevance although Slovenian is a neighbouring language. This is due to various factors such as the low prestige of Slovenian in Carinthia, the lower 'market value' (Bourdieu) of Slovenian spoken by a smaller and economically less powerful speech community compared to German, and the fact that the Austro-Yugoslav border was for almost 50 years a rather hermetical border separating two different ideological systems. Only when the border gradually lost this connotation in the late eighties and economic relations with Yugoslavia and later the Republic of Slovenia intensified, some knowledge of Slovenian became an advantage on the Carinthian labour market. An indicator for this slightly augmenting interest in Slovenian is the increasing number of participants in Slovenian language courses for adults and of pupils from German speaking families learning Slovenian in schools.

Nevertheless, with regards to domain distribution, Slovenian in Carinthia is practically reduced to the private or semi-private. Whereas Slovenian is functional in families, to some extent in peer groups, in local

Slovenian associations and in the church, the school in its present form cannot guarantee a language-preserving function. In the public discourse, the administration and the media Slovenian only plays a marginal role. There are also considerable differences in language use between different generations. Whereas in the elder generation the different local Slovenian dialects are currently used, the younger generation seems to be less proficient in this code; sociolinguistic research describes dialect and language loss among young people (Lausegger, 1993).

Within the core group Slovenian remains the language of the family. But as Slovenian plays only a minor role in official situations, socio-linguistic evidence suggests that even in these families there is a strong tendency towards code-switching when it comes to certain topics. As the school system on a secondary level only provides restrictive access to Slovenian as a medium of instruction, older school pupils even in Slovenian-speaking families often tend to speak German among them-selves and, where school-related topics are concerned, also with their parents. Media also have a strong influence on language shift. Through radio and TV German has made its way into practically all households. Audience research shows that media reception in Slovenian is only a supplement to a situation of media reception almost exclusively in German. As watching TV is often an activity that regroups different members of the family, conversations for which TV programmes are triggers have a relatively important role. Such conversations have a tendency to be either in German or to be marked by interferences from German or by code-switching to German (Busch, 1999). Another factor influencing language use in families is the fact that Slovenian is commonly only spoken in intimate situations, i.e. when no German speakers are present. Especially in areas of the bilingual region where there is developed tourism with privately run pensions and hotels this can cause temporary language shift in some families (Lausegger, 1993).

A domain in which Slovenian is still functional to a high degree is the church with its related social activities. Historically the gifted Slovenes often became priests establishing a militant intellectual elite which has fought to sustain the language group and its activities. It is estimated that 95% of the population in southern Carinthia is Catholic and that a quarter of these people attend church regularly, but secularisation is also in progress. Within the ecclesiastical structure there is a certain degree of autonomy for the Bishopric with regard to Slovenian. In about 80% of the parishes both German and Slovenian are used side by side and in the remaining 20% there is a tendency to separate the relationship between the two languages. The church also plays an important part in cultural activities with church choirs, groups for children, adult education and other activities conducted in Slovenian (Williams, 1997: 18f).

Slovenian as an official language

Minority rights for Slovenes in Carinthia are recognized under Article 7 of the State Treaty of 1955 and are granted territorial principles. Therefore minority rights such as access to education in Slovenian also follow territorial principles, and are thus not bound to personal declaration. Austria has signed, but not yet ratified, the Council of Europe's Charter for Regional or Minority Languages (1992) and has signed the Framework Convention for the Protection of Minority Rights (1995). Both of these documents guarantee some basic linguistic rights. The Austrian Constitutional Law, the State Treaty and the *Volksgruppengesetz* (Ethnic Group Law) of 1976 do not contain any direct guarantee of protection for the ethnic group itself, but to some extent regulate language use. The result is that there is a multitude of different laws and regulations concerning language use. Nevertheless, the absence of any coordinated language planning and language policy in Austria very often leaves questions of language use and language planning to party politics.

There are 35 municipalities in the bilingual area of Carinthia. In all of these 35 municipalities parents have the right to ask for bilingual education for their children, and Slovenian can be used in the churches. Only 6 of these communes have topographical signs in both languages throughout the whole municipality, some more have bilingual topographical signs on part of their territory. In 14 municipalities Slovenian is recognized as an official language in communal matters. Residents of these municipalities are also entitled to use Slovenian when dealing with officials in the District Internal Offices. These provisions also apply for the use of other official services such as revenue service, state farm bureau, public employment office and school district board. On the municipal level Slovenian may be used after a written application has been filed. Not all officials are able to speak Slovenian. Municipalities do not automatically publish official documents, announcements and recommendations in a bilingual format (Ethnic Group Report, 1996: 69f). In fact, local practice depends to a large extent upon the attitude of particular officials. Only in 9 municipalities Slovenian can be used when dealing with the local police. In court Slovenian can be used in three district courts and in the state court house in Klagenfurt. A German-Slovenian dictionary with jurisdictional terms does exist, but only very few laws are translated.

From this summary description it is obvious that it is not easy to know in which official situation when and with whom it is possible to speak Slovenian. Therefore, numerous residents forego their right in this area.

Slovenian in the media

The Slovenian-language printed press includes the Carinthian weeklies *Nas tednik* (official organ of the Council of Carinthian Slovenes), *Slovenski vestnik* (published by the Central Federation of Carinthian Slovenes) and *Nedelja* (official organ of the Catholic church). There are other magazines such as family magazines and municipal papers published on a monthly or quarterly basis. There is no daily newspaper in Slovenian published in Carinthia. The delivery of dailies from neighbouring Slovenia is unreliable and often delayed. Editors in Carinthia publish an average of 50 books annually in the Slovenian language. The regional public service radio station provides a daily programme of about 50 minutes and public service TV broadcasts half an hour in Slovenian on Sundays. Since 1998 there has been a 24-hour programme provided by a private station which includes programmes from Radio AGORA (bilingual) and Radio Korotan (exclusively in Slovenian). Equally, since 1998 the TV programmes from the Republic of Slovenia are available (with a decoder) on satellite in Carinthia. The Carinthian Slovenian media have always been confronted with a difficult financial situation. Newspapers this small are not interesting for the advertising market and only very modest state subsidies are granted. The only exception is private radio which is subsidised by the Federal Chancellery.

Among the producers of Slovenian media in Carinthia one can notice a certain tendency towards auto-censorship. Especially TV producers are very much aware of the fact that German-speaking Carinthians also occasionally attend these programmes. Therefore producers, but also their audience, do not want conflicts within the minority to be raised in these programmes. The Slovenian TV emission has to fulfill the somewhat contradictory expectations of being representative in a positive sense for the minority community in the eyes of the German-speaking audience and of creating social cement for the minority community. Therefore programmes often show elements of both, promotional films and home videos.

Those who are active and engaged in cultural and social activities of Slovenian organizations read minority language papers regularly (each of the three weeklies has a circulation of about 3000 per copy). Radio and TV guarantee anonymous reception and play an important role for those who do not want to declare themselves members of the minority community (up to 20,000 people watch TV programmes in the Slovenian language on Sundays).

As there is only little offered in Austrian media in the Slovenian language and as media from neighbouring Slovenia do not play an important role among the Slovenian population in Carinthia, media habits among the minority audience resemble those among the majority. Most of the time spent in the presence of media is spent in a German-language context. Minority media are built into the daily media routine as a complement. Current affairs, international and national politics are followed in majority language media. As the daily media contact is mostly contact with the German language, this also has considerable consequences for the language situation in the region.

Analysis of the manifest content of the Slovenian weeklies published in Carinthia shows that in both papers reports about the 'internal' life of the minority group are the most important issue. Approximately three quarters of the available space is dedicated to such articles. Reports about international issues, Austrian politics and regional affairs are rather insignificant. The only field that has relatively more weight than in German language media is information about neighbouring Slovenia and the Alpe-Adria region. Topics that are regularly present in dailies or weeklies such as health care, environment and technology are almost excluded. Whereas in the past printed media in Slovenian showed a similar profile to media in the majority language, covering a wide range of topics, they have gradually lost this function and developed into special interest media. The profile of the weekly Slovenian TV emission on the Austrian public service TV channel is amazingly parallel to the profile of the papers. The specialization of the Slovenian media also corresponds to the expectations of recipients. Both papers have a regular column with congratulations for readers who celebrate birthdays, marriages, and so on. Radio request programmes with the same kind of congratulations have the highest popularity. In sum, minority papers, radio and TV programmes seem to be a kind of social cement replacing to some extent communication on the village square.

The specialisation of minority media certainly influences language use in all other domains. It is mainly through media that neologisms are introduced and consolidated and where the standard language is present in written and spoken form. Media developments might eventually also offer new chances for minority media. Satellite TV, digitalization in radio and TV and the internet - with its possibilities of easy access to printed and audio-visual material - will increasingly make available a wider range of programmes produced in different localities. Minority media can also potentially enlarge their audience beyond the local community to members of the community that have migrated.

Educational status

The minority school system reaches back to the times of the Austro-Hungarian monarchy. School was considered as a means of homo-genizing the heterogeneous population. Mother tongue teaching for the different language groups was only introduced in the first three grades of primary school in order to enable pupils to follow lessons in German as soon as possible. The Austrian school system was based on German and all other languages were only considered auxiliary and transitional.

When Austria was annexed in 1938 to the Third Reich, minority schools were abolished and minorities severely persecuted. In 1945 lessons in minority languages were taken up again and a new school system was introduced. In the Slovenian-speaking area all subjects in primary school were taught simultaneously in both German and Slovenian. All pupils from Slovenian and German language environments were supposed to learn both languages at school. But even in this period from the third grade onward German was the medium of instruction and Slovenian was only taught as a subject. Nevertheless, this was the only period in the history of Austrian minority schools that a minority language had some regional relevance for the majority population as well. Due to nationalistic German pressure in 1958 the compulsory bilingual school was abolished and parents had to declare whether they wanted their children to learn Slovenian at school or not. Despite the fact that minority rights were granted by law on a territorial principle, somehow a personal declaration principle was introduced. Pressure was exerted on parents to remove their children from Slovenian lessons. The result was that only about 20% of the children in the region attended bilingual lessons in primary school after 1958. In the following years this number fell down further. In the early eighties bilingual schools again became a topic in party politics. Nationalistically oriented German circles, backed up by the FPÖ (Freedom Party of Austria), demanded the separation of school children according to language criteria and the abolishment of common classes in primary schools. After long discussions an amendment to the Education Act was passed in 1988. This amendment foresees separate bilingual and monolingual classes, but enables the access to bilingual education for German-speaking children to be maintained. They are to be integrated into bilingual classes, if their parents register them. If the number of pupils is too low to run separate classes, a mixed class is to be established and a second teacher comes into the class for 10 to 14 hours.

Today 26.4% of the pupils or 1724 in absolute figures (according to the school statistics of 1999/2000) in primary school attend bilingual classes and another 89 pupils learn Slovenian as a subject in primary school. The increase of pupils in bilingual classes is partly due to the social and political changes that took place in the early nineties. The frontier between Austria and Slovenia was no longer considered as a frontier between two different political systems, partly due to the social movement in the eighties that emphasised solidarity and multiculturalism. Also the opening of a private and a public bilingual primary school in the regional capital Klagenfurt in the early nineties is an important factor. In secondary education the situation is more restrictive and the number of pupils attending Slovenian lessons reaches only a total of 1249 (school statistics of 1999/2000).

One of the main challenges for the educational system is that the level of proficiency in Slovenian is very heterogeneous when children enter school. Appropriate didactic methods and learning material to deal with this heterogeneity are lacking. Whereas in 1981 43% of the pupils entering school mastered Slovenian well and only 31% had no knowledge at all, in 1997/98 the corresponding figures were 21% with a good command and 58% without (*Jahresbericht*, 1997/98: 109).

Pre-school education
In the past few years, Slovenian organisations in Carinthia have paid more attention to pre-school education. The first kindergartens with bilingual or Slovenian groups were private. There are two kindergartens, established by Slovenian organisations in the town of Klagenfurt, and some more in other villages in the bilingual area. These kindergartens are subsidised through federal sources out of the special budget for minorities. Some of the municipal kindergartens are also bilingual or run bilingual groups. As the capacity of bilingual municipal kindergartens and of those run by Slovene organisations is insufficient, groups of parents and educators have founded autonomous groups.

The children's language backgrounds in kindergartens are very heterogeneous. Some speak Slovenian dialects at home, others a language close to standard Slovinian, and others do not speak Slovenian at home at all. Generally at the age of three, when children enter kindergarten, they have to some extent become acquainted with German. Questions of teaching methods are left to the personal initiative of the staff.

One example of such an initiative is the private, originally bilingual kindergarten *Ti in Jaz, Dvojezicni vrtec Borovlje/Ich und Du, Zweisprachiger Kindergarten Ferlach*. It was founded two years ago after the local authorities in Borovlje/Ferlach refused to offer bilingual education to children aged three to six. When the private kindergarten was founded it was decided to add English as a third language. The kindergarten group has about 25 children and is led by three kindergarten teachers: one full-timer, speaking only Slovenian with the children, another full-timer speaking all the three languages with the children and a part-timer who speaks only English with them. The kindergarten has been counselled by a university teacher and has worked out a concept (who speaks which language when with the children) and has produced a ten-minute professional video available in German, Slovenian and English. An ongoing research project aims at insight into the communication strategies of both the children and the kindergarten teachers.

Primary education

Education in Slovenian is integrated into the Austrian public school system. At primary level there are 81 schools in the bilingual area and in one public and one private school in the town of Klagenfurt bilingual education or learning Slovenian as a subject is possible according to Austrian school legislation. In the school year 1999/2000 Slovenian classes were actually only held in 64 of these schools.

The general primary school curriculum comprises a classical subject canon: mathematics, music, drawing, handicraft, physical education, local history, geography, biology, religious instruction and German. From the third grade onwards a modern foreign language (mostly English) is taught as a compulsory practical exercise without assessment. In bilingual schools Slovenian is part of the core curriculum. The curricula in German and Slovenian are parallel in their requirements. In the first three years of instruction both languages should be used to the same extent as a medium of instruction in all subjects. In the fourth year of primary education German becomes the only medium of instruction and Slovenian is taught as a subject in language lessons. The Austrian constitutional court decided in May 2000 that Slovenian should be used on an equal basis with German as a medium of instruction throughout primary school, i.e. also in the fourth year. The curriculum also allows another form of Slovenian language teaching in primary schools. In monolingual German classes Slovenian can be taught as an additional practical exercise during two hours a week without assessment.

In practice there are great differences in the amount of Slovenian instruction provided. The status of Slovenian in bilingual classes seems to be highly dependent on the pupils' command of the language when they begin school, on the commitment of bilingual teachers and on the involvement of parents in bilingual classes. On the didactic and methodological level there is a lack of funding for experimental classes and evaluative research; therefore teachers are to a large extent left to their own inspiration. The private bilingual school in Klagenfurt has successfully introduced the 'one-day-one-language method', i.e. one day all subjects are taught in one language and the following day in the other.

Until the beginning of the nineties textbooks in Slovenian were only available for Slovenian alphabetisation and language instruction. These textbooks were based on the assumption of a homogeneous language background, meant for pupils with a good knowledge of Slovenian. But the reality in the classroom was much more heterogeneous. To cope with these shortcomings individual bilingual teachers and groups of teachers took the initiative to work out new textbooks and teaching materials. The school authorities provided translations from standard primary school textbooks in German for practically all subjects. But many teachers consider simple translations of textbooks to be rather problematic as they invite pupils to use the textbook in their stronger language, which is increasingly German.

Secondary education

Although Austrian school laws grant the possibility to bilingual general secondary schools (*Hauptschulen*) or to schools where Slovenian is used as a medium of instruction, there are no general secondary schools where Slovenian is used as a medium of instruction. Slovenian is only taught as a subject. There are three different possibilities of registering for Slovenian lessons: demanding lessons in Slovenian according to minority school law, choosing Slovenian as a foreign language (alternatively to English) or taking Slovenian as an optional additional subject. As the number of pupils enrolled for Slovenian as a subject in general secondary schools is relatively low, the necessary number for differentiating is not reached in most schools and pupils are taught in one single group. Often even pupils of different ages have to be taught within one single group. The pupils' language background in these classes is very heterogeneous and teaching is very demanding. Only about 5% of the pupils (i.e. 240 pupils in the school year 1999/2000) in the bilingual area attend Slovenian language classes in general secondary education. Compared with the number of pupils registered for bilingual classes in primary schools (26.4%), there is a strong decrease between primary and general secondary education.

On the level of academic secondary schooling (*Allgemeinbildende höhere Schule*, AHS) there is only one school (in Klagenfurt) where Slovenian is a medium of instruction. This is the *Bundesgymnasium für Slowenen* (*zvezna gimnazija za Slovence*) founded in 1957. More than 3000 pupils have gone through this school since its foundation; approximately half of them have left with a matriculation examination (*Matura*). In the school year 1999/2000, 435 pupils were taught at the lower and upper secondary level together. In some academic secondary schools Slovenian can be chosen as a subject. In the school year 1999/2000, 336 enrollments were registered for this option. As in some schools the number of pupils enrolled for Slovenian as a subject is low, groups may comprise different ages and even different schools.

For most subjects taught in secondary schools text books in Slovenian are not available; therefore German books are in use. As all school books in Austria are state-subsidised, authorities argue that due to the small circulation school books in Slovenian for the different levels of secondary education would be too expensive. Another problem is that school books have to be renewed regularly and reprinted according to progress in science. Already existing books in subjects like Slovenian and history have become rather outdated. Cooperation with Slovenia concerning school books began only in 1990, when an Austrian schoolbook on economics was translated into Slovenian; this book is now also being used in vocational training in Slovenia. As the curricula in the two countries are generally not identical, school books from Slovenia cannot be used in Austrian schools.

One pilot project combining research and in-service teacher training in secondary school should be especially mentioned: the 'KUGY Class' at the Slovenian Grammar School of Klagenfurt/Celovec is probably the most daring experiment in multilingualism. It was established in 2000 after one year of preparatory activities for the teaching staff. In this class, 28 students from Austria, Slovenia and Italy, each of them with at least basic knowledge of German, Slovenian and Italian, are being taught the subjects of a regular Austrian grammar school with the only difference that the language of instruction varies from subject to subject. For some it is Slovenian, for others Italian, and for one or two German. Of course, each of these languages is also taught as a subject. In the first year teachers sometimes try to make sure that students do understand what is being discussed by providing translations from the main language of their subjects into the other two languages. In such cases, it is often students who provide translations from one language into the other.

A year before the experiment started, teachers began to prepare for trilingual instruction by taking Italian classes (each of the staff is bilingual, speaking Slovenian and German at first language level) and paying visits to Slovene and Italian schools in order to get acquainted with the school culture in the countries of origin of their future students. They also took part in seminars preparing the ground for team work and collective planning. In addition, they began to build up contacts for partnership with teachers and students in schools of both countries. All the students of the KUGY Class were called in a week before regular school began. They were given five days of intensive training in Italian and German with the help of Italian teachers so as to improve their oral skills in these two languages. The program included also language training during leisure time and in the evenings. This experience of full immersion, in which the staff of the KUGY Class was also involved, proved to be an ideal preparation for school. The original plan had foreseen a language tandem experience for all students, but since the Austrians prevail and since there are but a few Italians the original idea of forming tandems had to be abandoned for a more traditional form of language training. Students have been invited to form tandems with the students of their Italian partner class in Friuli-Venezia Giulia. For the sake of completeness it should be added that the students of the KUGY Class also have to learn English.

Vocational training

Non-academic vocational training in Austria is organized in a dual system of training in business or industry combined with a theoretical course at compulsory vocational schools. Except for agriculture and household, there are no schools in which Slovenian is a medium of instruction and there are no bilingual schools of this type. Some enterprises, in which Slovenian is currently used as a working language (e.g. trading companies, print-shops, book stores, tourism) take part in the apprenticeship training scheme. At compulsory vocational schools pupils can learn Slovenian as an additional subject. In the school year 1996/97 only 31 enrolments were registered.

In 1990 a higher bilingual secondary college for commerce was founded in Klagenfurt. Pupils enter this college at the age of 14 and follow five years of education. The matriculation examination at the end of this period grants access to university. Pupils successfully completing secondary vocational college are entitled after three years of professional experience to practice their own trade. The curriculum in the Klagenfurt college for commerce includes general education, vocational theory and vocational practice (in a school-run mock enterprise). Slovenian and German serve to an approximately equal extent as medium of instruction for all subjects. English and Italian are taught as foreign languages. In the school year 1999/2000 the school had an enrollment of 128 pupils. The other bilingual academic vocational school is a private school in St. Peter/Šentpeter, run by the church. This higher secondary college provides vocational training for tourism and similar branches. 110 pupils were enrolled in 1999/2000. There is also a considerable number of pupils from the neighbouring Republic of Slovenia in both schools.

Higher education
In the Austrian universities and art colleges, as well as in the recently established *Fachhochschulen* (post-secondary special subject colleges) the medium of instruction generally is German with the exception of particular courses (e.g. guest lectures) in different languages. At three Austrian universities (Klagenfurt, Graz and Vienna) Slovenian can be studied as a subject. Students can specialize in a degree in Slovenian philology, in teacher training for academic secondary school or in interpretation and translation.

At the different Austrian universities, especially at Klagenfurt University, the amount of research work done in this field increased in the eighties, when some departments specialized in intercultural education. In 1989 the standing Conference of Austrian Universities launched a broad study on the status of minorities in the country, including education. Several masters' and PhD theses have been written on topics related to minority schools and to the language situation in the bilingual area in Carinthia. Nevertheless there is a lack of in-depth coordinated research in this field.

Adult education
Adult education in Slovenian is left to the voluntary sector. There is a wide range of organizations and (church) institutions offering courses in adult education on different levels, which are not aimed at formal

qualifications. Activities in this field organised by Slovenian organisations and by the church have a long tradition. As secondary education in Slovenian was only introduced in the second half of the 20th century, these courses were for a long time the only possibility of further education in Slovenian. According to the needs and interests of their members, Slovenian cultural associations organize lectures, courses and seminars on different topics (e.g. culture, agriculture, literature, health or foreign language courses), where Slovenian is frequently a medium of instruction. Some of these cultural organisations have also built their own infrastructures for such courses and cultural activities. The two central Slovenian cultural organizations, *Slovenska prosvetna zveza* (SPZ) and *Krščanska kulturna zveza* (KKZ), also organize adult education courses on a regional level, especially seminars for managers of local cultural organizations.

As economic relations between the Republic of Slovenia and Carinthia have become more intensive, there is a growing demand of Slovenian language courses for the German-speaking population. These courses are mainly organized by the above-mentioned organizations. In addition to the voluntary sector, Austrian adult education centres offer evening classes at different levels. Most of these courses lead to an intermediate level; there is a considerable lack of courses on an advanced level. Slovenian language courses at Klagenfurt University, initially organized for students only, are more and more frequented by learners who are not enrolled as regular students, but wish to deepen their knowledge of Slovenian.

Until very recently there were hardly any teaching materials for Slovenian in adult education; teachers had to rely on their own initiative. In the past few years books and manuals for teachers in adult classes have been worked out in Slovenia based on modern communicative methods of language learning. Nevertheless these courses require adaptation by the teachers for the specific situation in Carinthia, as the original target group does not consist of people living in the bilingual region.

Conclusion

On the level of education, the greatest challenge for the future is the heterogeneous composition of bilingual and Slovenian classes at all levels of schooling. Whereas language acquisition in German progresses rapidly due to out-of-school factors, Slovenian language acquisition has to be specially fostered. Intercultural learning was established as a general principle in Austrian curricula on the primary as well as on the secondary level already in 1991/92. In practice still a lot remains to be done in this field. Language awareness training, fostering of metalinguistic competences (e.g. transfer and translation between the two languages) and developing strategies for understanding could be steps towards the educational aim of intercultural learning. Another field in which additional efforts are necessary is taking measures to bridge the gap between primary and secondary education. There is a dramatic decrease in enrollment for Slovenian and bilingual education on the secondary level. In the past more attention has generally been paid to Slovenian and bilingual education on the primary level than all the other areas of education. These deficiencies should be worked upon.

In most Western European countries where minority languages are in contact with a majority language, long-term maintenance is the exception rather than the rule. There is a tendency to go from monolingualism in the minority language to transitional bilingualism on the individual and societal level, and finally to the majority language. The reduction of domains in which the minority language is functional seems to be a key factor for language loss. Especially when the family domain is affected, the shift rate is likely to be very high (De Bot, 1996: 581). This is the case for Slovenian in Carinthia. Nevertheless, there are some encouraging facts, such as the rising interest for the Slovenian language among German speakers. This can be seen in the increasing number of pupils enrolled for bilingual classes and the increasing number of adults attending Slovenian language courses. With the recently installed full bilingual radio programme in Slovenian and German, the situation is also improving in the media field.

Reversals of language shift or even language revival have been achieved to some extent in regions where adequate language policies and language planning have been introduced, as it is the case e.g. in Wales. In Austria the absence of such measures has been a constant throughout the years. Measures to raise the prestige of Slovenian in public domains and especially among the German-speaking population in the region will be of crucial importance.

References

Austrian Centre for Ethnic Groups (1996) *Ethnic group report*. Vienna: Austrian Centre for Ethnic Groups.

Busch, B. (1996) *Lepena. Ein Dorf macht Schule. Eine Mikrountersuchung sozialer und kultureller Gegensätze*. Klagenfurt.

Busch, B. (1999) *Der virtuelle Dorfplatz. Minderheitenmedien im Prozeß der Globalisierung*. Klagenfurt.

Charter for Regional and Minority Languages (1992). European Treaty Series 142.

De Bot, K (1996) Language loss. In H. Goebl, P. Nelde, Z. Stary and W. Wölck (eds) *Kontaktlinguistik. Ein Handbuch zeitgenössischer Forschung* (pp. 579-585). Berlin/New York: De Gruyter.

De Cillia, R. (1998) *Burenwurscht bleibt Burenwurscht. Sprachenpolitik und gesellschaftliche Mehrsprachigkeit in Österreich*. Klagenfurt.

Framework Convention for the Protection of Minority Rights (1995). European Treaty Series 157.

Institut für empirische Sozialforschung (IFES) (1990) *Vertretung der slowenischen Volksgruppe in Kärnten*. Wien.

Lage und Perspektiven der Volksgruppen in Österreich (1989). In *Bericht der Österreichischen Rektorenkonferenz* (pp. 89). Wien.

Lausegger H. (1993) Situationally motivated speaking habits among Carinthian Slovenes. *Slovene studies* 115 (1-2), 87 - 99.

Mercator Education (1997) *Slovenian language in education in Austria*. Dossier established by Brigitta Busch. Leeuwarden: Mercator Education.

Minderheitenschulwesen (1998) *Jahresbericht des Landesschulrat für Kärnten über das Schuljahr 1997/98. Abteilung VII*. Klagenfurt: Minderheitenschulwesen.

Reiterer, A. (1996) *Kärntner Slowenen: Minderheit oder Elite?* Klagenfurt.

Williams, G. (1997) *Slovene in Austria*. Unpublished manuscript in view of the Euromosaic extension. Bangor.

Wodak, R., De Cillia, R., Reisigl, M., Liebhart, K., Hofstätter, K. and Kargl, M. (1996) *Zur diskursiven Konstruktion von nationaler Identität. Forschungsbericht*. Wien.

The national minority languages in Sweden

LEENA HUSS

In the past few years, a debate has been going on about the status of historical and regional minority languages in Sweden, which was a non-issue up until the nineties as no official minority language policy had existed. This debate, initially triggered by Sweden's entering the European Union in 1995 and the pressure exercised on the State by some Swedish minority groups, that same year resulted in the Minority Language Committee being assigned to investigate whether Sweden could ratify the Council of Europe Framework Convention for the Protection of National Minorities and the Council of Europe Charter for Regional or Minority Languages (see first chapter of this Volume). In December 1997, the Committee released a report which proposed ratification of both conventions and recommended that all varieties of Finnish, Romani and Sami spoken in Sweden be considered national minority languages (SOU, 1997: 192-193).

The recommendations of the Committee were met with bitter opposition on the part of some Jewish, Tornedalian and Sami groups. According to the report, it was not possible to ascertain a continuous presence of Yiddish long enough to legitimate the inclusion of Yiddish in the category of historical languages in Sweden - a conclusion questioned by the promoters of Yiddish. The concern of the Tornedalians was that their language, Meänkieli (also known as Tornedalen Finnish), was not included as a language in its own right but merely as a dialect of Finnish, which was seen as a great setback by Tornedalian language revivalists. The situation was somewhat similar with regard to Sami, as protests were voiced against the fact that all three Sami varieties spoken in Sweden - North, Lule and South Sami - were covered by the general label Sami. The representatives of the small and extremely endangered South and Lule Sami languages wanted their own varieties to be treated as separate languages in order to counterbalance the relative dominance of North Sami in Sweden.

The committee report was circulated for comment and in the two-year discussion that followed, the inclusion of Yiddish as well as the view of Meänkieli as a language rather than a Finnish dialect gradually gained support. In June 1999, a Government Bill titled *Nationella minoriteter i Sverige* (National minorities in Sweden) (1998/99: 143) was released in Sweden and a unified policy towards national minorities was proposed. The historical minority languages taken up were Finnish, Meänkieli, Romani, Sami and Yiddish.

Swedish policies vis-à-vis immigrants and immigrant languages

The very existence of a report of this kind was a token of a total re-orientation in the official view of the languages spoken in Sweden. For the first time, the State was willing to recognise that some other languages than Swedish had special positions as historical languages within the Swedish territory. In a European perspective, Sweden has long been an exception, because its efforts have been concentrated on immigrants and immigrant languages while its historical minorities have largely been ignored.

When immigration to Sweden accelerated in the sixties and seventies, an awareness grew in certain circles that the State had a moral responsibility for the well-being of those who had chosen to come to work and stay permanently in Sweden (Runblom, 1995). An official Swedish policy towards immigrants was formed during the following years, resulting in 1975 in the introduction of the principles of 'equality, freedom of choice and cooperation' as a basis for this policy. With regard to the linguistic and cultural rights of the immigrants, the freedom of choice principle was of special importance as it was interpreted as the right to choose to what extent one wished to retain one's original culture or to embrace the Swedish culture. Language was seen as an important cultural aspect and in order to emphasize the freedom of language choice, the Home Language Reform was launched in 1977/78, giving immigrant children the right to study their own languages within the Swedish school system. In this and several other respects, Sweden was seen to have shifted from a model of assimilation to a multiculturalist model which tolerated and even invited cultural diversity. In many countries in Europe, Sweden became known as a social laboratory and a model welfare state with pragmatic social solutions, even in the domain of immigrant policies (Runblom, 1995).

During the period when the new Swedish immigrant policy was taking shape and the rights of linguistic subgroups were discussed, the historical minorities did not get any special attention. In some respects, they gained through immigration, for instance they could now apply for home language instruction in the school. In the Swedish Instrument of Government of 1974, 'religious and ethnic minorities' were granted the right to maintain and develop their cultures and no distinction was made between immigrants and historical minorities. However, there seemed to be an underlying assumption that the social and cultural needs of the latter, in those days primarily understood as the Finnish and Sami-speaking populations in northern Sweden, were after a long time of assimilation and integration in society best met by general cultural policies applying to all groups.

Ethnic revival in Sweden

The official abandonment of assimilationist immigration policies in Sweden in the seventies coincided with a new type of minority activity in many parts of Europe and beyond. Historical minorities in various countries were experiencing an ethnic revival and minority-political actions were carried out to secure the maintenance and development of formerly neglected and even stigmatized minority cultures and languages. In the Nordic countries, the Sami were the first to mobilize themselves and in the late seventies and early eighties, there was a veritable explosion of literary and artistic interpretations of Sami culture. The Swedish Tornedalians joined the ethnic revival movement somewhat later, in the eighties, when the first Tornedalian cultural organisation was founded. In the wake of the official multiculturalist immigrant policies in Sweden, these two historical minority groups saw their chance to make their voices heard.

The third group joining the ethnic revival movement in Sweden was a group with considerable difficulties to define its own minority position. It was the Sweden Finnish group, by far the largest immigrant group in Sweden and Scandinavia but at the same time a group with very long linguistic roots in Sweden. From the Middle Ages to 1809 Finland was part of Sweden and even after that period continuing migration movements tied the two countries together. The Baltic Sea and the Gulf of Bothnia in no way blocked movement of people but rather facilitated it, and the outcome was a Swedish-speaking population along the western and southern coastal regions in Finland, and their mirror-image in Sweden, Finnish-speaking groups all over the middle and northern regions of Sweden.

As an argument used vis-à-vis the Swedish government, the position of the Sweden Finns is in contrast with that of the Swedish-speaking population in Finland. Finland Swedes as the former dominant class have retained considerable cultural and linguistic rights in Finland (see Østern in this Volume). From the latter half of the 19th century, when Finland was a Grand Duchy of Russia from which it gained independence in 1917, until the sixties or seventies, speakers of Finnish in Sweden were subject to harsh assimilation policies. The situation in the seventies when Finnish labour immigration to Sweden reached its peak, was that there was an old Finnish-speaking minority in the Tornedalen area along the northern Swedish/Finnish border, whereas the *Värmland* Finns (also called the Forest Finns) had lost their last-known Finnish mother tongue speaker in the seventies. Värmland Finns were descendants of Finnish settlers welcomed by the Swedish Crown to settle in the Middle Scandinavian woods to cultivate uninhabited lands. Their history dates back to the 16th and 17th centuries, while the eastern Finnish variety spoken by them survived for 400 years, finally dying out in the sixties or seventies. In other places, such as Stockholm, where the Finnish language had had a continuing history dating back to the late Middle Ages, linguistically assimilated generations were continuously replaced by newcomers from Finnish-speaking areas. In the rest of Sweden, large numbers of Finnish immigrants arrived in the late sixties and early seventies.

A decade later, in the late seventies and the eighties, part of the Finnish-speaking immigrant group became more and more language-conscious, demanding an increase in Finnish-medium school instruction and child care for Finnish-speaking children. On the part of the State, Sweden Finns were treated as an immigrant minority among many and demands of more mother-tongue medium activities for this group were sometimes seen as militant nationalism (e.g. Bratt Paulston, 1992). Some Sweden Finnish language activists started emphasizing that Finnish had roots in Sweden just as firm as Swedish had in Finland, and that they should be treated accordingly. For the Swedish authorities, this was a totally new way of thinking, with potentially fatal consequences, as Sweden Finns were the largest minority language group by far, numbering some 450,000 individuals. To provide Finnish-language services for them on a large scale could prove costly and this could also form a precedent for other immigrant groups who might wish to follow the same path. Motions submitted to the Swedish parliament were rejected on the grounds that all immigrants should be treated equally and therefore Sweden Finns could not expect any preferential treatment. This opinion was also reflected in the mass media.

Within the Sweden Finnish group, the new minority identity had emerged little by little. In their former country, the Finnish-speaking immigrants had belonged to the linguistic majority population, and when they moved to Sweden, many of them brought with them a typical majority attitude 'When in Rome ...'. They accepted the assimilatory policies employed by the Swedish authorities as a matter of fact and it was only later, when the Swedification of the second and third generations was well under way, that concern about the fate of the Finnish language surfaced. At the same time, the national organization of the Sweden Finns (_Ruotsinsuomalaisten Keskuliitto_, RSKL) had come to the conclusion that the principles of 'equality' and 'freedom of choice', guaranteed by the new immigration policy and giving immigrants the same rights as Swedes, were not enough to safeguard the cultural and linguistic interests of minorities. From the eighties onwards, the RSKL partly changed its goal of securing the social and political interests of the Sweden Finns and began to emphasize the importance of maintaining Finnish language and culture as key factors for the future of the Sweden Finnish minority.

The case of the two diaspora minorities, the Roma and the Jews, is different. The Roma have a long history of outsidership in Swedish society, illustrated for instance by the fact that they became sedentary as late as the sixties when municipalities received special financial resources for Roma housing purposes. It was also then, for the first time, that the Swedish Roma children were allowed to go to school. Today, the situation is different but the Roma still face problems which are much greater than those of most other minority groups in Sweden. The Working Group for Roma Issues (_Romer i Sverige_, 1996: 243) discusses the serious difficulties of the Roma with regard to education, the labour market and social questions and proposes measures which are all geared to the reclamation and rehabilitation of Roma language and culture in Sweden. They propose, among other things, a Roma cultural centre, special support for publishing literature in Romani, mother tongue instruction in Romani in school, training of mother tongue teachers of Romani, scholarships for training jobs oriented to cultural maintenance, and support for Roma organizations. This shows that there is a growing opinion among (at least part of) the Roma that the previous immigration-political measures and other measures targeting the Roma population have failed in their task to integrate the Roma into the larger society. The measures proposed above reflect a wish among the Roma to join the ethnic revival movement going on in Sweden.

After a number of years of rapid assimilation of Jews in Sweden after World War II, an upsurge of Jewish ethnic consciousness started in the fifties, resulting among other things in the establishment in 1955 of an all-Jewish school in Stockholm, the Hillel School, and of a Jewish Center in 1963. However, the Jews in Sweden seem to have assimilated rapidly and a total absorption of the Jews into Swedish society has according to Runblom and Tydén (1990: 200) only been hindered by the vitalising effect of new Jewish migrant groups entering the country. Today Jews are considered to be well-integrated in society and they have higher education than Swedes in general, although there are also signs of an increasing in-group interest in Jewish culture. This is demonstrated for instance by a growing number of pupils in the Hillel school and the great popularity of special summer camps for Jewish youth (Runblom & Tydén 1990: 199). However, Yiddish as the in-group language seems to have been of minor interest until the mid-nineties, although its new status of national minority language may alter the situation.

From two to five historical minority languages in Sweden

Of all Nordic Sami, the Norwegian Sami population had attained the highest level of minority rights in the late eighties and early nineties and as such served as a source of inspiration for the Sami in Finland and Sweden. Increasing cooperation between the Nordic Sami as well as European and global cooperation between minorities and indigenous peoples were other inspiring and supporting factors in the past few years, when the Swedish Sami embarked on linguistic revitalization. The Tornedalian and Sweden Finnish revitalization movements also gained by international minority cooperation. In 1995 when Sweden joined the European Union, the European Bureau for Lesser Used Languages officially recognised Finnish and Sami as historical minority languages in Sweden, causing large headlines in some daily newspapers. The position of Finnish (outside the Tornedalen area in northern Sweden) as a historical minority language had been questioned by several commentators, but the fact that it was confirmed in a larger European forum strengthened the position of Sweden Finnish language activists and accelerated their work for linguistic revitalization.

The assignment of the Minority Language Committee in 1995 was, as mentioned above, one result of European cooperation and integration. As recommended by the Council of Europe, two diaspora languages - Romani and Yiddish - were included in the languages to be investigated. If the situation of Finnish and Sami had been of marginal interest to the State, Romani and Yiddish had previously attracted no attention at all, and their inclusion was to many Swedes a great surprise. Groups of experts were to investigate whether the presence of these languages in Sweden was long enough to qualify them as historical minority languages. The task was by no means easy as practically no previous research existed on language maintenance among these groups and the experts had to start from scratch. Finally they came to the conclusion that Romani (all varieties) had historical status in Sweden, whereas Yiddish was ruled out.

However, in the Government Bill mentioned above, the number of minority languages seen as historical was raised to five, through the re-inclusion of Meänkieli and Yiddish. Although these deviations from the view expressed in the Minority Language Committee report were not totally uncontroversial, the Bill was passed by Parliament on 2 December 1999, resulting in an official recognition of five historical minority languages as from January 2000.

The current status of the historical minority languages of Sweden

Size of ethnic groups and number of speakers

Gathering statistical information on the size of various ethnic groups in Sweden on the number of people speaking a minority language is extremely difficult as there has been no census with questions about ethnic origin or language since 1930. The only official statistical sources available are data on persons born abroad, or foreign citizens, or children of (one or two) parents who were born abroad or are foreign citizens. As historical minorities by definition have a long presence in their host country, this information is of little use. As a consequence, figures given in the literature are based on more or less haphazard estimates made using various calculation methods. The figures given in this section are mainly based on expert reports included in the Minority Language Committee report (SOU, 1997: 192), as further elaborated and updated in

Table 1   Estimated sizes of the national minority groups in Sweden and the
number of the speakers of minority languages (1999)

National minority groups		*Speakers of minority languages*	
Sweden Finns	400,000-450,000	Finnish	250,000
Tornedalians	75,000-80,000	Meänkieli	50,000-60,000
Sami	15,000-20,000	Sami	10,000
Roma	15,000-20,000	Romani	10,000
Jews	20,000	Yiddish	5,000-6,000

Hyltenstam (1999), and probably represent the most reliable sources to be
found today.

Those identifying themselves as Sweden Finns today are mostly first,
second or third generation immigrants who live mainly in cities and
industrial centres all over Sweden. The largest concentration of Finns,
70,000-80,000 persons, is found in the greater Stockholm area.
Tornedalians, in contrast, have their historical origins and family histories
in the northern parts of Sweden. Exceptions in this respect are found in
the many inter-ethnic families with one Tornedalian and one Finnish
parent. In most of these cases Tornedalian men are married to or co-habit
with women from the Finnish side of the border - an extremely common
phenomenon in Tornedalen. The opposite, Tornedalian women marrying
or co-habiting with men from the Finnish side, are rare. The Finnish
spouses have probably acted as important language revitalisers in their
own families and local communities, having mostly arrived in Sweden as
monolingual Finnish-speakers. Still mutually comprehensible, Finnish
and Meänkieli have interacted and blended through the years and this
has strengthened the local variety vis-à-vis Swedish during the many
decades (roughly during 1888-1968) when all Finnish varieties were
forbidden in Swedish schools and heavily stigmatized by the society at
large.

The Sami are an indigenous people living in the Nordic countries and
in the Kola Peninsula, Russia. In Sweden they speak three languages:
North, Lule and South Sami. North Sami dominates by far, while South
Sami with some 200-300 speakers and Lule Sami with 700-800 are
extremely endangered. Lule and South Sami are also spoken in Norway
by approximately 1000 people each. North Sami is spoken in Sweden,
Norway and Finland (approximately 9000, 25,000 and 4000 speakers
respectively). The Sami have traditionally lived in the northern parts of

Sweden, but nowadays there are large groups of Sami living in Stockholm and a couple of other cities. The traditional livelihood of the Sami, reindeer-herding, is becoming rarer and nowadays only about 10% of the Swedish Sami are engaged in it.

Rather like the Sweden Finns, the present Jews and the Roma groups mainly consist of immigrants of first, second or third generation. The first Jews came to Sweden in the 17th and 18th centuries. At the end of the 19th century, new groups of Jews arrived, mostly from Eastern Europe. After World War II, Danish, Norwegian and other Jewish refugees came to Sweden, many of them later continuing their journey to other countries. At the end of the eighties more than half of the Jews, some 9000, lived in Stockholm (Runblom & Tydén, 1990: 195-199).

The Roma in Sweden cover three main groups: an early group, today called the 'Swedish Roma', which started coming to Sweden at the beginning of the 16th century, a group of Kalé Roma from Finland who started coming to Sweden in 1954 when the common Nordic labour market was created, easing migration between Finland and Sweden, and last, several groups of non-Nordic Roma who have migrated to Sweden since the sixties. The number of 'Swedish Roma', the Kelderash, is estimated at 2500, the number of Kalé at 3000 and the rest of the Roma groups in Sweden (mainly Lovara, Sinte and Xoraxane) at 10,000 individuals. In addition to that, there is also a group of some 10,000 Travellers, whose origin in Sweden is still being discussed. According to the present Swedish minority policy they are included in the Roma group (*Romer i Sverige*, 1996: 4).

Sociolinguistic status of national minority languages

Language use and in-group views
For practically all speakers of the five national minority languages of Sweden, the present linguistic situation can be characterized as diglossic. National minority languages are mostly or exclusively used in the private domain, while Swedish greatly or exclusively dominates public life. Another feature common to these minorities is that - newcomers, first-generation immigrants and refugees excluded - language use shows the pattern typical to endangered languages: the older the person, the more minority language fluency and use; the younger the person, the less fluency and use. In most cases, speaking a minority language equals being bilingual (or multilingual), as there are - newcomers and first

generation immigrants again excluded - practically no monoglot minority language speakers left.

Finnish, Meänkieli and Sami are supported by an ethnic and linguistic revitalization movement led by the national organizations of the Sweden Finns (RSKL), the Tornedalians in Sweden (_Svenska Tornedalingars Riksförbund-Tornionlaaksolaiset_, STR-T) and the Swedish Sami Parliament respectively. Among all these minorities, the greatest language-related concern is the ongoing language shift in the child and young adult generations which has not been halted or reversed by the present system of 'home language' or 'mother tongue' instruction in school, nor by other kinds of existing transitional bilingual programmes provided by the Swedish school (Janulf, 1998; Svonni, 1993; Winsa, 1999). Today, linguistic revitalization is increasingly carried out by in-group efforts aiming at introducing and strengthening minority language competence among children, such as Maori-inspired 'language-nest' kindergartens, language immersion camps, adult minority language literacy programmes and creative writing workshops (see Huss, 1999). Revitalization is also reflected in the growing number of inter-ethnic families choosing the minority language as the home language or one of the home languages. During the years before the ethnic revival, the majority language was typically chosen as the only language in inter-ethnic families (Huss, 1999: 99-102).

As far as attitudes are concerned, the situation of Finnish, Meänkieli and Sami has improved and the stigma historically attached to them is gradually fading away. Among Sami-speakers, this may partly be due to the official status of Sami in the northern municipalities of Norway and Finland since 1992 and the establishment of the Swedish Sami Parliament in 1995. In Finland, the Sami Parliament was established in 1973 and in Norway in 1989. Among Finnish- and Meänkieli-speakers, the revalorisation of the minority language and culture led by the minority organizations has probably been a contributing factor. Language has gained importance as a core value (Smolicz, 1992) in the Finnish, Sami and Tornedalian cultures in parallel with the strengthening of the ethnic revival movement. This has caused conflicts between those who claim that language competence is vital for minority identity and those who maintain that ethnicity without language is of equal worth. For the ethnic activists, the challenge is to accommodate the latter group which may have an important role to play in a successful revitalization process.

As far as the two other minorities, the Roma and the Jews, are concerned the situation is somewhat different. Until now, their minority language maintenance efforts have not been as visible in society as those of the Finns, the Sami and the Tornedalians. Yiddish-speakers are the group that has until now been the least visible among the historical language minorities discussed in this chapter. This is the outcome of the general Jewish integration strategy applied in Sweden: the creation of in-group supportive networks financed by the group, independent of the host state (Boyd & Gadelii, 1999: 316). In some homes, Yiddish has been transmitted from parents to children, while in others, Swedish became the family language early on. In some Jewish associations in Sweden, Yiddish has played and still plays a fairly important role (Boyd & Gadelii, 1999: 317-318). The discussion that arose about Yiddish in connection with the work of the Minority Language Committee seems to have activated a group of language revivalists and caused a debate on the importance of Yiddish as a cultural core value among Swedish Jews. Some Jews view Hebrew, the official language of Israel, as the most important Jewish language and consider Yiddish a language of the past and of the Holocaust. The fact that Yiddish has now been recognized as a national minority language will probably strengthen the support for it and enable the Yiddish language activists to work more efficiently.

A factor complicating the Roma in-group attitudes vis-à-vis maintaining and developing Romani in Sweden is the character of a secret language attached to it. There has been a certain reluctance among the members of the group to allow publication of dictionaries and text books for use outside the group, or to organize mother tongue instruction in Romani. At the same time, the language has been and still is a core value of the Roma culture and, in adulthood, a sign of belonging to the group (Fraurud & Hyltenstam, 1999: 243). There has been the understanding, as described by Vuorela and Borin (1998: 60-61) for the Finnish Roma, that children will learn Romani as part of growing up, simply because it is the insider language of the community. According to them, starting to learn Romani is a sign of choosing Roma identity in the same way as a Roma girl starts wearing her Roma dress at a certain age to show that she chooses to live like the Roma and obey the rules of Roma culture. In recent years in Sweden, however, part of the Roma have begun to see their own language as severely endangered and in need of help from outside, even at the risk of exposing it to non-Roma. For them, the Swedish ratification of the Council of Europe Charter and Framework Convention represents enhanced possibilities of maintaining and devel-oping Romani in Sweden. As far as the Kalé Roma from Finland are concerned, the situation is further complicated by the fact that Finnish is spoken as a mother tongue by most if not all of them and functions in Sweden as a new secret language and therefore, perhaps, partly as a core value. The situation may be similar for non-Nordic Roma groups who came to Sweden being bilingual in Romani and one or several other languages.

Minority languages in media and literature

As mentioned previously, all five national minority languages of Sweden are mainly used in the private sphere and lack totally or partly many important domains of use. Today, this is a serious threat to these languages as the tendency in the Nordic countries seems to be that public domains in language maintenance have taken on a more central role than before. Due to modernization, national majority languages have forcefully entered everyone's immediate linguistic environment, and the progress of a minority language into the public sector is the key concern of a revitalization movement. Two important domains to get access to are the mass media and fictional literature. Below, a short presentation of the status of the five national languages in these domains is given.

Sweden Finnish is the national minority language used most widely in the media in Sweden. There are a couple of hours of daily radio broadcasts in Finnish, a daily ten-minute TV news broadcast and half an hour of other TV programmes in Finnish. In North Sami, there is a half-hour radio broadcast and an hour of youth and children's programmes every Saturday, but the number of Sami TV programmes still remains low, approximately 20 hours per year. Two new digital radio channels, one for Finnish and one for Sami, are being developed. For Meänkieli, the offerings are much smaller. The Swedish radio broadcasts three hours per week in Meänkieli and once a week the daily Finnish morning programme includes a quarter of an hour in Meänkieli. The first three Meänkieli-medium TV programmes in history, half an hour each, were broadcast in 1999-2000. So far, there have been no Yiddish or Romani-medium radio or TV broadcasts in Sweden.

The Sweden Finnish press includes several weekly newspapers, a large number of bulletins and journals of various organizations and associations, the Finnish journal of the Swedish Church, a cultural magazine and journal of the Sweden Finnish Language Council. Sweden Finnish literature published so far comprises some 250 volumes of prose and poetry. There is only one Sami magazine in Sweden, with mostly Swedish text but including small parts in (mostly North) Sami. Sami literature in turn is mainly published in Norway but Sami authors in

Sweden and Finland also have the opportunity of publishing their works in Norway. About 30 Sami titles are published every year, most of them school books. The number of novels in Sami is still modest, some 20 titles. Tornedalians also have their own magazine, half in Meänkieli and half in Swedish. The first novel in Meänkieli was published in 1985 and since then some 30 volumes, including fiction and poetry, collections of Tornedalian folklore and children's books have been published. As far as Yiddish and Romani are concerned, the number of publications is very small. Gröndahl (forthcoming) mentions in her presentation of Swedish minority literatures five titles for Yiddish (prose and poetry) and for Romani only some school materials and a couple of children's books translated from Swedish. Runblom and Tydén (1990: 199) mention that short-lived Yiddish-medium papers were published during World War I and during the latter half of the forties for Eastern Jewish trans-migrants and other Jewish newcomers.

Minority language planning in Sweden
The use of Sweden Finnish in the media has been greatly facilitated by the fact that there is a 25-year old tradition of Sweden Finnish language cultivation in Sweden. The Sweden Finnish Language Council (*Ruotsinsuomalainen kielilautakunta*) has created new terminology and compiled numerous word lists in different fields, has contributed to the development of dictionaries, and has given advice to the general public concerning language use. According to the philosophy of the Council, the Sweden Finnish official (mainly written) language is to follow the Finnish standard norm used in Finland, while the Council refrains from suggesting any norms for the everyday spoken language used by the Sweden Finnish. Since the beginning of 2000, the Council has shifted from mere language cultivation to more general language planning work, including both corpus planning, status planning and acquisition planning activities to strengthen the Sweden Finnish language. Recently, the Language Council and the Federation of Tornedalians (STR-T) have discussed language cultivation cooperation between the two minorities. Meänkieli so far has no language cultivation body but there are plans to establish such a body in the near future.

The Swedish Sami also have their own Sami Language Board (*Sámi giellaraddi*), established in 1994 by the Swedish Sami Parliament. In addition to the usual board members, it also comprises special consultants for Lule and South Sami whose task is to propose measures to strengthen the position of the Sami languages in the traditional South Sami and Lule Sami areas in Sweden.

Yiddish and Romani have no language cultivation bodies yet. The Sweden Finnish Language Council has recently launched the idea of establishing a common language planning and research body for Swedish, the majority language, and for all five national minority languages (Huss, 2000). It would enhance the possibilities of cooperation between the various language groups and greatly facilitate the development of language cultivation for the three languages - Meänkieli, Romani and Yiddish - which still lack systematic language planning. A model of this kind of overall agency for several national languages has been in use in Finland since 1976.

Educational status of national minority languages

The option of one or two weekly mother tongue lessons, i.e. instruction in the mother tongue as a subject, is available for all school children with another mother tongue than Swedish, if there are at least five children in the municipality opting for it and if it is possible to find a teacher in that language. Statistics on 'home language pupils', since 1997 officially called 'mother tongue pupils' (i.e. pupils in the Swedish school with other languages than Swedish as the medium of daily communication with at least one parent, see Boyd in this Volume) give information about the number of school children taking part in mother tongue lessons in different languages. However, the circumstances can vary considerably in regard to the way these figures are arrived at: they depend on the extent to which the school informs parents about the mother tongue option, the possibilities of organizing mother tongue instruction for all pupils who are interested in taking part in it, or the exactness of recording pupils in fact attending mother tongue lessons. The figures available concerning the number of pupils entitled to mother tongue instruction and the number of pupils attending mother tongue lessons in the compulsory school in 1998/99 are given in Table 2.

The Finnish group has been offered mother tongue instruction (until 1998 called 'home language instruction') since the sixties and the rate of participation within this group has been relatively high. Today (2000) it has dropped to little over 40%. During the seventies and early eighties, there were also Finnish mother tongue classes (with instruction through the medium of Finnish and Swedish) and classes with 50% Finnish and 50% Swedish pupils where the former received instruction through the medium of Finnish in some subjects. The number of pupils attending

Table 2 Number of national minority language pupils entitled to mother tongue instruction and attending mother tongue lessons in the compulsory school (1998/99) (Source: National Board of Education, February 2000)

Languages	Entitled	Attending
Finnish *	14,362	6,101
Romani	826	217
Sami **	511	345
Yiddish	-	-
Hebrew	144	52

* No distinction is made between Meänkieli and Finnish in northern Sweden and consequently there are no figures available for Meänkieli.
** No distinction is made between the three Sami varieties spoken in Sweden: Lule, North and South Sami.

Finnish mother tongues classes today is approximately 900, while there are no figures available for the latter form of bilingual classes. Both of these bilingual models (and mother tongue instruction) were subject to severe cuts in the late eighties and early nineties. Partly as a reaction to this, 14 independent Finnish schools have since then been founded in Sweden. This became possible when the Conservative government in power in the early nineties eased the regulations concerning the establishment of such schools. One of these schools has a Meänkieli profile and is situated in Tornedalen. All of these schools are bilingual in the sense that at least 50% of the instruction must be given through the medium of Swedish. The total number of pupils attending these schools is approximately 900. However, there is a strong opposition against independent ethnic schools in Sweden, mainly against Muslim profile schools but also against other independent schools, and in some municipalities these schools are openly opposed by local politicians.

The Sami are the only minority group in Sweden with a state-initiated special school system. The history of the Swedish Sami schools dates back to the 17th century when instruction of the young Sami in Christianity and literacy was provided by the Church. The six Sami schools of today have a total number of 186 pupils (1999), a low figure considering the total number of Sami in Sweden (see above). Until the nineties, the Sami language did not have any prominent place in the curriculum of these schools, while Sami-profile instruction was given in subjects such as arts and crafts or music. It was not until the nineties, particularly in 1993 when a dissertation was published (Svonni, 1993) stating that there was a rapid language shift going on among school-age Sami children, that a wider public was made aware of the looming death of the Sami language in Sweden. Bilingual programmes were designed and applied in several of the Sami schools and so far they seem to have increased the amount of instruction given through the medium of Sami. Nevertheless, the programmes retain a transitional character, with most Sami in primary school and more and more Swedish when the children advance to higher levels. In secondary school, Sami is taught only as a subject. What is available for the great majority of Sami children and youngsters, i.e. those who attend the municipal schools, are the weekly mother tongue lessons offered to all minority children (345 Sami pupils in 1999), or in some schools 'integrated Sami instruction', implying mother tongue instruction combined with Sami-profile instruction in a couple of other subjects (170 pupils in 1999). The total number of pupils receiving some kind of instruction in or through the medium of Sami in 1999 was approximately 700 (source: The Sami School Board, 1999).

There has been mother tongue instruction in Romani since the seventies and to a certain extent mother tongue teachers of Romani have been trained. Concerning Roma children (and even Tornedalian and Sami pupils), the regulations of mother tongue instruction have been more generous than concerning other minority children because the requirement that the home language be used as a language of everyday communication with at least one parent has not been applied. Mother tongue classes with fewer than five pupils are also possible. In addition, Roma pupils have the right to study more than one home language other than Swedish - a right not available to other minority language groups. To facilitate the teaching of Romani at school, a normative word list was produced in the seventies in some Romani varieties spoken in Sweden. The scarcity of teaching material is still a great problem, although the National Board of Education, that also produced the word list, has since that time initiated several development projects to remedy the situation. They have resulted in a small number of Swedish books for children and adolescents translated into some Romani varieties as well as a couple of readers and other teaching materials. The teaching of Romani at school also faces the special difficulty caused by the tradition of Romani being the secret language of the Roma. The attitudes towards school among the Roma are mixed: some of them see school as a threat to Roma culture, while others are worried about the fact that many Roma children drop out of school at an early stage. The Working Group for Roma issues in Sweden (*Romer i Sverige*, 1996: 7) proposes to search for a concept which would unite Roma values and Swedish education and enable active cooperation between the Roma and the school in order to avoid further drifting apart of the two.

In the Jewish Hillel School in Stockholm, established in 1955, the focus has in addition to mainstream school content been on Jewish history and culture as well as Hebrew, while Yiddish has not been included in the curriculum. Neither does Yiddish seem to have been included in the child and adolescent programmes of Jewish congregations in Sweden. Runblom and Tydén (1990: 199) maintain that Yiddish was actually never very widely spread among Swedish Jews except for a couple of short periods during World War I and during the second half of the forties. Their estimation of the situation prevailing in the late eighties, when their book was compiled, was that the Yiddish tradition was kept alive mainly by a small number of elderly Jews. Today, there is no Yiddish mother tongue instruction in any Swedish school.

University level education in Finnish as a subject has a long tradition in Sweden and Finnish is today offered by four universities (Lund, Stockholm, Umeå and Uppsala). Special courses in Meänkieli on a small scale have recently been taught in two universities (Luleå and Stockholm). University level education in Sami (even that is a phenomenon with a long tradition in Sweden) is offered at three universities (Luleå, Umeå and Uppsala) and it is possible to study all three varieties: Lule, South and North Sami. Romani and Yiddish have until now not been taught as subjects at university level.

Linguistic pluralism for Sweden?

In the course of years, an increasing interest and involvement in linguistic revitalization has become apparent among several historical minorities in Sweden, beginning in a couple of core areas or among groups of ethnic activists and spreading gradually to other areas and groups, like ripples in a pond. The cultural and linguistic revival movements have had to concentrate their efforts on two distinct fronts: among the minorities themselves and among the corresponding majorities, the latter of whom have to be persuaded to grant or strengthen some basic minority rights if linguistic and cultural maintenance is to become a realistic goal.

European integration and the existence of international minority rights instruments, such as the Council of Europe Charter for Regional or Minority Languages, are factors that have in a very decisive way changed Sweden's official view of historical languages within its own territory. The Government Bill finally released in 1999 and the ratification of the two Council of Europe Conventions resulting from it have been welcomed by the minority groups concerned and high hopes are held for future measures proposed in the Government Bill. Nevertheless, some critical voices within the same minorities have been raised to the effect that a mere ratification will not alter the situation much unless minority members seize the opportunity of accelerating their previous language revitalization efforts, now with official support from the State.

As proposed in the Bill, a Swedish recognition will lead to a number of measures geared to strengthening the historical minorities and their languages in Sweden. Among these languages, Finnish, Meänkieli and Sami in certain municipalities in northern Sweden are considered to have a historical and geographical basis and therefore more comprehensive measures are proposed for them. In these municipalities, individuals are entitled to use their original languages, orally or in writing, in contacts with courts of justice and administrative authorities, and these are to answer (orally) in the same language. Examples of other measures proposed for the municipalities where Finnish, Meänkieli and Sami have official status are minority language medium pre-school activities and care for the elderly.

The nationwide measures proposed by the Bill comprise a number of efforts to make all historical minorities more known to the Swedish public and to support their cultural and linguistic activities. In the field of education it is proposed that the provision of information about national minorities and their languages be included in the national curricula for primary and secondary schools as well as after-school centres. The National Board of Education is also to pay particular attention to the further development of mother tongue instruction for the national minorities. Research and university level instruction in Finnish, Sami and Meänkieli as well as the corresponding minority cultures are to be continued and developed, and the need for research and education on Romani and Yiddish culture and language are to be investigated.

The recent developments in Sweden undoubtedly offer increased opportunities for maintaining and revitalizing historical minority languages. However, some weaknesses in the Government Bill give rise to alarm. One of these is the fact that no legally-based or other protection is offered to minority language-medium instruction in the compulsory school system. Instead, instruction of the mother tongue as a subject is suggested to be followed up and it is seen as a sufficient way of guaranteeing long-term minority language maintenance. As representatives of the national minority groups have frequently pointed out, the existing model of mother tongue instruction in the Swedish mainstream school is by no means sufficient if the aim is to guarantee long-term minority language maintenance in Sweden. Schooling through the medium of other languages than Swedish is, however, a most controversial issue in Sweden and remains the most serious problem for those in favour of minority language support. As several of the national minority languages already are extremely endangered, the question of minority language medium education is crucial and it is possible that also other minorities than the Sweden Finns and Tornedalians will take the opportunity of founding independent schools with a minority culture profile. Nevertheless, in a society like the Swedish, independent schools face an uncertain future and placing the responsibility of language maintenance on such schools rather than on the mainstream school system implies that the issue has not fully been accepted by the State. It is true, as Fishman (1991) and several others have pointed out, that the school alone can hardly reverse ongoing language shift - the language choices made by individual parents are also critical - but the roles of family and school are closely intertwined and mutually dependent, and for long-term language survival cooperation is urgently needed.

In addition to the status of national minority languages in school education discussed above, other weaknesses in the Government Bill could be mentioned as well. However, if seen - as the title of the Minority Language Committee Report ('Steps Towards a Minority Policy') suggests - as the (first) steps towards a reorientation with regard to historical minorities, the recognition of these minorities and their languages is a good starting point for renewed efforts to support linguistic pluralism in Sweden. As before, the greatest responsibility in language maintenance and revitalization lies with the minorities themselves, but now they are more officially sanctioned than they have ever been before.

References

Boyd, S. & Gadelii, E. (1999) Vem tillhör talgemenskapen? Om jiddisch i Sverige. In K. Hyltenstam (ed.) _Sveriges sju inhemska språk - ett minoritetsspråksprespektiv_ (pp. 299-328). Lund.

Bratt Paulston, C. (1992) _Forskning och debatt om tvåspråkighet. En kritisk genomgång av svensk forskning och debatt om tvåspråkighet i invandrarundervisningen i Sverige från ett internationellt perspektiv._ Stockholm: Skolöverstyrelsen.

Fishman, J. (1991) _Reversing language shift. Theoretical and empirical foundations of assistance to threatened languages._ Clevedon: Multilingual Matters.

Fraurud, K. & Hyltenstam, K. (1999) Språkkontakt och språkbevarande: romani i Sverige. In K. Hyltenstam (ed.) _Sveriges sju inhemska språk - ett minoritetsspråksprespektiv_ (pp. 241-298). Lund.

Gröndahl, S. (forthcoming) Invandrar- och minoritetslitteraturer i Sverige. Från förutsättningar till framtidsutsikteer. In S. Gröndahl (ed.) _Möten i gränsland: Minoritets- och invandarlitteratur i nordiskt perspektiv._

Huss, L (1999) _Reversing language shift in the far North: Linguistic revitalization in Northern Scandinavia and Finland._ Acta Universitatis Upsaliensis. Studia Uralica Upsaliensia 31. Uppsala.

Huss, L. (2000) Kielenhuolto ja kotimaiset kielet. _Kieliviesti_ 2/00, 3-4. Stockholm: Sverigefinska språknämnden

Hyltenstam, K. (ed.) (1999) _Sveriges sju inhemska språk - ett minoritetsspråksperspektiv._ Lund.

Janulf, P. (1998) _Kommer finskan i Sverige att fortleva? En studie av språkkunskaper och språkanvändning hos andragenerationens sverigefinnar i Botkyrka och hos finlandssvenskar i Åbo._ Stockholm: Studia Fennica Stockholmiensia.

Nationella minoriteter i Sverige. Regeringens proposition (1998/99). Stockholm.

Romer i Sverige. Situationsbeskrivning (1996). Unpublished report. Norrköping: Statens Invandrarverk - Nordiska Zigenarrådet.

Runblom, H. (1995) Swedish multiculturalism in a comparative European perspective. In S. Gustavsson & H. Runblom (eds) _Language, minority, migration. Yearbook 1994/1995 from the Centre for Multiethnic Research_ (pp. 199-218). Uppsala Multiethnic Papers 34. Uppsala: Uppsala University.

Runblom, H. & Tydén, M. (1990) Judar. In I. Svanberg & H. Runblom (eds) _Det mångkulturella Sverige. En handbok om etniska grupper och minoriteter._ Stockholm (second edition).

SOU (1997). _Steg mot en minoritetspolitik. Europarådet konvention om historiska minoritetsspråk. Betänkande av minoritetsspråkskommittén._ Stockholm.

SOU (1997) _Steg mot en minoritetspolitik. Europarådets konvention för skydd av nationella minoriteter. Betänkande av minoritetsspråkskommittén._ Stockholm.

Smolicz, J. (1992) Minority languages as core values of ethnic cultures: A study of maintenance and erosion of Polish, Welsh, and Chinese languages in Australia. In W. Fase, K. Jaspaert & S. Kroon (eds) _Maintenance and loss of_ minority languages (pp. 277-305). Amsterdam/Philadelphia. Studies in Bilingualism 1

Svonni, M. (1993) Samiska skolbarns samiska. En undersökning av minoritetsspråks-behärskning i en språkbyteskontext. Acta Universitatis Umensis. Umeå Studies in the Humanities 113. Umeå.

Vuorela, K. & Borin, L. (1998) Finnish Romani. In A. Ó Corráin & S. Mac Mathúna (eds) Minority languages in Scandinavia, Britain and Ireland (pp. 51-76). Acta Universitatis Upsaliensis. Uppsala. Studia Celtica Upsaliensia 3.

Winsa, B. (1999) Language attitudes and social identity. Oppression and revival of a minority language in Sweden.

Swedish in Finland

ANNA ØSTERN

Swedish is presently one of the two official languages in Finland. The majority of the inhabitants in Finland is Finnish-speaking but a minority speaks Swedish as its first language. The number of bilingual families (one parent Finnish-speaking, the other Swedish-speaking) is increasing. The Swedish spoken in Finland is one of the five regional varieties of Swedish. Swedish belongs to the Germanic language family and is one of the Nordic languages which have much in common. Swedish is understood in all Nordic countries by about 20 million people. The Swedish spoken in Finland has the same standard and norms as the Swedish spoken in Sweden. However, one can decide from a person's intonation whether s/he is a Finland-Swede. One can also decide, due to intonation differences, from which part of the Swedish-speaking part of Finland a person comes, i.e. whether a person comes from Ostrobothnia, Åland or the southern part of Finland. The oral language of about 30-40% of the Finland-Swedes consists of different Swedish vernaculars. But the norm for the Finland-Swedes is standard Swedish, which is also the medium of instruction in the Swedish-based school. It is important for the Finland-Swedes that written Swedish in Finland does not differ from written Swedish in Sweden.

Demographic and sociolinguistic stratification

The total population of Finland is about 5.2 million people. The Finnish society is going through a strong phase of internationalisation right now. Through Finns who move and work abroad and who come into contact with people talking different languages and belonging to different cultures, pluricultural understanding is increasing. Within the country, there are about 100,000 immigrants, speaking about 120 different languages. As a result, the Finnish society is changing from a homogeneous monoculture into a pluricultural society (cf. Liebkind, 1994; Nyberg, 2000).

The government form of 1919 postulates that Finnish and Swedish are the two national languages of the country. In the foundation law of 1922 the regulations regarding language use are specified in detail. About 5.6 % (296,000 persons) of the population state Swedish as their mother tongue. The number of persons who speak Swedish as one of their languages in Finland is estimated at about 600,000. Persons who consider Swedish to be their mother tongue are usually bilingual with at least sufficient knowledge of Finnish; quite often they are trilingual with English being the third language. In a description of regional languages in Europe the present situation in Finland is described as follows:

> Finnish and Swedish are the official State languages. However Swedish (*svenska*) is a lesser used language and is spoken along the southern and western coasts and on the Åland islands. There is a Sami community which speaks Lapp (S‡megiella) in the north of the country and a community of gypsies scattered throughout Finnish territory. There are two other autochthonous minorities, a Russian language and a Tatar language, spread throughout the country. (EBLUL, 1999).

There are special laws protecting the autonomy of the Åland Islands where about 25,000 Swedish-speaking inhabitants live. Åland got a Swedish population already in 500 a.c. The Swedish immigration to Finland is otherwise assumed to be from the age of crusading and the early middle age (1100 and 1200 century). Thus the Swedish language in Finland has got roots far back in time, not least to the six hundred years during which Finland was a part of Sweden (until 1809).

The Swedish-speaking population is about 296,000. In 1880 the Swedish-speaking population was 294,900 persons and at that time constituted 14.3% of the total population of Finland. Because of the doubling of the Finnish-speaking population during the 20th century, the Swedish-speaking population has relatively decreased to about 5.6% (1996), although it has remained almost the same in numbers. The decrease in the relative number of Swedish-speaking people in Finland can partly be explained by emigration. Since 1950 about 60,000 Finland-Swedes have emigrated, mostly to Sweden. The decrease in percentage of Swedish-speaking people is to a lesser degree dependent on language shift to Finnish. Since 1950 the net number of persons who have shifted from Swedish to Finnish is about 1000.

The social stratification in the Finnish society is equal for the Finnish-speaking and the Swedish-speaking population. It differs very much to what extent it will be possible to use Swedish as a language of communication in stores, offices, religious matters, social welfare and health care (cf. Finnäs, 1996, Østern, 1997).

About 50% of the Finland-Swedes are a majority in their municipalities and the other half is a language minority living under strong influence from Finnish. There is a small number of municipalities in Ostrobothnia and Åboland which are unilingually Swedish. All municipalities in Åland are unilingually Swedish.

According to Finnäs (1996) more babies are born in bilingual families than in monolingual Swedish families. This means that the language situation in Swedish-based schools is experiencing very powerful changes.

Through a variety of brochures the Finland-Swedish Assembly (*Svenska Finlands folkting*) has actively informed bilingual families about the possibility to choose a Swedish-based school. One brochure points out that parents within two months of their child's birth are to register the child's language. In the brochure 'We have the right to choose!' (*Folktinget*) it is sait that 'Every citizen of our country has the right to choose which is his or her mother tongue'.

According to Finnäs (1996), bilingual families register their children as Swedish-speaking to an increasing part. If the mother is Swedish-speaking, the percentage exceeds 70%; if she is Finnish-speaking the percentage is about 50%. Grannabba (1999) has investigated patterns in the motivations of bilingual families for choosing a Swedish-based school for their children and concludes that parents generally want to give their children the possibility of bilingualism.

Educational system and support structure

The educational system in the Swedish-speaking parts of Finland is not different from the system in the rest of Finland. The main characteristic of the organisation of teaching at all levels for the Finland-Swedish population is the principle of language shelter. In addition to the Finnish school system, a parallel school system exists in Swedish. The minority schools have commonly native speakers of Swedish as teachers and the language of the school is Swedish.

About 98% of the schools (at all levels) is run publicly by the local authorities. The schools are funded by the state up to 60-70% of the costs.

The rest of the costs are funded by the local authorities. The public obligatory school in Finland consists of grades 1-9. Children enter school at the age of seven. The state regulates the school system through laws. Students do not pay fees; this is true for all levels of the school system. Exceptions to this rule are some adult education institutions. In six very dominantly Finnish-speaking cities there exists a so-called 'private' Swedish school. But these schools are financed in the same way as the other public schools. Very few schools are actually privately run by organisations (one Steiner school and a Montessori kindergarten).

Central as well as local authorities are involved in education. The primary, secondary and upper secondary school systems have been regulated by central laws since 1984. The National Board of Education is generally not normative, but the board has a statutory right to decide upon evaluation and grading. The task of the board is to develop the educational system through different developmental projects and to work out the framework curriculum for comprehensive schools and for senior secondary schools (1994). The framework curriculum for pre-schools dates from 1996.

The local authorities work through a council of education. In this council the local curriculum for the different school levels is decided upon. With the reform of the national curriculum in 1994, the local educational councils were given greater responsibility and more freedom to decide upon the school programmes than before. It is also decided locally how to control the qualitative standard of local schools.

The National Board of Education gives advice to the ministry of education on education policy. The National Board of Education has a separate department for minority questions on Swedish, Sami and Romani, on returnees as well as on the education of refugees. The National Board of Education predominantly supports schools through the development of the curriculum. It is also developing national educational standards for different age groups. A special council controls the national standard of grading for graduates from upper secondary schools (*studentexamensnämnden*). The council formulates the extensive examinations for graduating students. The outcomes also serve as an entrance test to university and higher vocational education.

The Swedish Assembly in Finland (*Svenska Finlands folkting*) has a support function for information about the Finland-Swedish population. There is also an organization of Swedish municipalities (*Svenska kommunförbundet*) for administrating the local policy in Swedish-speaking areas. The Swedish-based cultural foundation (*Svenska kulturfonden*) offers grants for projects and research on the Swedish language and culture in Finland.

The major Swedish-based university of Finland is Åbo Akademi University. The university has a special task in taking care of the needs of education and research among and for the Finland-Swedes. Thus there exists the Institute for Swedish sociological research in Finland, which continuously carries out demographic research on the Swedish-speaking population in Finland. One part of Åbo Akademi is located in Vaasa under the name of the Ostrobothnian campus of Åbo Akademi (*Österbottens högskola*). A centre for research on and production of teaching materials for Swedish-based schools (*Svenska läromedelscentret*) has recently been established at the Ostrobothnian campus.

The department of teacher education in Vaasa fulfils its responsibilities by maintaining close contact with all the Swedish-based regions of Finland, being sensitive to the number of teachers required and providing courses and research in most of the various fields of specialisation offered by the Finnish-based teacher education departments.

In the following sections the Finland-Swedish educational system is discussed in more detail from a longitudinal perspective.

Pre-school education

Day care institutions in Finland are regulated by the day care law of 1973. The law obliges local authorities to arrange day care according to the needs of the municipalities for children between six months and six years of age. The law underlines the importance of upbringing and caring more than that of teaching. The day care institutions are under the supervision of the Ministry of Welfare and the board of welfare (*socialstyrelsen*). These institutions are organised by the local authorities. They are not free of charge; parents pay according to their income. The institutions are divided on a language base in Swedish-language and Finnish-language institutions. Some are bilingual with separate language groups. For six-year-old children there is a voluntary pre-school offer either in day care institutions or in primary schools. There are some situations where pre-school education is organized within primary schools (local authorities have to apply to the National Board of Education). The pre-school is then integrated with grades 1 and 2. There is a cost-free offer for all six-year-old children of a pre-school year. The framework curriculum for pre-schools has been published by the National Board of Education in 1996.

The kindergarten teacher is commonly a native speaker of Swedish, but usually s/he is also fluent in Finnish. This is typical for the urban bilingual areas in Finland, where Swedish-speaking families often live in a Finnish-speaking context. The parents want their child to go to a Swedish-based day care group in order to give the child a chance to speak Swedish more fluently when primary schooling starts.

For Finnish-speaking pre-school children there exists in some areas the possibility to take part in an immersion programme where the medium of instruction is Swedish. The target group are unilingual Finnish-speaking children, but the idea is that these children will become functionally bilingual in Swedish and Finnish through the immersion programme. Most research in the immersion field is carried out at Vaasa University. The concept of immersion was implemented in the Finnish-based school system in Vaasa and the first immersion pupils are now in upper secondary schools.

All kinds of instructional material from Sweden are available for the Swedish-based pre-school. Teaching material is also constantly being produced in Finland by publishers who use Swedish as their main publishing language (*Editum/Schildts och Söderströms*). Also the faculty of education at the Swedish university in Finland (Åbo Akademi) publishes didactic material for pre-school teachers.

Primary education

Primary school in Finland caters for pupils aged 7-12 (grades 1-6). In 1998 there were 4200 children enrolled in the first grade of Swedish-based primary schools. In a report about the situation in the Swedish-based primary schools in the school year 1998/1999 the National Board of Education concludes that classes are much more mixed linguistically today than during the eighties. The numbers of pupils in Swedish-based schools have increased by almost 30%, from 3200 pupils in 1980 to 4100 pupils in 1998. According to the investigation still two out of three pupils in Swedish-based schools come from completely Swedish-speaking homes. Especially pupils from Swedish-speaking homes in the higher grades speak Finnish regularly. The National Board of Education concludes that about 30% of the pupils in Swedish-based schools speak a Swedish dialect. The pupils are almost without exception from Ostrobothnia. In all Swedish-speaking regions of Finland there are pupils from families where other languages than Swedish and Finnish are spoken (about 2% of the pupils). According to the teachers' estimates about 19% of the pupils in Swedish-based schools do not speak Swedish fluently. Teachers also estimate that 56 % of the bilingual pupils speak Swedish unimpededly.

The law for primary and secondary education (1983) underlines the nature of a common basic education. Schools are public schools regulated by the law of general compulsory learning (*läroplikt*). Based on the framework curriculum for comprehensive schools every school is supposed to develop its own local curriculum. In the principles for the curriculum for primary and secondary schools (called '*grundskola*') the subjects to be taught are defined. In the framework curriculum of 1994 (for grades 1-9) the values on which to found teaching are described according to the United Nations Declaration of Human Rights (a lasting development, national cultural traditions as well as internationalism, values and moral, health and welfare). These aims hold nationwide. However, there is a great freedom of choice to decide on the contents of teaching and on how to profile local schools. There has recently been a change from primary schools focused on rules to primary schools focused on aims to achieve.

Schools are of vital importance for the cultural identity of a small minority like the Swedish-speaking population in Finland. The language of instruction in Swedish-based schools is Swedish. Primary school teachers in Swedish-based schools speak Swedish fluently. If a teacher with another mother tongue than Swedish wants to teach in a primary school, s/he has to pass a Swedish language test.

There are 251 Swedish-based primary schools. In 1998 there were about 25,000 pupils enrolled in these schools. The number of bilingual children in Swedish-based schools increased rapidly in the nineties. One third of the pupils (about 8000) speak standard Swedish and about 20% (5000) speak a Swedish dialect. About another 10% use the vernacular when talking to peers. About one third (8400) come from bilingual homes and speak Swedish as well as Finnish. About 5% (200) of the pupils come from monolingual Finnish families. About 2% of the pupils have another mother tongue than Finnish or Swedish. In the national registration of language for children of bilingual families in the seventies, about 40% of the children were registered as Swedish-speaking; in the nineties about 60% of the children were registered as Swedish-speaking.

On the so-called language islands, 70-90% of the pupils come from Finnish-speaking homes. On the other hand, there are many rural schools where almost none of the children know Finnish at all. Instead, most of the pupils in the rural areas speak a Swedish vernacular. When they go to school they are supposed to learn standard Swedish.

In Swedish-based primary schools there is a course called 'strengthened mother tongue Swedish' (*förstärkt modersmål*) for pupils from bilingual homes where Finnish is the dominant language and the child is not quite fluent in Swedish. Some 2% of the pupils in Swedish-based primary schools come from monolingual Finnish-speaking homes. For the pupils who have Finnish as mother tongue, there is an offer of Finnish as mother tongue (*modersmålsinriktad finska*). The other pupils learn Finnish as their first foreign language. The teaching of Finnish as a subject starts in grade three. In Finnish schools pupils can choose to learn either Swedish or English as their first foreign language. Most pupils choose English from grade three and Swedish from grade seven. The learning of Swedish is obligatory for Finnish-speaking pupils and the learning of Finnish as a foreign language is compulsory for Swedish-speaking pupils. Only on the Åland Islands pupils may choose Finnish on a voluntary basis. In Swedish-based schools the medium of instruction is Swedish unless a foreign language is being taught.

For immersion programme schools in Finland the medium of instruction is also Swedish during the first three years; then gradually the teaching partly takes place in Finnish. In a few cases, immersion programmes in English are used in Swedish-based schools. In one case immersion in Finnish is tried out for a Swedish-based primary school located in Jakobstad (Østern, Sjöholm & Smeds, 1999).

In primary Swedish-based schools, Swedish is integrated in all subjects. The importance of linguistic awareness is stressed and material to help the teachers is developed for that purpose. The books used for teaching different subjects are mainly produced in Sweden and Finland. Many of the lecturers in didactics at the Swedish-based teacher education center also produce books for different subjects.

There are some 22 Swedish-based institutions for various types of special education (training schools for severely handicapped children, training vocational schools, schools for visually handicapped children and so on). The main trend is integration of pupils in special education into mainstream schooling. Every primary and secondary school has a special needs teacher to consult. Especially in primary schools the special needs teacher is a companion-teacher for speech-training and for support of children with reading and writing difficulties.

Secondary education

Grades 7-9 are part of the obligatory school system (grades 1-9 are called *grundskola*). From 1997 the administrative barriers between primary and secondary schools have been taken away. In grades 7-9 the teachers are subject teachers. The teaching in these grades is based on the framework curriculum for comprehensive schools. Every secondary school has its own local curriculum. At this stage the study advisor is a central person who gives advice about studies beyond the obligatory period of schooling: either a vocational school or a gymnasium.

Swedish as a subject is taught at least during 2-3 hours weekly and concerns writing, reading of literature, oral communication skills and grammar. In secondary schools the same type of support for language learning can be given as in primary schools. The Swedish-based section of the National Board of Education has developed national tests for mathematics, for Finnish as a foreign language and for Swedish oral communication in grade 9. These tests are offered on a voluntary basis. Swedish-based publishers such as *Editum/Schildts* and *Söderströms* produce teaching material for secondary schools. Also teaching material from Sweden is widely used.

Upper secondary education

The law for upper secondary education (gymnasium) dates from 1992. In the law the goals for this type of secondary education are described. The teaching in the gymnasium is based on studies in lower secondary education. The regulations for the subjects taught are described in a decree from the Ministry of Education (1993). The National Board of Education has published the framework curriculum for upper secondary education in 1994.

Upper secondary education takes commonly place during three years for 16-18/19 years old pupils. Recently the system has developed away from fixed year groups into a flexible system with course studies. For instance, the obligatory number of courses in Swedish as a mother tongue in Swedish-based schools is six: language and communication, creative text production, text and language structure, Finland-Swedish and Nordic, literature as a mirror of contemporary society, and language and literature as power factors.

In the gymnasium, a course called strengthened mother tongue Swedish for bilingual pupils can also be taught. The aim of the course is to offer bilingual pupils a possibility to reach the same proficiency level in Swedish as monolingual Swedish pupils.

In Finnish-based senior secondary schools Swedish is taught as a subject. Swedish is described in the Finnish-based national curriculum (1994) as part of the students' general education. Swedish language proficiency, it is said, gives the students Nordic cultural capital and strengthens their cultural identity of which the bilingualism of the country is a part.

Swedish-based upper secondary schools are monolingual in Swedish. In two cities there is a Swedish-based gymnasium (in Vaasa and in Helsinki) with one group of students receiving their teaching to a large extent in English (international baccalaureate). This group consists of 50% Swedish-speaking students and 50% Finnish-speaking students.

Four of the Swedish-based gymnasiums, each one of them in dominantly Finnish-speaking cities, are called 'private' or 'substituting' schools. Here the students to a large extent use Finnish as their language of communication outside the school and also inside school when not talking to a teacher. In these schools the use of Swedish as medium of instruction is underlined. The upper secondary schools are part of second-stage education. Another type of second-stage education is formed by vocational education schools.

Vocational education

There exist 52 Swedish-based basic vocational training schools in Finland. Usually they offer courses during 1-3 years. Pupils can go from secondary schools to this type of education. Vocational schools are often part of a polytechnic type of school which offers higher professional education.

Since 1996 there are three Swedish-based polytechnic type of schools, called AMK institutions (*yrkeshögskola*). Three more AMK institutions are bilingual and have Swedish- as well as Finnish-based classes or mixed groups. Programmes at AMK institutions are for instance available in technology, health, art, youth work, business management, hotel and restaurant management. The characteristic feature of an AMK institution is that the teaching is strictly directed towards higher vocational education and not towards research.

Swedish is used as medium of instruction in Swedish-based vocational schools. In bilingual institutions, such as business management schools or hotel and restaurant management schools, some subjects are taught in Finnish and some in Swedish. Swedish as a subject is taught in all Swedish-based vocational schools and AMK institutions.

Higher education

The major Swedish-based university for higher education is Åbo Akademi University. Another Swedish-based university institution is the Swedish Business Management School. A third Swedish-based institution at university level is the School for Social Studies and Welfare at the

University of Helsinki. Some other universities are bilingual and offer some teaching in Swedish: the University of Helsinki, the Technical University, the Theatre Academy, the Music Academy and the University of Vaasa.

Åbo Akademi University requires as a rule native-like competence in Swedish from its students. Some 25% of the students are predominantly Finnish-speaking but they have passed a test in Swedish, which is supposed to be a guarantee that these students can study in Swedish. Academic teaching is offered in Swedish from the undergraduate to postgraduate level. At the bilingual universities of Helsinki and Vaasa Swedish and Finnish are taught side by side. At the university of Vaasa Finnish-Swedish translators are trained. The summer universities and the open university work in close contact with the Swedish and bilingual universities; they also offer distance courses at university level.

Adult education

Adult education is offered in adult education institutes. These institutes teach a large number of different courses, many of them as leisure time interests such as arts education and language courses. Some of the centers teach vocational courses for people without employment. The Swedish language association for adult studies organises distance studies.

Of special interest for the minority culture are the 17 folk high schools in Finland where young people usually study for two years in order to gain a deeper understanding of a special field of interest. This kind of schooling is supposed to be 'a school for life'.

Adult education in Swedish is offered in 30 civic institutes (*medborgar- och arbetarinstitut*), one correspondence institute (*brevinstitut*), 40 vocational schools/institutes which also offer adult education, 3 centres for adult education, 17 folk high schools, 2 upper secondary schools and 10 in-service centres at universities and colleges. There are 3 Swedish-based summer universities. Furthermore there are 2 study centres. Many of these institutes offer bilingual programmes.

The Swedish-based adult education institutes gradually become more bilingual and offer subject studies in Swedish as well as in Finnish. Students often come from both language groups. A visible minority of the students are refugees. Swedish as a subject is offered in Swedish-based as well as in Finnish-based adult education institutes.

Teacher education

Finland has 21 universities. At the faculties of humanities there is an offer of studies of Swedish as a subject. There are chairs for Swedish in Åbo (Turku), Helsinki, Tampere and Vaasa. Teacher education is provided by universities at the faculties of education. Finland-Swedish teachers receive their education from the faculty of education at Åbo Akademi University. Since 1974, this faculty has been located in Vaasa as an integral part of the Ostrobothnian campus of Åbo Akademi. The main reason for locating the faculty of education in Vaasa was that the region to a great extent is Swedish-speaking and thus can provide easy access for student-teachers to Swedish-based schools and classes. A special professional development school (*Vaasa Övningsskola*) is part of the faculty of education as the department of teacher education.

Contemporary teacher education in Finland is an outcome of almost thirty years of development. Class teacher education was transferred to the universities in 1974. A decree from 1979 states that the degrees of class teacher and subject teacher for comprehensive and upper secondary schools should be equally extensive. In the new degree act on education (valid since 1995) the earlier strict boundary between class teacher degrees and subject teacher degrees has been eliminated. Since 1995, kindergarten teacher education takes place at the faculty of education. Swedish-based kindergarten teacher education is located in Jakobstad in Ostrobothnia and is part of the department of teacher education at Åbo Akademi University. Subject teachers for the Swedish-based school system take their one year of pedagogical studies in Vaasa. Likewise special education teachers and sloyd teachers have a master's programme in Vaasa. At the Swedish-based faculty of education a complete academic programme exists from initial teacher education to postgraduate studies in educational sciences.

The undergraduate education of teachers at Åbo Akademi is primarily devoted to the needs of the Swedish-speaking population in Finland. The faculty of education is responsible for the pedagogical part of all types of Swedish-based teacher education in Finland and thus functions as a safeguard for the vitality of an important minority culture in Finland.

At the Swedish-based faculty of education at the Ostrobothnian campus of Åbo Akademi University about 700 students are enrolled as teacher students. Per year about 60-80 students graduate with a master's degree in educational sciences and become qualified either as class teachers, special education teachers or sloyd teachers. In 1996, the first 45 kindergarten teachers with a bachelor degree graduated from the faculty.

faculty. It is also possible to take a master's degree in education, especially in early childhood education. Four to five persons take a licentiate grade in educational science yearly, and approximately three persons per year take their doctoral degree in educational sciences. Åbo Akademi also gives extra teacher education in Helsinki.

Subject teacher competence for Swedish-based schools can also be acquired at the University of Helsinki. The studies in didactics in Helsinki are mainly offered in Finnish but the training periods are at Swedish-based schools. Some students take their master's degree at a Finnish university and then they take a test in Swedish (native-like proficiency is required) to gain qualifications for teaching in the Swedish-based school system.

Educational research

For decades Swedish-speaking inhabitants of Finland have been the focus of empirical research. Today there exists an extensive body of research in the field of education, carried out at universities and especially in the faculty of education at Åbo Akademi University. Some of the emphasis has been on issues of language and identity. A large-scale project at the Department of Teacher Education is centered around language and communication in a pedagogical perspective (Østern & Sjöholm, 2000). The relationship with the majority language is explored through research on bilingualism and education (Brink & Eriksson, 1997; West, 1999; Østern, 2000). Finland-Swedish culture and identity are central issues in the research (Koivunen & Rosenblad, 1999: Østern, 2000). The Institute for Swedish sociological research in Finland provides researchers and authorities with updated demographic information about the Finland-Swedish population and about attitudes and changes in attitudes among the minority and majority population (Nyman-Kurkiala, 1996). Studies in language shift and language loss are another theme of vital interest (Tandefelt, 1996). The National Board of Education supports research on the evaluation of learning in schools. Some crossnational comparative studies concerning learning have gained great interest. Immersion programmes are continuously monitored by researchers at Vaasa university. Nordic research networks are also important for Finland-Swedish educational research.

Prospects

The Swedish population is, compared to other language minorities, a vital group in Finland, partly due to legislation that protects the language. Another reason are the deep historical roots of Swedish in Finland and its cultural capital. Artists from the Swedish community contribute to the cultural spectrum of Finland through literature, music, dance, theatre, film and crafts.

A key issue for the Finland-Swedish minority is the choice of language(s) in bilingual families and above all the choice of the school language for their children. The quality of education in Swedish-based schools will decide on the future of the Finland-Swedish minority as a language group. The quality of the Swedish-based educational system is high and can thus contribute to a high self-esteem among the Finland-Swedish community. The challenges for Swedish-based schools include the handling of language heterogeneity among their pupils and the transformation to meet the expectations of a society in rapid change. Areas of future strength can also be found in the fields of cultural and linguistic competence, international cooperation, the use of multimedia and parallel forms of instruction.

Finland is a relatively small country and has for several years been part of the European Union. Thus, the language skills with which we provide the next generation will constitute an important policy issue. The language programme we have in Finland is therefore indeed a first priority question. In fact, comparatively many hours have been allocated to language teaching in Finland. We assume that a growing number of adolescents in Finland, especially in urban settings, will consider themselves trilingual (Finnish, Swedish and English) rather than bi-lingual. By the increasing internationalization (often via English) and by receiving refugees, old language frontiers will be transcended and new language patterns will emerge.

References

Brink, D. and Eriksson, S. (1997) *Man kan inte simma på svenska i Kotka*. Ett utvecklingsperspektiv på självuppfattning, språkbruksmönster och attityder till svenska hos elever i en svenskspråkig skola i en finskspråkig miljö. Vasa: Pedagogiska fakulteten vid Åbo Akademi.

European Bureau for Lesser Used Languages (1999) *University in Diversity*. Brussels: EBLUL.

Finnäs, F. (1996) *Finlandssvenskarna*. Helsingfors: Finlands svenska folkting.

Grannabba, H. (1999) *Mönster i tvåspråkiga familjers val av svenskspråkig skola för sina barn*. Vasa: Pedagogiska fakulteten vid Åbo Akademi.

Koivula, A. and Rosenblad, L. (1999) *Språköelevers förhållande till det svenska språket och elevernas Finlandssvenska identitet*. Vasa: Pedagogiska fakulteten vid Åbo Akademi.

Liebkind, K. (1994) Maahanmuuttajat ja kulttuurien kohtaaminen. In K. Liebkind (ed.) *Maahanmuuttajat. Kulttuurien kohtaaminen Suomessa*. Helsinki: Gaudeamus.

Nyberg, K. (2000) *Flyktingbarn, skola och integrering. En studie i flyktingbarns skolsituation i SvenskFinland*.Vasa: Pedagogiska fakulteten vid Åbo Akademi.

Nyman-Kurkiala, P. (1996) *Ung och Finlandssvensk. Forskningsrapport nr 32*. Vasa: Institutet för Finlandssvensk samhällsforskning, Åbo Akademi.

Østern, A. (2000) Mitt språkträd - blivande lärare berättar om sin språkliga och kulturella identitet. In S.E. Hansén and G. Eklund-Myrskog (eds) *Att spana i tiden*. Vasa: Pedagogiska fakulteten, Åbo Akademi.

Østern, A. and Sjöholm, K. (2000) Flerspråkiga undervisningsmiljöer förändrar lärarrollen. *Meddelanden från Åbo Akademi* 1.

Østern, A., Sjöholm, A. and Smeds L. (1999) *Recitation, berättande och fiktionsskrivande, samt läsförståelse och självbild i modersmålet hos elever i finskt språkbad respektive elever i svenskspråkig klass i slutet av årskurs fem. Mellanrapport 3*. Vasa: Pedagogiska fakulteten vid Åbo Akademi.

Tandefelt, M. (1996) *På vinst och förlust. Om tvåspråkighet och språkförlust i Helsingforsregionen. Rapport 35/1998*. Helsingfors: Svenska handelshögskolan.

West, M. (1999) *Det tog ju en tid att lära sig svenska. Tio invandrarelevers språkliga situation i en österbottnisk kontext*. Vasa: Pedagogiska fakulteten vid Åbo Akademi.

Part II

Immigrant languages in Europe

Immigrant languages in Sweden

SALLY BOYD

Sweden, in contrast to most other European countries has a longer tradition of an explicit policy of support for immigrant minority languages (hereafter: IML's) than for historical and regional minority languages, with the possible exception of Sami (cf. also Huss' contribution to this Volume). There are a number of reasons for this, among them the fact that Sweden was a country of migration to other parts of the world during the late 19th and early 20th centuries. These migrants achieved economic success in North America for example by acquiescing to the assimilation policy of the day. Sweden's status as a country of primarily sending rather than receiving migrants, together with its geographic marginality in Europe and lack of colonial contacts, meant that the domestic population was relatively homogeneous and fairly unaware of ways of life in other parts of the world. The political and geographic marginalization of historical minorities, together with the assimilation policies which were carried out toward them during this period left these groups in a rather weakened position, as compared to other European minorities (cf. Huss in this Volume).

Sweden became a country of immigration primarily during the sixties and early seventies. During this period, the economic boom led to a need for labour to industry, and migration was dominated by persons from Finland and from Southern Europe seeking employment. During the seventies, after labour market migration was restricted, the main form of migration was family tie migration. Refugees were also admitted during the seventies, many of them from Latin America or Eastern Europe. In the eighties refugee migration dominated, and the number of persons coming from parts of the world experienced as more culturally distant, e.g. the Middle East, increased. During the nineties refugee migration has been restricted by various measures, and the only major new group of migrants has been refugees from the former Yugoslavia, primarily from Bosnia and Kosovo. Since the conclusion of the war in Bosnia and Sweden's membership of the EU, the number of refugees and family tie migrants has decreased somewhat.

Demographic data

As of the turn of the year 1998/1999, there were just over a million persons living in Sweden who were either born abroad or who were born in Sweden with foreign citizenship. This figure can be compared with the total population figure of just under nine million persons. Thus the population with foreign background constitutes approximately 11% of the total population. A somewhat higher figure is sometimes quoted, which includes children under 18 born in Sweden to parents at least one of whom was born abroad, even if the child is a Swedish citizen. These children are entitled to immigrant minority language instruction (hereafter IMLI) in school, if a language other than Swedish is used in communication with the child in the home (see below). The figures in Table 1 show the official number of persons who were granted residence permits in Sweden and the number of persons officially considered to have left the country each year since 1991.

Table 1   Migration to and from Sweden since 1991, in thousands (Source: Statistisk årsbok för Sverige 2000, Table 84 and 85)

Year	Permits granted	Departures	Net immigration
1991	49.7	24.7	25.0
1992	45.3	25.7	19.6
1993	61.9	29.8	32.1
1994	83.6	32.6	51.0
1995	45.9	33.9	12.0
1996	39.9	33.8	6.1
1997	44.8	38.5	6.3
1998	49.4	38.5	10.9

The reception of a relatively large number of refugees from Bosnia and other regions of ex-Yugoslavia accounts for the large number of residence permits granted in 1993 and 1994. Although refugee migration has been restricted by various measures during the nineties, both before and after the war in Bosnia, the number of permits granted remains relatively high due to Nordic migration, which does not require residence or work permits, and family tie migration (see below). The number of departures has increased gradually during the 1990's due to the economic recession.

Many of those leaving are probably Nordic citizens. Table 2 divides the new migrants to Sweden in 1998 into categories according to the official reasons for granting a residence permit.

Table 2   Official reasons for migration in 1998, number of persons in thousands (Source: Statistisk årsbok för Sverige 2000)

Nordic citizens	19.7 (no residence or work permit required)
Refugees	8.2
Family ties	21.7
Labour market	0.4
European Economic Space	5.7
Students	2.6
Adoptions	0.8
'Adjustment' *	-9.8
Total	49.3

* This negative figure has to do with the discrepancy between agencies handling applications for residence and those registering new residents.

Table 2 shows that refugees and their families, together with Nordic migrants dominate the new arrivals in Sweden. Table 3 shows figures for the ten most common countries of origin. With the exception of Finland and possibly former Yugoslavia (including Bosnia-Herzegovina), residents with foreign background in Sweden come from a large number of different countries of origin. The various national groups are thus relatively small. This fact makes provision of IMLI in schools relatively difficult, especially in municipalities outside of the three major urban areas (see below).

Table 4 shows figures for the number of children in compulsory schools entitled to IMLI for the school years 1993/94 to 1998/99, as well as the number and percentage of pupils participating in this instruction and in instruction in Swedish as a second language (L2). Table 4 indicates that while the *number* of pupils entitled to and participating in IMLI is increasing, the *percentage* of pupils participating in both IMLI and Swedish as a second language is gradually decreasing in compulsory education. It can be added that the number of children entitled to IMLI who are attending so-called independent schools has increased in the same period from just over 2000 in 1993/94 to almost 6000 in 1998/99.

Still, this constitutes only 5% of all pupils entitled to IMLI. Table 5 shows the number of pupils attending IMLI in compulsory schools in the ten languages with the greatest number of pupils.

Table 3   Most common countries of origin of foreign born and foreign citizens residing in Sweden in 1997/1998, in thousands (Source: Statistisk årsbok för Sverige 2000, Table 80)

Finland	225
Ex-Yugoslavia *	76
Bosnia-Herzegovina	54
Iran	52
Norway	50
Denmark	45
Poland	42
Germany	41
Iraq	41
Turkey	36
All others ca.	400

*   Excluding immigrants from Bosnia-Herzegovina, once this nation was recognized by Sweden.

Table 4   Pupils entitled to and receiving IMLI and L2 Swedish from 1993-1999

School year	Entitled pupils	IMLI participants		L2 Swedish participants	
		abs. no.	% of entitled	abs. no.	% of entitled
1993/94	102,284	58,801	57.5	56,170	54.9
1994/95	111,720	61,306	54.9	62,219	55.7
1995/96	109,924	60,338	54.9	61,599	56.0
1996/97	111,351	60,745	54.6	58,533	52.6
1997/98	115,846	62,100	53.6	59,930	51.7
1998/99	119,352	62,671	52.5	58,210	48.8

Table 5   Pupils receiving instruction in the 10 most frequently studied IML's in Swedish compulsory school

IML	Abs. no.	% of entitled	% of instruction outside school hours
Albanian	4,189	64.8	65.5
Arabic	10,031	64.2	59.5
Bosnian/Croation/Serbian	6,935	50.2	67.1
English	2,525	50.7	55.6
Farsi	4,543	63.3	69.8
Finnish	6,101	42.5	33.3
Kurdish	2,189	56.1	55.9
Polish	2,347	51.8	65.7
Spanish	5,385	55.1	61.3
Turkish	2,652	53.2	62.6
Other (tot. 113 languages)	15,730	47.1	61.1

Table 5 shows that the participation rates for the ten most frequent IML's varies between just over 40% for Finnish up to just under 65% for Albanian. While Finnish pupils participate to a somewhat lower degree than other pupils, a relatively high proportion of instruction for them is held during regular school hours. These figures probably reflect the 'split' within this group: some Finnish-speakers consider language as a core value of ethnicity and it is in large part due to the efforts of this group that IMLI was instituted in the first place (see below). Since the Finnish minority is relatively large and well-organized, with a relatively good supply of trained teachers, it is possible to organize instruction as part of the regular school day. At the same time, other members of the group, particularly within the younger generation, are oriented towards linguistic assimilation. Therefore, the interest in studying Finnish may be relatively weak, despite the fact that instruction is offered as part of the regular school programme.

It is difficult to explain the variation in the proportion of instruction offered outside the school day. It probably depends on a number of factors such as the extent to which pupils with the same IML tend to live in the same areas and attend the same schools, the availability of qualified teachers (who can perhaps also teach other subjects and thus demand to teach IML during the regular school day) and the mobilization of the group around the issue of IMLI. Participation rates are relatively high for more recently-arrived groups such as Albanian-, Arabic- and Farsi-speaking pupils. They are probably equally high for Bosnian-speaking pupils, but since the figures in Table 5 include speakers of Serbian and Croatian, thus including pupils whose parents migrated as early as the sixties, the participation rate is lower than would be expected if it only included the recently-arrived Bosnian-speaking pupils.

Language maintenance and language shift

It is difficult to summarize the situation as regards processes of language maintenance and shift. If we define language maintenance and shift based on language use, several studies of the topic have indicated a gradual language shift among most groups of immigrants, with some groups shifting more rapidly than others (Boyd, 1985). The shift process has taken place despite a relatively generous policy towards integration of immigrants both in the field of education (see below) and political participation, at least as it stands in the relevant documents. Integration in the labour market has been slow, particularly since the eighties, and this has perhaps retarded second language acquisition among adults in some groups, as this source of contact between majority and minority has been limited for these groups.

In a project carried out at the end of the eighties and beginning of the nineties, which studied the situation for immigrants from North America, Finland, Turkey and Vietnam to (or for the Finns *within*) the Nordic region, it was found that the minority language was maintained best by the Turkish- and Vietnamese-speaking communities studied, while the English- and Finnish-speaking communities used the majority language more frequently than the other two groups. These latter groups reported greater bilingual proficiency than the former two groups, who expressed concern primarily for the children's proficiency in the majority language, but also for their maintenance of the minority language. It is difficult to generalize these results to other immigrant groups. Many groups show a significant heterogeneity, so that, for example, for some immigrants in Sweden with Finnish background, maintenance of Finnish is extremely vital, for others it is of little importance. The same can be said of more recent refugees from Bosnia and Kosovo.

As these four groups were all studied in at least two Nordic countries, the effect of the host country on language maintenance could also be measured. It was found that the Finnish minority in Sweden were more successful at maintaining the minority language than they were in Norway, but that North Americans in Finland and Denmark used English more frequently than North Americans in Sweden. For the Vietnamese- and Turkish-speaking groups, there was little difference between mainte- nance of the language in the two countries studied. The Vietnamese in Norway were similar to those in Finland and the Turks in Sweden to those in Denmark in terms of language maintenance and development of the respective majority languages. All four groups expressed a strong loyalty to their respective IML, but gave different reasons for this loyalty (Holmen *et al.*, 1995). The more economically secure and integrated groups tended to emphasize the importance of the IML maintenance; the more economically marginalized groups tended to emphasize the importance of the majority language, e.g. in regard to education of the younger generation. However, as mentioned above, it is difficult to generalize even within a single group.

The Turkish- and Vietnamese-speaking groups seemed to uphold a rather strict separation of which language should be used in different domains, a situation which according to Fishman's concept of diglossia ought to encourage language maintenance. There was considerably more variation in this regard among the English- and Finnish-speaking minorities. The success with which the communities managed to maintain their IML seemed to have little to do with whether the domains of use of the two languages were strictly separated or overlapping (Boyd & Latomaa, 1996). Rather it depended on network structure and economic factors. The Turks and Vietnamese were in many cases marginalized in terms of jobs and housing in relation to majority society. They could only find housing in areas with members of their own and other immigrant minorities, where few Swedes lived. Even the workplace was an environment where few if any Swedes were present in other than supervisory roles. The majority of the Finnish and North Americans, on the other hand were working and living side-by-side with members of the majority. The Turkish and Vietnamese children grew up in an environ- ment which required them to use their mother tongue actively, while the North American and Finnish children in many cases grew up in families where only one parent actively used the minority language, the other parent being a majority member. These children, at least while they were young, had trouble seeing the value of IML maintenance. The greater value accorded English and Finnish by majority groups in the Nordic region did not seem to facilitate maintenance of these languages, as compared to Turkish and Vietnamese, at least in the short term.

Since these studies were carried out, several things have happened which have probably affected the conditions for IML maintenance, although no systematic studies have been carried out in this field during the later nineties. During the early and mid-nineties Sweden went into a recession, which increased the problems experienced by the refugee migrants from the eighties, many of whom had academic educations, in getting employment. These migrants were routinely sent to a series of language courses and job-training courses, many at a high school level or below. Both types of courses rarely led to employment. When employers were asked why they were reluctant to employ non-Swedes, language proficiency was often mentioned as a reason for not calling foreign-born doctors, teachers, engineers and other academically trained persons to interviews or not hiring those interviewed. Various programmes to facilitate the labour market integration of migrants were started, but as the labour market as a whole was in recession, few programmes were successful. IML proficiency was rarely mentioned as an asset for immigrants seeking employment. Instead, insufficient knowledge of Swedish (and sometimes of English) was one of the major reasons given for denying immigrants employment and many programmes to facilitate integration included courses in Swedish.

As the labour market improved towards the end of the nineties, the focus turned instead toward the segregated housing situation. The outer suburbs of the three largest cities in Sweden - Stockholm, Göteborg and Malmö - became increasingly economically depressed and increasingly dominated by relatively recently arrived immigrants, refugees and their families. This has been and still is experienced as a major problem by politicians and large segments of the society as a whole. In the late nineties nationally-funded programmes were started at the municipal level to increase 'integration' of the residents of these neighbourhoods. The programmes aimed at activating the residents in projects to improve life in areas such as housing, participation in school activities, crime prevention, day care or health care. Unfortunately, many of these projects were short-term, poorly planned and not adequately evaluated when they were finished. Few, if any of the projects aimed directly at language-related goals, and those that did had improvement in Swedish as a goal, rather than IML development. One project in the field of day care, for example, aimed at bringing very young children and their mothers to the day care institution. Once the children and mothers were accustomed to the environment, the mothers participated in classes in Swedish as a second language in an adjoining locale while the children were cared for by the pre-school staff. Few, if any of these municipally run but state-funded projects were initiated and run by the residents themselves. Few if any addressed the question of IML maintenance. IML's have been viewed increasingly as an obstacle to 'integration'.

In addition to support for education in IML's (see below), the Swedish state has provided some support in the areas of mass media and for voluntary organizations. Huss (this volume) mentions the support for Sami and Finnish programming on radio and television. The Swedish Radio broadcasts weekly in nine other immigrant languages: Polish, Arabic, Albanian, Serbian/Croatian/Bosnian, Turkish, Spanish, Farsi, Assyrian/Syrian and Somali. Except for the Somali broadcast (15 minutes), these broadcasts total between one and two hours per week. There are also weekly broadcasts in Swedish, both on radio and television aimed primarily at immigrant minority audiences. The Immigrant Institute in Borås lists a total of 200 periodicals currently published in Sweden in a total of some 50 IML's. Many of these publications receive support from the state. Books, including books for children, are made available to public libraries in a range of different languages through the Library Service. About half of these books are published in Sweden, the other half in the various countries of origin.

Immigrant organizations also receive support from local municipalities and their national parent organizations from the Swedish state. The Immigrant Institute has compiled a list of about 50 nationwide organi-zations. On the local level, there are many more, some of which are part of the nationwide organizations, but many of which are not. It is virtually impossible to generalize about the political agenda of so many diverse organizations and the extent to which IML maintenance is an important issue for them.

Policy in the field of education

The first official policy regarding immigrant residents in Sweden was formulated in the mid-seventies (*Invandrarutredningen*, SOU, 1974: 69), and IML's played a very central role in this policy statement. Among other things, this policy provided for a linguistic 'freedom of choice', which allowed immigrants and their children to choose to what extent they wished to retain the language and culture of their country or region of origin and to what extent they wished to adopt Swedish language and culture. Although it is easy to be critical of this rather static and simplistic view of language and culture, this at least was a policy which recognized the value of bilingualism and biculturalism as well as the value of the language and culture of immigrant groups in the country. The goal of the policy as regards language was that of 'active bilingualism'.

Probably the most important concrete measure proposed regarding language in that document was the provision of 'home-language instruction', i.e. IMLI, for children in the pre-school, compulsory school and upper secondary school, one or both of whose parents had a first language other than Swedish. The report stated that immigrant children had the right to study the mother tongue of their non-Swedish parent(s), and that municipalities had the obligation to provide this instruction within the regular school day. Once this commission report was published, a heated debate ensued among educators and other academics as to how this instruction should be carried out most effectively, both in terms of pedagogical and organisational effectiveness, so that the goal of active bilingualism could be attained for as many immigrant pupils as possible. There was a strong but rather quiet grass-roots opposition among members of the Swedish majority to the institution of this instruction 'top down', as Sweden has a long tradition of political measures directed towards all citizens, not specific groups, and this tradition is particularly strong within the field of education. The number of independent schools at this time was extremely small, and those that existed were generally open to all students, not particular religious or minority groups. (A notable exception is the Sami schools, see Huss, this Volume.)

By the early eighties a number of different forms of IMLI emerged, which have been described in more detail elsewhere (see also Broeder & Extra, 1999; Boyd, 1993; 1994/1999). The forms of instruction included what can rightfully be considered to be bilingual classes, where IML's functioned as one of the languages of instruction, as well as instruction half in IML and half in Swedish. These forms of instruction instituted during the last half of the seventies gave Sweden an image of unusual progressiveness and generosity towards its immigrant minorities at the time. However, this instruction was not particularly widespread, even when it was at its peak, at about 1980. The most common form of IMLI was instruction during two hours per week, in regular school time, given in small groups by a peripatetic teacher. These forms of instruction were supplemented by introductory classes, mainly focussing on Swedish as a second language, for newly arrived pupils and a comprehensive programme of instruction in Swedish as a second language both for new arrivals and other minority children deemed by the school to need this instruction. Although the intent of the 1974 report had been to encourage instruction in more truly bilingual forms than the supplementary two hours per week model, this latter model survived as by far the most common one up until the end of the eighties at least.

Two things happened at the beginning of the nineties which led to a significant deterioration in the practice and status of IMLI in Sweden. First, a right wing populist party called *Nydemokrati* (New Democracy) gained popularity and managed to win some seats in the Swedish parliament. This party was clearly negative to immigrants and new refugee migration, though not openly calling for a total stop for migration or the dismantling of all special programmes for immigrants or their children. IMLI was a favourite target of politicians in this party. It was argued that it was too expensive and only led to a slower acquisition of the majority language and thereby also integration in the wider community. These politicians also claimed that the 'privilege' of IMLI led to animosity on the part of majority pupils, parents and teachers. Although the party did not survive in the parliament more than one term (three years), due primarily to internal conflicts, their more openly hostile attitude towards the relatively generous policy regarding immigrants had important effects both on the general public and on elected officials. Many Swedes previously did not really dare to express such xenophobic attitudes in public. It was now felt that these opinions could be more openly expressed. Protests against this party and its policy were voiced by many, including the academic community. At the same time, some of the more established political parties adopted a more restrictive policy both toward new refugee migration and toward special programmes for immigrants resident in Sweden such as IMLI, after this party emerged.

The second occurrence at about the same time was that the Swedish National Audit Office published an investigation of IMLI (RRV, 1991) which, based on a shoddily done 'audit' of instruction for immigrants and their children, recommended that funding for this instruction be sharply cut back. The investigation was critical of both IMLI and in Swedish as a second language, but the cutbacks it suggested affected IMLI more than Swedish as a second language instruction (see e.g. Hyltenstam & Tuomela, 1996). Although the report's recommendations did not receive the support of the parliament, which argued that these decisions should be taken at the municipal level, major cutbacks were carried out anyway by many of the municipalities. In a single year (1991/92 compared to 1992/93), the number of hours taught decreased by 33%, while the number of pupils decreased by only 8%. In 65% of all municipalities, IMLI was now carried out partly or solely outside of the ordinary school day (Hyltenstam & Tuomela, 1996: 23). The emphasis in the political rhetoric of the first half of the nineties at least shifted strongly toward the importance of Swedish as a second language, and due to the general economic crisis of this period, IMLI was often considered to be an expensive luxury.

Since that time, the picture has deteriorated further for IMLI within the public schools. The number of pupils participating has increased slightly year-by-year, while the number of eligible pupils has increased more dramatically. New options for integrating IMLI into the school pro-gramme have been instituted, again from above, e.g. 'pupil's free choice' or 'school choice'. The first of these implies that pupils can take IMLI as an elective, instead of e.g. extra instruction in physical education, home economics or computer science. The second option implies that schools can decide to have an 'IML profile', offering a greater amount or range of IML's. However these options have rarely if ever been utilized by pupils or schools. Instead, the proportion of pupils receiving IMLI after school hours has increased. With all the uncertainty (and poor working conditions) associated with IML teaching, few teacher trainees who are proficient in an IML have opted to include it as a subject for their qualification. It is no longer possible to become a teacher in IML alone, but only in combination with other subjects. At the same time various groups of parents and leaders from within immigrant communities have started independent publically-funded schools which employ IML's as the medium of instruction. This development has been met with apprehension by many politicians who favour the 'comprehensive school' model of education, where all pupils attend the same school and receive basically the same education.

The most recent development is that beginning in 1997, the school subject 'home language' is now called 'mother tongue'. The aim was to raise the status of this subject in school, and emphasize the parallels between IML for minority pupils and Swedish for majority pupils. Unfortunately, the change in terminology has thus far not led to an increase either in the quantity or quality of IMLI for most pupils. There are several reasons for this. One is that the parliamentary School committee stated in their official investigation in the same year that the concept 'mother tongue' be restricted to the language which is the pupil's 'actual first language, i.e. the language in which a child has learned to speak and understand and which during a long period of time has been the child's colloquial language' (SOU, 1997: 121, cited in Huss, 1998: 27). While it is suggested that the status of the school subject 'mother tongue' should be improved for students who have an IML as first language, and made more comparable to that of Swedish as mother tongue, the number of pupils eligible to receive this instruction is at the same time reduced. In part this is achieved by the stricter definition quoted above, as it excludes pupils for whom the IML is not the primary colloquial language in the family, and in part by the fact that each pupil is eligible for instruction in only *one* language as mother tongue (including Swedish). Pupils who are considered to have an IML as a mother tongue are entitled to instruction in this language in school, and to instruction in Swedish as a second language. But the new provision excludes the large proportion of pupils who have a Swedish-speaking parent or for other reasons can be considered to have attained native speaker proficiency in Swedish, but nonetheless have acquired an IML at home from one or both of their parents. These pupils are prevented from receiving instruction in both IML *and* in Swedish as mother tongue. Pupils with an IML as mother tongue become increasingly marginalized, as their numbers decrease and as they are excluded from the instruction in Swedish as mother tongue.

According to information from a number of knowledgeable sources, the terminology change has not led to any dramatic increase in the number of pupils receiving IMLI during school hours. The majority of pupils are still receiving IMLI two hours a week outside of school time (in the late afternoons and evenings), while those attending schools with a large proportion of IM pupils are in some cases able to receive IMLI during the regular school day, but not in combination with instruction in Swedish as mother tongue. The proportion of pupils receiving instruction with IML as the medium of instruction is very small, outside of the independent schools mentioned above. According to one of the sources referred to above, there is however some indication that increasing flexibility in teacher training programmes may lead to an increasing supply of teachers qualified to teach IML.

At the universities, educational programmes in the major IML's have not expanded during recent years. Instead they have had major problems surviving. For example, instruction in Finnish has been discontinued in Göteborg and recently also in Lund. While universities seem eager to expand their programmes in languages such as Japanese and Chinese, the interest in and support for IML teaching is not as great, although several major IML's are languages of value in business and commerce as well as for the minority communities. Some of the departments of e.g. Arabic and Spanish, because they are small, have difficulty providing courses both for Swedish students who often have limited proficiency and are mainly interested in studying these languages for literary or historical purposes and for native speakers who may have pedagogical or other interests in studying their mother tongues. The lack of demand for IML teachers in the school has also decreased the demand for IML university courses.

Future developments

It is encouraging that some efforts have begun to be made to equate IML's and (mother tongue) Swedish as subjects to be studied in the school. It is unfortunate that this reform has the 'either-or' quality described above, which leads to an unfortunate bifurcation of the student body in many schools and decreases the number of pupils who will opt for IMLI. There has been relatively little public discussion of this proposal since it was made in 1997. Rather, it seems that many minorities are opting to start independent schools, and to attend the increasing number of English medium schools, instead of continuing to fight the uphill battle of integrating mother tongue instruction in an otherwise Swedish comprehensive school programme.

What has led to more public debate is the decision on the part of the Government to develop an official policy for promoting *Swedish* in Sweden. The National Language Board of Sweden published an official proposal for this policy in 1998. This document points to the weakening of Swedish in Sweden due to the influx of other languages, primarily English, into domains such as education, science, information technology or culture. A number of language planning proposals are made, many of which are damaging to language promotion and maintenance efforts of both historical, regional and immigrant languages in Sweden (see Boyd & Huss, 1999). By opposing English linguistic and cultural imperialism, the policy proposals also would have assimilatory effects on other linguistic minorities in Sweden. For example, the policy document declares that the 'normal' language of education in Sweden should be Swedish. It recommends that teachers seeking employment in Swedish schools should be tested for their Swedish language proficiency before being hired. Swedish is furthermore described as the major means for immigrants and refugees to become integrated into Swedish society. It is difficult to ignore the parallels between this policy effort, the English-only movement in the US and similar popular movements in France. Many linguists find it disturbing that this movement to strengthen Swedish comes so close in time to the proposal to ratify the Council of Europe's Treaty protecting historical and regional minority languages. The policy proposal seems to be one more step in a direction away from the progressive multicultural visions of the commission of the mid-seventies which gave Sweden its undeservedly progressive image in the field of immigrant minority policy in general and educational policy in particular.

References

Boyd, S. (1985) Language survival. A study of language contact, language shift, and language choice in Sweden. PhD thesis, Department of Linguistics, Göteborg University. *Gothenburg monographs in linguistics* 6.

Boyd, S. (1993) Immigrant minority languages and education in Sweden. In G. Extra & L. Verhoeven (eds) *Ethnic minority languages in Europe*. Clevedon: Multilingual Matters.

Boyd, S. (1994/1999) Sweden: Immigrant languages and education. In R.E. Asher & J.M.Y. Simpson (eds) *The encyclopedia of language and linguistics, Vol. 8*, (pp. 4423-4424). Oxford: Pergamon Press. Revised and uppdated for B. Spolsky (ed) *Concise encyclopedia of educational linguistics*. Oxford: Pergamon.

Boyd, S. & Huss, L. (1999) En helhetssyn på språken i Sverige behövs! *Språkvård* 3.

Boyd, S. & Latomaa, S. (1996) Language contact in the Nordic Region. A re-evaluation of Fishman's theory of diglossia and bilingualism? *Nordic journal of linguistics* 19 (2), 155-182.

Broeder, P. and Extra, G. (1999) *Language, ethnicity and aducation. Case studies of immigrant minority groups and immigrant minority languages*. Clevedon: Multilingual Matters.

Holmen, A., Latomaa, S., Gimbel, J., Andersen, S. and Jørgensen, J. (1995) Parent attitudes to children's L1 maintenance: a cross-sectional study of immigrant groups in the Nordic countris. In W. Fase *et al.* (eds) *The state of minority languages. International perspectives on survival and decline*. Lisse: Swets & Zeitlinger.

Huss, L. (1998) En ny syn på 'hemspråk' och 'modersmål' i den svenska skolan? *Multiethnica* 23.

Hyltenstam, K. and Tuomela, V. (1996) Hemspråksundervisningen. In K. Hyltenstam (ed.) *Tvåspråkighet med förhinder? Invandrar- och minoritets-undervisning i Sverige*. Lund: Studentlitteratur

RRV (The national Swedish audit bureau) (1990) *Invandrarundervisningen i grundskolan. Revisionsrapport*. Stockholm: Riksrevisionsverket.

SOU (1997) *Skolfrågor. Om skola i en ny tid. Skolkommiténs slutbetänkande.* Stockholm: Deptartment of Education.

Swedish Central Bureau of Statistics (SCB) (2000) *Statistisk årsbok för Sverige* (Statistical yearbook of Sweden).

Immigrant languages in federal Germany

INGRID GOGOLIN
HANS REICH

Immigration is a federal responsibility in Germany, whereas integration policy is at least partly under the responsibility of the States (*Länder*). Education especially, including education of immigrants, is a State domain. Accordingly, this chapter starts with an outline of the demographical situation, followed by an overview of the sociolinguistic situation, both concerning Germany as a whole. In the third section, which deals with education, we present the examples of three *Länder*:

- The example of the City State of Hamburg, a centre of massive immigration with changing educational policy.
- The example of Northrhine-Westphalia, Germany's largest State, comprising the conurbation of the Ruhr and other industrial centres with a high immigration rate, but also areas of a more rural character; educational policy in Northrhine-Westphalia has been devoted to linguistic diversity for a long time.
- The example of Hesse, also a State with different immigration patterns: the European metropolis of Frankfurt and the surrounding area as a centre of immigration and more rural areas with considerably lower immigration rates; in the past Hesse supported immigrant languages in schools, but things changed abruptly in 1999.

We conclude with some remarks on the future development of language policies in Germany.

Demographic data

About ten million inhabitants of Germany are of non-German origin and bi- or multilingual in the sense that they use German *and* one or more languages other than German in their everyday life. But as a matter of fact no reliable statistical data are available, neither on the ethnocultural composition of Germany's population nor on the sociolinguistic status quo in Germany. Neither can the number of speakers of languages other than German can be indicated reliably nor can the number of languages spoken by them be stated. The absence of such data is due to the self-conception of the German nation state. Until recently, despite all evidence, Germany considered itself to be a non-immigration country, which in the same vein meant: a monolingual country. Thus, official data are only available about non-German citizens (*Ausländer*) living in Germany, be it permanently or temporarily. These data are unsuitable for statements about cultural and linguistic plurality in Germany. Firstly, the equation of nation state and language is trivial and absurd. Secondly, a growing number of those who have immigrated to Germany possess German citizenship. They may be immigrants with the legal status of *Aussiedler*, i.e. immigrants from Eastern Europe who are able to prove that they are of German descent, or they may be naturalised immigrants from anywhere else who applied for German citizenship after having been in Germany for at least eight years, or they may be the spouse of a German citizen and have made use of the option to get a German passport.

Due to a change in citizenship legislation effective since January 1, 2000, the number of bi- or multilingual German citizens with an immigrant background will grow tremendously. Children of immigrant families who are born in Germany, automatically receive German citizenship now, and parents with non-German passports who have children below the age of seven can apply for German citizenship for them. Until the age of 23, all these 'Germans' are allowed to hold dual citizenship; afterwards they have to decide on one or the other. With this new legislation, Germany withdrew - although not totally - from the *ius sanguinis* as the basic principle of citizenship.

As we know from research, immigrants - even if they change their passports - do not necessarily give up their cultures and languages of origin. Therefore, no reliable statistical data on the demographic status of immigrant groups and immigrant languages and on distribution and vitality of these languages in Germany can currently be provided. All statistical information given below is therefore based on the inadequate criterion of citizenship; all other information can only be based on much weaker data, such as reasoned estimates or small-scale research, mostly in terms of regional case studies.

Post-war immigration
Immigration to Germany is a constant factor since the end of World War II. The first considerable pattern of immigration consisted of German nationals who came as refugees from Eastern European countries. Until

the early fifties, nearly 12 million of these refugees came to Germany, most of them with traumatic war and post-war experiences. Additional immigrants from the same regions came to Germany with the legal status of *Aussiedler*. Since the beginning of the fifties until 1999, nearly four million people belonging to this group immigrated to Germany, most of them Russian or Polish-speaking people. Germany faced a tremendous growth of the numbers of these immigrants after 1989, due to the collapse of the socialist systems. The political reaction to this collapse from German side was a restriction of immigration possibilities for *Aussiedler* and a cutback in subsidies for them. Today, the numbers of applicants for *Aussiedler* immigration to Germany are decreasing considerably.

The next large immigration flow to Germany is made up by the group of *Gastarbeiter*, guest workers who were mostly recruited in Mediterranean countries from 1955 on; in 1999 approximately 4.5 million people belonged to this group of immigrants. Bilateral contracts were signed until the early seventies with Italy, Yugoslavia, Morocco, Portugal, Spain, Tunisia, Turkey and, for a short time, Korea. In 1973, due to a massive economic crisis, a recruitment stop was enacted. Paradoxically, this led to a considerable rise in immigration from these countries - especially of children - because the reunion of families was still legal. In the year 2000 the German government revitalised this type of immigration, i.e. recruitment of workers from abroad. Now the aim is the recruitment of highly skilled workers, especially in the domain of communication and information technologies.

The *Gastarbeiter* immigration since the middle of the fifties concerned only the western part of Germany, the former Federal Republic. The former GDR also had made contracts for the recruitment of workforces with some countries: in the sixties with some Eastern European neighbours, after 1970 with Cuba, Vietnam and some African states. But the immigration to the GDR differs considerably from that to the Western *Länder*. Firstly, only a small number of *Vertragsarbeiter* (contract workers) came to the GDR - altogether no more than 90,000 until 1990, i.e. 1.4% of the number of persons employed. Secondly, the contract workers were submitted to a rigid rotation system; they had to leave the country after a strictly limited period of time and the reunion with family members or the foundation of a family was as unwelcome as other signs of integration (cf. Krüger-Potratz, 1991; Gruner-Domic, 1999).

The most recent type of immigration to Germany - so-called new immigrants - comprises asylum-seekers or other refugees, seasonal workers, and also people entering the country illegally. Obviously, there are no reliable statistical data on the latter type of immigration, but all estimations assume that their numbers are rising. In 1960, the proportion of non-German citizens in the Federal Republic of Germany amounted to 1.2%; in 1999, it amounted to around 10%, which is approximately 7.5 million people (cf. *Ausländerbeauftragte*, 2000).

As yet, the 'foreign' population is distributed unevenly over the *Länder*. Whereas the proportion of 'foreigners' in the Western *Länder* ('old' FRG) lies somewhere between 5% (Schleswig-Holstein) and 14% (Hesse, Berlin), none of the Eastern *Länder* count more than 2.5% of 'foreigners'. Most of them live in urban areas. The city of Frankfurt am Main has the largest proportion of 'foreigners' with more than 30% of the population; all major cities in Germany - Berlin, Cologne, Frankfurt, Hamburg, Munich - and the conglomerates - the *Ruhrgebiet* in Northrhine-Westphalia, the *Rhein-Main* area in Hesse - get close to this percentage of residents with foreign passports. A growing proportion of 'foreigners' is long-settling in Germany; 30% of them have been living there for 20 years or more, 50% for ten years or more.

Corresponding to this demographic situation, the number of 'foreign' pupils in German schools is also continuously growing. In 1997, approximately 1.2 million pupils with non-German passports attended the school system (approximately 10% of the student population). The number rose from approximately 670,000 to 960,000 between 1985 and 1995 in the compulsory school system, and it nearly doubled in the same period in the vocational school system (from approximately 120,000 to 220,000). With reference to passports, the German school system today still does not guarantee equal access to school success. Whereas nearly 30% of the pupils with German passports finish their school career with the *Abitur* - i.e. receive the final examination of highest value - this applies only to less than 10% of the 'foreign' pupils. And whereas less than 10% of the pupils with German passports leave school with the lowest type of exam (*Hauptschulabschluß*), this applies to more than 20% of the 'foreign' pupils. Generally speaking, the German school system distributes school success along ethnic lines.

Nationalities

Official statistics on Federal State level give detailed information about immigrants from 139 states of origin. About 25% of Germany's 'foreign' population are citizens of other EU member states. Their numbers rose until 1994 and have been stable since then. The highest proportions of EU members come from Italy (33% of EU members) and Greece (approximately 20%). Next are Austrians (10%), Portuguese (7.1%), Spaniards (7.1%), British citizens (6.2%) and people from the Netherlands (6.0%) (cf. *Ausländerbeauftragte*, 2000: 17).

The largest group of 'foreigners' in Germany, however, are Turkish citizens (1998: 30% of the 'foreigners'/2.11 million people, cf. *Ausländer-beauftragte*, 2000: 232), followed by people from the Republic of Yugoslavia (Serbia and Montenegro, 720,000 or 9.8%), Italians (612,000 or 8.4%), Greeks (363,000 or 5%) and people from Poland (283,000 or 3.9%) (*Ausländerbeauftragte*, 2000: 17).

Sociolinguistic evidence

It is rather difficult to determine which groups of immigrants in Germany can be addressed as linguistic communities. Obviously, the number of speakers plays a role, but this is not the only nor the decisive factor. Social conditions and political opportunities or obstacles play a role as well. In the end, however, it is the linguistic behaviour of the groups and the way they see themselves that matters.

Unfortunately, there has been and still is little language survey research in Germany. As we pointed out already, large-scale data on patterns of language use, degree of linguistic competencies, language maintenance or loss are not available, neither at the national nor at the state level, with the exception of the State of Hamburg. Only general impressions can be given. Below we refer to the size and social structure of the language groups, legal status and language maintenance, and the role of the media.

Size and social structure of the language groups

Speakers of the following languages reach a group size above 100,000 in Germany: Arabic, Bosnian/Croatian/Serbian, Dutch, English, Farsi, French, Greek, Italian, Kurdish, Polish, Portuguese, Romanian, Russian, Spanish, Turkish and Vietnamese. Out of these, Dutch, English and French can hardly be seen as immigrant languages, even though they also contribute to the linguistic diversity of Germany. On the other hand, there is no doubt that smaller groups such as speakers of Albanian, Chinese, Korean or Japanese function as linguistic communities in Germany and may at least partly be seen as immigrant languages. All these groups differ not only in size but also in social structure, linguistic behaviour and other aspects. Therefore, a comprehensive view is impossible. Three groups are presented here as typical examples.

The most important ethnolinguistic group are the Turkish-speaking immigrants. They form the most visible minority. Turkish shops - from fast food to travel agencies - are to be found in all towns. In the cities districts exist with high proportions of Turkish people, where life in the streets has a quasi-oriental character. In such quarters all goods and services that are necessary for everyday life - from medical provisions to books, gifts, toys, clothing, food and entertainment - are available 'in Turkish'. Children who grow up during their pre-school years in such an environment acquire Turkish nearly to the same degree of competence as monolingual Turkish children do in Turkey (Hepsöyler & Liebe-Harkort, 1991: 21-25; Pfaff, 1993: 126; Mehrländer *et al.*, 1996: Chapter 10.4). The problem here lies more in the acquisition of German as a second language. The birth rate of the Turkish population in Germany is still remarkably high, more than twice the birth rate of the German population (Statistisches Bundesamt, 1999: Table 3.29). There are a large number of religious, political, social or cultural associations and institutions where Turkish is spoken regularly. A new middle-class is emerging with Turkish entrepreneurs (not only in ethnic business), doctors, clerks, teachers and social workers (for details see Şen & Goldberg, 1994). Given these circumstances and taking into account that language loyalty in Turkish emigrant communities seems to be above average, as research in other countries also indicates (see Löfgren, 1991: Tables 3.14 and 4.12; Jørgensen & Holmen, 1994: 124-130; Tribalat, 1995: 47), it can be taken for granted that the Turkish minority in Germany is a vital and viable linguistic community.

Quite different from this is the situation of speakers of Bosnian/ Croatian/Serbian, quantitatively the second largest group of minority language speakers in Germany. Their starting conditions were not bad. The early immigrants had a relatively higher degree of education than other guest-workers and a relatively higher socio-economic status. They started as a self-conscious minority with good prospects. The Yugoslav wars deeply changed the course of their migration history. Refugees joined the former labour migrants, often in a state of desperation and with no other future prospect than a forced return to their destroyed home country. The political separation of the State of Yugoslavia troubled the political as well as the linguistic loyalties of the emigrants. Associations which referred to national rather than regional identity broke down and support by the official representatives of the country or countries of origin diminished considerably. Again, the birth rate might be a good indicator: it is far below the birth rate of the Turkish population in Germany (Statistisches Bundesamt, 1999: Table 3.29). The younger generation starts - as it seems - to turn away from the language of origin and there is little probability of a reversal of the language shift process, unless completely new conditions would arise.

The Italian-speaking community serves as the third example. Italian guest workers were the first to immigrate to post-war Germany and at that time had to bear all the weight of prejudice and marginalization. Being European Union citizens from the beginning, they had the opportunity of free movement and they made the most of that. Patterns of two-way migration are rather frequent amongst them. Although they have been residing in Germany longer than any other group of immigrants, their social status (as indicated by e.g. unemployment rates) is still below average. On the other hand, Italian is an official European Union language and cultural ties between Germany and Italy are traditionally close. Language maintenance in the group of Italian workers in Germany seems to be on an average level. At the same time, the Italian language and culture are represented in Germany by middle and upper class people as well. There are *Instituti di Cultura Italiana* in several places in Germany, which support the dissemination of Italian language and literature. But as far as we can see, they offer hardly any activities concerning the cultural and linguistic needs or expectations of Italian migrants in Germany. Italian high-brow culture, popular culture and immigrants' cultural expressions are all visible in Germany, but rather separated from each other. The position of the Italian government is not quite clear. Sometimes it seems that the high-brow cultural export is supported to the detriment of the migrants. Sometimes it seems that links are looked for between these two different target groups of Italy's external cultural politics, but even in this case it seems that language maintenance amongst migrant workers is seen as less valuable than the expansion of Italian as a 'foreign' language.

Legal status and language maintenance
German immigration and integration policies tend to legally define different groups of immigrants with different rights. These legal definitions affect the groups' self-perceptions and possibilities to act, including their actions with regard to the maintenance of language and culture. Two opposite examples are given here: Russian-speaking *Aussiedler* and Spanish-speaking guest workers.

In the former Soviet Union the German-speaking minority, whose ancestors had been living there during the tsarist and early Soviet periods on more or less homogeneous speech islands, was dispersed during the Stalin era, collectively suspected of fascism and oppressed heavily. They slowly recovered during the following decades, but could not and in most cases did not want to hinder language shift in the next and following generations. German became the language of the grandparents and was hidden in public. When, in the eighties, the chance arose to 'remigrate' to Germany, parents and children alike had to learn German. Since they were regarded and treated as German nationals under certain conditions, it was generally expected (also by most of the *Aussiedler* themselves) that they would stop speaking Russian after a short period of time. But, as researchers in bilingualism are very well aware, things are not as simple as that. Many *Aussiedler* families continue to speak Russian at home, but now avoid speaking this language in public, because this is seen as 'shameful bilingualism' (Berend, 1998: 47-50). Although there are - mostly local - German-Russian organizations and some ethnic businesses, the idea that there could be a stable Russian-speaking community in Germany is not shared by many. Because the *Aussiedler* are German citizens, they could claim minority rights with more prospect of success than any other immigrant group. They lack, however, self-confidence to act accordingly and probably will not survive as a linguistic minority.

The Spanish-speaking community may serve as the opposite example. Spanish guest workers entered Germany during the sixties and seventies, which was politically and economically a difficult time in Spain. After the end of Franco's dictatorship in 1975, many emigrants returned to Spain. Between 1975 and 1985 the Spanish population in Germany decreased by approximately 1000 persons per year. At the same time substantial support was given by the Spanish government and its representatives abroad to migrants who stayed in the host countries. Language maintenance was and is one of the aims of this support. When Spain became a member of the European Union in 1986, the Spanish language, which always had been an important European and global language, gained additional momentum for the emigrants. Arguments of utility and identity converged and a high degree of stable Spanish-German bilingualism was the result. Although the Spanish-speaking community is relatively small, it can be supposed that it will maintain its bilingualism in the future.

Role of the media

Newspapers are available in all important languages of immigrants in Germany. The wholesale trade offers more than 50 newspapers for 'guest workers', mostly imported from the countries of origin. But there are also special editorial offices in Frankfurt which edit eight specific German issues of important Turkish newspapers. The Russian-German community disposes of several bilingual newspapers of its own. Recently, several bilingual (mostly Turkish-German) magazines have emerged, directed especially towards immigrant youngsters and dealing with topics such as popular music, the job market and ethnic business.

The broadcasting services under public law transmit programmes in Italian, Turkish, Spanish, Greek and Serbian/Croatian (40 minutes daily per language). The television services under public law transmit two programmes weekly which are targeted towards the immigrant public, one in German, one in dual channel technique. In Berlin four private stations broadcast programmes in Turkish. Of greater significance are the tv programmes imported from the countries of origin by cable (e.g. TRT international) or via satellite.

Internet is used by immigrant associations and political speakers and by the immigrants press. Some of the presentations are monolingual in the language of origin, some bilingual with German as the partner language. But there are also bilingual sites with the language of origin and English as partner language (e.g. the Turkish newspaper *Milliyet*). Recently, a Turkish community website has been installed which offers general information, news, chats, discussion fora etcetera - all in both languages.

Education

Teaching of immigrant languages in supplementary lessons was introduced in the 'old' FRG in the late sixties. This teaching took place according to the following framework. Since 1964, 'foreign' children in Germany should in principle receive the same educational opportunities as German children. If it was considered to be advantageous for this aim, teaching of their language of origin (officially referred to as 'mother tongue teaching') could be provided in addition to the regular curriculum. The so-called 'mother tongue teaching' should, according to the relevant decrees, contribute to the social integration of the pupils 'for the duration of their stay in the Federal Republic of Germany' and at the same time 'preserve their linguistic and cultural identity'. The underlying agenda of these recommendations was, similarly to policies in other European immigration countries and the official European Union policy, an assimilation or rotation perspective.

The basic organisational measures for which the *Länder* could opt were the following:

- Supplementary teaching of the mother tongue as an offer for immigrant children attending mainstream classes. This teaching could take place in addition to the regular curriculum and school day and should not exceed five lessons a week.
- Mother tongue teaching in replacement of the first or second obligatory 'foreign' language (usually English or French). This special measure for 'foreign' pupils aimed at saving them from the burden of learning 'regular' foreign languages in case their German competencies were poor. In practice, the acceptance of this offer could mean a severe limitation of the potential school success, as the acquisition of the highest qualification (*Abitur*) is bound to a fixed catalogue of obligatory 'foreign' languages in Germany; none of the immigrant languages belongs to this catalogue. Therefore a 'foreign' pupil who accepted this offer was either excluded from the highest qualification or constrained to the additional learning of obligatory 'foreign' languages.
- 'Mother tongue' as a subject and as a medium of instruction in reception classes for pupils of the same nationality, in Bavaria referred to as 'bilingual classes'. This model was vehemently criticized as it turned out to be an excluding educational system for 'foreigners', providing them with a formal qualification which *de facto* was inferior and stigmatizing. This type of teaching is now disappearing.

Within the outlined framework the responsibility for organisation, financing and curriculum development could be assumed in two different ways:

- Five of the then eleven *Länder* (FRG before 1990) made themselves responsible for this teaching, i.e. Bavaria, Hesse, Lower Saxony, Northrhine-Westphalia and Rhineland-Palatinate.
- The remaining six *Länder* placed the teaching in the hands of the countries of origin. These *Länder* contributed to the teaching by a share of the costs, e.g. by providing classrooms free of charge. These *Länder* were Baden-Württemberg, Berlin, Bremen, Hamburg, Saarland and Schleswig-Holstein.

After the German unification, the East German *Länder* also introduced regulations for mother tongue teaching into their new school legislation, usually following the first model mentioned above. But as the actual numbers of immigrant children in the East German *Länder* are still very low, the teaching is realized only here and there, mostly in larger cities.

Since the character of immigration has changed, in some States the *status quo* has come under discussion. We can not go into a description and analysis of the school policies of all the 16 *Länder* with regard to immigrant languages (but see Gogolin *et al.*, 2000). Only three typical examples will be presented here: the cases of Hamburg, Northrhine-Westphalia and Hesse.

Hamburg

Of the 1.7 million inhabitants of Hamburg, approximately 280,000 (16%) have passports other than German. In the last decade, both the absolute and relative number of 'foreign' children in Hamburg's schools rose continuously. Whereas in 1987, 15.4% of the school population (ca. 25,000 children) had passports other than German, in 1998 this was 19.5% (ca. 33,000). In addition, about 6000 children from *Aussiedler* families or from bi-national parents had a migrant background. Nearly 40% of the 'foreign' children have Turkish passports; other large groups come from former Yugoslav states, Iran, Poland, Albania and some EU member states. The official statistics refer to the second-largest group of 'foreign' children in the category 'other nationalities'; more than 35% of these children belong to this group. As estimated by the Hamburg school board, this group contains around 100 different nationalities.

Since 1996, the Ministry of Education of the *Land* Hamburg has been trying to gather data on the number of languages spoken by children in the Hamburg school system. Every school is obliged to report these data to the statistical office of the ministry. According to these data, in the year 1999 around 90 languages were spoken by a total of 34,000 Hamburg school children with an immigrant background. The largest groups were Turkish (around 10,800 speakers), Russian (4500 speakers), Polish (2300 speakers), Farsi (2300 speakers) and Dari (1900 speakers), followed by Bosnian, Arabic and Serbo-Croatian. Unfortunately we must expect this information to be rather weak. From interviews with teachers and head teachers in case studies we know that many of them have no profound knowledge of the cultural or linguistic background of the children they teach. Very often, the equation of 'one state, one language' is used by teachers (as well as by other officials) as a rationale for their indication of a child's linguistic background. Therefore we must expect that the real variety of languages spoken by children in Hamburg schools is higher than the above mentioned figures.

As indicated before, Hamburg was one of the *Länder* which traditionally placed the teaching of immigrant languages in the hands of the countries of origin. In Hamburg the Consulates of these countries were responsible for the financing and recruitment of teachers. The responsibility for the inspectorate was shared between Hamburg and the respective country; the *Land* Hamburg contributed to the teaching by an allowance of roughly half a million DM per year and by providing class-rooms free of charge. In 1996, 104 classes for 'mother tongue teaching' of this type existed; 87 teachers appointed by foreign Consulates taught in these classes.

Since the beginning, this traditional policy - established in 1976 - was intensely criticized by political representatives of immigrants as well as by experts from the educational and research field. As a first reaction to this criticism, a measure in favour of children of Turkish origin was established in 1986. In order to 'safeguard their linguistic and cultural identity' (*Richtlinien und Hinweise für die Erziehung und den Unterricht ausländischer Kinder und Jugendlichen*, Hamburg, 1986: Par. 4), these children were conceded the possibility of taking part in five lessons of teaching in their mother tongue a week, two of which could be dedicated to Islamic religious instruction. The teachers, 35 on average since 1986 due to this measure, were appointed by the *Land* Hamburg; some of them worked in more than one school. Criticism of this policy did not stop after the introduction of the new measure; on the contrary. It was now argued, that the *Land* created an additional inequality which was not in conformity with the general principles of democratic education.

In 1997, an amendment of the general school legislation took place in the *Land*; some of the major critical arguments against the former language policies were reflected in the innovation process. The preamble to the new School Law says: 'Children and youngsters whose first language is not German, under consideration of their ethnic and cultural identity, have to be supported in such a way that they can develop their bilingualism and that they can actively take part in instruction as well as in school life' (translated *Hamburger Schulgesetz* of April 10, 1997: Section 3.3). The new Hamburg Government, consisting since 1998 of a coalition between the Social Democrat and the Green Party, started to put this into action by establishing a range of new measures. The most relevant one is the intention of taking over the responsibility for the teaching of all immigrant languages. Hamburg still allows the consulates to offer teaching and cooperates with those who do so, but the *Land* is establishing a procedure to make itself responsible for this teaching, if necessary together with the country of origin. The teaching may now take place within regular school hours, and as a rule the teachers will be appointed by the *Land* (mostly not as regularly employed teachers, however, but based on hourly wages). Furthermore, the *Land* is prepared to take over the inspectorate, also in those cases where the consulates are still responsible, and it is in the process of establishing special curricula for this teaching.

In order to realize the new policy, the following action programme was established:

• Mother tongue teaching in primary schools can now be integrated in the regular school day as part of the regular timetable; it is planned to extend this regulation also to secondary schools. The possibility for children to take part in this teaching is no longer dependent on citizenship of a country of origin representing a particular language, but on the parents' wish.

• The marks pupils receive in this teaching are mentioned in the pupils' school reports.

• The number of languages taught is going to be extended. In addition to Turkish, already offered are Kurdish, Dari, Farsi and Russian. It is planned to take over the teaching in Italian, Portuguese and Albanian from the respective consulates.

• The *Land* established an in-service training course for the teachers (most of them being native speakers of the respective languages, but not necessarily qualified teachers), aiming to impart special skills to them for the teaching of immigrant languages in a multilingual context.

• The *Land* established a system of examinations in immigrant languages. This measure aims to provide an opportunity to those pupils who do not have access to mother tongue teaching within the Hamburg school system to receive regular and officially accepted credits for their performance in extracurricular courses.

• The development of syllabuses and teaching material for the teaching of immigrant languages in a multilingual context has been started.

• The *Land* introduced two primary schools with bilingual programmes (one with German and Italian, one with German and Portuguese) in 1999/2000. The schools start teaching both languages from the first school day on and aim to achieve co-ordinated literacy for the children. The project is carried out in cooperation with the respective consulates which contribute to the programme by providing the teachers for Italian and Portuguese respectively. It is planned to expand the programme to other schools and other languages, e.g. Russian.

- A research project aimed at evaluation of the language skills of school beginners with a Turkish background in both Turkish and German was carried out in 1999.
- The school board offers German classes to immigrant parents, which can take place at the schools their children attend.
- The school board makes information brochures available about the Hamburg school system, with a special focus on language education, in different immigrant languages.

Given the recent decisions and measures planned or already established, the *Land* Hamburg is one - fortunately not the only - example of a possible change of basic political attitudes towards multilingualism in the German *Länder*. At least certain parts of the political sphere began to realize that multilingualism in German society (not only in Hamburg) is an undeniable fact and that it is unwise to react to this fact only in a declining manner. Moreover, the new policy towards immigrant languages is in best conformity with recent recommendations of the permanent Conference of Ministers of Education with regard to intercultural education. It is stated there that immigrant languages mean a profit for German society as a whole and for the schools, and that efforts should be made to increase this profit both for those children who live in bi- or multilingual families and for those who grow up monolingually in German.

Thus, we can draw a rather positive and promising picture about the prospects of immigrant language teaching in Hamburg in terms of taking steps towards 'moving away from a monolingual habitus' (cf. Gogolin, 1994 for this term). Nevertheless, it is impossible to make any predictions about the future development. There are also negative indications. Growing opposition against the recent political decisions can be perceived. It is argued that immigrant language teaching is too expensive for the Hamburg school system; that the promotion of bilingualism is no guarantee for better success in the dominantly German school; and that the recognition of multilingualism impedes the immigrants' integration into German society.

Northrhine-Westphalia

Around two million 'foreigners' live in Northrhine-Westphalia, i.e. more than 11% of the population. If we take children into account, their percentage of the population is twice as high. In 1997 about 22% of the children in Northrhine-Westphalia were 'foreigners' (*Landtag* Nordrhein-Westfalen, *Drucksache* 12/2552, November 10, 1997). Children of Turkish origin make up the largest group of 'foreign' children (about 47%). The proportion of 'foreign' children in kindergarten rose from 11.6% in 1993 to 14.8% in 1998. The population of 'foreign' school children increased by about 27% in the last decade. In absolute figures, Northrhine-Westphalia is the German *Land* with most school children of 'foreign' citizenship; one third of all 'foreign' children in Germany visit a school in this *Land*. Only 2% of the schools in Northrhine-Westphalia have no 'foreign' children in their school population (*Ministerium für Arbeit*, 2000).

As is usual in the German school system, the medium of instruction in Northrhine-Westphalian schools is German. In the secondary system at least one 'foreign' language - commonly English - is obligatory for all children. Exceptions have been made for 'foreign' children, in particular for those of Turkish origin, whose German is considered to be insufficient for a promising school career or for mastering an additional language; they may choose to take their home language instead. In this context the following languages are offered 'instead of the first foreign language': Greek, Italian, Portuguese, Spanish and Turkish. As already mentioned, the decision for this offer may lead children into a dead end school career because English is a prerequisite for the *Abitur* as the school-leaving exam of highest value.

As mentioned above, Northrhine-Westphalia is one of the *Länder* which took mother tongue teaching into its own responsibility. At first, it was offered only for the official languages of those countries with which bilateral agreements about the recruitment of workforces existed, i.e. for children of Greek, Italian, Moroccan, Portuguese, Spanish, Tunisian and Turkish citizenship and for children from former Yugoslavia. According to the pertinent decree, teaching should not exceed five lessons a week and the lessons could include aspects of the history of the country of origin and - in the case of Turkish and Greek - religious instruction. In practice, as we know from statistical data, the teaching rarely exceeded three lessons a week. The marks children get for this teaching are integrated in their school reports. In 1999, around 50% of the 'foreign' pupils in primary schools for whom an offer of mother tongue teaching was made took part in the lessons. For those children for whom no offer of instruction in the home language is made, the *Land* offers the possibility to pass extracurricular school-leaving examinations in their languages. Around 10,000 pupils a year make use of this offer. Languages in great demand are Russian, Polish, Vietnamese, Czech, Farsi, Urdu and Albanian.

In the meantime, the *Land* reacted to the changes of immigration processes and altered some of the regulations on mother tongue teaching. The possibility to participate in this instruction is no longer strictly bound to the nationality of a pupil; moreover, not only national languages are taught but also minority languages within the countries of origin, such as Kurdish. The relevant decree formulates the general objective of the instruction as follows: it should "contribute to the integration of linguistic minorities into (German) society and aim at the development of bi- or multilingualism as an essential element of intercultural education in an internationally mobile society" (*Landtag* Nordrhein-Westfalen, *Drucksache* 12/2552, 1997, 3). In order to improve and evaluate various options to realize these objectives in practice, the *Land* organized a number of model projects in schools, some of them under the auspices of European Union programmes in terms of 'Comenius'. One example is the project 'Opening of Mother Tongue Teaching' (1994-1997; cf. *Landesinstitut*, 1998a) which tried out possibilities of co-educating children with a bilingual back-ground in German and the pertinent language and children without basic knowledge of the latter. The evaluation of the project showed that this teaching was very successful in terms of intercultural objectives but less successful in terms of linguistic aims in a narrower sense.

Another innovative initiative in the *Land* was the project *Begegnungs-sprachen in der Grundschule* (Languages of Encounter in primary schools; cf. *Landesinstitut*, 1998b). With this project the *Land* offered an alternative to early 'foreign' language learning. *Begegnungssprachenunterricht* func-tioned in the sense of language awareness instruction. The participating primary schools were free to choose the language(s) of encounter: it could be English, but likewise a language or languages spoken by children in the school or a language of neighbours (e.g. Dutch in the German-Dutch border area). At a rhetorical level, this project was evaluated very positively. It was regarded as a very promising approach to primary school children's abilities and affections and as more convenient for them than traditional 'foreign' language teaching. At the same time the project was considered to be too demanding for teachers. Their prerequisites, i.e. knowledge as well as methodical competence for the development of children's abilities for appropriate interaction in multilingual settings rather than learning words and sentences of one specific 'foreign' language, were insufficient. Although the *Land* had initiated the development of teaching material, most of this concerned English as *Begegnungssprache* and was therefore hardly useful for all schools with other *Begegnungssprachen*, especially the languages of immigrant minorities in the *Land*. Not surprisingly, about 90% of the schools that took part in this experiment opted for English as *Begegnungssprache*. Likewise unsatisfactory was the in-service training of primary school teachers, who in their initial training are usually not confronted with the challenges of multilingual classrooms, for the purpose of their specific role in the teaching of *Begegnungssprachen*.

As a reaction to the ambivalent evaluation of the project *Begegnungssprachen*, a new policy was recently introduced. The newly elected government of the *Land* strengthens the role of English in primary as well as in secondary schools. Only recently, English was introduced as the first 'foreign' language in primary schools. Until now, primary schools opt voluntarily for the introduction of English; in the year 2000, about 3450 schools or 17,000 classes made use of this possibility. From the year 2003 on, English as first 'foreign' language will be obligatory in primary schools from the third grade on. Secondary schools were encouraged to offer subjects through in the medium of another language than German or to take part in model projects under the heading of bilingual schools, mostly with English and very few with French as the 'foreign' language of instruction. All these activities are accompanied by official statements that this policy is not meant as competitive towards immigrant languages. The teaching of English as well as the teaching of immigrant languages should contribute to the development of a multicultural and multilingual atmosphere in the *Land* and to a notion of equality of languages. It cannot be foreseen if the new policy of the *Land* will turn out as repressive for immigrant languages or - as it is officially declared - as beneficial to them.

Hesse

In 1996, about 28,000 children of foreign nationality attended kindergarten in Hesse, which amounts to 81.4% of the 3-6 years olds (as compared to 94.5% of the German population) (*Ausländerreport* Hessen, 1998: Table 5.3). The language usually spoken in kindergarten is German, but there are some kindergartens in the cities which employ bilingual educators also. In the same year, 107,000 pupils of foreign nationality attended primary and secondary schools in Hesse, which amounts to 15.5% of the total school population. The medium of instruction is

German. 'Foreign' languages are taught in all secondary schools and to an increasing degree also in primary schools, mainly English. There is one 'European' school in Frankfurt which offers a German-Italian bilingual branch from grade 1 on. The Hessian employers support a programme of bilingual vocational training with German and Italian/Greek/Portuguese/Spanish as partner languages.

As mentioned above, Hesse had decided to offer 'mother tongue teaching' to children of immigrants from the former recruitment countries of 'guest workers' in the form of supplementary lessons (up to five lessons per week) under the State government's responsibility. Attendance was voluntary. The teachers were employed by the State government but they were mostly educated in the countries of origin.

In the eighties the State of Hesse went ahead with curriculum development. It was ordinated in 1983 that 'mother tongues' should be seen as a 'regular learning area' and should be introduced into the timetable with two lessons in grade 1, three lessons in grade 2, and five lessons from grade 3 on. Pupils with the nationality of one of the former recruitment countries were obliged to attend these lessons, if offered at their own or a neighbouring school (with a minimum group size of ten pupils), unless a demand of exemption was made by the parents. This regulation was unique in the Federal Republic of Germany. The figures of pupils attending lessons of so-called 'heritage' languages went up from 54% of the target group in 1980 to 68% in 1985. In some years they were higher than 70%; in 1996 (last figure available) the rate was 62% (*Ausländerreport* Hessen, 1998: Table 6.14; Reich & Hienz de Albentiis, 1998: 22-24).

In the framework of this policy, syllabuses were developed for primary (1985) and secondary schools (1996). A centre for the teaching of 'heritage' languages was established in Frankfurt and became responsible for material development, in-service training and counselling. Lastly, in-service programmes were set up in order to give at least part of the mother tongue teachers a qualified teacher status in Hesse. In 1992 the restriction of mother tongue teaching to pupils of the former recruitment countries was done away with and other immigrant languages, including the languages of the *Aussiedler*, could be offered at schools as well. Mother tongue teaching was formally enacted in §8a (3) of the School Act as an ordinary subject matter in Hessian schools. Contents and aims were explicitly placed in a European and intercultural perspective. At that time, the teaching of immigrant languages had reached the best possible legal status in the *Land* Hesse.

The year 1999 revealed that the maintenance of this legislation was not assured. After a populist campaign against the (federal) bill on nationality which should make double nationality more accessible, the conservative party won the (regional) elections, formed a coalition with the liberals and took over government from the former Social Democrat - Green Party coalition. One of the first initiatives of the new government was to propose an amendment of the School Act in order to 'secure quality in Hessian schools'. Succinctly the bill says: *§8a Abs. 3 wird aufgehoben* (immigrant language teaching is abolished). In 1999 this bill was adopted by the Hessian Parliament.

It is an extreme case, but it shows what is to be feared in Germany. The results of devoted work in educational policy, referred to as a model for other States of the Federal Republic, was destroyed in a few months time. Neither conservative values nor any arguments of school quality can justify this decision. Not even financial reasons are convincing in this case. Since most of the mother tongue teachers cannot be dismissed over the next years, they have to be occupied with other activities in schools. One is forced to conclude that it was mainly ignorance relying on common sense which caused this disaster. Three decades of intercultural pedagogy - school practice, work of educationalists, official decrees and recommendations - were not enough to convince the political elite and the public opinion. As a result, a monolingual ethnocentric mind-set prevails.

Conclusion

Legislation in Germany is first of all characterised by indifference towards language issues at the constitutional level. The Constitution neither states a national language nor does it mention minority languages. In accordance with international conventions, however, it guarantees freedom of language choice, implicitly by the constitutional articles on free personal development (Art. 2) and freedom of communication (Art. 5), explicitly by the article on non-discrimination (Art. 3). As far as we know these human right principles of individual linguistic freedom are not severely violated in Germany.

In the constitutional discussion after the unification of the two German Republics it was proposed to introduce a new article on minority protection into the Federal Constitution, but this proposal met resistance from both the conservative and the progressive side and was finally rejected by the German Parliament. Constitutional jurisprudence, how-ever, keeps discussing this issue seriously (Robbers, 1994).

In three State Constitutions (i.e. in Brandenburg, Saxony, Schleswig-Holstein) minority rights are formally spelled out. They protect the indigenous minorities of Sorbs, Danes and Northern Frisians. In accordance with the European Charter on regional and minority languages and the prevailing positions in constitutional law, a sharp distinction is made between indigenous and immigrated linguistic communities, irrespective of demographic, cultural and pedagogical arguments. Only the Constitution of Saxony adds a section to the minority rights article indicating that the State respects the interests of those 'foreign' minorities whose members legally live in the country.

Consequently, all linguistic activities of immigrant groups rely on individual human rights. Within this framework room is given for associative and political action. Again, to our knowledge, associative action with regard to minority language maintenance is not severely hindered in Germany, but it has to be seen in the framework of rather restricted possibilities for political participation of immigrants in general. It is true that self-organisations can and really do get impressive work done in language maintenance, that in some important cases the official representatives of the countries of origin give considerable support and that the Ministries of Education are in generally not reluctant to ideas of linguistic diversity, preferably in a European context. But it is also true that the school system is not eager to integrate immigrant language teaching into the common curriculum, that huge differences in language prestige continue to be spread in the public opinion and that campaigns against immigrant language teaching are supposed to win votes in elections. The idea of a multilingual Germany is not prevailing, neither in political mindsets nor in the public opinion. As yet, much depends on the immigrant groups themselves. There are resources for language maintenance, there is a tradition of teaching immigrant languages in the regular school system (although it is not stable) and there are supporters of a policy of pluralistic integration, also with regard to language, in the social sciences (Schulte, 1998). In sum, the case for immigrant languages is not closed in Germany.

References

Ausländerreport Hessen (1998) *Bevölkerung, Ausbildung und Arbeitsmarkt.* Wiesbaden: HLT Gesellschaft für Forschung Planung Entwicklung.

Ausländerbeauftragte. Beauftragte der Bundesregierung für Ausländerfragen (2000) *Daten und Fakten zur Ausländersituation.* Berlin: Ausländerbeauftragte.

Berend, N. (1998) *Sprachliche Anpassung. Eine soziolinguistisch-dialektologische Untersuchung zum Russlanddeutschen* Tübingen: Gunter Narr.

Gogolin, I. (1994) *Der monolinguale Habitus der multilingualen Schule.* Münster/New York: Waxmann.

Gogolin, I., Neumann, U. and Reuter, L. (Hrsg.) (2000) *Schulbildung für Kinder aus Minderheiten in der BRD (1989-1999).* Münster/New York: Waxmann (in print).

Gruner-Domic, S. (1999) Beschäftigung statt Ausbildung. Ausländische Arbeiterinnen und Arbeiter in der DDR (1961 bis 1989). In J. Motte, R. Ohliger and A. von Oswald *50 Jahre Bundesrepublik - 50 Jahre Einwanderung. Nachkriegsgeschichte als Migrationsgeschichte* (pp. 215-240). Frankfurt/New York: Campus.

Hepsöyler, E. and Liebe-Harkort, K. (1991) *Muttersprache und Zweitsprache. Türkische Schulanfängerinnen und Schulanfänger in der Migration - Ein Vergleich.* Frankfurt am Main u.a.: Peter Lang.

Jørgensen, J. and Holmen, A. (1994) Sprogbrug hos tyrker i Danmark og Sverrig. In S. Boyd *et al.* (ed.) *Sprogbrug og sporgvalg blandt indvandrere i Norden. Bind 1: Gruppebeskrivelser.* København: Danmarks Lærerhøjskole.

Krüger-Potratz, M. (1991) *Anderssein gab es nicht. Ausländer und Minderheiten in der DDR.* Münster/New York: Waxmann.

Landesinstitut für Schule und Weiterbildung/Bezirksregierung Düsseldorf (Hrsg.) (1998a) *Wie Kinder miteinander und voneinander Sprachen lernen. Öffnung des Muttersprachlichen Unterrichts zur Förderung und Weiterentwicklung der Mehrsprachigkeit in Europa.* Bönen: Verlag für Schule und Weiterbildung.

Landesinstitut für Schule und Weiterbildung (1998b) *Wege zur Mehrsprachigkeit. Informationen zu Projekten des sprachlichen und interkulturellen Lernens 3.* Soest: Landesinstitut für Schule und Weiterbildung/im Selbstverlag.

Löfgren, H. (1991) *Elever med annat hemspråk än svenska.* Malmö: Lärarhögskolan.

Landtag Nordrhein-Westfalen (1997) *Drucksache 12/2552 vom 10.11.1997 und Amtliche Schuldaten.*

Mehrländer, U., Ascheberg, C. and Ueltzhöffer, J. (1996) *Repräsentativuntersuchung 95: Situation der ausländischen Arbeitnehmer und ihrer Familienangehörigen in der Bundesrepublik Deutschland.* Berlin/Bonn/Mannheim: Bundesministerium für Arbeit und Sozialordnung.

Ministerium für Arbeit, Soziales und Stadtentwicklung, Kultur und Sport (2000) *Zuwanderungsbericht NRW.* Düsseldorf.

Pfaff, C. (1993) Turkish language development in Germany. In G. Extra and L. Verhoeven (eds) *Immigrant languages in Europe* (pp. 119-146). Clevedon: Multilingual Matters.

Reich, H. and Hienz de Albentiis, M. (1998) Der Herkunftssprachenunterricht. Erlasslage und statistische Entwicklung in den alten Bundesländern. *Deutsch lernen* 1, 3-45.

Robbers, G. (1994) Ausländer im Verfassungsrecht. In E. Benda, W. Maihofer and H. Vogel (eds) *Handbuch des Verfassungsrechts der Bundesrepublik Deutschland* (2. Aufl.) (pp. 391-424). Berlin/New York: De Gruyter.

Schulte, A. (1998) *Multikulturelle Einwanderungsgesellschaften in Westeuropa: Soziale Konflikte und Integrationspolitiken*. Bonn: Friedrich-Ebert-Stiftung.

Şen, F. and Goldberg, A. (1994) *Türken in Deutschland. Leben zwischen zwei Kulturen*. München: C.H. Beck.

Statistisches Bundesamt (1999) *Statistisches Jahrbuch für die Bundesrepublik Deutschland 1999*. Stuttgart: Metzler-Poeschel.

Tribalat, M. (1995) *Faire France. Une enquête sur les immigrés et leurs enfants*. Paris: La Découverte.

Immigrant minority languages in the Netherlands

TIM VAN DER AVOIRD
PETER BROEDER
GUUS EXTRA

This chapter goes into the status of immigrant minority (henceforth IM) groups and IM languages in the Netherlands from a demographic, socio-linguistic, and educational perspective. The demographic perspective focusses on the role of language and ethnicity in multicultural population statistics, the sociolinguistic perspective on the distribution and vitality of IM languages, and the educational perspective on the status of IM languages in both primary and secondary schools. Empirical data will be presented from large-scale language surveys among 41,603 pupils from 109 primary and 26 secondary schools carried out in The Hague, one of the largest multicultural cities in the Netherlands.

Demographic perspective

In this section our focus is on criteria for the definition and identification of (school) population groups in a multicultural society, in terms of nationality, birth-country, self-categorization, and home language use. Moreover, we well present empirical data with respect to birth-country and home language criteria, derived from the above mentioned survey studies.

Demographic data and criteria
As a consequence of socio-economically or politically determined processes of migration, the traditional patterns of language variation across Western Europe have changed considerably over the past decades (cf. Extra & Verhoeven, 1993; 1998). Many industrialized Western European countries have a growing number of IM populations, which differ widely, both from a cultural and from a linguistic point of view,

from the mainstream indigenous population. In spite of more stringent immigration policies in most European Union (EU) countries, the prognosis is that IM populations will continue to grow as a consequence of the increasing number of political refugees, the opening of the internal European borders, and political and economic developments in Central and Eastern Europe and in other regions of the world. It has been estimated that in 2000 at least one third of the population under the age of 35 in urbanized Western Europe has an IM background.

For various reasons, reliable demographic information on IM groups in EU countries is difficult to obtain. For some groups or countries, no updated information is available or no such data have ever been collected at all. Moreover, official statistics only reflect IM groups with legal resident status. Another source of disparity is the different data collection systems being used, ranging from national census data to more or less representative surveys. Most importantly, however, the most widely used criteria for IM status - nationality and/or country of birth - have become less valid over time because of an increasing trend toward naturalization and births within the countries of residence. In addition, most residents from former colonies already have the nationality of their country of immigration.

Given the decreasing significance of nationality and birth-country criteria, collecting reliable information about the composition of IM population groups in EU countries is one of the most challenging tasks facing demographers. Complementary or alternative criteria have been suggested in various countries with a longer immigration history, and, for this reason, with a history of collecting census data on multicultural population groups. In English-dominant countries such as the USA, Canada, and Australia, census questions have been phrased in terms of self-categorization ('To which ethnic group do you consider yourself to belong?') and home language use.

In Table 1, the four criteria mentioned are discussed in terms of their major advantages and disadvantages (see also Broeder & Extra, 1998: 4). As Table 1 makes clear, there is no single royal road to a solution of the identification problem. Different criteria may complement and strengthen each other. Given the decreasing significance of nationality and birth-country criteria in the European context, the combined criterion of self-categorization and home language use is a potentially promising long-term alternative.

Table 1   Criteria for the definition and identification of population groups in a multicultural society (P/F/M = person/father/mother)

Criterion	Advantages	Disadvantages
Nationality (NAT) (P/F/M)	• objective • relatively easy to establish	• (intergenerational) erosion through naturalisation or double NAT • NAT is not always indicative of ethnicity/identity • some (e.g. ex-colonial) groups have NAT of immigration country
Birth-country (BC) (P/F/M)	• objective • relatively easy to establish	• intergenerational erosion through births in immigration country • BC is not always indicative of ethnicity/identity • invariable/deterministic: does not take account of dynamics in society (in contrast to all other criteria)
Self-categorization (SC)	• touches the heart of the matter • emancipatory: SC takes account of the person's own conception of ethnicity/identity	• subjective by definition: SC is also determined by the language/ethnicity of the interviewer and by the spirit of times • multiple SC possible • historically charged, especially by World War II experiences
Home language (HL)	• HL is a significant criterion of ethnicity in communication processes • HL data are corner-stones of government policy in areas such as public information or education	• HL is a complex criterion: who speaks what language to whom and when? • language is not always a core value of ethnicity/identity • HL criterion is useless in one-person households

For the reasons mentioned before, it is not easy to give a complete and reliable overview of the actual size of the IM population in any of the European Union countries. What is typical of the Netherlands, in contrast to neighbouring countries like Germany and Belgium, is that some IM groups have had Dutch nationality since birth, due to the country's colonial past (cf. Extra & Vallen, 1997). These include all Antilleans (> 90,000) and most of the Surinamese (> 260,000), who came to the Netherlands in the last few decades from former Dutch colonies in the Caribbean, and the so-called *repatriates* from the former Dutch East Indies (the present Republic of Indonesia; > 280,000), who arrived in the Netherlands after Indonesia's independence.

The Dutch Ministry of the Interior has attempted to reduce the increasing erosion of statistics pertaining to IM groups in the Netherlands by proposing the following three determinants in all municipal population statistics (cf. Fernandes Mendes, 1991): 1) birth-country of person, father, and mother; 2) nationality of person, father, and mother; 3) self-categorization. Obviously, the combined birth-country criterion only suffices for first- and second-generation groups. Furthermore, the (combined) nationality criterion has limited value because many IM groups have or obtain Dutch nationality. The third criterion, self-categorization, led to many objections being raised by both minority and majority groups in the Netherlands because of its subjective loading, the possibility of multiple self-categorization, and the potential misuse of the data collected. Ultimately, parliamentary support was given to the Ministry of the Interior for an introduction of the combined birth-country criterion in all municipal population statistics, although it was recognized that this criterion would lead to a diminishing identification of IM groups over time (cf. Dales, 1992: 17). It was also recognized that other criteria could be relevant for specific purposes or domains. Explicit reference in this context was made to the relevance of the home language criterion for the domain of education (cf. Dales, 1992: 12).

As mentioned before, the combined birth-country criterion does not solve the identification problem. The use of this criterion leads to non-identification in at least the following cases:

- A growing number of third- and later-generation groups (e.g. Moluccans and Chinese in the Netherlands).
- Different ethnocultural groups from the same country (e.g. Turks vs. Kurds from Turkey).
- The same ethnocultural group from different countries (e.g. Chinese from China vs. Vietnam).

- Ethnocultural groups without territorial status (e.g. gypsies).
- People that have lived in more than one country (e.g. refugees).

A more sophisticated way of defining and identifying population groups in an increasingly multicultural society would be crucial for government policy in general and for educational policy in particular. In 1997 (Uitleg, 1997), the Dutch Ministry of Education defined six categories of secondary school pupils, belonging to IM groups, with access to extra funding for L2 classes and/or mother tongue instruction. In Table 2, the utilized criteria for IM pupils in Dutch secondary education are mentioned and compared.

Table 2   Categories of and criteria for IM pupils in secondary education (Ministry of Education, Uitleg, 1997)

Category	Criteria
1 Mediterranean pupils	Country of birth or nationality of both parents
2 Moluccan pupils	Language, culture, and tradition
3 Surinamese and Antillean pupils	Language, culture, and tradition
4 Gypsy pupils	Language, culture, and tradition
5 Non EU-pupils	Mother tongue and country of birth of the pupil
6 Eastern European pupils	Country of birth of the pupil

Apparently, the traditional criteria of country of birth and nationality are not sufficient for identifying all groups. For some categories of pupils, language, culture, and 'tradition' are the criteria for identification; for pupils from outside the EU, mother tongue and country of birth are considered relevant. The criteria refer alternately to country of birth, nationality and/or language; moreover, they are alternately related to parents (1) or pupils (5/6), whereas in other categories any such point of reference is missing (2/3/4). It does not come as a surprise that secondary schools experience many difficulties in collecting the requested data for the Ministry of Education on the basis of these criteria.

The impact of birth-country vs. home language criteria

In cooperation with the Ministry of Education and Sardes (Utrecht), we have started to collect and gradually extend home language statistics on primary and secondary school pupils in an increasing number of Dutch municipalities. The rationale for this joint enterprise derives from three types of considerations:

- The relevance of home language statistics for demographic, socio-linguistic, and educational purposes.
- The absence of such data at the national level.
- The increasing role of municipalities as educational authorities, due to processes of decentralization of national responsibilities and finances.

A first extensive home language survey was carried out amongst almost 35,000 primary school pupils in five cities in the south of the Netherlands (see Broeder & Extra, 1995; 1998). In 1999 and 2000 follow-up surveys have been carried out at almost all primary schools in ten large and medium-sized cities across the country. The outcomes of an accumulative analysis of this data base will be reported on in 2001. In addition, in the context of a first pilot study, similar data have been collected at almost all schools for secondary education in The Hague, one of the largest multicultural cities in the Netherlands (see Aarssen *et al.*, 1998). Here we will focus on the data collected in The Hague at both primary and secondary schools. Table 3 gives a comparative overview of the kernel data.

Table 3   Kernel data of the home language surveys carried out in The Hague

Criteria	*Primary Schools*	*Secondary Schools*
Year of data collection	1999	1997
Number of participating schools	109 out of 142 schools	26 out of 30 schools
Sample	27,900 pupils (68% of estimated total)	13,703 pupils (72% of estimated total)
Reference to home languages besides Dutch	13,662 pupils (49% of sample)	6,153 pupils (45% of sample)
Number of traced home languages	110	75

Tables 4 and 5 are cross-tables which report on the outcomes of the combination of the birth-country and home language criterion for the two samples respectively. The samples have been divided into three generations. G1 consists of pupils who were born outside of the Netherlands. In G2, the pupils were born in the Netherlands but one or both of their parents were born abroad. The third group consists of those pupils who, like their parents, were born in the Netherlands; both native Dutch pupils and third generation immigrant pupils are part of G3.

Table 4   Outcomes of the birth country x home language criterion for the primary school survey (BC = birth-country of PFM = person/father/mother; NL = the Netherlands; HL = home language)

Generation	G1	G2	Other (including G3)	Totals
Criteria	BCP≠NL	BCP=NL BCFM≠NL	BCPFM=NL	
HL=Dutch	349	2,599	10,206	13,154
	1.3%	9.8%	38.6%	49.8%
HL≠Dutch	3,184	9,540	538	13,262
	12.1%	36.1%	2.0%	50.2%
Totals	3,533	12,139	10,744	26,416
	13.3%	46.0%	40.7%	100%

Table 5   Outcomes of the birth country x home language criteria for the secondary school survey (BC = birth-country of PFM = person/father/mother; NL = the Netherlands; HL = home language)

Generation	G1	G2	Other (including G3)	Totals
Criteria	BCP≠NL	BCP=NL BCFM≠NL	BCPFM=NL	
HL=Dutch	116	1,037	6,367	7,520
	0.9%	7.6%	46.7%	55.2%
HL≠Dutch	2,437	3,286	387	6,110
	17.9%	24.1%	2.8%	44.8%
Totals	2,553	4,323	6,754	13,630
	18.7%	31.7%	49.6%	100%

The lower totals for HL≠Dutch in Table 4 compared to Table 5 are caused by missing combined values. When we compare the different generations in Tables 4 and 5, we notice that the proportion of G1 in the secondary school sample is larger than the proportion of G1 in the primary school sample (18.7% versus 13.3% respectively). The same is true for the third subgroup of pupils (49.6% versus 40.7% respectively). These figures can be considered a reflection of a tighter immigration policy (for G1) in recent years and the relatively strong presence of indigenous Dutch pupils in the third subgroup in the secondary school sample. In both the primary and secondary school survey, we notice that for G1 the mismatch between the birth-country and home language criteria is small. In the primary school survey 349 G1 pupils out of 3533 (9.9%) report to have Dutch as their home language; in the secondary school survey this is 4.8% (116 out of 2437 pupils).

Home languages other than Dutch are on the increase between the two samples. In the secondary school sample, 44.8% of all pupils report another language instead of or next to Dutch at home. For the primary school sample, this figure rises to 50.2%. The group of pupils who report another language at home and who themselves and their parents were born in the Netherlands are in both samples relatively small (2% and 2.8% respectively). However, when we also take G2 into consideration, we notice a steep rise in the proportion of pupils whose country of birth does not 'match' their home language; for the secondary school sample, this concerns 3673 informants (26.9%), whereas in the primary school sample this percentage rises to 38.2% (10,078 informants).

In Table 6, we present results which elaborate on this mismatch between birth-country and home language. On the basis of the birth-country criterion (pupil/father/mother/combined criterion), the numbers of pupils are presented for whom there is a match or mismatch between home language and country of birth. In cases of mismatch, the country of birth is the Netherlands, yet the home language is not Dutch. The proportion of mismatches in relation to matches is given in the third and sixth column. Table 6 makes clear that there is a good to very good match between birth-country and home language when the birth-country of the father or mother or when the combined criterion is applied. However, when the birth-country of the pupil is taken into consideration, we see that there is a fast rising number of mismatches between birth-country and home language. Not only is there a sharp contrast between this criterion and the other three criteria, but there is also a significant difference between the primary and secondary school surveys for this

Table 6   Mismatches for the birth country x home language criteria for the two samples (BC = birth-country)

	Primary school survey			Secondary school survey		
Birth-country criteria	mismatch	match	mismatch proportion	mismatch	match	mismatch proportion
BC pupil	10,273	16,634	0.618	3,648	9,769	0.373
BC mother	1,257	23,213	0.0542	675	12,286	0.0549
BC father	1,325	22,739	0.0583	710	12,067	0.0588
BC PMF	512	22,896	0.0224	362	12,015	0.0301

criterion (0.618 versus 0.373 respectively). From these figures, it can be derived that identification of multicultural population groups on the basis of the combined criterion is at this moment relatively unproblematic, but that within five to fifteen years, when the present group of pupils will become parents themselves, the picture will have changed dramatically.

Figures from an additional analysis of first grade children in the primary school sample show that the mismatch proportion passes a score of 1000. When we focus on one particular group, this effect comes alive very graphically. The Chinese community in the Netherlands is known for its relatively long history of migration in the Netherlands and, in spite of this, for its relatively high language vitality. Table 7 shows the effects of the use of the two discussed criteria for identification.

Table 7   Outcomes of the birth-country x home language criteria for Chinese pupils in the primary school sample

	Birth country pupil		Combined birth country	
Criteria	BCP≠NL	BCP=NL	BCFMP≠NL	BCFMP=NL
HL=Dutch	5	5	9	1
	7.6%	7.6%	13.6%	1.5%
HL≠Dutch	9	47	56	0
	13.6%	71.2%	84.8%	0.0%

In Table 7, it becomes clear how badly the birth-country criterion matches the actual language use of Chinese pupils, when the focus is only on the pupil's country of birth. For more than two-thirds of the pupils (71.2%), a mismatch can be observed. When we look at the figures for the combined birth-country criterion and the home language criterion, we notice that no mismatch of this type can be observed (0.0%). A comparison of these figures shows that the birth-country criterion loses significance very rapidly for ethnocultural minority groups which show high levels of language vitality.

Sociolinguistic perspective

In this section, our focus is on the distribution and vitality of IM languages in the Netherlands, as derived from the language surveys discussed earlier. Here again, we will report on the data collected in The Hague at both primary and secondary schools (see Table 3). The span of the data base offers a good opportunity for a pseudo-longitudinal analysis. Some of the results will be presented below. For a detailed description of the outcomes of these surveys, we refer to Aarssen *et al.* (1998) and Van der Avoird *et al.* (1999).

Design and method of the language surveys in The Hague
The questionnaire designed for the surveys started with a number of background questions on the pupil and school. Then the question was asked whether, at the pupil's home, any language other than Dutch was used. Those who answered 'yes' to this question were asked to specify both a home language profile and a school language profile. Those who answered 'no' were only asked to specify a school language profile. The questions used were as follows:

- *Pupil and school profile*:
  age, sex, name/ location/ type of school, grade, and birth-country of pupil/ father/mother.
- *Screening question*:   Are any other languages than Dutch ever used in your home? If the answer is yes: fill out both the home language profile and the school language profile. If the answer is no: fill out the school language profile only.

- *Home language profile*:
language repertoire:	Which other language(s) is/are used in your home instead of or next to Dutch?
language proficiency:	Which of these home language(s) can you understand/ speak/ read/ write?
language choice:	Which language do you usually speak at home with your mother/ father/ younger siblings/ older siblings/ best friends?
language dominance:	Which language do you speak best?
language preference:	Which language do you like to speak most?
- *School language profile*:
participation:	Which language(s) do you learn at school?
need:	Which language(s) do you not learn at school, but would you like to learn at school? In which language(s) do you take classes outside of school?

Table 8 presents the major birth-countries of the pupils and their parents who participated in the two language surveys. As Table 8 makes clear, 85% of the primary school pupils (n=23,695) were born in the Netherlands. In the previous generation, 45% of the mothers (n=12,587) and 44% of the fathers (n=12,377) were born in the Netherlands. A comparison of the primary and secondary school surveys reveals that, in the latter, relatively fewer pupils were born in the Netherlands (i.e. 80%, out of 13,703 pupils), whereas relatively more parents were born outside the Netherlands: 55% of the mothers (n=7554) and 54% of the fathers (n=7439). Morocco, Turkey and Surinam are the three countries where most of the other pupils and their parents were born, followed at some distance by the Dutch Antilles/Aruba. Other countries where many parents were born, are Somalia, Pakistan, China/Hongkong and Indonesia. For the primary school population, the number of mothers born in Germany and Colombia is relatively high compared with the number of fathers born in these countries.

Home language profiles

First we refer to the kernel data already summarized in Table 3. Of the 27,900 pupils that took part in the primary school language survey, 13,662 pupils (49%) reported that, at home, one or more other languages are used in addition to or instead of Dutch. In these pupils' homes, a total number of 75 different languages are used. Of the 13,703 pupils that took

Table 8   Distribution of birth-countries in the surveys in The Hague

Birth-country	N pupils	Primary school survey			Secondary school survey		
		Pupil	Mother	Father	Pupil	Mother	Father
The Netherlands	34,651	23,695	12,587	12,377	10,956	7,554	7,439
Turkey	1,352	851	3,483	3,645	502	1,104	1,113
Morocco	1,037	535	2,776	2,872	574	1,152	1,175
Surinam	1,047	578	3,756	3,537	469	1,729	1,717
Dutch Antilles/Aruba	482	340	684	695	142	199	217
Somalia	190	125	216	199	65	65	63
Irak	163	126	140	156	37	45	48
Pakistan	150	91	328	391	59	147	170
Afghanistan	106	59	68	74	47	48	48
China/Hongkong	99	40	201	197	56	156	157
Iran	94	44	57	69	50	56	52
Great Britain	85	47	90	94	38	58	65
Germany	85	55	146	85	30	65	58
Indonesia	79	29	245	273	50	357	324
Colombia	76	40	104	45	36	40	24
Other/Unknown	1,907	1,245	3,019	3,191	592	928	1,013
Total	41,603	27,900	27,900	27,900	13,703	13,703	13,703

part in the secondary school language survey, 6153 (45%) reported that, at home, one or more other languages are used in addition to or instead of Dutch. In these pupils' homes, a total number of 110 different languages are used. In all, there are more than 24,000 references to languages, which means that at some pupils' homes, more than one language other than Dutch is used. In tracing and classifying the languages, the Catalogue of Languages of the ILEA (1990) and the Ethnologue database on the Internet (Grimes, 1996) were very helpful.

Table 9 gives an overview of the 15 most frequently mentioned languages in each of the two surveys, i.e. the number of times pupils mention a particular language as their home language. This number reflects the size of the language group.

Table 9   Distribution of home languages in the surveys in the Hague

Ranking	Primary school survey	N	Secondary school survey	N
1	Turkish	3,666	Hind(ustan)i	1,304
2	Hind(ustan)i	2,339	English	1,185
3	Arabic	1,879	Turkish	1,159
4	Berber	1,830	Berber	967
5	English	1,219	Arabic	858
6	Sranan Tongo/Sur.	886	French	323
7	Papiamentu	682	Sranan Tongo/Sur.	699
8	Kurdish	399	Kurdish	301
9	Spanish	379	German	255
10	Urdu	273	Papiamentu	238
11	French	256	Spanish	237
12	Chinese	245	Chinese	181
13	Somali	224	Javanese	160
14	German	189	Moluccan-Malay	147
15	Pakistani	123	Urdu	96

A comparison of the two lists in Table 9 shows striking similarities, in that 13 of the 15 languages were mentioned by both primary and secondary school pupils. Somali and Pakistani occur only in the top 15 of the primary school population, whereas Javanese and Moluccan-Malay occur only in the top 15 of the secondary school population. The frequency order in which the languages are listed shows that Papiamentu and Urdu take a relatively high position in the primary school list, and that German, French, and English take a relatively high position in the secondary school list.

In a more detailed analysis and comparison of the different languages mentioned in Table 9, the survey data supplied relevant information on the basis of which profiles of the different language groups could be established. In Aarssen *et al.* (1998) and Van der Avoird *et al.*(1999), a detailed language profile is presented for each of the 15-20 largest language groups, based on the following dimensions:

- Language monopoly: the extent to which the language in question is the only language used at home, instead of or in addition to Dutch.
- Language proficiency: the extent to which the language is understood.

- Language choice: the extent to which the language is used in interaction with the mother.
- Language dominance: the extent to which pupils speak this language best.
- Language preference: the extent to which pupils prefer to speak this language.

Since the concept of ethnolinguistic vitality was introduced by Giles *et al.* (1977), the focus has been on its determinants rather than on its operationalisation. In our case, the operationalisation of ethnolinguistic vitality is derived from the language profiles. In Tables 10 and 11, the five above-mentioned language dimensions are compared as proportional scores, i.e. the mean proportion of informants per language group that indicate a positive response to the questions under consideration. The (decreasing) language vitality index in the final column of Tables 10 and 11 is, in its turn, the mean of these five proportional scores. Obviously, the index chosen is arbitrary in the selection and operationalisation of its constituent dimensions, and in the equal weighting of these dimensions. Nevertheless, there is a statistically significant positive correlation between the language vitality indices calculated for 19 languages of the primary and secondary school surveys (rho = 0.835, df = 17, p<.001).

Also on the different language dimensions there are strongly positive correlations between the primary and secondary school samples. According to the language vitality index, Chinese, Turkish and Urdu belong to the most vital languages in both primary and secondary schools. As yet, Somalian and Pakistani only take a vital position at primary schools; these languages do not have a top 15 position at secondary schools. The reverse can be observed for Moluccan-Malay, French, and German, which only take a top 15 position at secondary schools. The fact that English, French, and German have low vitality is related to the fact that their status is more established in the school context than in the home context. It can be seen in Table 11, in particular for secondary schools, that for all three languages, relatively high proficiency scores go together with relatively low scores on language choice.

The language vitality indices do not necessarily reflect the differences in migration history of the different language groups. A comparison of the vitality indices in Tables 10 and 11 with the distribution of birth-countries in Table 8 reveals that a relatively high language vitality may also emerge for groups whose members mainly belong to second and/or third generations, such as the Chinese and Moluccan-Malay language groups.

Table 10   15 major languages in the primary school survey in The Hague, in decreasing order of language vitality (in %)

Language group	N	Language monopoly	Language proficiency	Language choice	Language dominance	Language preference	Language vitality
1 Turkish	3,666	90	97	87	55	49	75.6
2 Somalian	224	84	95	91	51	50	74.2
3 Pakistani	123	81	92	81	50	56	72.0
4 Chinese	245	90	91	80	50	44	71.0
5 Urdu	273	72	94	75	41	45	65.4
6 Berber	1,830	69	94	80	42	41	65.2
7 Papiamentu	682	79	87	58	38	45	60.8
8 Arabic	1,879	63	89	62	39	40	58.6
9 Portuguese	122	80	80	52	20	39	54.2
10 Spanish	379	70	84	56	25	35	54.0
11 Ghanese	119	52	87	62	30	29	52.0
12 Hind(ustan)i	2,239	82	87	37	17	30	50.6
13 Kurdish	399	32	84	52	16	35	43.8
14 English	1,219	52	79	30	20	35	43.2
15 Sranan/Sur.	886	55	75	29	13	32	40.8

Table 11   15 major languages in the secondary school survey in The Hague, in decreasing order of language vitality (in %)

Language group	N	Language monopoly	Language proficiency	Language choice	Language dominance	Language preference	Language vitality
1 Chinese	181	74	97	93	59	62	77.0
2 Turkish	1159	50	93	92	61	60	71.2
3 Urdu	96	29	93	93	51	61	65.4
4 Berber	967	15	92	93	49	52	60.2
5 Kurdish	301	4	83	89	52	47	55.0
6 Arabic	858	18	88	75	42	49	54.4
7 Papiamentu	238	27	83	56	45	54	53.0
8 Hind(ustan)i	1304	44	94	47	23	32	48.0
9 Spanish	237	21	81	55	33	49	47.8
10 Moluc.-Malay	480	39	85	45	17	42	45.6
11 Sranan/Sur.	699	21	92	35	20	43	42.4
12 English	1185	22	81	32	26	48	41.8
13 French	323	16	67	31	26	36	35.2
14 German	255	23	75	21	18	25	32.4
15 Javanese	160	20	74	25	7	15	28.2

Language monopoly

For the primary schools, Turkish (90%), Chinese (90%), and Somalian (84%) have the strongest monopoly position: there is little or no competition with other languages spoken at home, apart from Dutch. On the other hand, Sranan (55%), English (52%) and in particular Kurdish (32%) share their position as home languages relatively often. For the secondary schools, a different picture emerges. In general, it seems that the languages have a weaker monopoly position among secondary school pupils compared to primary school pupils. Chinese (74%) and Turkish (50%) have the strongest monopoly position. For the other languages mentioned by the secondary school pupils, fairly low figures can be found. Arabic (18%) and Berber (15%) have the weakest monopoly position; they often co-occur. Likewise, Kurdish (4%) is generally used next to Turkish. Sranan (21%), English (22%) and French (16%) often play a role as *lingua franca* with other languages.

Language proficiency

The reported oral skills are relatively well developed among all language groups. For primary schools, the lowest scores for language under-standing are 79% of the pupils in the English language group and 75% of the pupils in the Sranan language group. For secondary schools, the percentages of pupils who report that they are able to understand the pertinent language are relatively low for the German language group (75%), the Javanese language group (74%) and the French language group (67%).

Language choice

The dimension of language choice in Tables 10 and 11 reflects the interaction with the mother. The language choice indices show the broadest spread of values among the language groups. At primary schools, in particular the pupils within the Somalian (91%), Turkish (87%) and Pakistani (81%) language groups use the pertinent language in interaction with their mother. At secondary schools, the 'mother language' takes an even more prominent position within the Chinese (93%), Urdu (93%) and Berber (93%) language groups. The order of the language groups according to the language choice index neatly reflects the order according to the general language vitality index. Aarssen *et al.* (1998) and Van der Avoird *et al.* (1999) also present figures concerning language choice in interaction with other family members. The findings confirm a widely attested pattern of language shift. The mother functions commonly as the gate keeper for language maintenance, whereas the father takes a strong second position in this respect. Dutch is used more frequently in interaction with siblings than in interaction with parents.

Language dominance and language preference

The narrowest range in values can be observed for the survey data on language dominance and language preference. The language dominance dimension at primary schools varies from Turkish (55%) and Somalian (51%) with the highest percentages of pupils who report that they are dominant in the pertinent languages, to Kurdish (16%) and Sranan (13%) with the lowest percentages of such pupils. For secondary schools, the language dominance dimension varies from Turkish (61%) and Chinese (59%) to Moluccan-Malay (17%) and Javanese (7%). At first sight, the language dominance dimension seems to match the language preference dimension. This, however, is *not* the case. An intriguing picture emerges. In Aarssen *et al.* (1998: 73) a more detailed analysis was carried out of the survey data on language dominance vs. preference at secondary schools. Those pupils were selected who indicated that their best language was not their preferred language or vice versa. The mismatch between reported language dominance and language preference is evident for all language groups. The three language groups with the proportionally highest numbers of pupils with a preference for Dutch, but dominance in another language, were the Chinese (19%), Turkish (16%), and Arabic groups. On the other hand, many pupils in the Spanish (23%), English (23%) and Moluccan-Malay (21%) groups report that they speak Dutch best, but prefer to speak another language.

Educational perspective

In this final section, we address the status of IM languages in Dutch education. Because schooling in the Netherlands is compulsory for all children from 5-16 years old, the focus is on both primary and secondary education. For an overview of the status and use of major IM languages in the Netherlands, we refer to Extra and Verhoeven (1993).

IM languages in Dutch primary education

IM language instruction (henceforward IMLI) for IM children at Dutch schools has a remarkable history of implementation. For large groups of pupils, IM languages were introduced as a subject and/or medium of instruction in 1974, without previous curriculum development, without teacher guidance and inspection, and even without a legal base. Table 12 presents a nation-wide overview of IMLI enrolment figures in different years, according to statistics of the Dutch Ministry of Education. In the context of a policy of decentralization of educational responsibilities towards municipal authorities during the nineties, no nation-wide enrolment figures have been collected or published after 1993. As Table 12 makes clear, enrolment is subject to both temporal and inter-group fluctuations.

For various reasons, the implementation of IMLI has been conceived as a complex task for schools. Firstly, given the multicultural and multilingual composition of many primary schools, this task is not restricted to the implementation of bilingual programmes, but it is extended to arranging multilingual education. Practical experience with and empirical evidence on education in a bilingual context can therefore only be transferred to a limited extent. Secondly, there is large variation

Table 12   Enrolment of IM children in IMLI in 1990 and 1993 (Ministry of Education)

	1990			1993		
Birth-country	*N total*	*N IMLI*	*%*	*N total*	*N IMLI*	*%*
Morocco	38,867	27,506	71	41,373	28,205	68
Turkey	38,294	31,328	82	42,619	33,002	77
Moluccan Islands	4,755	1,726	36	397	1,559	39
former Yugoslavia	2,989	807	27	4,474	1,129	25
Spain	2,721	914	34	2,244	706	32
Italy	2,529	262	10	217	271	13
Cape Verdian Islands	2,462	1,031	42	2,189	417	19
Portugal	1,506	508	34	189	1,095	58
Greece	815	318	39	855	261	31
Tunisia	671	69	10	969	298	31
Total	95,609	64,469	67	102,753	66,943	65

in the type and degree of bilingualism of IM children, both within and across different ethnocultural groups. Viewed from an intergenerational perspective, these differences have increased steadily over time, with language dominance patterns tending to shift towards Dutch. Thirdly, embedding IMLI for a variety of target groups in the school curriculum is no easy task. Some IM groups receive IMLI in addition to the core curriculum, whereas other groups receive it instead of having instruction in other core-curriculum subjects. Finally, the feasibility of IMLI is often questioned in cases where there is a relatively small demand from small-sized and/or widely scattered groups.

Developments in this much-debated domain of Dutch education should be evaluated against the background of a policy perspective on IM children in terms of socio-economic and second-language deficits rather than ethnocultural differences. In the early seventies, the deficiencies of low-SES children in all primary schools were targeted by the Ministry of Education. Consequently, schools with many low-SES children received funding for additional teaching personnel. While the influx of IM children from low SES-families in Dutch schools increased sharply in the seventies and eighties, IM policy became exclusively associated with the struggle to eliminate educational deficiencies at the cost of recognizing ethnocultural differences. The equalization of IM policy and deficit policy in the Netherlands is not a universal phenomenon. Australia and Scandinavia are good examples of areas in which multicultural policy concepts for IMLI have been proposed in terms of language resources rather than language problems (cf. Clyne, 1991 and Ministerial Advisory Council, 1994 on LOTE = *Languages Other than English* in Australia; Home Language Reform, 1976 in Sweden and Nordic Roads, 1997).

In 1992, the CALO report *Ceders in de tuin* (*Cedars in the garden*), an advisory report for the Dutch Ministry of Education, proposed a reconsideration of current concepts in educational policy on IM children. The CALO report argued for a change in the conceptualization of IMLI from a deficit to a cultural perspective. The chosen perspective has different consequences for the target groups, goals, target languages and evaluation of IMLI. In Table 13 previous and proposed policy concepts in this domain are compared on each of the dimensions mentioned.

Table 13 Immigrant Minority Language Instruction from a deficit vs. multicultural perspective

Dimensions	IMLI from a deficit perspective	IMLI from a multicultural perspective
Target groups	Temporary facility for low-SES children from first/second generation	Structural facility for children with a non-Dutch home language, independent of SES and generation
Goals	Primary focus on auxiliary goals: bridging the home/school gap and contribution to second language learning or school success	Primary focus on intrinsic goals: contribution to first language learning
Target language	Home language	Home language or standard language of source country (optional)
Evaluation	In terms of school success in other subjects, in particular second language proficiency	In terms of first language proficiency

Since 1974, access to IMLI in Dutch primary schools has been granted to the following target groups: children who have at least one parent of Moluccan or Mediterranean origin (the latter originating from one of the eight Mediterranean countries with which bilateral labour contracts have been concluded in the past) and children of at least one parent with a recognized refugee status. The list has been indicative of multiple policy restrictions. Firstly, it was meant to be exhaustive in terms of source countries and/or target groups. Secondly, it was meant as a temporary facility, with a focus on first/second generation children of IM groups. Finally, the list took a deficit perspective by excluding higher SES groups like the Chinese, and by excluding Antillean and Surinamese children who are more or less fluent speakers of Dutch as a result of the colonial status of Dutch in the respective source countries. Chinese children have explicitly been excluded from IMLI, because of the government's view that it has not been demonstrated that the Chinese community in the Netherlands has an SES comparable to the Mediterranean target groups (Ministry of the Interior, 1983). The CALO (1992) proposal was that both the SES criterion and the generation criterion be disregarded and IMLI be allowed for all children who make use of another language at home, in addition to or instead of Dutch, in contact with at least one of the parents.

The goals of IMLI have traditionally been formulated in auxiliary terms. In this policy conception, IMLI's main contribution should be to bridge the gap between the home and school environment and to promote second language learning and/or school success. Only rarely has the primacy of intrinsic goals in terms of promoting first language proficiency been advocated. Yet, it is interesting to note that the notion of IMLI at the secondary school level in terms of intrinsic goals had, in fact, been accepted previously and more widely. The National Examination Board for Turkish and Arabic at secondary schools defined in detail the target proficiency level for these languages. The CALO (1992) argued for the primacy of intrinsic instead of auxiliary goals in both primary and secondary schools.

The choice of the target language variety for IMLI has in the past led to the problematising of programmes in which the home language of IM children diverges widely from the standard language of the source country. This is so, in particular, for Moroccan children who often speak a Berber variety at home. In cases of home and standard language divergence, the CALO (1992) proposed a conditional right of option for parents of primary school children and for youngsters at secondary schools, derived from the principles of cultural self-orientation and freedom of choice. At this time, the only groups who are receiving non-standard language instruction are Moluccan children (who learn Moluccan-Malay instead of standard Indonesian) and Syrian-Orthodox children from Turkey (who may opt for Aramese instead of Turkish).

Evaluative studies of IMLI programmes for IM children ultimately suffer from a bias similar to that of many American studies on bilingual education as they primarily focus on the effects of IMLI on L2 learning and/or school achievement in other subjects. From this perspective, progress in L1 proficiency, *per se*, is rarely considered and measured in terms of overall school success. The empirical evidence for IMLI effects on L2 learning and/or school achievement is rather ambiguous (cf. Appel, 1984; Teunissen, 1986; Driessen, 1990) and there are very few empirical studies of IMLI effects on L1 proficiency. While Aarts *et al.* (1993) report that Turkish instruction has a positive effect on the Turkish proficiency of Turkish primary school children in the Netherlands, similar positive effects of Arabic instruction did not emerge for Moroccan children (cf. also Driessen, 1990).

Recent educational policy in the Netherlands can be characterized in terms of a growing tendency towards decentralization. Consequently, the responsibilities and tasks of the Ministry of Education, municipalities and schools are being redistributed in an attempt to find a new balance. In the context of this decentralization tendency and in reaction to the CALO (1992) report, the Ministry of Education got parliamentary support in 1998 for changing the law regarding IMLI at elementary schools. The new law aims at compromizing between the deficit perspective and the cultural perspective, outlined in Table 13, while allowing the auxiliary goals of IMLI for younger children (grades 1-4) at curricular hours and the intrinsic goals for children in any grade only at extra-curricular hours. Table 14 gives an outline of the basic properties of the present IMLI legislation.

In the view of the Ministry, municipalities should have responsibility for public information about IMLI goals and facilities, for IMLI needs-assessment, for a selective distribution of the local IMLI budget across local priority languages and across local schools, for interscholastic cooperation on IMLI for smaller language groups and for the role of IM groups (both parents and self-organisations) as actors rather than just target groups for the implementation of a municipal IMLI policy. Notwithstanding the above, much remains unclear and uncertain about the newly assigned roles of the Ministry, municipalities and schools in the implementation of IMLI. Whereas the roles of the latter two are spelled

Table 14 Goals and status of IMLI in different stages of elementary schooling according to present IMLI legislation (1998)

Stage	Grades 1-4		Grades 5-8
Goals	Auxiliary: in support of learning Dutch	Intrinsic: in support of IML learning	Intrinsic: in support of IML learning
Status	at curricular hours	at extra-curricular hours	at extra-curricular hours

out in great and complex detail, the responsibilities of the Ministry remain vague and uncommitted. Moreover, serious concerns have been expressed about the extra-curricular status of the intrinsic goals of IMLI, about the restrictive municipal budgets that are made available and about the local expertise and commitment presently available for implementing the new law.

IM languages in Dutch secondary education

In contrast to primary education, and in conformity with other European countries, Dutch secondary education is organized in diverging types of schooling, and the scheduling of more than one language as target language of learning is common practice. Secondary education in the Netherlands is organized at the levels of VBO (technical and vocational education), MAVO (lower general education), HAVO (higher general education) and VWO (pre-university education), or combinations of these levels during the first year(s) of secondary education. At the VBO/MAVO level, English is compulsory together with French or German. English, French and German are compulsory subjects in the first three years of HAVO/VWO, and Latin and Greek are optional languages at the VWO level.

IM languages may be offered as optional or additional subjects. Government funds are made available if at least four pupils take a particular IM language for at least two hours per week. Schools may also cooperate in organizing such education for each other's pupils. During the period 1995-2000, between 8000 and 9000 pupils made use of these facilities yearly. Table 15 gives an overview of the distribution of pupils across languages and school years, according to statistics of the Ministry of Education.

Table 15 Distribution of pupils across languages and school years in Dutch
secondary education (Ministry of Education)

Languages chosen	1995/1996	1996/1997	1997/1998	1998/1999	1999/2000
Albanese	28	56	64	15	15
Arabic	3,601	3,784	3,644	3,394	3,962
Aramese	30	23	-	-	-
Chinese	-	-	26	24	11
English	-	28	30	35	35
French	-	1	13	17	21
Hebrew	-	58	-	-	-
Italian	1	15	25	34	33
Moluccan-Malay	30	17	17	13	12
Portuguese	253	212	328	272	288
Russian	-	-	4	17	22
Serb./Croat./Bosn.	249	204	222	248	263
Spanish	48	80	70	75	45
Turkish	3,746	3,678	3,530	3,414	4,206
Urdu	-	-	50	47	20
Vietnamese	24	15	-	-	-
Total	8,010	8,171	8,023	7,605	8,888

Not surprisingly (see also Table 12), Table 15 shows that Turkish and
Arabic are by far the most frequently chosen languages. For this reason,
the Ministry of Education focussed on developing facilities for the
learning and teaching of these two languages over the past years. To
mention the most important facts chronologically:
- In 1984, teacher training programmes were initiated for Turkish and
  Arabic at teacher training colleges in Rotterdam and Amsterdam,
  respectively.
- Since 1987, Turkish and Arabic have been offered as optional or
  additional subjects in secondary education.
- Since 1991 and 1993, detailed descriptions of language proficiency
  requirements have been made available and updated for VBO/MAVO
  and HAVO/VWO.
- In 1995, the first final certificates for Arabic and Turkish were made
  available at HAVO level.

- In 1996, the same happened at VWO level.

This chronology of events was accompanied by a number of other facilitating developments in terms of curricula, learning materials, dictionaries and language tests for Turkish and Arabic in secondary education. Moreover, facilities were made available by the Ministry of Education for supporting secondary schools in implementing these subjects (see also Van Hooff, 1998).

Özgüzel (1994) did a study on the attitudes of school principals, teachers of Turkish, and Turkish pupils and their parents towards Turkish in secondary education. Table 16 gives an overview of possible reasons for Turkish pupils (n = 168) to take Turkish as school subject.

Table 16 Arguments for taking Turkish as school subject (Özgüzel 1994: 104)

Do you take Turkish:	yes	%	no	%
• because you want a good job in which Turkish can play a role?	108	64.7	59	35.3
• because you want to communicate better with speakers of Turkish?	118	71.1	48	28.9
• because you feel obliged to your parents?	31	18.7	135	81.3
• because you think you will get higher marks for Turkish than for another modern foreign language?	52	31.1	115	68.9
• because you want to improve your writing in Turkish?	96	57.5	71	42.5
• because you have a Turkish background?	124	74.3	43	25.7

Both symbolic arguments (ethnocultural self-definition) and utilitarian arguments (communicative and labour value) play an important role.

Turkish and Arabic are *de iure* available for all pupils in secondary education, but these subjects are *de facto* rarely chosen by pupils other than those with a Turkish and Moroccan background. As yet, little empirical evidence is available on the variation in language proficiency of those first and/or second generation pupils who opt for Turkish or Arabic. The same holds for how teachers of Turkish and Arabic deal with such variation in their daily classroom practice.

Although various facilities have been made available by the Ministry of Education for Turkish and Arabic as secondary school subjects, not all eligible schools actually ask for such facilities. This reluctance may derive from a variety of more or less publically pronounced arguments, such as lack of need, lack of qualified teachers, lack of status (in contrast to English, French, German, Latin, or Greek) or competition with (and teacher jobs) for any of these languages. Some school principals state that Turkish is superfluous at their school, because 'our Turkish pupils have sufficient proficiency in Dutch' (*Commissie Examenprogramma*, 1994). Both the 'lack of need' and the 'lack of teachers' arguments are curious, given the fact that only four pupils are needed for the introduction of Turkish or Arabic at school and that many qualified teachers of these languages are looking for jobs. Unfamiliarity with the facilities and *rationale* for Turkish and Arabic in secondary education and the problematic status of these languages in primary education seem to be mutually reinforcing factors. As a result, Turkish and Arabic, and the teachers of these languages, have not yet acquired equal status with other subjects and teachers at secondary schools.

A pilot study on the implementation of new languages at secondary schools

As a result of the outcomes of the previously discussed language survey carried out at secondary schools in The Hague (Aarssen *et al.*, 1998), a follow-up study has been set up on the *status quo* and implementation of non-traditional new languages at secondary schools in the same city. This pilot study is based on cooperation between the local educational authorities, the local center for educational support (HCO), Babylon (Tilburg University) and the Ministry of Education. The study aims at a process evaluation of the *status quo* of newly introduced languages in the school years 1999/2000 and 2000/2001. During the former year, the focus was on Turkish, Arabic, and Spanish; during the latter year on Turkish, Arabic, Spanish and Hindi. Data have been collected in terms of pre-structured interviews with the most relevant actors, in particular school directors, teachers of both traditional and new school languages, and (non-)participating pupils. Moreover, classroom observations will be carried out on the basis of prepared protocols. The outcomes of this study are expected to be published in 2001, and they are expected to be relevant for a nation-wide implementation of new languages as optional subjects at Dutch secondary schools.

References

Aarssen, J., Broeder, P. & Extra, G. (1998) *Allochtone talen in het voortgezet onderwijs. Bouwstenen voor lokaal taalbeleid.* Den Haag: VNG Uitgeverij.

Aarts, R., Ruiter, J. de & Verhoeven, L. (1993) *Tweetaligheid en schoolsucces. Relevantie en opbrengst van etnische groepstalen in het basisonderwijs.* Tilburg: Tilburg University Press.

Appel, R. (1984) *Immigrant children learning Dutch. Sociolinguistic and psycholinguistic aspects of second-language acquisition.* Dordrecht: Foris.

Broeder, P. & Extra, G. (1995) *Minderheidsgroepen en minderheidstalen.* Den Haag: VNG Uitgeverij.

Broeder, P. & Extra, G. (1998) *Language, ethnicity and education. Case studies on immigrant minority groups and immigrant minority languages.* Clevedon: Multilingual Matters.

CALO (Commissie Allochtone Leerlingen in het Onderwijs) (1992) *Ceders in de tuin. Naar een nieuwe opzet van het onderwijsbeleid voor allochtone leerlingen.* Den Haag: Staatsuitgeverij.

Clyne, M. (1991) *Community languages. The Australian experience.* Cambridge: Cambridge University Press.

Commissie Begeleiding Invoering Examenprogramma Arabisch en Turks (1994) *Onderzoek naar de groei van de vakken Arabisch/Turks in het voortgezet onderwijs.* Utrecht/De Meern: Inspectie van Onderwijs.

Dales, I. (1992) *Registratie en rapportage minderhedenbeleid.* Den Haag: Staatsuitgeverij.

Driessen, G. (1990) *De onderwijspositie van allochtone leerlingen.* Nijmegen: ITS.

Extra, G. & Vallen, T. (1997) Migration and multilingualism in Western Europe. A case study in the Netherlands. In W. Grabe (ed.) *Multilingualism* (pp. 151-169). Cambridge: Cambridge University Press. Annual Review of Applied Linguistics 17.

Extra, G. & Verhoeven, L. (eds) (1993) *Community languages in the Netherlands.* Amsterdam: Swets & Zeitlinger.

Extra, G. & Verhoeven, L. (1998) Immigrant minority groups and immigrant minority languages in Europe. In G. Extra & L. Verhoeven (eds) *Bilingualism and Migration* (pp. 3-28). Berlin: Mouton de Gruyter. Studies on Language Acquisition 14.

Fernandes Mendes, H. (1991) *Concept-nota registratie en rapportage minderhedenbeleid.* Den Haag: Staatsuitgeverij.

Giles, H., Bourhis, R. & Taylor, D. (1977) Towards a theory of language in ethnic group relations. In H. Giles (ed.) *Language, ethnicity and intergroup relations* (pp. 307-348). London: Academic Press.

Grimes, B. (ed.) (1996) *Ethnologue. Languages of the World.* 13th Edition. Dallas: Summer Institute of Linguistics (Internet version: www.sil.org/ethnologue).

Home Language Reform (1976). Norrköping: Statens Invandrarverk.

ILEA (1990) *Catalogue of languages spoken by ILEA school pupils.* London: ILEA Research and Statistics Branch.

Ministerial Advisory Council on Languages other than English (1994) *Report to the Minister of Education.* Melbourne: Directorate of School Education.

Ministry of the Interior (1983) *Minderhedennota.* Den Haag: Staatsuitgeverij.

Nordic Roads to Multilingualism (1997) *How to help minority children to become multilingual.* Helsinki: Hakapaino Oy.

Özgüzel, S. (1994) *De vitaliteit van het Turks in Nederland.* PhD thesis, Tilburg University.

Teunissen, F. (1986) *Een school, twee talen.* PhD thesis, Utrecht University.

Uitleg (1997) Informatie over culturele minderheidscategorieën voortgezet onderwijs (cumi-categorieën VO) en op leerlingenadministratie vereiste documenten. *Uitleg* 5/6, 19-2-1997 (gele katern).

Van der Avoird, T., Bontje, D., Broeder, P., Extra, G. & Peijs, N. (1999) *Meertaligheid in Den Haag. De status van allochtone talen thuis en op school.* Utrecht/Tilburg: Sardes/Babylon.

Van Hooff (1998) *Arabisch en Turks. Vakgids voor directies en docenten in het voortgezet onderwijs.* Amersfoort: CPS.

Community languages in the United Kingdom*

VIVIAN EDWARDS

This chapter provides an overview of community or heritage languages in the UK. The terms 'community' or 'heritage' languages are chosen in preference to the term 'immigrant languages' used in many chapters in this volume because the vast majority of speakers in question are second, third or even fourth generation of settlers in the UK. Discussion will focus on two main areas of sociolinguistic interest. The first concerns the distribution of minority languages, as well as difficulties in making accurate estimates of numbers of speakers. The second relates to language maintenance and shift and, in particular, the role of formal teaching in both community and mainstream schooling in helping to ensure that minority languages are transmitted to the next generation.

Numbers and distribution of speakers

Precise numbers of speakers of community languages are very difficult to establish. According to the 1991 UK Census, ethnic minorities make up some 5.5% of the population, and are concentrated mainly in industrial and urban areas, especially in the south-east of England and Greater London. The ten census categories for ethnicity - White, Black Caribbean, Black African, Black Other, Indian, Pakistani, Bangladeshi, Chinese, Other Asian and Other - are, however, weak indicators of the diversity of the UK population and, because no question was included on language (other than Welsh), it is not possible to extrapolate from census data to the number or size of different language communities. Nor is ethnicity an automatic guarantee that a respondent is bilingual.

Until very recently, the three main sources of information on linguistic diversity in the UK all dated from the eighties. The first is the Rosen and Burgess (1980) small scale study of the *Languages and dialects of London school children*. The second, *The other languages of England* (Linguistic Minorities Project, 1985), was set up to study mother tongue teaching and the changing patterns of bilingualism, drawing on data collected in three main centres - Bradford, Coventry and London. The third source is the language censuses conducted by the Research and Statistics Department of the Inner London Education Authority (ILEA, 1978; 1981; 1983; 1985; 1987). These censuses were able to demonstrate not only the range of languages spoken but also the changing profiles of the different communities over time. For instance, the number of Bangladeshi pupils trebled between 1981 and 1987, at which time they represented over a quarter of all pupils with a home language other than English and the largest linguistic minority in London.

With the disbanding of ILEA this data collection exercise came to a close. The last census published in 1989, however, gives an interesting indication of the extent of diversity. Over 25% of children reported speaking a language other than or in addition to English; and 180 different languages were identified. Some commentators (e.g. Nicholas, 1994) argue that even this very large number represented a significant underestimate. Although all schools are now required to report on the ethnicity of pupils, they are not required to collect data on language. It has therefore been impossible to estimate with any degree of confidence the numbers of speakers of community languages.

Diversity in London

The publication of a new survey of the languages of London school children (Baker & Eversley, 2000) thus represents an exciting landmark for those concerned to chart the nature and extent of diversity in present day Britain. The Languages of London Project was part of the wider Logosphere research programme to develop new methods of language mapping using Geographical Information Systems (GIS). It brings together information on well over 300 home languages (almost twice as many as reported in the last ILEA Language Census) spoken by more than 850,000 school children from all 32 London Boroughs and the City of London itself.

Predictably, those responsible for this most recent survey encountered many of the difficulties encountered by earlier writers (see, for instance, Alladina, 1985; Nicholas, 1994). Nomenclature remains a persistent problem: in 3.26% of the responses, it was not possible to determine the language spoken. Sometimes children offered a name related to a country (e.g. Nigerian, Ghanaan); sometimes they gave the name of a place (rather than a country) or made a transcription error; on other occasions, they gave no language name at all. Although the proportion of 'unclassified'

Table 1   Top ten home languages of London school children (Source: Baker &
Mohieldeen, 2000: 5)

Rank	Language name	Percentage
1	English	67.86
2	Bengali+Sylheti	4.51
3	Panjabi	3.32
4	Gujarati	3.19
5	Hindi/Urdu	2.91
6	Turkish	1.74
7	Arabic	1.23
8	English-based Creoles	1.20
9	Yoruba	1.16
10	Somali	0.93

languages was usually quite small, 21.8% of respondents in Hillingdon
and 15.85% of respondents in Newham fell into this category. Since even
very young bilingual children are usually able to label their languages,
the most probable explanation for misreporting of this kind is uncertainty
about the questioner's motives. If the teacher has not previously
demonstrated an interest and respect for other languages, children are
likely to give a guarded response. This might well include the assumption
that the teacher neither knows about nor is interested in the finer details
of their situation - hence answers such as Ghanaan rather than Akan, or
Pakistani in preference to Urdu.

An interesting innovation was the selective - though principled - use
of Dalby's (1999) classification of 'outer languages', 'inner languages' and
'dialects' in making decisions about language names. Dalby considers
Danish, Swedish and Norwegian, for instance, as three inner languages
constituting an outer language which he terms Nordic-East. However,
speakers themselves insist that we are dealing with three separate
languages and, for this reason, Baker and Mohieldeen (2000) classify them
as such. In contrast, in the case of Akan, Ashanti, Fante and Twi, all
names for languages spoken in Ghana, a different solution is adopted.
Dalby (1999) considers Ashanti to be a dialect of Twi, and classifies Twi
and Fante as inner languages which together constitute the Akan outer
language. Some boroughs give figures only for Akan and any division
between Fante and Twi would therefore be purely arbitrary. For this

reason, it seems preferable to combine all the languages under the outer language, Akan.

Bengali and Sylheti pose rather different problems. Many Bangladeshis come from the Sylhet region where a variety called Sylheti, closely related to Bengali, is spoken. No information is available, however, on the proportion of speakers of Sylheti. Six boroughs record separate figures for Sylheti and Bengali; seven combine speakers of the two languages into a single figure; the rest record only Bengali. For this reason, Baker and Mohieldeen (2000) amalgamate speakers of the two varieties.

Statistics for speakers of English-based creoles are even more problematic. These varieties are spoken in Guyana, Jamaica and most of the Virgin Islands down to Trinidad and can justifiably be considered as a single language. However, a wide variety of terms was used in reporting, including Jamaican Creole and Trinidadian Patwa or Patois. Eleven boroughs which almost certainly have children from homes where an English-based creole is spoken appear to have reported all children of African-Caribbean heritage as English speakers, while other boroughs seem to assume that all African-Caribbean children are speakers of an English-based creole. There is also a lack of clarity as to what precisely constitutes an English-based Creole: many children use features which mark their speech as Black without necessarily employing the full range of phonological and syntactic features which would be expected in a Caribbean setting (Edwards, 1986; Sebba, 1993).

Welsh is another language for which there would seem to be significant underreporting. According to Baker and Mohieldeen (2000) there are 66 Welsh-speaking children in London schools, whereas a company investigating the viability of making the Welsh-speaking Sianel Pedwar Cymru television station available in London estimated that there were 20,000 speakers. Baker and Anderson (in press) argue that even if only half of these lived in the boroughs included in the survey, it would be reasonable to assume that there were as many as 2000 Welsh-speaking school children in London. It should also be remembered that the only Welsh medium school in the capital - the London Welsh School - is independent and therefore was not included in the survey.

There are clearly serious shortcomings with the data set, including problems arising from the design and administration of the questionnaire and lack of information on children attending independent and special schools. None the less, this survey marks an important advance in our understanding of linguistic diversity. Most significant, Storkey (2000) has used the school children data as the basis for the calculation of numbers of adult speakers of community languages. Making adjustments for age structure, fertility and migration patterns based on information from the London Research Centre, it has been possible for the first time to produce upper and lower estimates of the total number of speakers for the languages of London.

Table 2   Estimated total numbers of speakers (to the nearest hundred) of the top 10 languages in London (Source: Storkey, 2000: 65)

Rank	Language	Lowest estimate	Highest estimate
1	English	5,737,400	5,636,500
2	Panjabi	143,600	155,700
3	Gujarati	138,000	149,600
4	Hindi/Urdu	125,900	136,500
5	Bengali+Sylheti	119,000	136,300
6	Turkish	67,600	73,900
7	Arabic	49,500	53,900
8	English Creoles	46,300	50,700
9	Cantonese	45,100	47,900
10	Yoruba	43,300	47,600

Close study of the language maps of London highlights various issues which have received little attention to date. For instance, the fact that above average numbers of speakers for a given language are generally found in adjoining boroughs suggests that people prefer to live in areas where cultural and linguistic contact with other members of their community is easier; and there is evidence that this pattern holds for both more recently arrived and well-established groups.

Given the tremendous fluidity of populations, Li (2000) also points to the usefulness of information on language for social and health policy:

In London, where one in five residents are from black and ethnic minority communities, up-to-date information on ethnicity is of particular importance, both for the assessment of needs and the planning of services. The data collected by London schools on the languages other than English spoken by their children at home may provide a useful proxy for the population distribution and the size of these communities until the next census. (Li, 2000: 83)

The Languages of London Project is thus an important landmark in the continuing search for more accurate information on the nature and extent of linguistic diversity. While Storkey (2000) points out that the quality of the data is likely to improve over time as systems are introduced and initial data collection problems resolved, Baker and Sanderson (2000) emphasise the need for positive attitudes towards multilingualism within schools.

Edwards (1995; 1998) draws attention to the ways in which language surveys can actually promote such positive attitudes. While they can, of course, be planned and carried out by teachers as a largely administrative exercise, it is possible to transform the process by involving children. Surveys offer valuable experience of devising questionnaires and collecting and analysing data. Children can also help to design and produce displays of the findings. Most important, making children an integral part of the project gives them a real sense of belonging to a multilingual community. A consistent finding of informal school-based surveys is that children speak many more languages than was previously thought. This observation applies both to schools where there is one large minority group - and where teachers assume that this is the only language spoken other than English - and to schools where there are only very small numbers of bilingual children. Language surveys increase awareness of the extent of diversity in the school. They also have the effect of raising the profile of other languages. They enhance the status of bilingual children and give them the opportunity to demonstrate their skills. At the same time, they broaden monolingual English-speaking children's horizons and increase their awareness of language.

Linguistic diversity outside London

It is to be hoped that developments in linguistic mapping in London will act as a spur for other areas of the UK, where information remains, to say the least, sketchy. It is generally agreed that settlers from the Indian subcontinent - and in particular Panjabi, Urdu, Gujarati and Bengali speakers - constitute the largest linguistic minority communities both within and beyond the capital. Panjabi-speaking Sikhs are usually held to be the biggest of these south Asian groupings. The most important areas of settlement outside London are the West Midlands and the northern cities of Leeds and Bradford. Pakistani Muslims from the Mirpur district of Azad Kashmir also speak a variety which is mutually intelligible with the Panjabi spoken by Sikhs, but claim Urdu as the language of religion and high culture. They are spread throughout the UK but have important settlements in the south, the Midlands and the north of England. Gujarati speakers are generally held to form the second largest south Asian community. They are scattered throughout the country with particular concentrations in Greater London and the Midlands. Bengali speakers consist of a small, mainly Hindu, community from Indian West Bengal and a much larger Muslim Bangladeshi community which is concentrated in the London boroughs of Tower Hamlets and Camden, though smaller settlements are also to be found in cities such as Coventry and Bradford.

The Chinese form another numerically important group, although they differ from the large south Asian communities in that their patterns of settlement are far more dispersed. Most came to the UK in the fifties and sixties to escape high levels of unemployment in Hong Kong following the requisition of land from farmers for development purposes and an influx of refugees from the People's Republic of China during the Cultural Revolution. About 70% of Hong Kong Chinese speak Cantonese which also serves as a *lingua franca* for speakers of languages such as Hakka and Hokkien. Other ethnic Chinese include a refugee community of approximately 25,000 from Vietnam who also use Cantonese as a *lingua franca*, and a small numbers of Chinese professional professionals from Singapore and Malaysia, mainly speakers of Putonghua, who often came originally to the UK as students.

Community language teaching within the communities

Formal language classes organized by religious and other bodies within the minority communities burgeoned from the late seventies onwards. The Directory of Mother Tongue Teaching (LMP, 1985), for instance, reports classes in 18 different languages for over 8500 pupils in just three inner city Local Education Authorities (LEAs). These classes continue to thrive, often in spite of chronic shortages of funds, teaching materials and professional development opportunities for teachers.

Sources of funding for community language teaching are an ongoing concern. As we shall see below, pressure from the European Union and the publication of the 1985 Swann Report resulted in a more sympathetic response on the part of LEAs to requests for help from community organizations. It is important to note, however, that such support has always been minimal. LMP (1985) reports that the majority of classes included in the Directory of Mother Tongue Teaching received no help of any kind. Similarly, Bourne (1989) makes it clear that the main form of support for community classes was free accommodation. Other sources of funding for community language classes include charitable foundations such as the Sir John Cass Foundation, the Trust for London and the National Lotteries Charities Board.

The availability of suitably trained teachers is another recurrent issue. Teachers of community languages come from many different backgrounds. Some are qualified teachers, already working in mainstream schools; some have worked in schools only in the country of origin; the only qualification for many others will be that they themselves speak the community language in question. This diversity of backgrounds raises a range of issues.

Teachers trained abroad or with no formal qualifications may adopt a style of classroom management and an approach to learning and teaching which differ in important respects from those prevalent in British schools. This is not necessarily a problem in itself, since children are quite capable of adjusting to one style of teaching in the mainstream and another in a community context (Edwards, 1998). However, it is possible to argue that both mainstream and community school teachers would benefit from a better understanding of the learning experiences of all the children with whom they work. Qualified teachers who work in both mainstream and community contexts play an important role in mediating the learning environment in British schools to less experienced colleagues, both by example and by offering in-service training.

National networks of community language teachers offer increasing numbers of opportunities for professional development. The Chinese community is a useful case in point. Two associations currently co-ordinate Chinese classes. The UK Confederation of Chinese Schools, incorporating almost a hundred member schools, teaches through the medium of Cantonese and serves the longer standing Hong Kong Chinese community. The much smaller and more recent Chinese Teaching Group of the UK Chinese Students and Scholars Association (CSSA) teaches through the medium of Putonghua. Most pupils are the children of students from the People's Republic of China, although, following recent political developments, growing numbers of Hong Kong families are keen for their children to learn Putonghua. Liaison between the two associations is good and both provide a range of support for teachers in the form of conferences and seminars. An Ran (1999), for instance, discusses a seminar organized by the CSSA on teaching methods in which participants concluded that teachers in community classes should aim for a synthesis of Chinese and British teaching methods which speak to the experience of the children.

Various local and national initiatives also offer direct and indirect support for community language teachers. The Resource Unit for Supplementary and Mother Tongue Schools is an initiative set up in 1997 to bridge the gap between mainstream and voluntary sector schools. In addition to computer and photocopying facilities specifically tailored to the needs of community schools, it offers help on staff development, teaching and learning materials and evaluation and assessment. It is also involved in the production of guidelines for supplementary and mother tongue schools; and a directory of mother tongue schools. The Association for Language Learning is another association which encourages teachers of different languages to come together, for instance, for the purpose of materials production.

The Centre for Information on Language Teaching and Research (CILT) produces two series of information sheets on community languages: *Community Languages in Britain* is aimed at non-speakers of the languages; *Sources and Resources* lists teaching resources held in the CILT library and key contacts, such as professional associations. They also publish a twice yearly *Community Languages Bulletin*, which is a valuable forum for the exchange of information and ideas. The University of Reading AIMER (Access to Information of Multicultural Education Resources) database provides separate listings of resources on Bengali, Chinese, Gujarati, Panjabi and Urdu (www.ralic.reading.ac.uk).

Some progress is also being made in the area of curriculum development. Ali and McLagan (1998), for instance, provide a suggested curriculum framework for the teaching and learning of a community language as mother tongue for pupils aged 5-11. It is important to remember, however, that teachers in the UK are often dealing with languages taught widely in many other countries. The Internet is likely to be an increasingly important source of information, ideas and resources. In a review of useful sites, Anderson (1997) draws attention, for instance, to a range of resources for community language teaching.

Community language teaching within mainstream schooling

Although most community language teaching takes place within minority communities, mainstream schools have had varying levels of involvement over the years. There has often been a certain tension between the aspirations of teachers at a grassroots level and official attitudes which have veered between qualified support and indifference.

The 1976 draft Directive of the Council of the European Community on the Education of the Children of Migrant Workers was an important catalyst for the development of community language teaching within mainstream schooling. For the first time, there was discussion of the need for member states to teach the language and culture of migrants' children as part of the normal curriculum. In the UK, the Directive met with considerable resistance. Teacher organizations objected on the grounds that expansion in this area was unacceptable at a time of educational cutbacks and teacher unemployment, while the government foresaw problems related to costs, the difficulty of providing teachers and the inability of a decentralized education system to implement the Directive.

A revised - and considerably 'dumbed-down' - version of the Directive was published in 1977. It called on members states simply to 'promote' community language teaching and to offer tuition only 'in accordance with their national circumstances and legal systems'. There is little evidence to suggest that the government were willing or able to achieve even these very modest aims (Bellin, 1990). An EC (1984) report on the implementation of the Directive confirms this assessment. While 80% of eligible children in the Netherlands were receiving 'mother tongue teaching' at school, only 2% of children from linguistic minority children in the UK had access to state provision of this kind.

However, the appearance of the Directive at least succeeded in placing community language teaching on the agenda of mainstream educators for the first time. It is certainly the case that LEAs began to offer material support for community-run classes during this period. Community language teaching become part of the curriculum in small but growing numbers of schools. However, the publication of the Swann Report in 1985 represented a considerable setback. It argued that community languages were ultimately the responsibility of minority communities, and that support from LEAs be limited to the provision of accommodation, grants for books and teaching materials, in-service courses and advice from the advisory service. Bourne (1989) reports that three quarters of English LEAs responding to her survey were offering some level of support, but that this mainly took the form of free accommodation.

Today community language teaching remains the main responsibility of ethnic minority communities themselves. However, three factors - Britain's membership of the European Union, the importance of global trade and the shifting balance between world languages - give some reason to be optimistic about the future of community languages in mainstream education. Of these, Britain's entry into Europe has possibly had the most obvious impact on attitudes towards other languages. The Maastricht Treaty makes provision for the development of 'the European dimension in education through the teaching and dissemination of the languages of the Member States'; one of the general objectives for education of the white paper on 'Teaching and learning: towards the learning society' (EU, 1995) is to develop proficiency in three Community languages. Plurilingualism is also one of the policy objectives of the Council of Europe (Jones, 1998).

Entry into Europe has also had important implications for trade. Whereas the English-speaking nations provided the traditional markets for the UK, 60% of British exports are now destined for the European Union (Anderson, 2000); and the most important new markets are likely to be in the Far East and China (Hagen, 1998). Because of the ready availability of a well-educated multilingual workforce, London is emerging as an increasingly important centre both for pan-European customer service centres and the coordination of geographically dispersed operations in marketing, sales, human resources, finance and information technology (Land, 2000).

There has been intermittent pressure on government to diversify language provision in schools in response to the challenge of global markets, including initiatives such as the British Overseas Trade Board's (1979) report on languages and export performance, and Parker's (1986) report on oriental languages. Official policy on this question, however, has been rather contradictory: the Department of Education and Science (1988), for instance, accepted the validity of arguments for diversification of the modern foreign language curriculum and acknowledged the need for speakers of Japanese, Chinese and other Asian languages. However, it was not considered cost effective to provide teaching in these languages for pupils of compulsory school age. The creation of Language Colleges in England and Wales has been rather more successful in this respect: at the time of writing 58 colleges were teaching 18 languages other than French, German and Spanish. The growing support for diversification is also suggested by the Nuffield Foundations' Inquiry (Moys, 1998), endorsed by the prime minister, the head of the CBI and other public figures, into the UK's needs over the next 20 years.

The third factor which supports arguments for diversification in language teaching is the shifting balance between world languages. Numbers of native speakers of English will soon be outnumbered by speakers of English as a second language. Graddol (1998) also points to two further likely developments in the next 50 years. The first is that Arabic, Hindi/Urdu and Spanish are likely to have similar numbers of native speakers as English, leading to a 'cartel' of languages rather than the pre-eminence of English; the second is that other regional and national languages are likely to gain rather than lose speakers, leading to an increased awareness of the importance of languages such as Vietnamese and Polish.

An important factor in the debate on diversification in language teaching is the relative status of different languages. Despite their historical legacy of multilingualism, the British often behave as though monolingualism is the norm. English has been used as an instrument of social cohesion and control, both internally and in the colonies. Its current position as the international language of communication helps to reinforce both notions of superiority and the feeling that it is unnecessary to learn other languages.

Yet bilingualism has always been desirable amongst the social elite. The ability to read and write Latin, for instance, was associated with English intellectuals for hundreds of years; and, even today, it is predominantly the middle classes who send their children to French immersion programmes in Canada and to 'Welsh schools' in anglicized areas of Wales. The bilingualism of less powerful members of society, in contrast, is often undervalued or overlooked. European languages such as French, German and Spanish tend to be viewed a great deal more favourably than, for example, Indian languages such as Panjabi, Gujarati and Bengali (Edwards & Redfern, 1992). This widely reported perception of a linguistic hierarchy is supported by current education legislation. The national curriculum accepts 20 languages as the foundation subject languages. The list, however, is divided into the official languages of the EC and non-EC languages; students may choose a non-EC language only if they have already been offered the chance to study an official EC language.

Two developments have had a major impact on the provision of community language teaching in the mainstream. The first was the implementation in 1988 of a national curriculum which required such extensive changes in teaching practice that attention was effectively deflected from issues concerning linguistic and cultural diversity (Edwards, 1998). The second was the change in regulations concerning Section 11, the main source of additional funding in schools with significant numbers of children of New Commonwealth origin. Since first introduced in 1966, Section 11 monies had been used not only to support the teaching of English as a second language but also for anti-racist initiatives and community language teaching. The new rules required an exclusive emphasis on English teaching, leading to an inevitable erosion of community language teaching within the mainstream. At the secondary level, community languages, as documented above, continue to be taught as subjects. At the primary level, a small number of LEAs promote transitional bilingualism (Bourne, 1989) and employ bilingual staff to support new arrivals in their learning of English. There are many isolated examples of schools which continue to offer community languages as part of their programme of extra-curricular activities or in language awareness activities for all children. Overall, however, the ability of mainstream schools to support the bilingual development of children from linguistic minority communities has been seriously impaired by recent developments.

Common concerns for community and mainstream contexts

Two aspects of community language teaching impact upon teachers and children in both mainstream and community contexts: assessment and resources. Assessment emerges as a recurrent theme in discussions of community language teaching. The ability to speak, read and write another language is important 'currency' within mainstream education when translated into qualifications such as GCSEs and A-levels. Examination boards have provided syllabuses in a growing number of languages, though recent moves to remove 'uneconomic' languages such as Turkish and Arabic were only abandoned after extensive community lobbying. The fact that many universities do not accept community languages as entry qualifications threatens to compromise the viability of school-based A-level classes in more popular community languages (Sneddon, 2000).

Anderson (in press) points out that there is no national database which records the languages which are taught in the supplementary school sector for which no examinations are available. Minority communities have responded to the issue of accreditation in a variety of ways. The London-based Gujarati Academy offers its own examinations (see Dave, 1991) which are currently being brought into line with GCSE and A-levels. Some community language students are also making use of the Alternative Syllabus for Contemporary Languages (ASCL) provided by the Institute of Linguists. The thirty languages which have been assessed across all five levels of the syllabus include Arabic, Thai and Vietnamese.

Another recurring problem for the teaching of community languages is the shortage of suitable teaching materials. Very often books and courses produced in the home country fail to speak to the experience of locally-born children and the linguistic level for any given age range is far too advanced. As a result teachers have to spend a great deal of time in lesson preparation and the production of resources, an inefficient process which could be handled more effectively on a centralized level.

Materials development in the UK has tended to take place in a fairly haphazard way. Two major initiatives have been targeted at community language teaching in mainstream schools. The Inner London Education Authority, the European Commission and the Schools Council jointly sponsored the Mother Tongue Project (Tansley, Navaz & Roussou, 1985; Tansley, 1986) which developed resources for teaching Bengali and Greek at the primary level. The 'Community Languages in the Secondary School Curriculum Project' produced materials for the diverse situations encountered in the mainstream by teachers of Urdu, Panjabi and Italian. In addition, there has been a range of local initiatives. Bourne (1989), for instance, describes how one LEA supported teacher secondments and drew on supplementary training funds to produce a course in Urdu. The textbooks which the team developed were made available for sale both within and outside the LEA.

There has also been a marked growth of minority language publishing in the UK. Specialist publishers such as Mantra, Magi, Roy Yates and Partnership Publishing have led the way, demonstrating that there is indeed a market for children's books in both single language and dual language (English plus community language) format. Dual language books represent perhaps the most important multilingual resource in many classrooms. For sound economic reasons, these are often adaptations of existing good quality picture books in English. The success of the adaptation is, however, variable (Multilingual Resources for Children Project, 1995). The second language has to be fitted into the space available and is sometimes printed over a coloured background; the net effect is that it looks less 'important' than the English, thus defeating one of the main objectives of attempts to make books in community languages available to children. The range and quality of dual language books, however, is constantly improving (Edwards & Routh, 1999) and there is evidence of serious efforts to ensure that 'the other languages' are given equal status with English.

In a world where access to electronic communication is becoming increasingly common, it is easy to overlook the fact that, in many schools, the most important producers of multilingual resources for children are teachers, parents and children, and not commercial publishers. Projects like the Multilingual Word-processing Project based at the University of Reading (Chana, Edwards & Walker, 1997; 1998) have charted the potential of the new technologies for involving parents and others in the production of stories and other learning materials in a range of languages.

Conclusion

Accurate information on ethnic and linguistic diversity is essential for many aspects of economic, social and educational policy making. Because of the nature of the questions included in censuses and other surveys, it has been very impossible until recently to gauge the quality of estimates either of the number of languages spoken in the UK or the size of different speech communities. The application of GIS techniques in the mapping of the languages of London school children, however, has set important markers for the future development of data collection in this area. A range of problems remain which centre largely on the use of non-specialists for the collection of language data. None the less, there can be little doubt that the quality of information will improve as new systems ensure greater consistency in data collection. It is certainly to be hoped that the lessons learned during the Languages of London project will be rapidly applied to other parts of the UK and beyond.

An understanding of the nature and extent of linguistic diversity is, of course, simply the starting point for policy makers. Equally important is an appreciation of the impact of diversity both on the host society and more recent settlers. As the more recently arrived linguistic minorities have become established and have developed more political power, they have begun to articulate both the central role of language in their individual and collective identities and the kind of support which is necessary to transmit these languages from one generation to the next.

The response from both the wider community and official quarters has tended to be highly variable. The overarching view would seem to be one of tolerance without commitment, and responsibility for language maintenance has been placed very firmly on the communities themselves. It remains to be seen whether commercial imperatives such as membership of the European Union and the forces of globalization have at least a modifying effect on attitudes of this kind.

Note

* This chapter develops and extends issues first raised in 'Community languages' in G. Price (ed.) (2000).

References

Ali, A. and McLagan, P. (eds) (1998) *Curriculum framework for mother tongue teaching to Bengali for pupils 5-11 years.* London: CILT and Tower Hamlets.

Alladina, S. (1985) Research methodology for language use surveys in Britain: a critical review. In P. Nelde (ed.) *Methods in contact linguistic research* (pp. 233-240). Bonn: Dümmler.

Anderson, J. (1997) Keeping in touch through the Internet. *The community language bulletin* 1, 8-9.

Anderson, J. (2000) Which language? An embarrassment of choice. In K. Field (ed.) *Issues in modern foreign languages teaching.* London: Routledge (in press).

Baker, P. and Eversley, J. (eds) (2000) *Multilingual capital: the languages of London's schoolchildren and their relevance to economic, social and educational policies.* London: Battlebridge Publications.

Baker, P. and Mohieldeen, Y. (2000) The languages of London's schoolchildren. In P. Baker and J. Eversley (eds) *Multilingual capital: the languages of London's schoolchildren and their relevance to economic, social and educational policies* (pp. 5-60). London: Battlebridge Publications

Baker, P. and Sanderson, A. (2000) Towards obtaining better data on the languages of London's schoolchildren. In P. Baker and J. Eversley (eds) *Multilingual capital: the languages of London's schoolchildren and their relevance to economic, social and educational policies* (pp. 87-90). London: Battlebridge Publications.

Bellin, W. (1990) The EEC Directive on the Education of the Children of Migrant Workers: a comparison of the Commission's proposed directive and the Council directive together with a parallel text. *Polyglot* 2, fiche 3.

Bourne, J. (1989) *Moving into the mainstream: LEA provision for bilingual pupils.* Windsor: NFER.

British Overseas Trade Board (1979) *Foreign languages for overseas trade: report of the study group*. London: BOTB.

Chana, U., Edwards, V. and Walker, S. (1997) Hidden resources: multilingual wordprocessing in the primary school. *Race, ethnicity and education* 1 (1), 49-61.

Chana, U., Edwards, V. and Walker, S. (1998) In their own write: wordprocessing in Urdu. In P. Goodwin (ed.) (1999) *The literate classroom* (pp. 99-105). London: David Fulton.

Dalby, D. (1999) *The Linguasphere register of the world's languages and speech communities*. Hebron, Wales: The Linguasphere Press.

Dave, J. (1991) The Gujarati speech community. In S. Alladina and V. Edwards (eds) *Multilingualism in the British Isles* (Vol.2) (pp. 88-102). London: Longman.

Department of Education and Science (DES) (1988) *Modern languages and the school curriculum: a statement of policy*. London: HMSO.

Edwards, V. (1986) *Language in a black community*. Clevedon: Multilingual Matters

Edwards, V. (1995) *The other languages: a guide to multilingual classrooms*. Reading: Reading and Language Information Centre, The University of Reading.

Edwards, V. (1998) *The power of Babel: Teaching and Llarning in multilingual classrooms*. Stoke-on-Trent: Trentham Books.

Edwards, V. and Redfern, A. (1992) *The world in a classroom: language and education in Britain and Canada*. Clevedon: Multilingual Matters.

Edwards, V. and Routh, C. (1999) Recent multilingual resources for children. In R. Stones (ed.) *A multicultural guide to children's books 0-16+* (pp. 12-13). London and Reading: Books for keeps and the Reading and Language Information Centre, The University of Reading.

European Communities (EC) (1984) *Report on the implementation of Directive 77/486/EEC on the education of children of migrant workers*. Brussels: EC.

European Union (1995) *Teaching and learning: towards the learning society*. Brussels.

Graddol, D. (1998) Will English be enough? In A. Moys (ed.) *Where are we going with languages?* (pp.24-33). London: Nuffield Foundation.

Hagen, S. (1998) What does global trade mean for UK languages? In A. Moys (ed.) *Where are we going with languages?* (pp. 14-23). London: Nuffield Foundation.

Inner London Education Authority (ILEA) (1978; 1981; 1983; 1985; 1987) *Language census*. London: Research & Statistics Department, ILEA.

Jones, S. (1998) How does Europe promote languages? In A. Moys (ed.) *Where are we going with languages?* (pp. 6-13). London: Nuffield Foundation.

Land, A. (2000) Languages speak volumes for global business. In P. Baker and J. Eversley (eds) *Multilingual capital: the languages of London's schoolchildren and their relevance to economic, social and educational policies* (p. 71). London: Battlebridge Publications.

Li, P.L. (2000) An indicator for health needs of minority ethnic communities in the capital. In P. Baker & J. Eversley (eds) *Multilingual capital: the languages of London's schoolchildren and their relevance to economic, social and educational policies* (p. 83). London: Battlebridge Publications.

Linguistic Minorities Project (LMP) (1985) *The other languages of England*. London.

Moys, A. (ed.) (1998) *Where are we going with languages?* London: Nuffield Foundation.

Multilingual Resources for Children Project (MRC) (1995) *Building bridges: multilingual Resources for Children*. Clevedon: Multilingual Matters.

Nicholas, J. (1994) *Language diversity surveys as agents of change*. Clevedon: Multilingual Matters.

Price, G. (ed.) (2000) *Languages of Britain and Ireland*. Oxford: Blackwell.

Ran, A. (1999) *Learning in two languages and cultures: the experiences of mainland Chinese families in Britain*. Unpublished PhD thesis, University of Reading.

Rosen, H. and Burgess, T. (1980) *Languages and dialects of London school children*. London: Ward Lock Educational.

Sebba, M. (1993) *London Jamaican: Language systems in interaction*. London: Longman.

Sneddon, R. (2000) *Language and literacy in the multilingual family*. Unpublished PhD thesis, University of London.

Storkey, M. (2000) Using the schools language data to estimate the total numbers of speakers of London's top 40 languages. In P. Baker & J. Eversley (eds) *Multilingual capital: the languages of London's schoolchildren and their relevance to economic, social and educational policies* (pp. 63-66). London: Battlebridge Publications.

Swann, L. (1985) *Education for all*. London: HMSO.

Tansley, P. (1986) *Community languages in primary education*. Windsor.

Tansley, P., Navaz, H. and Roussou, M. (1985) *Working with many languages: a handbook for community language teachers*. London: School Curriculum Development Committee.

Maghrebine Arabic in France

DOMINIQUE CAUBET

After the recognition of *Arabe dialectal* (colloquial Arabic) as a *langue de la France* (language of France), together with Berber, Yiddish, Romani and West Armenian, the status of Maghrebine Arabic has been evolving fast under the labelling of 'non-territorial languages' since 1999. This chapter will try to define the place this language holds in France. When dealing with questions of status, actual use, and learning and teaching, one should not use the word 'Arabic' without a qualifier such as Classical Arabic, Standard Arabic, Colloquial Arabic, Moroccan Arabic and so on. I will examine the notion of Maghrebine Arabic (MA), and then discuss demographic trends regarding the extension of Maghrebine Arabic in France and its sociolinguistic settings. Moreover, I will analyse the educational status of MA in relation to Modern Standard Arabic (MSA) at primary, secondary and university levels, and the evolution on the front of the French *baccalauréat*. I will conclude with the new situation created by the recognition of MA as a language of France.

Terminological issues

With respect to the Arabic 'cluster' (David Cohen calls it *l'élément arabe*), it is not neutral to decide what is a language and what is a dialect. From a linguistic point of view, MSA, Moroccan Arabic and Algerian Arabic form separate linguistic systems that function differently, especially at the level of syntax or such categories as aspect or nominal determination; this is enough for me to decide that they are different languages, with, more often than not, lack of intercomprehension (between e.g. Algerian Arabic and MSA or Yemeni Arabic and Moroccan Arabic). Therefore I claim that Moroccan Arabic, Algerian Arabic, Tunisian Arabic and indeed Classical Arabic are separate languages.

The status of Maghrebine Arabic is different. One must not forget - and this is largely disregarded - that there is a traditional literary *koine*, which differs completely from Classical or Standard Arabic, and which seems to be common to the whole Maghreb. It is mostly transmitted by oral tradition, *melhun, maâluf,* or poetry; it differs from everyday speech and requires oral learning like any literary language. It is elaborate, archaic, and has specific syntactic constructions and vocabulary. It is used and understood throughout Morocco, Algeria and Tunisia. Cohen (1994: 11) defines it as follows (my translation): '(...) the common interpretation of 'diglossia' contributed to the ignorance of this fundamental fact: the different groups of Arabophones, Muslims, Jews, Christians, possessed important types of literature, poetry, prose, chronicles, etc., composed in literary *koine*-s, covering vast areas of understanding, and presenting the same traits of archaism and formalism as any literary language in the world. This is where the diglossia of the people stood'. This literary elaborate level was and is still often used by people who cannot read or write MSA, mostly in the old cities, such as craftsmen, barbers, shopkeepers, and also some people of Bedouin tribes. Today, this variety is used by the new creators in the theatre, poets and songwriters. This traditional version is generally protected by the various countries of the Maghreb as part of their national patrimony.

Independence, by closing the borders, helped reinforce the existence of national *koine*-s, which clearly allows us to speak nowadays of Algerian Arabic, Moroccan Arabic and Tunisian Arabic. In the last thirty years, the development of transport, social mobility and exodus from the country-side triggered contact and mixing of the various local dialects. Koinisation was also produced by the media and the circulation of music (songs); local accents and lexical peculiarities remain, but do not affect the existence of a national *koine*, which obviously includes variation. Recent research in sociolinguistics refers to changes in the ways of speech of border regions of Morocco, such as Oujda, where, outside the family circle, young people tend to adopt the *koine* rather than stick to the local dialect. Moreover, one of the Maghrebine dialects of Arabic has developed into a national language inside Europe, i.e. *il malti* (Maltese). Of course the circumstances were very different from those of Muslim countries where the link with CA cannot be broken, and from those of Arab countries where MSA has been developed parallel to CA. Since the independence of the island, Maltese has been the national language of Malta. It is written in Latin script and fulfils the same spectrum of requirements as any other national language. There is literary Maltese, standard Maltese, a normative grammar, an official spelling, and there are dialects. Although from a linguistic and historical point of view Maltese is a dialect of Arabic, it is nowadays recognised as a language of its own, without reference to Arabic. This shows that any 'dialect' can develop into a 'language', if the political situation allows for it.

More and more voices today claim that the Maghreb has a specific culture in the Arab world. It is not as monolithic as some of its political leaders claim; indeed, its history is plural on the religious level (with strong Jewish, but also Christian or Animist communities) and on the level of origin (Berber, of course, but also Phoenician, Roman, Norman, Vandal, Arabic, Turkish, French, Spanish, Italian, Maltese ...). Up to now, there is a linguistic plurality for different domains: two mother tongues (Berber and Algerian Arabic, Moroccan or Tunisian Arabic), Classical Arabic for religion, MSA at school, French at university, and Spanish, Italian, or English. Codeswitching is also a very common phenomenon among the socio-cultural elite of (Maghrebine Arabic/French) bilinguals. Codeswitching is stigmatised, but it is also a sign of social success envied by those who do not master it. This plurality also applies to the French situation, if one looks at it closely.

Historically, the relations between France and North Africa go back to 1830. The French Jews who came from Algeria and who have had French nationality since 1870, with the *Décret Crémieux* are now completely integrated in French society. Although North African Arabic is no longer the mother tongue of those born after 1962, some of them now publicly claim their origin and their culture. Forty years after the war of Algeria, both communities (Muslim immigrants and Jewish repatriates) are slowly accepting the fact that they can share emotions via a culture, that of North Africa, inside a plural France.

Demographic trends

There are no official language figures, because there is no census concerning mother tongues in France; so one can only work by approximation. The figures for January 1994 show a total of 1,393,165 inhabitants in France originating from the Maghreb, who still retain their nationality of origin: 572,652 Moroccans, 614,207 Algerians and 206,336 Tunisians (cf. EuroStat, 1997). To these, one must add the people who have French nationality. Other figures give, for people of Moroccan origin (1992), 689,020, 69% being born in Morocco and 31% in France (see Masthoff, 1998: 14). This may include (it is not specified) people with French nationality.

It is still impossible from these figures to decide which language they speak: North-African Arabic or Berber? An estimation is given by Chaker (1997) for the Berberophones of Algerian origin, which he estimates to represent 40% of the people of Algerian origin (2 million, 2/3 with French nationality in 1996); from this one can deduce that the number of Arabophones of Algerian origin is around 1,200,000. For Morocco he claims that 50% of the immigrants could be Berberophone; this would mean about 275,000 Moroccans according to EuroStat, and 350,000 according to Masthoff. To this we must add the Tunisians (200,000), which gives a total of 1,700,000; when adding those who have French citizenship, 2 million seems reasonable as an approximation. For Berberophones, the figure given by Chaker for France is about 1 million. Recently, a much higher figure appeared in *Le Monde de l'Education* (Dec. 1999: 47), stating that 4 million people speak Arabic in France; this is probably exaggerated (no source was given). An interesting estimation for younger generations, as to the mastering of Maghrebine Arabic and Berber at the age of 18-20 years, is the number of students taking *Arabe dialectal* as an optional test for the French *baccalauréat*. Table 1 gives the figures of registered candidates for 1998 and 1999 (*baccalauréat général et technologique*).

Table 1   French *baccalauréat*, with partition of candidates taking North African languages

1998	Total registered	Total Maghrebine Arab	Total Berber
bac général	354,652	4,181 (1.17%)	
bac technologique	178,743	4,188 (2.34%)	
Total	533,395	8,369 (1.57%)	1,083 (0.20%)

1999	Total registered	Total Maghrebine Arab	Total Berber
bac général	344,243	4,663 (1.35%)	
bac technologique	185,368	5,174 (2.79%)	
Total	529,611	9,886 (1.87%)	1,751 (0.33%)

Since a number of youngsters do not register for the *baccalauréat*, the actual percentage is probably higher, at least 2 to 3% of an age-bracket (estimated 676,000), i.e. 15,000 to 20,000, which is a very high figure. As to the vitality of MA, the rate of success at the exam is quite high (72%), indicating a mastering of the language, especially given the fact that the test was written (1995-1999). MA is still known and spoken in younger generations. Indeed, the reason why this test became written instead of oral is that the candidates were too numerous (around 10,000). The *académies* could not find enough teachers to test the students orally and threatened to stop organising the exam in 1995 (see Caubet, 2000). This must be considered as another proof of the vitality of MA in France.

The vitality of MA and its culture in France

As we have seen, Maghrebine Arabic is spoken in the families in France where it is transmitted orally. More often than not, the speakers are not proud of their mother tongues, which are referred to as 'dialects, patois', and the noble language, for ideological and religious reasons, is Classical Arabic. Fortunately, there are circumstances in which the mother tongues can regain pride and a positive image. The fashion for youngsters is very much inspired by the looks of youths of North African origin, and so are the ways of speech. Cultural productions, music, films and dance have been very present as well on the French cultural scene since the late nineties. Paris is said to be the capital of world music. This is certainly the case for raï and rap in various languages, such as French, English, Occitan, Breton or Algerian Arabic. Artists like Khaled, Mami, Faudel, Rachid Taha, Zebda, the *Orchestre National de Barbès*, Amazigh Kateb (Kateb Yacine's son) and his group Gnawa Diffusion, whose fame is national, convey a very positive image for youngsters who can be proud to show that they know these rhythms and understand the language. Several comedians have been very successful in the last three or four years, e.g. Gad Elmaleh, Jamel Debbouze, Mohand Fellag, Eric et Ramzi, Elie Kakou, Elie Semoun, of Muslim or Jewish origin, and before them, Smaïn and Michel Boujenah. A number of films have had heroes of Maghrebine origin, mostly in the suburbs, e.g. *La Haine, Raï, Taxi, le Gone du Chaâba*. There are also many films on the Jewish community, Alexandre Arcady's films, but also *La vérité si je mens!* (a popular success in 1998). A series of words and expressions have entered the variety of French slang, which is spoken by everyone in the suburbs. The general intonation of suburban French sounds strangely North African. In the mid nineties, several books were published on the theme of the language of young people (see, e.g. Girard & Kernel, 1996). Words such as *zarma* (as if, so-called), *kiffer* (to like), *gaori/gouère* (non-Muslim), *foutre la darwa* (mess up), *khalouf* (pork), *r'nouch* (cops < snakes), and many more have entered the language of youths in the suburbs, but also the centres of towns.

We have seen that in France a great number of citizens speak North African Arabic. Also one must not forget the Jewish communities who are now completely integrated, but retain memory of their 'Maghrebinity'; we know that about 140,000 Jews among one million people left Algeria in 1962. The North African dialects transmitted in the families are often very conservative. People tend to speak the way they spoke when they left their country, some 30 years ago, regardless of the changes that have occurred since then in the countries of origin. It is very interesting for Arabic dialectology that one can find varieties that have disappeared in the Maghreb. It is even more so for the Jewish dialects, which are hardly spoken in the Maghreb anymore. Another phenomenon has been observed in Moroccan communities: Berberophone families have been known to change their family language to Moroccan Arabic as a conscious family policy (see El Minaoui, 1998).

In France, codeswitching is very common in these bilingual communities. Among the parents, MA is generally the matrix language and French is embedded, whereas the children often have French as their matrix language and MA is embedded. Recent research has also shown that the home language can affect the intonation of French, even when the children only have a receptive knowledge of the language. All this is very much linked to identity problems that have recently been described (see El Minaoui, 1998; 1999; Melliani, 1999 and Caubet, 1998).

Teaching MA and CA in France

France has a long tradition of teaching Classical Arabic and Colloquial Arabic. It dates back to the 16th century in the *Collège des Lecteurs Royaux*. Arabic was even introduced in secondary education in 1700 when it was taught by the Jesuits in what was to become the prestigious *Lycée Louis le Grand* (see Dumortier, 1996). In 1795 Bonaparte created *L'école spéciale des langues orientales* where four languages were taught at first, among which Arabic; Colloquial Arabic was part of the syllabus at the earliest stage.

France was then interested in the Middle East, and the introduction of North African Arabic coincides with the colonisation of Algeria from 1830. The teaching of Arabic in secondary education dates back to the beginning of the 20th century, and the question of what exactly should be taught has been debated since.

Primary education

At French primary schools, Arabic is being taught within two different frameworks, the first being ELCO (*éducation de langue et culture d'origine*), and the other, more interesting but very limited, as foreign languages subject. A number of studies have been done on ELCO (see Obdeijn & De Ruiter, 1998). The languages were introduced in France on the basis of bilateral agreements with the countries of origin, i.e. Tunisia in 1974, Morocco in 1975, and Algeria in 1981. The teachers are recruited and paid by the countries of origin. The introduction of ELCO was linked to migration. Initially, these programmes aimed at training the children in case they would go back to their home countries. At first, there was no discussion of this argument. Since the children were supposed to return, they simply had to be taught in the same language as in the countries of origin, with the same programmes. Table 2 gives an overview of primary school enrolment.

Table 2 Overview of primary school enrolment (Sources: Masthoff, 1998 and DEP, *Direction de l'Evaluation et de la Prospective*)

Country	Children at school	ELCO 84/85	Children at school	ELCO 90/91
Algeria	196,419	36,345	150,025	12,000
Morocco	137,754	10,427	157,073	28,000
Tunisia	48,155	8,471	49,678	9,100
Total	382,328	55,243	356,776	49,100

In 1996, there were 35,306 Moroccan children taking ELCO. There were 228 Moroccan teachers in France in 94/95, and 277 in 96/97 (see Masthoff, 1998). There were 450 teachers for all three Maghreb countries in 1998. The figures for Moroccan and Tunisian pupils have been stable since 1992, but the number of Algerian pupils has decreased tremendously.

When it became clear that there would be little return migration, the question came up whether the mother tongues should not be taught instead of MSA, but there was strong opposition on the part of the authorities of the countries of origin (see Neyreneuf, 1997; Berque, 1985). In a report to the Minister of Education, Berque (1985) recommended to introduce *langue et culture d'apport*, instead of *origin*. This teaching should concern all the children in the class and not only those of North African origin, and they should receive an introduction into the plurality of civilisations. This idea was so revolutionary at that time that it was not even considered. Fifteen years later, this question came back on the scene with a similar rationale. All citizens are presumed equal in France, whatever their origin, and all children should be given the same treatment at school and be taught the same subjects.

Experiments are being carried out in primary schools within the programme launched in 1995 for the introduction of foreign languages in all primary schools. Most schools chose English, but the official list comprises a choice of six possible languages, i.e. English, German, Spanish, Italian, Portuguese and Arabic. In the latter case, Colloquial Arabic was officially chosen by the *Inspection d'arabe* for this programme. Moroccan Arabic was chosen in Montpellier in 1996 and in Mantes-la-Jolie in 1997 (see Caubet, 1999). In both cases, secondary school teachers were seconded to do this. Both experiments were carried out with all the children in the class. This meant a lot of persuasion on the part of the teachers for the parents to accept it. But once accepted, it proved to work out very positively. The children of North African origin felt proud that their culture had a place at school and that their parents approved of the choice. Only a few parents of French origin in Montpellier were reluctant, but most of their children had no prejudice and felt happy to learn a new language.

Since the debate on traditional ELCO seems to have come to a dead end, the question is now as to whether such ELCO should be maintained at all. It is clear that most Maghrebins will stay in France, and ELCO seems to be obsolete for them, and felt as a means to maintain a kind of control by the countries of origin over communities in France. What was experimented in Montpellier and Mantes, might be promoted much more, given the fact that all children in France are part of the plural culture.

Secondary education: the case of Algeria and France

Arabic was taught in Algeria in the *Médersa-s* in the second part of the 19th century, but the systematic introduction of Arabic in public Algerian education dates back to the new instructions for the teaching of *langues vivantes* in 1902, probably inspired by William Marçais who was then Director of the *Médersa* in Algiers. This situation is different from all European countries, where Arabic could only be learned at university level. The Algerian instructions clearly separate what they call *Arabe littéraire* from *Arabe dialectal*. They are taught separately, and make use of different textbooks (see Desparmet, 1907 for the programmes, see *Revue Universitaire*, 15 April 1905). This situation prevailed until the independence of Algeria in 1962. One could take MSA as a first language (first year of secondary education) and Colloquial Arabic as a second language (third year). Already in 1930, there was an attempt to change the programmes and to rule out Maghrebine Arabic, which Marçais (who was then Professor at the *Collège de France*) violently opposed (see *Revue de l'Enseignement Public*, 1930 and 1931; incidentally, this is the first time the concept of diglossia was used to describe the situation of Arabic). Colloquial Arabic stayed on the syllabus until 1962.

Since 1962 and until recently, the only Arabic taught in secondary education in France is what is strangely labelled *Arabe littéral* (MSA). It was only taught in the best *lycées* of Paris or the provincial capitals in Southern France, along the lines of the Orientalist tradition. Children of the elite also chose Chinese or Russian. The arrival of migrant populations completely changed this situation, first by significantly increasing the number of pupils, and secondly by entailing the migration of the teaching of Arabic towards the suburbs which both at the social and educational levels soon transformed into ghettos. This triggered a reaction whereby parents stopped choosing Arabic as a language of the roots for their children (from 1991), and decided to adopt English as a language of social promotion for their children rather than Arabic. In fact, there was also disappointment as to the difficulty of learning MSA. It meant putting in a big effort, with the learning of a new graphic system, and it had the paradoxical result that the children were put in the ghetto classes of the *collège*, because Arabic was only taken by children of North African origin. So the investment was soon regarded as not profitable from a social perspective. In four years time, between 1990 and 1994, the number of pupils taking MSA decreased by 50%. The statistics only go back to 1982, but we know that, from 1973/1974 to 1983/1984 the figure was multiplied by ten (see Dumortier, 1996). Since 1983 had about 10,000 pupils, we can deduce that the figure in 1973 was around 1000. Table 3 gives a longitudinal overview of MSA enrolment in French secondary schools.

Table 3   MSA enrolment in French secondary schools (first, second or third language, adapted from Dumortier (1996), completed by figures from Midad (CNDP)

82/83	83/84	84/85	85/86	86/87	87/88	88/89	89/90	90/91
8,000	10,000	12,000	13,000	14,000	10,000	10,000	12,000	13,000

91/92	92/93	93/94	94/95	95/96	96/97	97/98	98/99	99/00
10,500	7,929	7,500	6,557	6,500	?	5,700?	5,643	5,993

The *agregation* dates back to 1906, but the *Capès* (qualifying exams for teachers, the first being more prestigious) was only initiated in 1976; its creation is linked to the policy of family reunion from 1974, whereby wives and children massively started to arrive in France. Like all *langues vivantes*, MSA can be chosen as first, second or third language (LV1, 2 or 3, respectively in first, third or fifth year of secondary education). As LV1 or LV2, it was only chosen by children of migrant origin, and in LV3 by more mixed audiences; LV1 is regressing fast:

Table 4   MSA enrolment as LV1-3 (Source: Midad (n. 8 and 11) - Direction de la programmation et du développement - Ministère de l'éducation nationale. (*Collège* represents the first four years, *lycée*, the next three years; *lycée professionnel* is oriented towards professional)).

1998 - LV1: 991 LV2: 2,845 LV3: 1,886		
collège: 2,017	*lycée*: 3,683 (général et technologique)	*professionnel*: 175

1999 - LV1: 778 LV2:? LV3: 1,903		
collège: 2,101	*lycée*: 3,605 (général et technologique)	*professionnel*: 187

A recent trend among the *Inspection d'arabe*, responsible for secondary education, tends to state that Arabic should be taught in secondary education 'in its globality', i.e. to pretend that Colloquial Arabic should be taught. When one looks closely at the instructions and programmes, this is far from obvious. One finds formulations like 'the teacher will take advantage of his knowledge of Colloquial Arabic and that of his pupils dynamise the class (*Orientations pour l'enseignement de l'arabe en collège*, *nouveaux programmes, Ministère de l'éducation nationale,* January 1996). And when one looks up the programme in the same *Orientations* ..., Colloquial Arabic is not mentioned. Recently, a new wording came up, containing a double negation: 'So one can not say that Colloquial Arabic is not being taught'.

Although it is interesting that the Inspection considers the introduction of Colloquial Arabic in secondary education, the teachers have received no training whatsoever to do so. If Maghrebine Arabic was to be taught properly by the teachers, who are either of French (38% in 1992 according to Masthoff, 1998: 25) or Oriental origin (no figures), they should be trained and the contents of the programmes should be defined clearly, including the phonetics and morphosyntax of North African Arabic. This new trend has had devastating results when applied to Colloquial Arabic at the *baccalauréat* (see below). As a conclusion, it can be claimed that Maghrebine Arabic (or any other Arabic dialect) is not being taught as such in secondary education.

In 1996, together with five other universities, CERBAM-INALCO entered a programme for home language tuition (Comenius project 26358-cp-1-96-1-c2, *Home Language Instruction for Turkish and North African Children,* coordinated by Tilburg University). Teams from five European countries (France, Germany, the Netherlands, Britain and Spain), are working on four home languages, i.e. Moroccan Arabic, Rifian Berber, Turkish and Kurdish. The French team started to work on a handbook and a textbook for 16-18 years old, as a preparation for the *baccalauréat* (see Benjelloun, 1998). The textbook for 12-14 years old is under print. The pilot study was carried out in two French *Lycées, Lycée La Hotoie* in Amiens (in 1996 and 1997) and *Lycée Polyvalent* in Toulouse (in 1998). It was a great success, because a number of pupils who were not taking MSA came to the classes and received an introduction to Arabic; they did fairly well at the exam and were able to gain some pride as well.

University education

For a long time Arabic was taught essentially at the *Ecole des Langues Orientales* (now INALCO) in Paris. The first chair was occupied by Antoine-Isaac Silvestre de Sacy (1795-1838) who taught both *Arabe littéraire* and *Arabe vulgaire,* as was specified in the decree creating the institution (see Labrousse, 1995: 60). Dom Raphaël de Monachis was nominated as *professeur adjoint d'Arabe vulgaire* (Egyptian Arabic; Champollion was his student in 1807) from 1803 to 1816. In 1819, an actual chair was created labelled *Arabe vulgaire* and this lasted until 1916.

The present-day situation with two chairs for Colloquial Arabic, one for *Arabe Maghrébin* and one for *Arabe Oriental* dates back to the beginning of the century (respectively 1916 and 1909; see Colin, 1948). INALCO now offers a full curriculum in Maghrebine Arabic (Licence BA since 1993; Maîtrise MA since 1996). It also offers DEA (*Diplôme d'études approfondies*; one-year diploma previous to PhD) and Doctorates (PhD) in Colloquial Arabic. Classical Arabic is being taught in a number of universities in France, but nowhere else is there an official status for Colloquial Arabic. Usually (but not always) the students are given a few hours of initiation, but can only graduate in MSA/CA. In the past, there was a chair for *Arabe dialectal* and one for Berber at the University of Algiers. They were both suppressed at the time of independence in 1962.

The optional *arabe dialectal* at the *baccalauréat*

This test is part of the numerous options a candidate can chose in order to gain a few extra marks at the *baccalauréat*. Since the beginning of the 20th century, the French *baccalauréat* has allowed people who have knowledge of a home/second language to take this test. Until 1994, this was an oral test, where all one needed to prove was that one could take part in a conversation. Because the number of candidates became too large (in particular those with a MA and Berber background), and the exams very difficult to organise, the choice was made, under the influence of the *Inspection d'arabe*, to transform the oral test into a written one (see Caubet, 1997; 1999; 2000). INALCO was chosen by the Ministry of Education to organise the exams and to evaluate the results for a list of 29 languages, including *Arabe dialectal* and Berber. From the beginning, Maghrebine Arabic has represented 65% to 77% of all written papers in all optional languages. Table 5 gives a longitudinal overview of evaluated papers.

For *Arabe dialectal*, a choice of transcription was offered in Arabic and Latin script being a simplified version of what linguists use. The written exam had another interesting result: students were surprised and proud to realise that their mother tongue could be written and that they could actually read it.

Unfortunately, in September 1999 we learned that this *Arabe dialectal* had been ruled out by the *Inspection d'arabe* from the test, without any consultation with INALCO who organised the exam. It was replaced by a test in Arabic (without qualifier), presupposing knowledge of MSA; the candidates should write ten pages of documents in MSA. Knowing that this test is by definition not prepared at school, one wonders where the pupils could have learned to read MSA, because it is not transmitted in

Table 5 Longitudinal overview of evaluated papers for the *baccalauréat* (% between brackets)

Languages	1995	1996	1997	1998	1999
Maghrebine Arabic	5,225 (65.1)	6,976 (74.9)	7,517 (74.9)	8,253 (77.7)	9,296 (75.5)
Algerian Arabic	2,097 (40.0)	2,374 (34.0)	2,570 (34.2)	2,638 (32.0)	2,848 (30.6)
Moroccan Arabic	1,983 (38.0)	3,157 (45.2)	3,380 (45.0)	3,866 (46.8)	4,231 (45.6)
Tunisian Arabic	1,045 (20.0)	1,448 (20.7)	1,567 (20.8)	1,749 (21.2)	2,127 (22.8)
Arabic script	2,058 (40.1)	2,465 (35.3)	2,527 (33.6)	2,510 (30.4)	2,171 (25.5)
Latin script	3,071 (59.9)	4,511 (64.7)	4,990 (66.4)	5,743 (69.6)	6,348 (74.5)
Total 29 languages	7,958	9,312	10,035	10,624	12,317
Berber	1,448 (18.2)	1,143 (12.3)	1,277 (12.7)	1,083 (10.2)	1,750 (14.2)
Oriental Arabic	155 (0.2)	172 (0.18)	216 (0.2)	230 (0.2)	225 (0.2)
27 other languages	1,173 (14.7)	1,030 (11.0)	1,025 (10.2)	1,058 (9.9)	1,046 (8.5)

the families. Moreover, since the test is now labelled *Arabic*, all the pupils taking Arabic at school (i.e. those who should be able to read MSA) are excluded from the optional test (you can take the same language twice), whereas until 1999 they could choose MSA plus MA as an option (*Arabe littéral* and *Arabe dialectal* being considered as two languages).

Arabe dialectal has been tested independently from *Arabe littéral* since 1902 in France. This suppression is a direct application of the new trend of Arabic 'in its globality' referred to before. It penalises the pupils, and one wonders what the teaching of Arabic has to gain from such a rigid position. For 2000, the number of registrations has gone down tremendously, i.e. 4441 for *arabe* (= MSA + *Arabe dialectal*) instead of 10,111 (*Arabe*

Table 6   French *baccalauréat*, registration of candidates taking 'Arabic' (no qualifier)

2000	Total registered	Total Arabe Maghrébin
bac général	345,013	2,110 (0.61%)
bac technologique	189,037	2,331 (1.23%)
Total	534,050	4,441 (0.83%)

dialectal only) in 1999. The new test shows a drastic reduction, from 1.57% of the candidates in 1998, 1.87% in 1999, to 0.83% in 2000 (see Table 1).

An inspection of the new test has been launched to measure the implications of the change; the first figures show that only 25 to 30% (compared to 1999) took the test (i.e. a decrease of 70% of the registered candidates). It is hoped that the Ministry will reconsider its decision and restore the 1999 test for 2001. Moreover, this decision appears to be in complete contradiction with the government's position on the European Charter for Regional and Minority languages, where *Arabe dialectal* has been listed as one of the languages of France.

The European Charter for Regional and Minority Languages

Several reports were ordered by prime minister Lionel Jospin before the signing of the Charter of the Council of Europe on 7 May 1999: one on the political significance was written by Bernard Poignant (1998), the second one on the constitutional significance by Guy Carcassonne (1998). The Carcassonne report opened an interesting breach, differentiating between migrant languages which are excluded from the Charter, and non-territorial languages (my translation): 'This means it could apply only to those languages which are both spoken by a significant number of French citizens, and which are not the official language of another country. (...) The crossed application of both criteria would lead to a list that would be short, but would concern a great number of people, because not only Romani and Yiddish, but certainly Berber should be on the list'. Guy Carcassonne includes Berber, but explicitly excludes Arabic (without a qualifier): 'The situation of Arabic is very different [from Berber], not because of the very high figure of French citizens who have it as one of their mother tongues, but because of the international situation. (...) Since

Arabic is today the sixth language spoken in the world, i.e. ahead of French, it is difficult not to see it as a foreign language, whichever criteria we use'.

Carcassonne considered Arabic as a monolithic whole, as is often the case in the international context. Bernard Cerquiglini (1999), director of INALF (*Institut National de la Langue Française*) and vice-president of the *Conseil Supérieur de la Langue Française*, was asked in December 1998 to list the languages that could qualify for France's signature of the Charter. He handed in his report in April 1999. To the surprise of many, he numbered 75 languages, among which he defined five languages 'without a territory', i.e. not the official languages of particular countries. Apart from Berber and *Arabe dialectal*, he mentioned Yiddish, Romani chib and Western Armenian. In doing so, he was the first to give recognition to the actual mother tongues spoken in the communities originating from the Maghreb. This decision will no doubt have some serious implications for MA. It has been recognised officially, is integrated into the regional languages network, and it may benefit from some concrete measures, such as its slow introduction in primary education. Its status has definitely changed, and it is fascinating to witness such a process.

Conclusion

MA's position should in theory now be stronger, but this is also the time chosen to rule it out from the *baccalauréat*, thus showing a contradiction inside the government, with a progressive attitude on the part of the Prime Minister and the Ministry of Culture, but a very conservative position on the part of some of the services of the Ministry of Education. A new Minister of Education was chosen in March 2000, Jack Lang; he is said to have an open-minded attitude on the issue of regional and minority languages. France is a very special place as far as North African Arabic is concerned. The shared (although painful) history is of course the reason for this. France is a country which is beginning to realise that its culture has become plural. Gently, but surely, the culture of North African origin is taking more and more space in French society. In this context, *Arabe dialectal* has become an official *langue de la France* and on the whole this evolution can only be extremely positive.

References

Benjelloun, S. (1998) _El-lu a dyali: el-Çarabiya el-ma ribiya 2_ (2 volumes, 1 cassette audio). Tilburg: Syntax.

Berque, J. (1985) _L'Immigration à l'école de la Rébublique. Rapport au Ministre de l'éducation nationale._ CNDP, La Documentation Française.

Carcassonne, G. (1987) _Etude sur la compatibilité entre la Charte européenne des langues régionales ou minoritaires et la Constitution._ La Documentation française, 8 Septembre 1998 (http://www.admifrance.gouv.fr).

Caubet, D. (1997) L'épreuve d'arabe dialectal au baccalauréat: passage à l'écrit - Bilan comparatif des sessions 1996 et 1995. In M. Tilmatine, _Enseignement des langues d'origine et immigration nord-africaine en Europe: Langue maternelle ou langue d'Etat?_ (pp. 163-172). Document pédagogique Erasmus, INALCO/ CEDREA-CRB.

Caubet, D. (1998) Alternance des codes au Maghreb: pourquoi le français est-il arabisé? _Plurilinguismes 14, Alternance des langues et apprentissage en contextes plurilingues._ Paris: CERPL, Université René Descartes, 121-142.

Caubet, D. (1999) Arabe maghrébin: passage à l'écrit et institutions. _Faits de langue_ 13, Parole orale/Parole écrite: Formes et Théories, 235-244.

Caubet, D. (2000) L'épreuve facultative d'"arabe dialectal" au baccalauréat 1995: passage à l'écrit + débat. _L'Arabisant_ 34, 53-67.

Cerquiglini, B. (1999) _Les langues de la France._ Site de la Délégation à la Langue Française (http://dglf.culture.fr).

Chaker, S. (1997) La langue berbère en France, situation actuelle et perspectives de développement. In M. Tilmatine (ed.), _Enseignement des langues d'origine et immigration nord-africaine en Europe: Langue maternelle ou langue d'Etat?_ (pp. 15-30). Document pédagogique Erasmus, INALCO/CEDREA-CRB.

Cohen, D. (1994) Préface. In D. Caubet and M. Vanhove (eds) _Actes des premières journées internationales de dialectologie de Paris._ INALCO.

Colin, G.S. (1948) L'arabe vulgaire à L'ecole nationale des langues orientales vivantes. _Cent-Cinquantenaire de l'Ecole des Langues Orientales._ Paris: Imprimerie Nationale, 95-112.

Desparmet, J. (1907) _Enseignement de l'arabe dialectal d'après la méthode directe._ Première période, classe de 6ème, Alger, Adolphe Jourdan, 2ème édition 1907 (1ère éd., 1904-5).

Dumortier, B. (1996) L'arabe dans l'enseignement secondaire français: éléments pour un approche géographique. _L'école et les discontinuités territoriales,_ Ifrési, L.G.H, Lille 1.

El Minaoui, L. (1998) _Approche sociolinguistique du codeswitching dans une famille immigrée installée en France._ Unpublished mémoire de Maîtrise, INALCO.

El Minaoui, L. (1999) _L'alternance codique chez un travailleur immigré d'origine marocaine installé en France depuis 30 ans: trois langues en présence, tamazight, arabe marocain, français._ Unpublished mémoire de DEA, INALCO.

Girard, E. and Kernel, B. (1996) *Le VRAI langage des jeunes expliqué aux parents (qui n'y entravent plus rien...)*. Albin Michel.

Labrousse, P. (ed.) (1995) *Deux siècles d'histoire de l'Ecole des langues orientales*. Editions Hervas.

Masthoff, P. (1998) La France. In H. Obdeijn and J.J. De Ruiter (eds) *Le Maroc au cœur de l'Europe – l'enseignement de la langue te culture d'origine (ELCO) aux élèves marocains dans cinq pays européens* (pp. 13-67). tilburg: Syntax.

Melliani, F. (1999a) *Immigrés ici, immigrés là-bas. Comportements langagiers et processus identitaires: les cas des jeunes issus de l'immigration maghrébine en banlieue rouennaise*. Unpublished Thèse de doctorat, Université de Rouen.

Melliani, F. (1999b) Le métissage langagier comme lieu d'affirmation identitaire. *LIDIL 19*, numéro coordonné par Jacqueline Billiez, 59-77.

Neyreneuf, M. (1997) Négociation franco-marocaine pour l'enseignement de langues et cultures d'origine (ELCO). In M. Tilmatine (ed.) *Enseignement des langues d'origine et immigration nord-africaine en Europe: Langue maternelle ou langue d'Etat?* (pp. 65-68). Document pédagogique Erasmus, INALCO/CEDREA-CRB.

Neyreneuf, M. (2000) L'enseignement des langues et cultures d'origine (ELCO). *L'Arabisant 34*, 11-17.

Obdeijn, H. & De Ruiter, J.J. (eds) (1998) *Le Maroc au cœur de l'Europe – l'enseignement de la langue te culture d'origine (ELCO) aux élèves marocains dans cinq pays européens* Tilburg: Syntax.

Poignant, B. (1998) *Langues et cultures régionales*. La documentation française, 1er Juillet 1998 (http://www.admifrance.gouv.fr).

Moroccan children and Arabic in Spanish schools

BERNABÉ LÓPEZ GARCÍA
LAURA MIJARES MOLINA

Although Spain continues to be a country with a high percentage of emigrants, it has over the last fifteen years also become a country that attracts immigrants. According to the last available data, on 31 December 1998 there were 719,647 newcomers with a work permit living in Spain whereas the number of Spanish people living abroad was 2,134,773 in 1995 (OPI, 1998/1999). This change has caused an increase in the numbers of newcomers in Spain and, likewise, their children's presence in the Spanish school system. This situation has led to the development of programmes to improve the conditions for these new citizens in Spain, as has been done in other countries of Europe. Some of these programmes are aimed at the children of immigrant workers. These programmes are especially significant as they are dedicated to a population whose fundamental rights have been guaranteed by all European governments. Although the goals of these programmes vary, the education of the second generation of immigrant workers is one of the areas most often considered when developing programmes directed to newcomers.

The educational programmes directed towards immigrant minority children are commonly based on intercultural theories about education. These programmes are intended to maintain and develop a multicultural society. For this reason, one of the main aspects of these programmes is to guarantee that schools will not only teach the national language of the country of immigration, but also the languages and cultures of the countries of origin of immigrant children. In Spain, European guidelines have led to programmes of *education des langues et cultures d'origine* (ELCO), currently directed only towards children of Moroccan and Portuguese origin. Although the Portuguese ELCO programme is not the focus of this study, we would like to present some information about it. In the 1996/97 school year, Portuguese ELCO was developed in Asturias, Burgos, Cantabria, León, Madrid, Zaragoza, Galicia, Navarra and País Vasco in 78 schools with 65 Portuguese teachers. The teaching of

Portuguese reached 6087 children, distributed across those with Spanish nationality 4161, Portuguese nationality 1674, and others 252 (*Informe sobre el estado y la situación del sistema educativo 1996-1997*, 1998).

The focus of this chapter is on Arabic as an immigrant minority language for Moroccan children in Spanish education. The reason for studying this programme is that it is currently the only public programme that acknowledges, within the context of the school, the language of the largest immigrant group. Bearing in mind that it is not possible to study Arabic in secondary schools and only in some primary schools through this ELCO programme, we can easily understand the unstable teaching status. This study can help us to better understand the sociolinguistic context of Moroccan children who attend schools in Spain. Bilingual programmes have been developed before in Spain. The implementation of bilingualism in the autonomous regions has been realised through regional minority language programmes. Therefore, the debate about bilingualism in schools is not new. Although immigration has changed the general scene with regard to the issue of bilingualism, we should not forget about the linkage between the status of regional and immigrant minority languages.

Intercultural education in the Spanish school system

Diversity has become a matter of pedagogical reflection in schools, and has led to a new intercultural approach to education. This new approach entails a further step away from previous monolingual and monocultural educational policies. Intercultural education is the new framework in which diversity is viewed in the schools. This new way of understanding education is based on recognising, accepting and valuing different cultural realities in the school by including in the curriculum previous learning experiences of minority children. This supposes that equal opportunities are enhanced and that advantage is taken of the richness that diversity implies. For more information about intercultural education in Spain we refer to Carbonell i Paris (1995), Jordán (1994), Juliano (1993) and Santos Rego (1994).

Although intercultural education deserves a wider and richer perspective, this concept seems to have been pushed by the continuous development of the migration phenomenon. It is the result of an initiative of the European Social Foundation, intended to avoid the problems of integration that can be experienced by children of immigrant origin. These problems are related to loss of the mother tongue and the subsequent cultural identity weakness (Comisión Europea, 1995). Integration is considered crucial to avoid problems related to labour exclusion and to reduce risks of marginalization, school absence and failure rates of these children who are supposedly more exposed to such dangerous outcomes. From an intercultural perspective, it is obvious that knowledge of the mother tongue is an important aspect in the integration or lack of integration of foreign minors in the host countries. Initially, this teaching was intended to provide these children with an adequate education that would help them if they returned to their country of origin. However, given the fact that the idea of returning is increasingly out of line with the expectations of the immigrant population, justification for this teaching has shifted to the knowledge and valorisation it provides of different cultural realities in the school, thus helping the pupils' integration.

In Spain, different educational laws, in particular the *Ley Orgánica del Derecho a la Educación* (LODE) and the *Ley de Ordenación General del Sistema Educativo* (LOGSE), advocate the integration of pupils from other cultures. These laws state that pupils should respect individual freedom, develop tolerance and solidarity, acquire habits of democratic coexistence and respect, fight against inequality and discrimination for reasons of race, sex, religion or opinion, and become trained to achieve peace, cooperation and respect for diversity. Based on these existing premises and with the support of European initiatives related to minority education mentioned before, the educational services of the Spanish state have promoted the development of ELCO programmes. This development has also been made possible by the flexible framework introduced in the last educational reform. This reform allows the existence of an open curriculum adapted to the characteristics of individual schools. In the case of children of Moroccan origin, the largest immigrant minority group in the Spanish school system, intercultural perspectives of education have been realized through the ELCO Moroccan programme.

ELCO for children of Moroccan origin

The status of the programme

As a result of the bilateral Spanish-Moroccan Cultural Cooperation Programme, a home language and culture teaching programme was set up for Moroccan children in July 1994. The main objectives of the programme were to teach the Arabic language and Moroccan culture as well as to improve school integration of the pupils concerned. This approach was also meant to improve self-esteem and to reduce ethnic prejudice and ethnocentric behaviour. In order to achieve these goals, a coordinated effort was made, dividing the responsibilities of the programme between the Spanish and Moroccan governments. Morocco is in charge of coordinating the Moroccan teachers and their wages, as well as outlining the pedagogical materials for the programme. Spain is in charge of the actual implementation of and support for the programme in public schools with a high number of Moroccan children.

The programme can be implemented in two different ways: outside (mode A) and inside (mode B) the regular timetable. In mode A, Arabic language and Moroccan culture teaching are provided during one hour or an hour and a half, twice a week, outside the normal school timetable. In mode B, Arabic language and Moroccan culture teaching are integrated in the school day; Moroccan children usually receive Arabic instruction during the hours in which religion is taught. In neither of the two modes, the subjects of Arabic language and Moroccan culture are officially assessed. This lack of assessment makes the academic status of the programme different from that of other subjects forming part of the school curriculum. This situation has contributed to a perception of ELCO as a secondary subject which is not given the importance that it truly merits. Moreover, the fact that the programme is administered by the Moroccan government and especially directed towards children of Moroccan origin is a reason to perceive this subject as different from the others. Finally, the fact that Arabic is offered only in primary school and that the state does not offer the possibility to continue this subject in secondary school, can be taken as a sign of the transitional nature of the programme.

Degree of participation

Moroccans are the largest immigrant community living in Spain. Since the regulation process for immigrants first revealed the presence of a large number of Moroccan immigrants in Spain in 1991 (López, Ramírez & Planet, 1996), this population has continued to grow. On 31 December 1998 the number of Moroccans living legally in Spain was 140,896 (OPI, 1998). The extraordinary regulation process for immigrants, that ended in July 2000, shows again an increase in the number of Moroccan people. Figure 1 shows the growth of the Moroccan population in Spain.

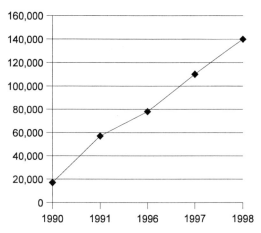

Figure 1   Increase in Moroccan immigration since 1991 (based on the data of the
Observatorio Permanente de la Inmigración and the _Atlas de la Inmigración
Magrebí en España_)

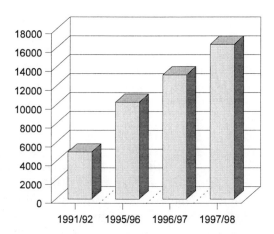

Figure 2   Increase in Moroccan children in Spanish schools (excluding university
level education; based on data of _Ministerio de Educación y Cultura
español_)

Due to family reunion and births, Moroccan children and youngsters represent the largest non-national group in the Spanish school system, and this group has experienced a major growth in the past few years. In the 1991/92 school year there were 5029 children of Moroccan origin in Spanish elementary schools (Ioé, 1996), whereas in the 1997/98 school year their number was 16,444. Due to the transfer of powers to the autonomous regions, the process of collecting data is very difficult and slow. For this reason the data for the 1998/99 and 1999/2000 school years are not yet available. For a detailed study of the development of Moroccan immigrant minors in Spain, we refer to López (1999).

With these data in mind, a comparison can be made with the number of children who received ELCO in the 1997/98 school year, i.e. a total of 1035 children in all Spanish programmes. We notice immediately how far away ELCO is from reaching all children that could benefit from this education. This is especially remarkable when we compare these figures to those related to the Portuguese-oriented ELCO. Of the 3869 Portuguese children in Spanish schools in the 1996/97 school year, 1674 children received this education. These data have been provided by the *Oficina de Planificación y Estadística, Ministerio de Educación y Cultura*. Although the Portuguese programme has a longer tradition, this comparison can be useful in understanding the limited status of Moroccan ELCO in Spanish schools. During the 1997/98 school year, the Arabic language and Moroccan culture teaching programme was implemented in Madrid, Barcelona and Las Palmas. Only in Madrid some of the programmes were integrated into the regular school time table. More information on the implementation of Moroccan ELCO in Spain is given in Franzé (1999). Table 1 gives an overview of the curricular status of the Moroccan ELCO programme and the degree of participation.

There are also other initiatives that non-governmental organisations and associations have developed in order to offer Arabic teaching to children of Moroccan origin. With regard to non-governmental organisations that teach Arabic, data are not yet available. A significant programme is that offered by the Moroccan Immigrant Workers Association in Spain (ATIME). It has been developed through an agreement with the Spanish Ministry of Education and Culture. This association conducts its programme in public schools outside the school timetable a couple of times per week. Members of the association voluntarily teach the children. Most of the time these teachers are graduates without specific training for Arabic language teaching. Also, the courses are given without standardized materials.

Table 1 Curricular status of the Moroccan ELCO programme and degree of participation (based on data of the *Centro de Investigación y Documentación Educativa*, CIDE)

	Madrid	Barcelona	Las Palmas	Total
Outside the school timetable	199	383	97	679
Integrated into the school timetable	356			356
Pupils	555	383	97	1,035
Schools	28	18	5	51
Teachers	10	6	2	18

With regard to language teaching in secondary school, Spain cannot be favourably compared to other European countries where Arabic language teaching is an optional subject. Spain does not offer such a possibility. As yet, the Spanish option of foreign language learning is limited in almost all public institutions to English or French.

Objectives of the programme

The learning of the mother tongue by immigrant children is considered essential in facilitating integration into the host society. European guidelines based on recent research on mother tongue learning show that such learning is considered crucial for children's cognitive development and also for their future language learning (Baker, 1997; Skutnabb-Kangas, 1998). The ELCO programme, in addition to incorporating the linguistic contents to be taught, also includes the cultural contents that children should learn in the schools. Actually, the programme distinguishes between linguistic, cultural and intercultural objectives. The first objective for pupils is to achieve basic linguistic competence that will allow them to improve both oral and written skills. With regard to culture, the objectives are to locate and explain the most important characteristics of Moroccan society and also of the Arabic and European worlds. Concerning the intercultural perspective, the objectives are for Moroccan children, by taking into account their cultural identity and language of origin, to develop in an affective and intellectual way that will allow them to achieve harmonic integration into the new society (*Ensamble pédagogique*, op. cit.).

The implementation of the programme

We aim to make an analysis of the Moroccan ELCO according to the two branches that constitute the programme, i.e. Arabic language teaching on the one hand and Moroccan culture teaching on the other. Although the branch concerned with Arabic language teaching is the main focus of the programme, the branch associated with the teaching of culture should not be forgotten. An analysis of these two ELCO branches can help us to understand the status of Arabic as an immigrant minority language, and also to understand the position of Moroccan children within the framework of the Spanish school system.

Not only is ELCO the only existing public programme in Spain recognising Arabic as an immigrant minority language, it also tries to establish a relationship between the knowledge of this language and the socio-educational results of the children who take part in the programme. It is understood that children of Moroccan origin have specific needs that decisively influence the outcome of their school careers. In order to analyse the two branches, we have carried out fieldwork on the Arabic language and Moroccan culture teaching programme in schools located in the centre of Madrid.

From mother tongue to classical Arabic
The first important issue to be analysed is what language is being taught in the schools as the 'mother tongue' of children of Moroccan origin. The language that actually is being taught is classical Arabic. In order to understand what this means, it is necessary to outline the linguistic situation in Morocco. By doing so, we will be able to better understand how the ELCO programme in Spain is being articulated.

Although the official language in Morocco is classical Arabic, there are other languages which should more realistically be considered as the mother tongues of Moroccans. These languages are different Moroccan Arabic and Berber dialects. French and Spanish also have also a very important presence in Morocco because they were the main languages spoken during the Protectorate. Classical Arabic is the first language in the hierarchy of languages in Morocco because it has a legal status that the other languages lack. However, it is a highly formal language which is used only in official contexts. As Boukous (1995) says, this split has provoked 'non-mother tongues, in particular classical Arabic and French, to be first in the hierarchy of language use, while rejecting the mother tongues, the Amazighe and the Arabic dialect'. According to the same author, this hierarchical classification of language varieties in Morocco distinguishes between 'strong languages', i.e. classical Arabic and French, and 'weak languages', i.e. Moroccan Arabic and Berber dialects. This distinction is known as diglossia. Practically the only contact Moroccan children have with classical Arabic occurs in the schools where they learn it as a foreign language. The distance between the capability in classical Arabic versus the mother tongues of the children is proportional to the number of years that these children have been receiving formal education in their country of origin.

Until the independence of Morocco in 1956, French was the main school language of the country, except in religious school centres. After the independence, various educational reforms were designed to achieve complete Arabization of the curriculum, the introduction of Arabic as the language of schools, and the *Moroccanization* of teachers. This process of Arabization has been implemented with varying degrees of commitment, and until today it has not been completely achieved (see also Merrouni, 1993). As Moroccan Arabic and Berber dialects are not legally recognised, their presence and recognition in the schools are virtually zero. However, the *Charte Nationale d'Education et de Formation* published by a National Committee in 1999 gives the Amazighe language a new status as an official language to be learned in the schools.

Even for Moroccan children in Morocco, in order to speak and write classical Arabic it is necessary to have much previous training. It is therefore obvious that to those Moroccan children socialised in another country, classical Arabic is even more alien. It is important to remember this fact in assessing the level of familiarity that these children have with the language that they now are learning at school. If we transfer this situation to the way ELCO is being implemented in Spain, we can see how the programme reproduces the language policy of Morocco. Children of Moroccan origin are not taught their mother tongue, but another different language. It is true that the different Moroccan dialects, though not the Berber ones, come from classical Arabic. These languages are, however, startlingly different, even though there exits a certain fundamental level of coincidence between both languages. As Boukous (op. cit.) says, 'Quant aux autres variétés, à savoir l'àrabe dialectal et l'amazige, elles constituent évidentmenent des systèmes linguistiques bien individualisés, elles possèdent chacune une grammaire comportant des règles bien precises....'.

Without denying the symbolic value that classical Arabic can represent for these children, it is obvious that in the case of Moroccan ELCO there is a contradiction between the theory on which the programme is based and the reality of the way it is being applied. As previously noted, in many cases these children learn a completely unknown language as if it were their mother tongue. This fact alone should be enough to rethink the basis on which classical Arabic is taught. If the main aim is that these children take advantage of the knowledge of their first language in order to organise their minds and to facilitate the learning of a second language or even the rest of their school subjects, it is evident that by teaching classical Arabic this goal can hardly be achieved. If the main goal for these children is to see their culture reflected in the schools, it will be necessary to analyse what is understood as Moroccan culture.

Diversity or difference?

As has been mentioned several times, learning the culture of the student's country of origin is the second theme upon which the ELCO programme is based. This learning has brought about the introduction of Moroccan culture in schools, supposedly endowed with the specific features that are the main characteristics of this immigrant community. These Moroccan elements have been defined in advance by the governing organisations and are in this form introduced in the schools. This fact has caused Moroccan children to be defined in the school context by their officially dictated *Morocanness*. According to Narrowe (1998), we are witnessing the construction of an immigrant culture that is being developed through a series of ethnic obligations that seem to be intrinsic to being Moroccan. Moroccan children are being defined as such by an outside definition of Moroccan ethnic identity (see Mijares, in press, about this issue and about stereotypes with regards to Moroccans). Furthermore, this definition, set in advance for children of Moroccan origin, has arguably been the source of problems that seriously affect these children in school. It is very common to listen to these children, living between two different worlds, and to say that they are neither Moroccan nor Spanish. These children are considered to be living between two worlds so culturally different that their situation can cause an identity crisis that might ultimately lead to school failure. These kinds of statements are a reflection of the persistence of the discourse that Edward Said defined as Orientalist. What is curious to prove is that in this case we are talking about the construction of the other's image. Moroccans as well as Spanish people are participants in this construction. These kinds of discourses are collected in Franzé and Mijares (1999). It is for this reason that the intention is for them to learn and preserve their culture and safeguard a Moroccan personality that seems to have very concrete features and is the common heritage of all the children of Moroccan origin.

The relation between school failure and teaching the culture of origin was widely discussed in France in the seventies. Studies on this relation have demonstrated that the reasons for the low school success among children of immigrant origin have been analysed much more in socio-economic terms than in cultural terms. Accordingly, it is necessary to note how children of Moroccan origin share school success and failure rates with indigenous children of the same socio-economic status (Camilleri, 1992). Although ELCO is an educational facility that intends to improve the children's academic results, this programme cannot only be conceived as an antidote against the possible school and social problems of the children to whom it is directed.

What seems to result from this characterisation of Moroccan children under the blanket definition of Moroccans is a need to introduce diversity in the schools. Moroccans seem to have fixed characteristics without having in mind their own perception as individuals. This mindset has caused the passing from an appreciation of diversity to an awareness of difference. Moroccan children are different because they are classified as Moroccans and immigrants before being thought of as children and pupils. From this perspective, the construction of a Moroccan identity in the schools is created through various intercultural activities. This is done by introducing elements that are based on a folkloric reading of Islamic practices such as the fasting of the month of Ramadan. Also the *Eid* or the Moroccan gastronomy seem to be key elements in the life of these children. Other folkloric elements such as henna, music or traditional clothes are very important in recreating Moroccan culture in the schools. Difference is constructed by means of these folkloric manifestations of Moroccan culture, while it is not specified which are the identity problems that affect these children. The vagueness and deficiency of the discourse related to Moroccan children in the schools confirms the idea of them being constructed as a piece of monolithic Moroccan culture. In this sense, the teaching of classical Arabic in the ELCO programme instead of the actual mother tongues confirms that Moroccan identity is invented in order to be taught to children.

Conclusions

At the moment, the Moroccan ELCO programme in Spain is the only public initiative that recognises Arabic as an immigrant minority language. Nevertheless, the current programme has been implemented with some fundamental contradictions that can result in unintended consequences.

On the one hand, the language that is being taught is not the mother tongue of the children towards whom the programme is directed. Instead of the different native dialects, Classical Arabic is being taught as their 'mother tongue'. This situation, which reflects the low status of Moroccan Arabic and Berber languages in Morocco, has been transferred to the Spanish schools. We should not forget that the Moroccan government manages the ELCO programme. The National Ministry of Education is only in charge of allowing the programme and engaging Moroccan teachers that will be in charge.

On the other hand, the discrepancy in skills between mother tongues and classical Arabic is greater when these children have only achieved a low level of schooling in their countries of origin. As has been explained with regard to Arabic teaching, this fact is crucial in order to understand to what level these children are habituated to classical Arabic. They may start the programme learning a totally unknown language. At home these children communicate within their family by means of a dialect. In the case of children who communicate in a Berber dialect, the distance will even be greater. It is crucial that this issue be assessed in order to know whether the objectives of the programme are being achieved or not.

It is also necessary to fix a set of evaluation criteria in order to know how effective the programme is. Such criteria do not currently exist. On the one hand, there is no check as to whether children are learning Arabic or not. On the other hand, there is no knowledge as to whether this learning, as currently operated, is giving the expected results. At this point, we could ask the following questions. Does ELCO contribute to the improvement of the educational careers of children? Does it help to facilitate better integration in the schools? And last but not least, does it help to achieve a sense of interculturality?

In the case of Moroccan ELCO as it is currently being implemented, we are in danger of achieving exclusion instead of integration. The cause of exclusion would be that objectives are not well defined, that the theoretical basis is lost when applied to the daily reality and that vital evaluation criteria are missing to recognise that we have lost our way.

Home language programmes directed to immigrant children should be considered important, but they must have a real and realistic status within the official curriculum in order to achieve the formulated objectives in a concrete manner.

References

Boukous, A. (1995) *Société, langues et cultures au Maroc. Enjeux symboliques.* Rabat: Publications de la Faculté des Lettres et des Sciences Humaines.

Camilleri, C. (1992) El problema de los efectos propios de la cultura en la escolaridad de los jóvenes nacidos de inmigrantes en Europa. In M. Siguán (coord.) *La escuela y la migración en la Europa de los 90.* Barcelona: Editorial Horsori.

Carbonell i Paris, F. (1995) *Inmigración: diversidad cultural, desigualdad social y educación.* Madrid: Ministerio de Educación y Ciencia.

Comisión Europea (1995) *Informe sobre la educación de los hijos de migrantes en la Unión Europea.* Luxemburgo: Oficina de Publicaciones Oficiales de las Comunidades Europeas.

Franzé, A. & Mijares, L. (coord.) (1999) *Lengua y cultura de origen: Niños marroquíes en la escuela española.* Madrid: Ediciones del Oriente y del Mediterráneo.

Informe sobre el estado y la situación del sistema educativo 1996-1997 (1998) Madrid: MEC

Ioé (1996) *La educación intercultural a prueba: Hijos de inmigrantes Marroquíes en la escuela Española.* Madrid: CIDE-MEC.

Jordán, J.A. (1994) *La escuela multicultural. Un reto para el profesorado.* Barcelona: Paidós.

Juliano, D. (1993) *Educación intercultural. Escuela y minorías étnicas.* Madrid: Eudema.

López, B.(1999) Niños marroquíes en la escuela española. In A. Franzé & L. Mijares (coord.) *Lengua y cultura de origen: Niños marroquíes en la escuela española.* Madrid: Ediciones del Oriente y del Mediterráneo.

López, B., Ramírez, Á. & Planet, A.I. (coord.) (1996) *Atlas de la inmigración magrebí en España.* Madrid: Eds. de la Universidad Autónoma de Madrid.

Merrouni, M. (1993) *Le problème de la reforme dans le système éducatif marocain.* Rabat: Editions Okad.

Mijares, L. (1999) Cuando inmigrantes y autóctonos comparten estereotipos: niños, escuela e imágenes sobre la inmigración marroquí en España. *Anales de Historia Contemporánea. Monográfico sobre Inmigración Magrebí y Escuela* 15, 167-177.

Narrowe, J. (1998) *Under one roof. On becoming a Turk in Sweden.* Stockholm: Studies in Social Anthropology.

Obdeijn, H. & De Ruiter, J.J. (coord.) (1998) *Le Maroc au coeur de l'Europe. L'Enseignement de la langue arabe et culture d'origine (ELCO) aux élèves marocains dans cinq pays européens*. Tilburg: Syntax.

Observatorio Permanente de la Inmigración (OPI) (1998/1999) Indicadores de la inmigración y el asilo en España. *Ministerio de Trabajo y Asuntos Sociales* 1 (May 1998); 6 (July 1999).

Said, E. (1995) [1978] *Orientalism. Western conceptions of the Orient*. London: Penguin Books.

Santos R. & Miguel A. (1994) *Teoría y práctica de la educación intercultural*. Santiago de Compostela: Universidade de Santiago de Compostela.

Romani in Europe

PETER BAKKER

In this chapter an overview of the status of the Roma in the European Union (EU) will be given, with a focus on the demographic, political, sociolinguistic and educational aspects of their language.

Although Romani is geographically the most widespread language in Europe, it is nevertheless a minority language. In this chapter the term *Roma* will be used for the people called *Gypsies* in English. Roma is one of several terms which the members of this group use for themselves. Other Gypsy groups call themselves *Sinti, Romanichal* or *Kalo*. All of them share the same language, which, like any natural language, consists of a number of dialects. This language is invariably referred to as *Romani* or *Romanes*, regardless of the ethnic name they use for themselves. The noun *Rom* (plural *Roma*) means 'husband, man' and in most dialects also 'Gypsy person'. The adjective *Romano/Romani* means 'of a Gypsy' and the adverb *Romanes* means 'in the way of a Gypsy'. *Romanes* is used for the language by the speakers. The term for the language, *Romani*, is an abbreviation of *Romani chib*, i.e. 'the Gypsy tongue or language'. The Romani language is most closely related to languages of North India, such as Hindi, Rajasthani and Punjabi. Romani is, after at least ten centuries of separation from the languages of India, no longer intelligible to speakers of those languages. From the fact that the language is of Indian origin, one can reasonably suppose that the ancestors of the Romani people are also from that area.

Where do Romani and the Roma come from?

The Romani language comes from India, but there is no proof that the members of the population group who were to become the European Roma was homogeneous when they left the Indian subcontinent. However, the striking homogeneity of the Romani language, including a universal set of loanwords from Iranian languages, Armenian and Greek, and other pervasive influences from Greek shows indisputably that the ancestors of the Roma must have formed one community during a sizable period (11-13th century? Western part of Asia?), from the moment they left the Indian subcontinent until the moment they spread through Europe from South-Eastern Europe. The best guess regarding the time the ancestors of the Roma left India is around 1000 AD, but several scholars maintain dates between 500 and 1000 years earlier.

It is certain that the Roma were present in South-Eastern Europe in the 13th century. From there they spread, usually in small groups of a few dozen people, throughout Europe. By 1550 virtually all European countries housed a minority of Roma. Since that time the Roma have had a continuous presence in Europe. The first century in Europe was relatively peaceful for the Roma, but during the 17th century many local authorities wanted to get rid of the Roma. This led to unremitting oppression, banishment and even genocide by the authorities. The period of the most brutal oppression was around 1700, when many Gypsies were killed by or at the instigation of the authorities. Despite this genocide, both the Roma and their language Romani survived all these centuries remarkably well. New groups of Roma arrived again in Western Europe in the second half of the 19th century. Many Roma were killed and a number of Roma communities were decimated before or during the second World War. Some Roma groups and individuals were assimilated into mainstream society. Others shifted to majority languages, or to local minority languages. This means that not all Roma continue to speak their ancestral language.

In some western European countries, probably partly in response to the oppression of the Roma and their language, a number of new languages developed which combine the Romani vocabulary with the structure of local languages. Prime examples are Sweden, Norway, the United Kingdom and Spain. In many cases these new languages continue to be called Romani. Sometimes, these mixed or intertwined languages are collectively called 'Para-Romani'. These should be actually distinguished from Romani which is one and the same language, with dialectal diversification.

The Roma should not be confused with Travellers and Caravan Dwellers. Even though some Roma live in caravans, there are clear historical, cultural and linguistic differences between Roma and these other groups. This chapter deals only with Roma and their language. It should finally be said that Romani is very different from Romanian, a Romance language of the Balkan, and that its name has nothing to do with the city of Rome or the name Romance.

Who are the Gypsies?

Gypsies (Roma) are an ethnic group. The Roma share with other ethnic groups a common history, a common language, a common lifestyle and a shared set of values. Even though the different groups have developed individual particularities, there are a number of Romani cultural traits and hygienic behaviour which recur in some form in all groups. The Romani universe is divided into two, in that 'lines are drawn between the Gypsy and the non-Gypsy, the clean and the unclean, health and disease, the good and the bad' (Miller, 1998: 201).

In the Romani system of values, some types of behaviour and objects have to be avoided. The upper part of the body is clean, the lower part unclean. Underwear should be therefore washed separately from clothes, and both separately from cloth used in the kitchen. Two sets of towels are used. Cracked kitchenware should not be used, pets who lick their own body are considered dirty and they cannot be touched. One should only eat food which has been prepared according to Romani rules. Roma cannot share toilets with others. There are many such unwritten rules of behaviour that must be followed by Roma and Sinti, at the risk of defilement. Defilement in turn can lead to forms of punishment by the Romani community, such as fines, temporary isolation, or in extreme cases banishment.

This system of values also has its impact on the transmission of the Romani culture, including the language. We will also discuss some of the consequences it has for Roma in the educational system. Such values are not found in any other linguistic minority in Europe. It is not the only difference between Roma and other European minorities.

Roma versus other minorities

Are the Roma a regional minority or an immigrant minority? The answer could be neither, or both. The Roma have been continuously present in almost all European countries for at least four and a half centuries. This appeared possible despite oppression, banishment, and even outright genocide. They are as much European citizens as those belonging to European regional language minorities. After so many centuries of presence and settlement in Europe one can hardly consider them immigrants: in 1550, when all European countries hosted Romani minorities, European settlement in North America or Australia had not yet begun. On the other hand, many Roma are more or less recent arrivals in the countries where they actually reside. One can think of, most recently, the Czech Roma in Scandinavian countries and Britain, or the Yugoslav war refugees of the ninetiess in several EU countries; before them, the Roma who came with the Yugoslav guest workers of the sixties, and the Sinti and Roma who left Germany to avoid Nazi persecution in the thirties and forties, and who settled in neighbouring countries; or the Lovari and Kalderash Roma who came to Western Europe after the abolition of serfdom in what is now Romania from around 1850. The foreign origin of these groups must not be taken as a sign of nomadism, however. The vast majority of these Roma were house-dwellers before they immigrated.

The situation of the Roma differs from that of all other minorities in Europe from a number of perspectives:

- The Roma are present in all countries of Europe, and in all countries they form a numerical minority.
- Even though they are a minority, they are altogether one of the largest ethnic and linguistic minorities of Europe, and certainly the geographically most widespread of all.
- Even though the ancestors of the Roma are originally from South Asia, there are no Romani speakers outside Europe (except for groups in Australia, the Americas and the western part of Asia, who presumably moved there via Europe); so they are a typical European minority, and the Asian origin of the Roma is not part of their oral traditions.
- The number of illiterates is exceptionally high among the Roma (50 to 80%), not only in their own language, but also in the majority language.
- A minority of Roma groups object to their language being subject to study, and they do not want outsiders to use, learn, write or teach it.
- The number of Roma who made a successful academic or intellectual career is proportionally much lower than for other linguistic minorities in Europe; a comparatively very small number of Roma people have finished secondary education; nevertheless, there are Roma who are e.g. university professors, company owners, journalists, doctors, legal prosecutors and brain surgeons.
- Wherever they are, the Roma are at the bottom of society, subject to prejudice and discrimination, and often living in poverty.
- Only a minority of the Roma do not live in houses. More than 80% of the Roma have been living in houses for at least 200 years, but some

still maintain a nomadic or partly nomadic lifestyle or they prefer to live on caravan sites.

- All non-immigrant minorities in Europe live in a certain region, but the Roma are spread over many different areas.
- There is not a single region, city or even a village in Europe where the Roma form a numerical majority. They are always a minority.
- Even though Roma profess many different religions, usually that of the region in which they reside, they also have their own value system and spiritual beliefs, as mentioned above.

In short, the Roma have a very low status wherever they reside; they are reasonably numerous in Europe, but at the same time they are a minority everywhere, often without resources for educational programmes.

Demographic status

It is difficult to obtain reliable statistics on the number of Roma and on the number of Romani speakers in different countries. The number of ethnic Roma is in any case higher than the number of Romani speakers since many Roma have shifted, in the recent or distant past, to other languages, or they have in a few cases created new means of communication. Estimates of the total number of Roma (including both speakers and non-speakers of Romani) vary between one and two million for the EU.

In the statistics documents regarding regional and minority languages in Europe, the presence of Romani speakers in EU countries is estimated as follows: Austria: 30,000; Germany: 70,000; Finland: 10,000; Sweden: 14,000. For other EU countries no mention is made of Romani - even though Romani is spoken in all EU countries. Most country reports ignore the Roma and their language.

The European Roma Rights Center has collected information concerning the number of Roma, and gives both official and recent numbers originating from the Report of the High Commissioner for National Minorities (HCNM) of the Organisation for Security and Cooperation in Europe (OSCE). Table 1 gives only their number for European Union countries. Please note that these refer to the numbers of Roma, not to the numbers of Romani speakers.

The figures in the last column are from Liégeois and Gheorghe (1995). The 'official' numbers are from a variety of sources, mostly estimates submitted to the UN Committee on the Elimination of Racial Discrimination in the late nineties. The numbers for the Netherlands include Travellers

Table 1   approximate numbers of Roma in EU countries (Source: OSCE, HCNM)

Country	Official numbers	OSCE	Minority Rights Group
Austria	95	15,000-20,000	20,000-25,000
Belgium	not available	10,000-15,000	10,000-15,000
Denmark	not available	2,000-3,000	1,500-2,000
Finland	10,000	7,000-10,000	7,000-9,000
France	not available	300,000-380,000	280,000-300,000
Germany	50,000-70,000	90,000-150,000	100,000-130,00
Greece	150,000-300,000	150,000-200,000	160,000-200,000
Ireland	10,891	20,000-30,000	22,000-28,000
Italy	130,000	100,000-120,000	90,000-110,000
Luxembourg	not available	100-200	100-150
Netherlands	20,000	35,000-40,000	35,000-40,000
Portugal	40,000	40,000-50,000	40,000-50,000
Spain	325,000-450,000	650,000-800,000	700,000-800,000
Sweden	20,000	15,000-40,000	15,000-20,000
United Kingdom	90,000	100,000-150,000	90,000-120,000

and Caravan Dwellers who are not Roma or Sinti, and the figures for Ireland comprise almost exclusively Travellers, who likewise are not Roma.

A different set of figures is given below, for all European countries, based on collective work by several experts on Romani (Bakker *et al.* 2000). The figures we give below in Table 2 are therefore from well-informed sources, but it is not easy to assess their accuracy. They also appear to differ slightly from those given above. Table 2 provides both absolute numbers, estimated for the numbers of Romani speakers per country, and the approximate percentage of the Roma population in the pertinent country who are speakers of Romani, i.e. in relation to the people who are Roma but who shifted to some other language. This Table does not give information on the number of Roma per country, neither does it give information on e.g. Travellers, Caravan Dwellers and other groups who are sometimes counted together with Roma in the statistics, but who are not speakers of Romani.

Table 2 Approximate number of Romani speakers in European countries (Source: Bakker et al., 2000)

Country	Appr. number of Romani speakers	Appr. % of the Roma who speak Romani	Country	Appr. number of Romani speakers	Appr. % of the Roma who speak Romani
Albania	90,000	95	Lithuania	3,700	90
Austria	18,000	80	Luxembourg	100	80
Belarus	27,000	90	Macedonia	215,000	90
Belgium	10,000	80	Moldava	56,000	90
Bos.-Herzegovina	40,000	90	Netherlands	7,000	90
Bulgaria	600,000	80	Norway	200	90
Croatia	28,000	80	Poland	50,000	90
Cyprus	650	90	Portugal	100	0
Czech Republic	140,000	50	Rumania	1,030,000	90
Denmark	1,500	90	Russia	405,000	80
Estonia	1,150	90	Serb.-Montenegro	380,000	90
Finland	3,000	40	Slovakia	300,00	80
France	215,000	70	Slovenia	8,000	90
Germany	85,000	70	Spain	100	0.01
Greece	160,000	90	Sweden	9,500	90
Hungary	290,000	50	Turkey	280,000	70
Italy	80,000	80	Ukraine	101,000	90
Kazakhstan	42,000	90	United Kingdom	1,000	0.5
Latvia	18,700	90			

If we count the number of speakers in the countries which belong to the European Union, we arrive at a number of Romani speakers of close to 600,000. The largest numbers are found in France, Greece, Germany and Italy. Some EU states with high population figures nevertheless have low numbers of Romani speakers (Belgium, the Netherlands). In some states the number of speakers is low despite the presence of a sizeable Roma community (United Kingdom, Spain), since many of the Roma who are descendants of the immigrants of the 16th century and earlier no longer speak Romani in those two states. They preserve an ethnic identity, but they lost the language in some cases already centuries ago.

From a demographic perspective, there is a rather low life expectancy among Roma compared to other populations, so that young people form a proportionally large part of the population. Conditions of poverty prevail. In short, reliable demographic data on Roma are impossible to obtain. There are perhaps two million Roma in the EU, some 600,000 of whom are speakers of Romani. In countries outside the EU, the proportion of Romani speakers among the Roma is invariably much higher than this EU average.

Political status

Romani is not an official language in the European Union. There are a few countries which have recognized Romani, however, and a few others where Romani is used in education, government publications or the media - albeit at a modest level. Outside the EU, Macedonia and the USA make their census questionnaires available in Romani.

A number of international institutions have drawn attention to the Gypsies in their documents, often focusing on the protection or development of the Roma. In some of these documents the language is explicitly mentioned. A range of international institutions have thus expressed support for and recognition of the Romani language. Among these institutions we can mention the United Nations, the European Parliament, the Council of Europe, the Committee of Ministers, the Standing Conference of Local and Regional Authorities of Europe (CLRAE), and the Conference on Security and Cooperation in Europe (CSCE). Many of their statements are given in Danbakli (1994). We briefly discuss some of the most explicit ones, in chronological order.

In 1981 the Standing Conference of Local and Regional Authorities of Europe called upon the governments of member states 'to recognise

Romanies and other specific nomadic groups such as the Samis as ethnic minorities and, consequently, to grant them the same status and advantages as other minorities may enjoy; in particular concerning respect and support for their own culture and language'. Two years later, in June 1983, the Council for Cultural Cooperation recommended 'that the Romany language and culture be used and accorded the same respect as regional languages and cultures and those of other minorities'.

In 1989, the Council of Europe and the Ministers for Education stated that 'Gypsies and Travellers currently form a population group of over one million persons in the Community and that their culture and language have formed part of the Community's cultural and linguistic heritage for over 500 years'; therefore they aim at stimulating 'teaching methods and teaching materials' with 'consideration for the history, culture and language of Gypsies and Travellers' and encourage 'research on the culture, history and language of Gypsies and Travellers'.

In the same vein, the Council of Europe on 22 May 1989 adopted a resolution on school provision for Gypsy and Traveller children. It mentions that there are over a million Gypsies and Travellers in the European Community and 'that their culture and language have formed part of the Community's cultural and linguistic heritage for over 500 years'. The document also expresses support for special educational programmes.

During the Copenhagen Meeting of the Conference on the Human Dimension of the CSCE in 1990 the participants explicitly recognized 'the particular problems of Roma (Gypsies)'. They stated further 'that persons belonging to national minorities, notwithstanding the need to learn the official language or languages of the State concerned, have adequate opportunities for instruction of their mother tongue or in their mother tongue, as well as, wherever possible and necessary, for its use before public authorities, in conformity with applicable national legislation'. National minorities should further have the right to 'freely use their mother tongue in private as well as in public' and to 'conduct religious educational activities in their mother tongue' and other such basic linguistic rights.

Perhaps the most important document is the European Charter for Regional and Minority Languages of 1992 which will be discussed below. In 1993 the Parliamentary Assembly of the European Parliament approved a recommendation on Gypsies in Europe in which it was stated that 'as a non-territorial minority, Gypsies greatly contribute to the cultural diversity of Europe', among others through their language.

European cultural diversity can be enriched when 'guarantees for equal rights, equal chances, equal treatment, and measures to improve the situation will make a revival of Gypsy language and culture possible' and therefore a European programme for the study of Romanes should be set up. The Assembly further explicitly stated that 'the provisions of non-territorial languages as set out in the European Charter for Regional and Minority Languages should be applied to Gypsy minorities'.

The Universal Declaration on Linguistic Rights, approved by a host of institutions and non-governmental organizations in Barcelona in 1996, seems to include a language like Romani, despite its emphasis on a territorial base. Article 1.4 'considers nomad peoples within their historical areas of migration and peoples historically established in geo-graphically dispersed locations as language communities in their own territory', where 'territory' in this case can be understood as the whole of Europe.

In February 2000, the Committee of Ministers of the Council of Europe stated: 'In the countries where the Romani language is spoken, oppor-tunities to learn in the mother tongue should be offered at school to Roma/Gypsy children'. This recommendation on the education of Roma/Gypsy children in Europe, adopted by the Committee of Ministers of the Council of Europe on 3 February 2000, was drafted by the Council for Cultural Cooperation of the Council of Europe.

The European Charter for Regional and Minority Languages of 1992 (Council of Europe, 1992) is now operative in the states that ratified it. It specifically mentions non-territorial languages, a label which would include Romani (even though one could argue that Romani is not non-territorial in that all of Europe is its territory). In fact, in the Explanatory Report Romani ('Romany') is explicitly mentioned as an example of a 'non-territorial language', to which some parts of the Charter can be applied (Articles 36 and 37). In June 2000, the Charter had been signed by 22 countries, among them 10 of the 15 EU states, and ratified by 10 states. In those states it is now official. Ratifying states list minority languages, and they can specify where (e.g. education, mass media) these languages can be used. Not all states mention Romani in the list of languages to which the Charter applies. These countries do: Finland ('Romanes'), Germany ('the Romany language of the German Sinti and Roma'), the Netherlands ('Romanes') and Sweden ('Romani Chib'). Norway and Switzerland do not mention the language. Due to the non-territorial nature of the language, not all articles of the Charter apply to Romani, and some countries have stated in detail which parts of the treaty apply to Romani.

None of the three non-EU states that ratified the Charter mentions Romani, even though the language is spoken by a sizeable minority in two states: some 28,000 in Croatia (seven other minority languages recognized) and 260,000 in Hungary (six minority languages recognized). No numbers of speakers are known for Switzerland, which recognized Italian and Romansch.

France has a special status in this respect. It has not ratified the Charter, but it declared in 1998 that it would specify the languages. A commission, that was set up to study the regional and minority languages of France, produced a report in which some 75 languages were listed for France - including overseas territories. 'Romani Chib' is one of the languages mentioned, and therefore potentially recognized (Cerquiglini, 1999). The Sinti, Vlax and Caló dialects are explicitly mentioned.

The OSCE has also devoted attention to the Roma and Romani, especially through the High Commisioner on National Minorities who published a detailed report on the Roma and Sinti of the OSCE countries (HCNM, 2000). It deals mostly with issues relating to non-EU countries. The HCNM also prepared a report on government positions on national minorities. All governments of the OSCE states were asked (among others) to report on their national minorities, and the results were synthesized in its report (HCNM, 1998). A few states explicitly mentioned the presence of Romani speakers.

In short, some documents state that the participation of representatives of the Roma/Gypsy community should be encouraged in the development of teaching material on the history, culture or language of the Roma/Gypsies. European institutions have shown a positive attitude towards the presence of Romani in Europe, and states are stimulated to respect the freedom to use Romani in private and public. It is recommended that Romani be used in the school system, for which educational material should be developed. In some EU states Romani is a recognized minority language, in others it is not.

Sociolinguistic status

The sociolinguistic status of the Roma differs from that of most other European linguistic minorities. Romani is, more than other European minority languages, a spoken language. Even though books and periodicals are being published in Romani, and the language is used on the Internet, the number of publications is much lower than for other minority languages with comparable numbers of speakers. Most of the printed works are children's books, local news magazines, or political and religious texts (see e.g. Matras, 1999 for discussion).

Like all other languages, it is transmitted from generation to generation, from parents to children. It is spoken by all generations. Children learn it as their first language.

Except for young children, virtually all Roma, men and women, speak at least one other language apart from Romani. In some cases they speak many. In Kosovo, for instance, where people had to learn the languages of more prestigious groups in addition to their own, many Roma spoke and speak not only Romani but also Turkish, Albanian, Gorani, and Serbian. An important difference with other minorities, however, is that the number of languages of wider communication used by Roma groups is much larger than in cases of other minorities. Breton speakers will all learn French, whereas Catalans and Basques who straddle language borders may use both Spanish and French in non-local communication. The Roma, however, are spread across many countries, and consequently the different communities do not have a specific second language in common. In fact, the Roma often do not only learn the pertinent state language, but also local minority languages if they live in a region of a linguistic minority. In terms of interstate communication this may create difficulties for those Roma who do not speak many extra languages. An additional problem in intergroup communication is that different majority languages serve as a source for borrowed words in regional varieties of Romani. Since borrowings for words such as 'refrigerator' or 'glasses' are taken from different languages in the regional varieties of Romani, these words tend to differ from one dialect to another, and they may form a barrier in intergroup communication.

This brings us to the problem that there is no widely used standard language or spelling system for Romani (see Matras, 1999 for discussion). In most cases, local journals or book publishers use a spelling system based on the official languages of the state they reside in. These spelling systems are not always compatible, but they often show remarkable similarities. There is a super-regional spelling system in which a number of Roma periodicals and some books have been published since such a system was first proposed on the Romani World Congress in the early nineties. So far this is used only in a minority of published material. In a number of regions local standards are used (e.g. in Slovakia and

Macedonia, and in the EU in Burgenland and Austria). However, knowledge of the written language is not widespread, and the number of people who actively write Romani is very small, perhaps a few hundred at most.

Is Romani an endangered language? It is not possible to give a straightforward answer to this question. We have mentioned the shift away from Romani. Taken as a whole, the language is not endangered. The fact that the language has been preserved in adverse circumstances for five to ten centuries is indicative of its strength. There are today millions of speakers, even if scattered through small communities all over Europe and elsewhere. In many communities it is the first language learned, and as such transmitted to the children. Nevertheless, some dialects have become extinct in the last fifty years, such as Laiuse in Estonia and Bohemian Romani in the Czech Republic, almost all speakers of which were massacred by the Nazis and their allies. The speakers of the Havati dialect in Croatia have all been killed, but it is still spoken by some escapees in Italy and Slovenia. In a number of communities, Roma have shifted to other languages, especially the Roma communities descending from the people who migrated to Western Europe before 1550. Also in otherwise vital communities, there appears to be a tendency to shift away from Romani. The main factors involved, as always, seem to be media and education in languages other than the mother tongue. Seen in that light, Romani should be considered as much endangered as many of the other minority languages of Europe.

On the other hand, in those communities that are committed to their language, Romani is vital, and that is probably the most common pattern. A study among school children in the southern part of the Netherlands showed that Romani, both among Sinti and among Roma, was the most vital of all ethnic minority languages studied. It was the strongest language, the language most often used with all family members including siblings, and the preferred language (Venes, 1995; Broeder & Extra, 1998).

Educational status

The status of the Romani language in the educational system differs from country to country. Most of the Euridyce reports (www.euridice.org/ Eurybase/Files/dossier.htm) fail to mention the existence of Romani speaking minorities in the educational system. Only for Austria the Roma are mentioned. In most countries, including those of the EU, Romani is not a recognized language. Nevertheless, there are schools where Romani is used. Educational material in Romani has been produced for several Romani dialects and in different European countries. Most of this was prepared by enthusiastic Roma, seldom with the support of local or state authorities. The use of these materials is often limited to one or two schools at least in the EU. Below an overview is presented of EU countries and the use of Romani in primary education, with information gathered from diverse, but undoubtedly incomplete sources.

Austria
Four dialect groupings present. Teaching material, comic books, dictionaries, story books, computer games, periodicals for adults and children, scientific studies have been produced or are being developed for Burgenland Romani dialect (most extensive) and the Lovari dialect (in development).

Belgium
Several dialect groupings present. No Romani teaching material has been produced. There seems to be no Romani language education in Belgium.

Denmark
The original Danish Romani population has been partly deported and has partly assimilated. In several places there are small communities of Roma, most of them from former Yugoslavia, and most of them arrived from the sixties onwards. Most of these are speakers of Vlax and Balkan dialects. Some families came from Slovakia, probably speakers of Slovak Romani. There is no teaching material, no formal Romani education. An initially successful experiment in Helsingør, where the largest Roma community of Denmark resides, collapsed in the early eighties not long after its start; parents resisted Romani teaching, apparently because the dialect used deviated from their own - even though there are three dialect groups represented in Helsingør (see Liégeois, 1998: 204).

Finland
Dialectally homogeneous, but endangered. Dictionary, teaching material. Well-organized community, who keep language education in their own hands. There is an official representative body of Roma who deal with issues relating to Roma and who advise the government. The cultural autonomy of the Roma is recognized in an amendment to the Finnish

Constitution. The treatment of Roma in Finland has been praised by several observers (e.g. Hannikainen, 1996). The Romani language is used in day-care centers, and it is possible to learn Romani as a voluntary subject in a few schools. Many *Kaale* (as they call themselves) are reluctant to share their language with outsiders. According to official figures, a few hundred of the ca. 1400 Roma children take Romani classes at present.

France
Dialectally diverse. Teaching material available for some varieties, mostly for adults. Also story books, dictionaries, grammars. Little or no use of Romani in schools. The Gypsy Research Centre of Paris has produced some educational material in a standardized form of Romani.

Germany
Some teaching material has been developed for Roma, one of them in three dialects. Occasional Romani teaching. Romani speaking teaching aides at some places. The Sinti object to outside involvement with their language.

Ireland
Number of Romani speakers is negligible. The Irish Travellers are not historically related to the Roma, and they have no knowledge of Romani.

Italy
Dialectally diverse. Teaching material, dictionaries and grammars have been produced for several dialects. Many linguistic studies. Nevertheless, school teaching in or about Romani seems limited (see Casile, 1988 for a regional study). Courses for adults have occasionally been taught as well.

Liechtenstein
Probably nonexistent. According to the Liechtenstein government, there are no minorities in Liechtenstein.

Luxembourg
Probably nonexistent, even though there is a modest number of Romani speakers in Luxembourg.

The Netherlands
Except for some more or less private initiatives, no teaching material has been produced - at least not published. Some periodicals and poetry were

published. Sinti resist outside involvement with their language, and Roma from former Yugoslavia lack the resources. Occasional small-scale teaching initiatives at a few primary schools.

Norway
There are a few hundred Lovara and Churara in Norway. There seems to be no recent teaching material, but some was produced in the seventies. There is an academically produced text collection of Norwegian Lovara, with a glossary. There is also a separate language locally called Rommani (a combination of Norwegian and Romani) for which printed teaching material exists.

Portugal
The number of Romani speakers in Portugal is negligible. No texts have been produced, and the descendants of the first immigrants have lost their language.

Spain
Most of the indigenous Gitanos (descendants of the immigrants of the 1500s) no longer speak Romani. They have developed a new language called Caló, of which Romani is a main component, used in a Spanish framework. Some teaching materials and several dictionaries exist for this variety. Knowledge of Romani is limited to Gitano intellectuals and more recent (not very numerous) immigrant groups such as Kalderash. A reconstructed Romani language is sometimes used in print (mainly periodicals, but also the Spanish Constitution), called Romano-Kalo, but this has more symbolic than communicative value.

Sweden
Sweden has recently recognized Romani in all its varieties (*Regerings-kansliet*, 1999). Song books, several teaching books, reading material, and a grammar have been produced, and more is being produced. Money has been reserved for Romani mother tongue teaching and mass media. Sweden is dialectally diverse: speakers of Finnish Romani, Kalderash and Balkan varieties are established groupings in Sweden. Some government documents have been translated into the Arli Romani (Balkan) and Kalderash (Vlax) dialects. Apart from these, there are also the descendants of the very first Romani immigrants, who call themselves Romani-Manusj. They no longer speak the same Romani, but a combination of Romani and Swedish, which is a distinct language. There is a dictionary

of this language, but no teaching material. It seems widely known among young people and also used in correspondence, including via the Internet.

United Kingdom
The descendants of the very first Romani speaking immigrants, the Romanichal, no longer speak Romani, but a combination of Romani and English, which they call Rommany. There is some educational material available in this language. There are also thousands of Romani speaking immigrants, i.e. speakers of different dialects. No educational material seems to have been produced by or with those groups.

In short, the use of Romani in primary education in the EU thus far seems to be marginal, both as a language used in class and as a teaching subject. The situation in secondary education is even worse: there seems to be no secondary school in the EU (in contrast to some Central European countries) where Romani is a teaching subject, or the language of instruction. At the university level, Romani has been studied and taught at least in Austria, Denmark, France, Germany, Italy and the United Kingdom in the last decade.

There is a network of researchers, consultants, parents, teachers and others who are involved in the education of Roma and Travellers, but the Romani language is seldom among their top priorities. Publications on Gypsy and Traveller Education rarely deal with linguistic issues in depth. All in all, a reasonable amount of teaching material for Romani has been produced. This has often been produced locally, for specific dialects, and generally has little or no impact on other Romani communities.

Thus far we discussed linguistic aspects of Romani education. Many Roma parents, however, avoid schools because they see schools as a threat to their Romani culture. Ian Hancock, himself a Rom, described these feelings in the following eloquent way (Hancock, 1999):

From the traditional point of view, formal schooling has not been regarded as a good thing. It requires that Roma enter the non-Romani world, which is seen as polluting and counter-cultural. Not only is the environment unclean - particularly with regard to the toilet and cafetaria facilities, but equally unacceptable would be the seating of boys and girls in the classrooms, and the topics addressed in the curricula. It would also require formally identifying oneself and filling out paperwork, and spending a fixed amount of time in a non-Roma-controlled environment. The classroom is seen as a place to learn to become *gadzikanime* or 'Americanized'; there is nothing in the school-books about Romani history or contributions, and when 'Gypsies' turn up in the classes they are invariably represented negatively in works of fiction - especially children's fiction (Hancock, 1988) - and the historical figures presented as heroes in Western culture are all too frequently the same individuals who sent Roma in exile or even to their deaths. Schools are seen not only as environments that do nothing to teach a child to be a better Gypsy, but which seem determined instead to homogenize and de-ethicise that child. Stories about children's interaction with domestic pets, for example, send a different message to the pupil from the values taught in the home.

It is clear that such attitudes will lead to situations in which school attendance is avoided, and this requires special attention from educators. Some Roma-focused educational material is being produced by the Gypsy Research Center, among others some history books, language primers and books on education (see e.g. Bakker *et al.*, 2000; Liégeois, 1998).

Further reading on Romani and Roma in English

Much of the literature on Roma and Romani contains mistakes and mis-leading information. Here is a very brief list of some recommendable literature on culture and language: a general book on Roma (Fraser, 1992), a book on Roma in Europe (Liégeois, 1995), an annotated bibliography (Tong, 1995), a collection of papers on Roma education (Centre for Gypsy Research, 1993). On the linguistic side there is an accessible grammar (Hancock, 1995), a thorough scientific study (Sampson, 1926) and a popular book on the Romani language (Bakker *et al.*, 2000). A study of recent Romani as a written language is Matras (1999). Halwachs and Menz (1999) put Austrian Romani projects in a European context. Several recent collections of scientific research on Romani are available from John Benjamins Publications, edited by Matras and others (1995; 1997). These volumes also contain several papers regarding developing literacy in Romani (see also Kenrick, 1996).

The Center for Gypsy Research in Paris publishes a free periodical called Interface relating to Roma, focusing on educational matters. It also produces books on Roma education, history, language and culture in many EU languages, including Romani. Furthermore, it published a book with official documents on Roma and Travellers (Danbakli, 1994). A recent study of the political situation of Roma in Europe is HCNM (2000).

Much more has been written on the language Romani. A bibliography on Romani linguistics which is being compiled by Peter Bakker and Yaron Matras comprises more than 1500 titles of books and articles which have appeared since 1900. Country-based selections are available upon request from Peter Bakker (linpb@hum.au.dk).

Conclusions

This survey of the status of Romani in the EU is a reason for both sadness and optimism. On the negative side, we can mention that quite a few European states do not recognize Romani. On the other hand, there is more and more recognition for the language as states are exploring the implications of e.g. the European Charter. Political organizations such as the OSCE also play an important role in awareness-raising about Roma and their language. From an educational perspective, it appears that many countries do allow for the use and teaching of Romani, but very few countries have been able or willing to implement anything. All initiatives appear to be small-scale projects. The situation for Romani is in many ways more complex than for other minority languages in Europe. We can mention the lack of a territorial base, the preference for different dialects rather than a standardized or different language, the severe social and/or institutional discrimination of the Roma, the lack of unity of the Roma and of widely supported Romani political organizations, ignorance and prejudice regarding Roma on the part of the authorities and the general public, an unusually high degree of illiteracy among Roma and last but not least a spiritual ideology which discourages education in schools run by non-Roma. In spite of all of this, the Roma have been able to preserve their language in exile, and it is still among the most vital minority languages in Europe.

Acknowledgements

I want to thank all the collaborators on the *What is the Romani Language?* book for providing much of the information contained in this chapter. I also want to thank M. Danbakli, B. Gudmander, G. Extra, D. Halwachs, L. Hegelund, E. De Koninck,

J.P. Liégeois, Y. Matras, A. Paulin, A. Venes and the participants of the Oegstgeest meeting in January 2000 for giving access to a number of additional sources.

References

Bakker, P., Hübschmannová, M., Kalinin, V., Kenrick, D., Kyuchukov, H., Matras, Y. and Soravia, G. (2000) *What is the Romani language?* Hatfield/Hertfordshire: University of Hertfordshire Press; Paris: Centre de Recherches Tsiganes, Interface Collection.

Broeder, P. and Extra, G. (1998) *Language, ethnicity and education. Case studies of immigrant minority groups and immigrant minority languages.* Cleveland: Multilingual Matters.

Casile, F.M. (1988) *The Romany language in primary education in Italy.* Leeuwarden: Fryske Akademy/EMU Project 33/34.

Centre for Gypsy Research (1993) *The education of Gypsy and traveller children. Action-research and co-ordination.* Hatfield/Hertfordshire: University of Hertfordshire Press.

Cerquiglini, B. (1999) *Les langues de la France.* Rapport au Ministre de l'Education Nationale, de la Recherche et de la Technologie, et à la Ministre de la Culture et de la Communication. [http://www.culture.fr/culture/dglf/lang-reg/rapport_cerquiglini/langues-france.html]

Council of Europe (1992) *European charter for regional or minority languages.* [http.//conventions.coe.int/Treaty/en/Treaties/Html/148.htm]

Council of Europe (1992) *European charter for regional or minority languages. Explanatory Report.*

Council of Europe (1997-2000) *List of declarations made with respect to treaty no. 148 - European charter for regional or minority languages.*

Danbakli, M. (1994) *On Gypsies: Texts issued by international institutions.* Paris: Centre de Recherches Tsiganes/Toulouse: CRDP Midi-Pyrénées.

Eurydice (1999) Selected information from Eurybase. *Information dossier: Comparative perspectives on regional and minority languages in multicultural Europe* (pp. 57-89). Amsterdam: European Cultural Foundation [from website: http://www.eurydice.org/Eurybase/Files/dossier.htm].

Fraser, A. (1992) *The Gypsies.* London: Blackwell.

Halwachs, D. and Menz, F. (1999) *Die Sprache der Roma. Perspektiven der Romani-Forschung in Österreich im interdisziplinären und internazionalen Kontext.* Klagenfurt: Drava Verlag.

Hancock, I.F. (1988) Gypsies in our Libraries. *Collection building* 8 (4), 31-36.

Hancock, I.F. (1995) *A handbook of Vlax Romani.* Columbus, OH: Slavica Publishers.

Hannikainen, L. (1996) The status of minorities, indigenous peoples and immigrant and refugee groups in four Nordic states. *Nordic journal of international law* 65, 1-71.

Hancock, I.F. (1999) *The schooling of Romani Americans: An overview.* Keynote paper read before the Second International Conference on Psycholinguistic and Sociolinguistic Problems of Roma Children's Education in Europe, Varna, Bulgaria, May 27-29 1999. [http://www.geocities.com/Paris/5121/ schooling. htm]

HCNM (1999) *Report on the linguistic rights of persons belonging to national minorities in the OSCE area.* The Hague: High Commisioner on National Minorities.

Interface. Gypsies and Travellers. Education. Training. Youth. Free quarterly periodical published by the Gypsy Research Centre in Paris in English, French and Spanish.

Kenrick, D.S. (1996) Romani literacy at the crossroads. *International journal of the Ssciology of language* 119, 109-123.

Liégeois, J-P. (1995) *Roma, Gypsies and Travellers. Socio-cultural data. Socio-political data.* Strasbourg: Council of Europe Press.

Liégeois, J-P. (1998) *School provision for ethnic minorities: The Gypsy paradigm.* Paris: Centre de Recherches Tsiganes/Hatfield: University of Hertfordshire Press.

Liégeois, J-P. and Gheorghe, N. (1995) *Roma/Gypsies: A European minority.* London: Minority Rights Group.

Matras, Y. (1999) Writing Romani: the pragmatics of codification in a stateless language. *Applied linguistics* 20 (4), 481-502.

Matras, Y. (ed.) (1995) *Romani in contact. The history, structure and sociology of a language.* Amsterdam: John Benjamins.

Matras, Y., Bakker, P. and Kyuchukov, H. (eds) (1997) *The typology and dialectology of Romani.* Amsterdam: J. Benjamins.

Miller, C. (1998) American Roma and the ideology of defilement. In D. Tong (ed.) *Gypsies. An interdisciplinary approach* (pp. 201-217). New York: Garland. [Originally published in F. Rehfisch (ed.) *Gypsies, Tinkers and other Travellers* (pp. 41-54). London: Academic Press].

OSCE (2000) *Report on the situation of the Roma and Sinti in the OSCE area.* The Hague: Organization for Security and Co-operation in Europe, High Commissioner on National Minorities.

Regeringskansliet (1999) *Nationella minoriteter i Sverige.* Faktablad, Kultur-departmentet, June 1999.

Sampson, J. (1926) *The dialect of the Gypsies of Wales.* Oxford: Clarendon Press. [Reprinted in 1968; out of print; available in some libraries]

Tong, D. (1995) *Gypsies. A multidisciplinary annotated bibliography.* New York: Garland.

Universal Declaration on Linguistic Rights (1996) Barcelona [http://www.troc.es/ mercator/CDML_E.htm].

Venes, A. (1995) *Onder ons gesproken. Een onderzoek naar taalgebruik en taalattitudes van Roma-en Sinti-Zigeuners in Nederland.* [Speaking amongst ourselves. A study of language use and language attitudes of Roma and Sinti Gypsies in the Netherlands]. PhD Thesis, University of Tilburg.

Part III

Outlook from abroad

Multilingualism and multiculturalism in Canada*

JOHN EDWARDS

Recent developments in Europe are of considerable interest for students of languages, cultures and identities. We see a continent coming together - not without the occasional hiccup, of course - while, at the same time, there has never been so much attention given to 'small' languages, to stateless cultures, to minority concerns generally. Although the focus of this chapter is on multilingualism and multiculturalism in Canada, the current European context will be dealt with first.

The current European context

Of course, there is a great deal of posturing in the presented domain, and in many instances only lip-service is paid to such matters. And, some of the recent relevant resolutions, charters and so on are vague, or without teeth, or essentially unimplemented. None the less, there *are* real questions being asked about social and political accommodations, about the coexistence of a large federal continent with a 'Europe of the Regions'. So there are policy matters to consider here, and theoretical issues about unity and diversity.

But, as well, there are practical agendas which can either drive policy or cause it to collect dust on the shelf, and which may pay little heed to theoretical concerns. Reactions to *de facto* multiculturalism - diversity on the street, as it were - may be more important, for instance, than academic treatises on multicultural accommodation as an acceptable liberal-democratic response to heterogeneity, or the enriching societal effects of linguistic and cultural mosaics. It is surely reasonable, when thinking about social issues, to keep an eye on what is happening outside the cloister. A small example of this has just been presented by Gil-White (1999): he reminds us that, in the midst of what he calls the 'circumstantialist/primordialist' controversy among students of ethnicity and nationalism, ethnic 'actors' themselves are strong believers in actual descent criteria.

The implication, then, is that informed discussions about matters of language and culture, particularly where these involve minority groups (or, more exactly, relations between minorities and majorities, and, to a lesser extent perhaps, those among minorities themselves), must be ones which link academia with actual life. This is not to say that theoretical treatments need follow mundane events, nor (of course) should we expect the latter to reflect the sometimes rarefied insights of the former. But there ought to be some connection: on the one hand, attending to what is actually going on must be a salutary exercise for any academic undertaking which has obvious applied facets; on the other hand, there *are* linkages between ideas and events and the former *do* influence the latter - if only from a distance (temporal or other). Again, any subject which sees itself as a potential policy resource has special responsibilities here.

Within the European context itself, there has of course been a great deal of discussion, coexisting with the unfolding of various events - some of them unpleasant, some of them violent - on the ground. This discussion ranges from political insights, to intellectual debates, to academic investigation. One example of each will suffice here, particularly since the territory covered is, by and large, very familiar. In 1993, Vaclav Havel reminded the Council of Europe that European federalism was far from a purely administrative or technical matter; it could not be built, he said, upon partisan ideas, and it required both a guiding ethos and - more interesting, perhaps - an underlying generosity of spirit. In the same year, the ACTA foundation in Barcelona presented the results of a little survey conducted among a score of intellectuals, in which the scholars were asked to reflect upon European integration and its ramifications. Of special interest were thoughts about the idea of some pan-European culture and how (if such a thing could be conceived) it might mesh with more local identities. The diversity of opinion - even among twenty respondents - was considerable and suggests a lack of some common intellectual understanding of continental federalism. Specifically, while there was some degree of agreement that a general European *heritage* could be said to exist, it was not thought likely that such a beast could become any sort of replacement for (say) national loyalties. And, still in the same year, a perceptive book on European identities (Macdonald, 1993) argued convincingly that we need to know more about the scope and depth of people's allegiances, and under which conditions local identities might peacefully and usefully exist alongside larger ones. The important point was also made that it becomes particularly vital to understand existing identities at a time when new supra-state institutions (and possibly allegiances) are in formation.

These few points cover the major part of the terrain quite nicely, but it is the last which is the most basic, the key to other matters. At a time when old orders are changing, when things are in a state of flux, when loyalties and identities are under question (if not actual attack) - in these circumstances, people are particularly sensitive to actual and potential identities. To put it another way: periods of transition are, by definition, unsettling and often painful, particularly where they involve the negotiation or re-negotiation of identities. When - during or after these changes - people are asked to endorse new social contracts they (not unreasonably) hope that their own concerns have been adequately aired. It is this sort of situation which characterises much of the current European linguistic and cultural scene, but it is not unique. In fact, it is but the latest manifestation of longstanding patterns of social movement, of refigured boundaries, of reworked allegiances and affiliations. But it is not only in history that one can find parallels for what is happening - there are contemporary settings, too, that are of interest. One of the most relevant of these is the Canadian. Before turning directly to this, however, I want to present a little vignette (which is *almost* Canadian!).

An adventure in identity

In May 1999, Makah whalers in northern Washington - just across the Strait of Juan de Fuca from Vancouver Island - killed a thirty-ton, ten-metre-long grey whale. Makah culture had historically been built around whaling, and became rich because of it. The decline of the grey whale population led to the abandonment of the hunt in 1926, but by 1994 the now-protected species had returned: it was removed from the endangered list and a renewed Makah hunt was sanctioned for 'cultural purposes'. Given the fierce worldwide debate over whaling, it is not surprising that it then took five years for the current hunt to take place, the beginning of another five-year period during which the Makah will be allowed to take twenty whales. It is also unsurprising that the initial kill was surrounded by heated and acrimonious debate, and it is clear that this debate will continue so long as whales are killed. On the one hand there is concern for aboriginal rights, and cultural continuity; on the other, there is disgust at what is seen as a totally unnecessary slaughter - regardless of the size of the whale stocks - and a reversion to practices which may once have been appropriate but which are now anachronistic and repugnant. As is often the case when age-old practices are dusted off for modern times, the Makah whale hunt was accompanied by the ironic and the bizarre.

The traditional cedar canoe used in the hunt had to be towed into position, and the ceremonial harpoon had to be augmented by .50-calibre armour-piercing weaponry. Makah whalers were photographed standing on the back of the dead or dying animal, wearing modern sneakers and giving what look like quite non-traditional clenched-fist salutes of victory. A large fishing vessel was needed to land the whale - which, on the way to shore, sank to the bottom and was retrieved only with the use of compressed air. For the official beaching, the carcass was lashed to the cedar canoe. Once on shore, the traditional blessings were followed by the butchering (done by an Inuit) and, while praising the revitalisation of their culture, many needed a cola drink to wash down the unfamiliar raw blubber (said to taste like a mixture of lamb stew, latex and vaseline). Not all the whale meat was eaten raw, of course: the preparation of traditional whale dishes is now being taught to Makah students with the help of a Japanese cookery book.

Most of the reaction to the hunt, however vehement, was un-surprising. Anti-whaling organisations saw it as trophy-hunting; one observer said: 'It used to be about food. Now, it's about fun. I felt total repulsion watching them ... doing back flips off the whale'. Many politicians also condemned the Makah hunt, sensing that the general public's antipathy to whaling is stronger than its support for aboriginal traditions. Other aboriginal groups tended to endorse the hunt - particularly supportive here were members of the Nuu-Chah-Nulth and other British Columbian tribes, some of whom want to resume whaling themselves. Some commentators not overly enamoured with environmentalism were also supportive, citing both adequate whale stocks and inadequate 'green' reasoning: 'There is no dishonour in what the Makah did this week', observed the *Port Alberni Valley Times*, a Vancouver Island newspaper. Another British Columbian journalist noted that the hunt was 'grotesque, courageous, tragic, defiant, bloody and strangely beautiful ... an act carried out against overwhelming odds' (see *Globe & Mail*, Toronto, 20 to 22 May 1999, for these and the following citations).

But not all responses were quite so predictable. Some environmentalist and animal-rights groups found it difficult to decide between support for traditional aboriginal practices and condemnation of the killing of wildlife. A similar line was taken in some of the subtler editorials. For example, Vancouver's _The Province_ pointed out that 'we've been teaching our children that whales are almost holy creatures, and ... to respect native culture. How will our teachers reconcile yesterday's butchery?' Not all native communities were behind the hunt, either: 'Going back to the old tradition for food, it doesn't add up. In order to get the young kids off drugs ... it's not necessary to kill a whale'. One Makah elder said, 'I don't see the point of it. I don't see no use for the meat ... They claim to be descendants of the great whalers, but that's long gone'. Still others pointed out that the Makah's case would be easier to defend if they were to use purely traditional methods, and put their elephant guns and motorboats aside.

A concluding, parenthetical note: the hunt, subsidised by the American federal government to the tune of $340,000 - to assist the Makah in the exercise of their historical treaty rights to whaling - is a lucrative undertaking. Every grey whale taken is worth half a million dollars. And, given agitation in other parts of the world for resumption of whaling, it has been suggested that the 'natives are really just stalking horses for the nefarious Norwegian and Japanese whalers'.

Perhaps it may be thought that the Makah whale hunt is a minor matter. Admittedly, it is not on a level with the higher reaches of ethnic interaction - ethnic cleansing, for example. It is also perhaps less important than state policies of multiculturalism, or referenda on bilingual education, or moves to protect endangered languages. But it is certainly food for thought (if not for many of the Makah), and it introduces some of the lesser-known players in the current Canadian drama. Besides turning the spotlight on the aboriginal 'actors', this episode is also important precisely because it _is not_ ethnic cleansing or a chapter in the application of some broad policy of social engineering - that is, it reminds us that matters of identity can be found across a very wide spectrum. There is another point here, too, one which I believe is often forgotten but which is important if only because - again - it broadens the argument.

Struggles for group recognition and group identity are often more poignant when the group in question feels that at least part of its culture is at some risk. This is why settings involving minority groups often show things in the boldest relief. It would be a mistake, however, to imagine that this topic is one of 'minority' interest alone; _all_ groups - large or small, weak or powerful - have stakes here. We can see this more clearly once we realise that struggles for the maintenance of group identity are not only to be understood in inter-group terms; there is also an *intra-group* dimension here. Quite apart from whether or not groups stand in fear of powerful neighbouring cultures, there exists the difficulty of maintaining valued traditions in a world increasingly full of homo-genising pressures. A desired continuity - one which usually stresses the original, the pure, the 'authentic' (dubious quantities though these often are, at least in the hands of commentators with particular axes to grind) - must contend with an equally desired modernisation, with broader and broader access, with mobility of every description. The Makah example is particularly useful here since these aboriginal people suffer both sorts of 'identity-in-transition' pressure: that which arises from strong external forces, and that which is created by processes of change within the group. For minority populations these two variants are not unrelated of course, whereas, for majority or 'mainstream' groups, only the latter need arise and - even where it does - it often reflects a more untroubled history, and one less disturbed by interruption or discontinuity.

Setting the stage

Recent Canadian social history shows both theoretical and applied aspects of the language-culture-identity linkage. Thus, formal institu-tional responses have been elicited by official perceptions of diversity and plurality, as well as by considerations of desired future developments. But at the same time, events have unfolded on the street, in the school, in the corridors of politics - events which have intertwined with official policies and directions, and which have sometimes overtaken them or, at least, tempered or modified them.

Most people are aware, I suppose, of the continuing tensions in Canada, tensions largely animated by the strained relationship between Quebec and the rest of the country. But fewer will know that the cast of this play comprises more than *Québécois* nationalists and anglophone federalists. The constitutional tensions which cause conflict between these two groups have prompted a much broader examination of the Canadian cultural and political landscape. It must be remembered, too, that not all francophones - whether within the Quebec provincial boundaries or beyond them - have sovereigntist sympathies, and the anglophone population does not simply comprise one monolithic entity. Besides these groups, the players include aboriginal Canadians (as the preceding vignette suggests) and 'allophones' - i.e. immigrants from neither English-nor French-speaking backgrounds. The issues under review include of course basic constitutional arrangements, which have been put on the agenda by the political rise of separatism in Quebec - but also all other matters touching upon language and culture: these include as we have seen the rights of indigenous 'first nations' and state policies involving official bilingualism and multiculturalism. All of these reflect concerns about group identity, its maintenance and its continuity. And finally here, it should be recalled that all these internal debates occur within a country which has historically struggled to define 'Canadian-ness' in a continent dominated by its powerful and rapacious southern neighbour.

Nationalism and sovereignty

In 1981-82, Canada's constitution was brought 'home' from Britain, a final act of severance. With it came a new *Charter of Rights and Freedoms*, one of whose sections outlined minority-language rights meant to apply to all citizens in an officially bilingual country. But Quebec was not a signatory, fearing a threat to its own linguistic authority which had, over the years, supported French. Nonetheless, as a province of Canada, it was bound by the *Charter*. This unsatisfactory political state of affairs gave rise to several attempts to bring Quebec back into the constitutional fold. These failed, however, and the failures stiffened and reinforced separatist resolve within the province: the sovereigntist *Parti Québécois* returned to power in 1994, held a referendum on independence in October 1995 (which failed by the narrowest of margins), and was re-elected as the provincial government in late 1998. Although, since then, the separatist cause seems to have run into some difficulties, tensions obviously remain and another referendum is a distinct possibility (see Edwards, 1994; 1997; in preparation).

I suggest that the course of recent events - insofar as these are fuelled by Quebec - basically involves two related matters: concern about the state of French language and culture, and nationalist political power. The first of these has had a longer life than the second but, without the addition of some degree of political clout, it typically remains a simmering frustration. *With* such an addition, of course, recipes for change become at least imaginable.

There is no doubt that francophone worries about *survivance* and fears of *disparition* are justified. The traditional Catholic *revanche des berceaux* has long since disappeared in a modernised and secularised Quebec society, and attempts to shore up a dwindling *francophonie* through selective immigration have not been entirely successful. Many recent French-speaking newcomers hail from cultures and societies very different from Quebec; many, indeed, are members of so-called 'visible-minority' groups; relatively few resemble or, it is assumed, see themselves as agents of social continuity for the *Québécois de vieille souche*.

In such a situation, nationalist appeals are seductive. The *Parti Québécois* has, in this regard, always taken pains to present itself as the modern face of nationalism, as standing for the democratic conception that all residents of the province (or the country it is hoped it will become) - francophone or not - are Quebeckers. In short, the sovereigntists have claimed that theirs is a *civic nationalism*. Unfortunately, various comments have suggested to some observers that, after all, it is the old ethnic variety which is on offer. The most notorious example here was provided by Jacques Parizeau who, as leader of the separatist party on referendum night in 1995, said 'It's true we have been defeated, but basically by what? By money and the ethnic vote'. I would say that, beyond the purely Canadian issues at stake here, the sovereigntist movement has fuelled the larger debate about whether such a thing as civic nationalism actually exists at all. This is not the place to discuss the matter in any detail, but it is surely worthy of note that civic nationalism has had its strongest following in (European) French intellectual circles (see Edwards, in preparation).

Whatever the proper status of Quebec nationalism, one thing seems very clear: Quebeckers - whether sovereigntist or not - have a sense of themselves as a nation or *un peuple*. Naturally, this sense is strongest among separatists. Lucien Bouchard, currently the leader of the *Parti Québécois* and the Premier of Quebec, observed several years ago that 'Canada is divisible because it is not a real country. There are two peoples, two nations and two territories. And this one [Quebec] is ours' (see *Globe & Mail*, 30 January 1996). Nationalist rhetoric here, to be sure, but not without some accuracy. Compared to Quebec, the rest of the country is a much more heterogeneous, multicultural mixture; the anglophone monolith is long since gone, interpenetrated as it has become by many other elements. And this, in turn, accounts for some of the frustration and some of the rhetoric on the sovereigntist side. That is, large numbers of people outside Quebec simply do not understand the *national* self-definition that is so important there; for them, Quebec is one province among ten and, while it exhibits obvious differences, it ought not to be given any more than other regions. There are many obvious seeds of misunderstanding here.

This, in absurdly truncated fashion, is the central act in the current drama. It hinges, as we can see, upon nationalism and, indeed, this is the enduring legacy of a country with not one but two 'founding peoples' or 'charter groups'. Those who see a 'Quebec problem' that must be 'solved' are simplistic in their analysis: the 'problem' here is part of the definition of the country and perhaps its only real 'solution' is the very rupture which the *Parti Québécois* and its admirers wish to effect. But, as we have seen, the *general* question of nationalism in the Canadian context has given rise to more specific debates over *types* of nationalism. And there is an even more pivotal matter in all this, one which allows us to bring in, as it were, some of the other players: the disputed territory which is called *'the rights of citizens in liberal democracies'*.

Aboriginals and allophones

It has become clear through the words and deeds of recent Quebec governments - not all of them sovereigntist in philosophy, by the way - that part of the nationalist project in that province involves the protection of *collective* rights (generally of a linguistic or cultural nature). And, *mirabile dictu*, this is not an issue about which Quebec politicians have been mealy-mouthed. In the winter of 1988-89, for instance, the Liberal (i.e. non-sovereigntist) Premier of Quebec, Robert Bourassa, argued that the parlous state of French language and culture - a tiny island in a huge anglophone sea - justified and, indeed, demanded action which elevated group protection over individual rights. In this case, he was referring to 'sign laws' which reduced or eliminated the place of English.

Opposing sentiment took both specific and general forms. Some simply said that Quebec was part of an officially bilingual country and had no right to deny its anglophone citizens any form or degree of (otherwise acceptable) linguistic expression. But for others, the issue was of broader and less localised import: is it not the case that, for a couple of centuries or so, democratic governments have held rights to inhere in individuals, and have shied away (largely, but not always totally) from according them on the basis of group membership? This issue has become informed by - but has also stimulated - academic discussions of a vitally important nature. It is beyond my purpose and scope here to deal with the insights and debates which are now hot issues within a number of disciplines - political science, sociology and social philosophy among them - but I must at least point out that, whatever their outcomes, these discussions are at last taking arguments beyond the level of 'special pleading', where they have long resided, and on to more general terrain.

Part, then, of the nationalist *Québécois* position - as of nationalist positions in general - is the argument for the protection of the collectivity, for the fairness of group rights. This stems from nationalist sentiment *per se*, but it is reinforced by the perceived 'slippage' of francophone culture. Furthermore, this slippage is seen to be exacerbated by the growth of the allophone population (see below). And further still, there is the bitterness that all this has happened to one of the two original Canadian 'charter groups' - which now looks as if it might become simply one among that large group of allophonic 'others'. This is the reason, incidentally, why resistance to official policies of multiculturalism has traditionally been strongest in Quebec.

Nationalist sentiment in Quebec has not gone unnoticed in other quarters and among other constituencies whose sense of identity is of current concern. The allophone population, for example, now constitutes some 30% of the overall Canadian population, and is roughly equivalent to the size of the francophone group. There is some feeling afoot that - whatever may have been the case at the time of the founding of the country - conditions have now changed, and francophone demands for special consideration are increasingly unreasonable. This coincides with a previously existing concern over the official multiculturalism policy (enshrined in a government act in 1988) which remains embedded in a bilingual (i.e. French-English) framework. What is to be made of a policy which apparently supports cultural diversity, but excises the language components? Furthermore, this presupposes that a central thrust among allophone groups is for cultural retention or some species of abiding 'street' multiculturalism. Evidence for this is waning, as Canada - despite its claim to be a 'mosaic' rather than a 'melting-pot' - exerts the familiar assimilative pressures on newcomers. In this setting, these tend (outside Quebec, at any rate) to move people towards the anglophone mainstream (which, of course, is itself in a considerable state of flux). Indeed, some of the well-known criticisms of multiculturalism (as policy, if not as *de facto* entity) - e.g. it acts against social unity, it is a balkanising force, governments ought not to actively encourage cultural retention, and so on - have been echoed by members of minority groups themselves (see, for example, the popular treatment by Bissoondath, 1994).

Allophone groups within the province of Quebec have been particularly sensitised by recent events. I have already cited Parizeau's remarks on referendum night, remarks that implied that the francophone destiny had been thwarted by the 'others' (since virtually all anglophone and allophone Quebeckers voted against the separatist option, and since the margin of defeat was so incredibly narrow, Parizeau's lament was essentially accurate). But accuracy is not always politically correct, nor need it always be the best basis from which to proceed. Things were exacerbated when other separatist commentators pointed to the Jews, the Italians and the Greeks as the ethnic stumbling blocks.

Aboriginal groups have also been galvanised lately. They have become increasingly adamant that, if any special arrangements are on offer - for instance, the formally recognised 'distinct-society' status that has animated Quebec sovereigntists (but which is of broad concern within the provincial population, even among those who remain committed to the federation) - they should be the obvious and first recipients. Their case certainly has the longest history, and their generally shameful treatment at the hands of white colonisers is also seen (in some eyes, anyway) to suggest redress. Among aboriginal groups within Quebec, an interesting situation has arisen. They would not wish to become part of a new break-away country, would request federal assistance, and would no doubt have a great deal of popular support in this. They have pointed out, then, that if Quebec nationalists can hold a referendum on secession, surely they (the James Bay Cree, for example) should be able to do the same. But nationalism has its own logic, and the sovereigntists are not about to accord to the aboriginal peoples the political options they claim for themselves. There are, of course, examples from other parts of the world of minority reaction to still smaller minorities.

Members of the aboriginal community have also reminded us of some lurking dangers in the principle of collective rights. As discussions were unfolding about increased native self-government, aboriginal women's groups protested, on the grounds that rights accorded on the basis of 'groupness' could enshrine elements of a traditional system inimical to them. One of the points here is that it is an error to assume that group interest can be conceived of in a monolithic way.

A note on linguistic and cultural social engineering

The two governmental policies most relevant in this discussion are official bilingualism (underpinned by the *Official Languages Act* of 1969) and the multicultural policy which Prime Minister Trudeau outlined two years later and which achieved legislative status with the *Multiculturalism Act* in 1988. Both can be seen in either altruistic or opportunistic lights. For example, was the OLA meant to give official substance to the actual state of affairs, in which French and English mainstreams were to continue and, where at all possible, intertwine via bilingual adaptations - or was it a bone thrown by an increasingly powerful anglophone community? Was the Multiculturalism Act a welcoming and openhearted recognition of the increasing diversity of Canadian society, of the ever more important role of the allophones, or was it another bone - this time, one to appease and appeal to 'ethnic' voters, an essentially empty gesture predicated on the belief that, if anything, it would expedite their passage into the anglophone current?

Whatever one's view here, both policies have had to cope with a rapidly changing society. Thus, Canada has *not* become noticeably more bilingual over the past thirty years or so - if anything, the linguistic polarities have sharpened. There is essentially a francophone stronghold in Quebec and a sizeable minority in New Brunswick but, outside those regions, assimilation has continued apace. Similarly, for all the rhetoric, the Canadian scene shows most of the elements of that 'anglo-conformity' seen for so long in America. The inescapable conclusion is that, short of draconian intervention, policies like these 'work' to the extent to which they build upon, reflect or reinforce actual or broadly desired states of affairs. Otherwise, they can easily become dwarfed by demographic and social trends - dwarfed and, increasingly, empty.

Discussion

In this context, one can only provide hints about deeper matters. Nonetheless, I think it is clear that the Canadian experience is both intrinsically interesting and of broader import. It is a country which has historically struggled to maintain itself - socially, politically, psychologically - and which, in addition, has had to grapple with internal matters of explosive importance; some of these have been present from the beginning, while others are of more recent provenance. It is a country that has both native and immigrant inhabitants; the latter group comprises both 'old' colonisers and 'new' Canadians - and the old guard here generally consider that they are by now essentially indigenous themselves. In this regard it is like other new-world 'receiving' states, but it is also unique: it is the only one in which the European mainstream flows in two channels, not a single one. For all these reasons, the Canadian experience is intrinsically rich - and it is this very richness which may have implications for policy and practice far beyond its shores. What are the important general conclusions here, and what do they suggest, then?

First of all, anyone who has paid the slightest attention to Canada over the last few years must be struck by the many instances and illustrations it provides of basic elements in sociolinguistic, sociocultural and other equations. And this is true, to varying degrees, of many other parts of the world - particularly in this *fin-de-millénaire* period which seems so particularly marked by identity negotiations of all sorts. I began this chapter by touching upon the western European context, but we could look at the ex-Soviet Union and its former republics, at the political reworkings in southern Africa, at the intense examinations of multiculturalism and pluralism in North America and the antipodes, at aboriginal movements in South and Central America, and so on. Each of these settings holds insights for us all. Of course, we have to make appropriate extrapolations. We also have to accept that, while every setting is unique, its uniqueness lies not in elements never found elsewhere but rather in particular combinations of elements that are, in fact, quite common.

Secondly, while official positions on linguistic and cultural matters can channel and give focus to poorly stated or inadequately understood desires, they can also run aground on the shoals of practice. Thus, they are similar to all other social-policy initiatives. The *particular* dangers here, however, arise because language and cultural pronouncements cut to the heart of 'groupness', because they can be construed (by some) as giving unfair advantages (to others), because there exists the possibility of 'freezing', via policy, things which are rapidly changing on the street, and so on. One obvious implication is to consider extremely carefully all such policies - preferably *prior* to implementation. Another is to consider whether formal policies are actually the best procedure at all: I have argued elsewhere that, sometimes, the most appropriate official action is no legislative action at all.

Careful examination of identities in transition will always repay the effort. Such identities are implicitly up for renegotiation: things have thawed a bit, and will perhaps resolidify in some altered form. It is surely obvious that, in such fluid times, close examination is called for - not only by those most personally involved, but also by officialdom, by policy-makers, by academics and others who may have something to contribute or something to learn. Jung felt that, before one can attain a meaningful psychological unity, it is necessary to examine and understand all the constituent parts of the psyche. One need not be a Jungian to see that this may also apply when we move from the individual to the group level.

One of the clearest points emerging from the Canadian context is the difficulty involved when two nations attempt to live together under one state roof. It can be done, of course, but apparently never without tension. We are faced with the possibility, then, of either renewed federalism - perhaps from a more sensitive and more informed basis - or partition. In either case, the political ramifications will be instructive.

We know that there are many more nations in the world than there are states. Even with radical re-arrangements, the likelihood is great that most will remain stateless entities. We should be prepared to examine more closely the conditions under which nations can successfully share a country. Or, to look at it on a smaller scale: we need better information about arrangements between minority and majority groups, as well as among minority groups themselves.

The Canadian experience also reminds us that no group is a seamless whole. While we often have no difficulty accepting that when we are thinking about large multicultural societies in general terms, we can easily fall into error when considering particular groups. This is especially so, perhaps, when these groups are small, subordinate, marginalised, or otherwise markedly 'non-mainstream'. If, even with the best will in the world, we apply what we imagine to be ameliorative or corrective measures - based upon collectivist principles - we run the risk of creating internal fissures, or of maintaining arguably undesirable social practices and traditions.

One possible implication of this is to renounce collectivist action altogether, and fall back upon those principles of *individual* rights that have characterised modern liberal-democratic regimes. This, however, may not satisfy everyone, particularly those who feel that there is some historical balance to be redressed, some old grievance to be resolved, some fundamental injustice to be reversed.

What are the important arguments here? The Canadian experience, and many others too, show that groups under pressure typically support collective action, and endorse the view that group rights can legitimately be accorded within liberal democracies. Well, one would expect this. Equally, one would expect that majority cultures, secure collectivities, mainstream groups would reject such views, perhaps under the heading of 'special pleading'. They might have some sympathy for groups that have clearly suffered in the past, and they might even be willing to see some very specific forms of compensation. But experience shows that they are unlikely to see official recognition of group rights (and government action which might result) as any sort of generally acceptable principle. Again, this is understandable.

Since different constituencies take predictably different positions on collective and individual rights, it is extremely useful (to say the least) that - as I have already mentioned in passing - we are now beginning to see fully-fleshed attempts to sort the whole matter out, to see if some general principles might be elucidated. Some commentators have suggested (to take one very specific example) that indigenous groups might merit consideration not given to immigrant ones. I cannot follow this up here - not even to examine the flaws in this simple example - but this is obviously a 'growth' area, and rightly so. It is also an area, we should remember, in which academic insights and theoretical illumination may count for nothing outside the academic grove.

When traditions and modernity meet, where is the continuity? What is the 'authentic' culture to be protected? One typically finds, at the very least, internal conflict over these matters - and this was certainly so in the Makah case discussed above. Some were adamant that, for the good of the culture, the old ways should be revived and maintained: what are Makah without whaling? Others argued that what once obtained might no longer do so, that times and conditions have altered, that cultural continuity ought not to rest upon static practices and values (quite a Barthian notion, in fact). There are generally two sub-strands to this last point: first, that it is simply inappropriate and, in the case of traditions like whaling, perhaps repugnant, to try to carry on the old ways; second, that even if it were appropriate, the resuscitation and preservation of old practices is unlikely to be able to compete with more modern cultural forms. The implication is that cultural continuity deserves just as much critical attention as does cultural disruption and discontinuity

Further points arise when we turn to minority issues which, apart from their intrinsic interest, often illuminate more general social processes. Minorities are important in this regard because their position - sometimes under assimilative pressure, but always at least potentially precarious - throws into relief matters which are sometimes more obscure elsewhere. As the Makah whale hunt demonstrates, there are internal discontinuities created by modernisation, and these are found within all groups. And we should not forget, as well, that many writers have in one way or another argued that societies are best judged in terms of how they treat their least powerful members.

Of course, the very definition of 'minority' can be difficult. Are the *Québécois* a beleaguered minority group, whose language and culture require concerted collective protection? Or are they better understood as the provincial majority group? And what would their status be, in this regard, were Quebec to become an independent country? Or, consider the anglophones: can they claim minority status in Quebec and, on that basis, see themselves as a put-upon group, forced to fight for its existence in a society dominated by francophones? The geographical and political context is paramount here and it is clear that particular contexts will be invoked by people so as to bolster particular positions, or to press particular claims.

Larger minorities may contain smaller ones. In the interplay among them, one often finds that sauce for the goose is not sauce for the gander. Francophone sovereigntists in Quebec, who wish to separate after a successful provincial referendum, deny that form of political expression to native groups. Issues of self-determination quickly become highly contentious in such settings, selective appeals to history are made, old treaties and agreements are invoked, the weight attaching to the 'we-were-here-first' principle is carefully examined - none of this, of course, sums to anything which is agreeable in all quarters. That is why it is understandable, if ominous, that a scenario looms in which elementary varieties of power - which need owe nothing to logical argument - will become dominant.

Conclusions

In this chapter, I have attempted to interweave - in a very cursory manner, of course - a number of threads. These include languages and cultures, majorities and minorities. My view is that any discussion of language must also say something about the broader culture of which language is a part. Similarly, one can only understand minority issues by paying some attention to the larger mosaic to which they contribute. This sort of coverage is required because discussions of minority languages and cultures are really discussions of identities. Of course, discussion of *any* language and culture - minority or not - is essentially a treatment of identity, but there is an obvious and marked poignancy to the matter where 'small' or 'at-risk' groups are involved. With this in mind, some proposals for policy-makers can be outlined here. These basically reflect the summaries provided in the preceding section.

First, in preparation for any policy, it is advisable to look very carefully at other contexts. Of course, each setting is unique, but this is not because its elements are found nowhere else; in fact, basic constituents are remarkably similar across settings. The uniqueness arises, rather, through particular *combinations* of essentially the same building blocks. The implication is clear: things can be learned.

It is possible that, in some situations, the best policy is none at all - that is, no legislated or official action. Part of this caution derives from the difficulties inherent in policies which are essentially aimed at *collectivities* - some within the group may feel slighted or affronted; others, without the group, may consider such policies unfair; and so on. I have noted already the example of aboriginal *women* and their concerns over native autonomy; I could add to this that the creation of Nunavut (in March 1999) for the Inuit has annoyed some other northern aboriginal groups - the Dene, for instance. Relatedly, policy-makers should be sensitive to the possibility - indeed, probability - that alterations in one area will have knock-on effects in others. That is why, for example, language-planning interventions often founder on larger shoals.

A sense of history is also vital - today's at-risk minority may have wielded power in the past, or may become the bully-boy of tomorrow. The broader point is that history is a moving picture, not a still life. Interventions in the social fabric are fraught with many perils, and one of these arises from the (sometimes laudable) desire to redress old grievances, to level various playing-fields, to shore up cultural slippage.

In particular, policies aiming to 'preserve and protect' must consider carefully just what is to be sheltered. Cultures may involve practices that are increasingly ignored within the group itself, or that seem anach-ronistic, or have negative effects upon neighbours. One of the many implications here is that the broadest possible range of viewpoints needs to be assembled and assessed.

The most basic point in all this - and one which policy-makers may forget, or may be nudged into forgetting by the more strident demands made by some interested constituencies - is that we are enmeshed here with matters of identity, matters of emotion. If linguistic management, for example, had to respond only to instrumental requirements, only to practical communicative issues, then things would be a great deal easier. The fact that language is so much more than a purely pragmatic medium, that it is an important part (the *central* part, some have wished to argue) of a sense of 'groupness', implies the need for greater caution and sensitivity than is typically reflected in official interventions.

Note

*   This text is an expanded version of remarks made at the International Symposium on Minorities in European Linguistic and Cultural Policies, sponsored by the University of Vienna and the Research Centre on Multilingualism (Brussels), and held in Vienna in November 1999.

References

ACTA Foundation (1993) *Europe: Els intellectuals i la qüestió Europea*. Barcelona: ACTA.

Bissoondath, N. (1994) *Selling illusions: The cult of multiculturalism in Canada*. Toronto: Penguin.

Edwards, J. (1994) Ethnolinguistic pluralism and its discontents. *International journal of the sociology of language* 110, 5-85.

Edwards, J. (1997) French and English in Canada: Before and after the Quebec referendum of October 1995. In W. Wölck and A. de Houwer (eds.), *Recent studies in contact linguistics*. Bonn: Dümmler.

Edwards, J. (in preparation) Sovereignty or separation? Political discourse in Canada in the 1990s.

Gil-White, F. (1999) How thick is blood? *Ethnic and racial studies* 22, 789-820.

Havel, V. (1993) Short-sighted stumbling toward a new Europe. *Globe & Mail* [Toronto], 30 November.

Macdonald, S. (1993) *Inside European identities*. Oxford: Berg.

Minority languages in the United States, with a focus on Spanish in California

REYNALDO F. MACÍAS

The purpose of this chapter is to provide a comparative perspective on a language minority group in a non-European state that might provide some insights to the development of language policies for a new and developing multicultural Europe. While it is useful to provide such a case study, I begin this chapter with some historical background information that helps frame the current policies and cultural debates about Spanish, and to a lesser degree other non-English languages, in California and the United States. I then proceed to describe more in detail the language demography of the nation, the school enrollments of minority and immigrant language speakers, and the official status of languages. A brief discussion regarding the language debates within the country completes the chapter.

Historical background

The language diversity of the north American continent on the eve of contact with Europeans has been estimated at over 500 languages. The number of these languages which have survived until today, is less than half. At the same time, colonial languages - English, Spanish and French - have become dominant and hegemonic throughout this region. English has become dominant within the United States as the legacy of the British colonies which declared their independence and formed the country. The progeny of the British colonists and other settlers and immigrants adopted English as the national (rather than official) language across generations. The history of Spanish, however, is different from that of English.

The history of Spanish in the Americas can also be traced to the contact between Europeans and the indigenous populations in these continents in 1492. Sociolinguists often divide languages in an area into three categories related to the history and settlement of the speakers: indigenous, colonial and immigrant languages. Unlike colonial languages in other parts of the world, Spanish in the 'Americas' became the native language of much of the indigenous, native-born majority over time. Through racial miscegenation and social restructuring, even the social self-image in parts of the continent became the new racially-mixed and blended people of *La Raza* (the people) or *mestizos* (bi-racial). One source indicates that the contribution to this new people was heavily skewed in favour of the indigenous stock - estimated at between 5 and 25 million in middle America alone on the eve of contact with Europeans (Wolf, 1966).

Even with the decimation of the indigenous population that took place within the two generations after contact, it is estimated that there were over three to five million indigenous people in middle America by the end of the 16th century. During the entire colonial period of 400 years, only 300,000 Europeans, and close to 275,000 people of African ancestry, entered this region (Wolf, 1966). So, while we can identify Spanish as a colonial language, it is much harder to make the case that current day speakers of the language are descendants of the colonizers alone, primarily so, or even equally so. The current day *mestizo* Spanish-speakers are primarily an indigenous 'group'. While this group may continue cultural practices and values of these historical indigenous populations, they contrast sharply with those currently identified indigenous groups who have maintained a continuity of indigenous culture, language and identification through the more than half millennium since 1492. The current Mexican and the other varieties of 'American' Spanish, however, also reflect vital contributions from the indigenous languages of the area.

The British colonies in the northeastern American continent declared independence in 1776, and the United States was founded in 1789, with the ratification of the Constitution by the 13 former British colonies. Between 1803 and 1848, the United States expanded from the eastern coast of north America 2500 miles to the western coast of this northern continent. In this expansion, it gained, through purchase and military conquest, a substantial amount of new territory, occupied in most instances with populations of indigenous groups and settlers. The United States often adopted the social and other organization of the prior sovereigns in these territories, especially if they were from previous colonial powers or other declared independent states (e.g. Mexico). Indigenous populations were most often forcibly moved west, and then ensconced by the national government on federal reservations.

Nearly two-thirds of the current mainland jurisdiction of the United States was, at one time, under a Spanish-speaking sovereign-Spain or

Mexico. In 1848, in fact, the United States gained more than 900 square miles of territory as spoils of the US-Mexican war. This ceded territory became all or parts of 13 states within the union, including California. Close to 100,000 Mexicans and another 100,000 American Indians were already settled on those lands. At the end of the 19th Century, the United States intervened in the Cuban war of independence from Spain, and in the process gained Cuba, Puerto Rico and the Philippines. It currently still includes Puerto Rico as part of its jurisdiction. In part, as a recognition of the prior sovereign in these areas, and also as a recognition of the predominantly Spanish-speaking populations of these conquered areas, the federal government of the United States recognized an official status for Spanish for varying periods of time, and for various purposes. It currently recognizes the official bilingual status, in English and Spanish, of Puerto Rico. Table 1 shows a brief historical profile of the Spanish speaking population within the nation.

While it is clear that the Spanish language has benefited from a continuous 'in-migration' of Spanish speakers, it is also clear that the principal introduction of Spanish speakers to the United States took place as a result of military conquest and territorial expansion in the 19th century. During the 20th century, the increase of the Spanish speaking population not only kept pace with the population growth of the country, but exceeded it. In 1900, the Spanish speaking population was estimated at 2% of the national population, while in 1990, it was estimated at over 8%.

Language demographic profile of the nation

The total national population increased 10% between 1980 and 1990, from 226 million to 248 million persons. The total number of persons who spoke a language other than English increased almost four times more greatly (38.6%) during this same decade (see Table 2). More than 31.8 million people (14% of the nation's population five years old and over) said that they spoke a language other than English in 1990, compared with 23.1 million (11%) a decade earlier. After English, Spanish was the most common language spoken in the US. Over half (54.4%; 17.3 million) of those who said they spoke a language other than English in 1990, reported that they spoke Spanish. In 1980, about 11.1 million persons spoke Spanish, 48% of all those who spoke a language other than English.

Table 1 Spanish speaking population in the United States, 1850-1990

Year	Total US population	Spanish speakers on mainland US	Population of Puerto Rico*	Total number of Spanish speakers N	% of total popul
1850	23,191,876	118,000	–	118,000	0.5
1860	31,443,321	170,000	–	170,000	0.5
1870	39,818,449	234,000	–	234,000	0.6
1880	50,155,783	333,000	–	333,000	0.7
1890	62,947,714	423,000	–	423,000	0.7
1900	75,994,575	562,000	953,200	1,515,200	2.0
1910	91,972,266	448,000	1,118,000	1,566,000	1.7
1920	105,710,620	850,800	1,299,800	2,150,600	2.0
1940	131,669,275	1,861,400	1,869,300	3,730,700	2.8
1960	178,464,236	3,336,000	2,349,500	5,685,500	3.2
1970	203,302,031	7,823,600	2,712,000	10,535,600	5.2
1980	226,642,199	11,745,400	3,141,880	14,887,280	6.6
1990	248,718,301	17,345,064	3,451,596	20,796,660	8.4

* Most of these numbers come from the respective census for the date. Total population counts come from: US Census Bureau (1999: 8, Table 1: Population and Area: 1790 to 1990). The data for 1980 and 1990 for Puerto Rico are 98% of the total population counts for the respective census of Puerto Rico. The percentage reflects the proportion of the population five years and older that reported speaking Spanish. The rest of the data comes from Macías (2000).

Table 2 Changes in the non-English speaking population between 1980 and 1990, US, by language and age groups (Source: Macías, 1993)

	1980 Total		1990 Total		Net change		
	N	%	N	%	N	% of change	% increase
Non-English language speakers	22,973,410	100.0	31,844,979	100.0	8,871,569	100.0	38.6
5–17 yrs	4,529,098	19.7	6,322,934	19.9	1,793,836	20.2	39.6
18+ yrs	18,444,312	80.3	25,522,045	80.1	7,077,733	79.8	38.4
Spanish	11,117,606	100.0	17,345,064	100.0	6,227,458	100.0	56.0
5–17 yrs	2,947,051	26.5	4,167,653	24.0	1,220,602	19.6	41.4
18+ yrs	8,170,555	73.5	13,177,411	76.0	5,006,856	80.4	61.3
Other	11,855,804	100.0	14,499,915	100.0	2,644,111	100.0	22.3
5–17 yrs	1,582,047	13.3	2,155,281	14.9	573,234	21.7	36.2
18+ yrs	10,273,757	86.7	12,344,634	85.1	2,070,877	78.3	20.2

Many of the non-English language speakers were also distributed unevenly throughout the country. The next most widely used language, after Spanish, varied by region - Italian and German spoken more frequently in the Northeast and Midwest, and French and Chinese in the South and West. Among non-English language speakers, Spanish was the prevailing language in 39 states and the District of Columbia. More than half of all non-English language speakers in 1990 were in three states: California (8.6 million), New York (3.9 million) and Texas (4 million). New Mexico had the largest percentage of non-English language speakers at 36%, followed by California with 32%. In 18 states the proportion of persons who spoke a non-English language was 10% or greater.

Spanish was ten times more widely spoken than French, which was spoken at home by 1.7 million in 1990, while the next most widely spoken non-English language spoken in the home was German at 1.5 million speakers, followed by Italian at 1.3 million and Chinese at 1.2 million. About 4.5 million persons spoke an Asian or Pacific Island language and nearly 332,000 spoke a Native North American language. The Census Bureau tabulations provided for 380 language codes in the 1990 census, 170 of which were Native North American language codes.

In addition to the question about speaking a non-English language, the Census questionnaire included a question on the person's ability to speak English. Using this question, one can construct profiles of oral bilingualism for the national population. The 1990 Census provided information on the English speaking ability of non-English language speakers, five years and older. The English speaking ability was reflected in answers of 'very well', 'well', 'not well', 'not at all'. If we divide these answers into two groups ('very well' and 'well' in one group, and 'not well' and 'not at all' in the second group), then we can combine them with the non-English language information and get a rough idea of the group bilingualism in the United States. Most language groups have a high degree of bilingualism, some as high as 90% (see Table 3). In the top 50 non-English languages, 21 language groups have more than 90% of their speakers who speak English very well or well. Most of these languages are European languages (e.g. Danish, Dutch, Swedish, Hebrew, Norwegian, Pennsylvania Dutch, Finnish, Czech, German). Some of the non-European languages included in this group were Cajun, Tagalog, Bengali and Hindi.

Those language groups with a low percentage of bilinguals, and a high percentage of non-English monolinguals (who speak English 'not well' or 'not at all'), include Miao (Hmong), Cambodian, Korean, Chinese, Viet-

Table 3 Languages spoken at home and ability to speak English, ranked for persons five years and over, 1990 (Source: US Census Bureau, 1993)

Language and rank	Total		% of NEL speakers who speak English			
	N	*%*	*Very well*	*Well*	*Not well*	*Not at all*
US population, 5+ yrs	230,445,777	100.0				
Speak English only	198,600,798	86.2				
Speak a non-English language	31,844,979	100.0	56.1	23.0	15.2	5.8
Spanish	17,339,172	54.4	52.1	21.9	17.5	8.4
French	1,702,176	5.3	72.0	18.7	8.8	0.5
German	1,547,099	4.9	75.1	18.4	6.3	0.3
Italian	1,308,648	4.1	66.8	21.7	10.2	1.3
Chinese	1,249,213	3.9	39.7	30.4	21.2	8.7
Tagalog	843,251	2.6	66.0	26.6	6.9	0.6
Polish	723,483	2.3	63.0	23.4	11.8	1.8
Korean	626,478	2.0	38.8	31.1	24.7	5.4
Vietnamese	507,069	1.6	36.7	35.0	23.3	4.9
Portuguese	429,860	1.4	54.7	22.4	16.6	6.3

namese, Thai, Russian, Spanish and Armenian. These groups all have more than 25% of their speakers who are monolingual in these languages. These groups tend to be from Asian origins, partly because they reflect a high number of recent immigrants to the country.

School enrollments of minority and immigrant languages speakers

Schools in many states, including California, require a home language survey of all new students. If there is a non-English language in the new students background, there is a determination of the student's English language ability, and sometimes of the proficiency in the language other than English. If a student with a non-English language background is fluent in English, (s)he is considered Fluent English Proficient (FEP) by the school. If the student is not able to speak, understand, read and write in English well enough to participate in an English-only classroom, then (s)he is classified as Limited English Proficient (LEP) or as an English Language Learner (ELL) (see Table 4 for the state summary of the numbers of students by these categories). There is no distinction made between immigrant languages and minority languages. In fact, there is a presumption that all non-English languages are spoken by immigrants.

The instructional services provided for the English language learners between 1980 and late 1998 were organized or described in four categories: 1) English language development alone with the goal of developing English language abilities (ELD); 2) English language development and specially designed academic instruction in English (SDAIE), which is designed to teach non-language subjects to English language learners while taking into consideration their limited abilities in English (not unlike sheltered English instruction); 3) ELD, SDAIE and primary (non-English) language support - usually oral and informal support for understanding instructions and social organization of the classroom; and 4) ELD and academic instruction using the primary language. The annual language census collected data on these services (see Table 5). Through 1998, these data indicated that 70% of the English Language Learners in the state received their academic instruction entirely in English. Bilingual instruction (using both languages for academic instruction), was not widespread. Even if one included the informal use of the primary language, only half of the students were in classrooms using the non-English language.

Table 4 English language learners in California public schools, K-12, spring 1999 (Source: California Department of Education, 1999, statewide summary data)

Language	English learners / LEP		Fluent English proficient		Totals	
	N	%	N	%	N	%
State enrollment					5,844,111	100.0
All non-English languages	1,442,692	100.0	758,363	100.0	2,201,055	37.7
Spanish	1,181,553	81.9	479,102	63.2	1,660,655	28.4
Vietnamese	41,456	2.9	34,443	4.5	75,899	1.3
Hmong	29,474	2.0	6,453	0.9	35,927	0.6
Cantonese	25,556	1.8	27,992	3.7	53,548	0.9
Philipino (Tagalog)	19,041	1.3	37,977	5.0	57,018	1.0
Khmer (Cambodian)	17,637	1.2	10,610	1.4	28,247	0.5
Korean	15,761	1.1	26,256	3.5	42,017	0.7
Armenian	12,726	0.9	9,945	1.3	22,671	0.4
Mandarin (Putonghua)	10,388	0.7	23,248	3.1	33,636	0.6
Russian	8,143	0.6	6,395	0.8	14,538	0.2
Punjabi	7,762	0.5	5,101	0.7	12,863	0.2
Lao	7,703	0.5	4,772	0.6	12,475	0.2

Table 5   Instructional services to English learners in California public schools, K-12, spring 1995-1999 (in %) (Source: California Department of Education, 1999)

	_1995_	_1996_	_1997_	_1998_	_1999_
English language development	14.8	13.5	11.5	11.4	10.6
ELD + SDAIE	14.5	16.0	19.9	21.8	28.5
ELD + SDAIE + primary language support	19.8	19.7	21.6	21.7	32.8
ELD + ASPL	29.8	30.2	29.7	29.1	11.7
Other or none	23.1	20.6	17.4	15.9	9.8
None	–	–	–	–	6.7

In June of 1998, California voters adopted Proposition 227, which mandated that English be used to teach English throughout California, and that English language learners be taught through a 'structured English immersion' approach for a period not normally to exceed a year. This proposition was widely promoted and seen as an attempt at eliminating the use of the non-English language for instruction in California public schools. By the end of the first year of implementation, spring 1999, nearly half of English language learners were in a structured English immersion classroom, while almost another third were in English language mainstream classrooms (see Table 6). About 12% of these students were receiving their academic instruction in the non-English language and English language development - almost the percentage who were in Proposition 227 alternative courses of study - and over a 17% drop from the previous year, 1998.

The conflict of the election over Proposition 227 has continued through the first year of implementation, with teachers, parents and lawyers lined up on various sides of the issue on how best to protect and teach limited English proficient students. Bilingual education in California, like in the rest of the nation, is a transitional programme, offered only until such time as a student acquires enough English language proficiency to participate in an English only classroom. There are a few programmes called dual immersion, which have as their goal the bilingualism and biliteracy of all the students in the programme. These programmes are only partly directed at students with limited English proficiency and are attractive to the dominant English monolingual as a way of developing second or foreign language skills and abilities, mainly in the elementary schools.

Table 6 English learners enrolled in California public schools, by type of instructional settings, spring 1999 (in %) (Source: California Department of Education, 1999)

	1999
Structured English immersion	48.7
Alternative course of study	12.4
English language mainstream-students meet criteria	28.9
Entlish language mianstream-parental request	3.1
Other	6.9
Total	1,442,692

There is very little direct programmatic relationship or interaction between English language learners and their educational needs and those students enrolled in foreign language study. The extent of foreign language study in California can be reported for the 1997-1998 academic year. There were a total of 759,635 students enrolled in 25,271 foreign language classes throughout the state, mainly in secondary schools (see Table 7). The Spanish language was the most extensively studied, with 77% of the statewide enrollment. It was followed far behind by French (14%), German (2.6%) and Japanese (1.1%). The state curriculum framework for foreign languages supports a communicative approach to instruction.

Official status of languages

As of the year 2000, the United States does not have an official, national or constitutional language. However, English is by and far the single language of government. The founders of the country's political structure avoided declaring an official national language because of the language diversity of the colonies/new states, and because there was a commitment to a political pluralism. While a number of the founders

Table 7 Foreign language enrollments, by language and type of classroom, in California public schools, 1997-1998 (Source: California Department of Education, 1999)

Language	First and second year	Advanced	Native speakers	Advanced placement-language	Advanced placement-literature	Total	% of total foreign language enrollments
Spanish	407,404	95,386	53,344	25,689	4,237	586,060	77.2
French	85,459	18,464	–	3,891	267	108,081	14.2
German	15,140	3,981	–	674	–	19,795	2.6
Japanese	6,837	1,494	–	–	–	8,331	1.1
Chinese	4,111	1,405	166	–	–	5,682	0.7
Latin	3,948	1,159	–	–	251	5,358	0.7
Italian	1,301	382	–	–	–	1,683	0.2

individually longed for a cultural unity, this was sacrificed for a belief that national unity could be fashioned from a political pluralism (*e pluribus unum*). A current movement, begun around 1980, has been pressing for declaring English the official language of the country, with little success so far. This movement has been far more successful in persuading various states to make such declarations, usually through popular plebiscites. Approximately 34 states, including California, have declared English the official state language, almost half of these since 1980.

The Congress has adopted several laws, however, since 1964, which give minimal civil right protections to non-English language speakers, under the colour of banning national origin discrimination. These laws allow for the use of non-English languages in electoral services, in federal criminal judicial proceedings, and they regulate the adoption of English-only rules in the workplace. The Congress has also adopted a Native American Languages Act (1990), with the purpose to provide for the maintenance and recovery of American Indian, Eskimo, Inuit, Hawaiian and Pacific Islander languages. However, the findings in this law, and the purposes to which it is dedicated, are not applicable to immigrant or non-English colonial languages.

None of the contemporary international human rights treaties or covenants to which the United States is a signator, and which address language rights or issues, are enforceable within the United States. California, having come to the United States as spoils of the war with Mexico in 1848, has had Spanish as well as English as official languages for different periods of time and purposes. In the California Constitutional Convention in 1849, the eight Spanish surnamed delegates and the immediate history of the area wielded much linguistic influence on the proceedings and the other 40 delegates. The Convention elected an official translator, and all resolutions and articles were translated before being voted upon. The final document was simultaneously published in Spanish and English (Leibowitz, 1971: 46-47). Act XI, Sec. 21, Misc. Provisions of the California Constitution of 1849, reads, in part:

> All laws, decrees, regulations and provisions which from their nature require publication shall be published in English and Spanish.

Many of these notices were published in newspapers throughout the state in order to comply with this Constitutional requirement, and thus, in-directly, provided the extant Spanish language press with a government subsidy. As the English language newspapers began to develop, they often included 'Spanish pages' in order to qualify for the money for the Spanish language notices as well.

At the time of statehood for California in 1851, 18% of all schooling in the state was private and Catholic (Leibowitz, 1971: 47). These schools were usually taught in Spanish, and, of course, consisted mostly of Mexicans. The Catholic schools were initially state-supported. In 1852, the state prohibited religious schools from receiving state funds. The State Bureau of Public Instruction, in 1855, went further in the area of schooling by stipulating that all schools must teach exclusively in English. The Catholic Church initially led the fight opposing the imposition of English in California schools, even by partially encouraging bilingual schooling, but soon after 1855, under the direction of the Baltimore Diocese, it was a primary proponent of assimilation (Leibowitz, 1971: 48).

After gold was discovered in California in 1849, a large number of Euro-Americans and European, Latin American and Asian immigrants flooded to the northern California mountains to look for their fortune, quickly displacing in numbers the indigenous populations. Southern California, however, remained 'Mexican' in population well into the 1870's. The state laws, however, were made in the north and not always favourable to what was perceived as the Mexican south. The California legislature of 1854, and the general issues of the day, were dominated by the anti-Catholic, anti-'alien' Know Nothing party. Language policies were one of the areas in which they sought to battle their 'enemies'. The California legislature passed laws requiring court proceedings to be in English, a $5/month 'foreign' miners tax (aimed at Mexicans and also the Chinese, who, beginning in 1847, were being drawn to California as cheap labour), a $50 head tax on immigrants ineligible for citizenship (Leibowitz, 1971: 48), and the 1855 'Pigtail' ordinance, 'which required the removal of queues from Chinese men convicted of breaking the law' (Castro, 1977: 94).

The racial tensions and conflicts in California reflected similar social strains in other parts of the ceded Mexican territory which has become the Southwestern US The race riots and lynchings and wanton disregard for Mexican life and Indian life (there was seldom a distinction made) expanded to include the Chinese. There were 50,000 Chinese in California by 1870. In 1870, the California State legislature also enacted a statute providing that all the schools in the state (religious and public) be taught in the English language (Leibowitz, 1971: 50). This law superseded the State Bureau of Public Instruction's similar regulation of 1855. In 1894, the

California legislature was busy amending its 1879 Constitution: to restrict the vote to those who could read and write English and to require official proceedings in all branches of government to be conducted and published in no other than the English language (Leibowitz, 1971: 50).

By the beginning of the 20th century, California had subjugated non-English languages, especially Spanish, which had a special status as the official language of the prior sovereign, English was the official language of instruction in the schools, English literacy was required for voting, and English was the language for administration of government. This was the language policy in California for most of the 20th century, until the Civil Rights movement of the sixties caused the federal passage of the Civil Rights Act (1964), the Voting Rights Act (1965) and the Bilingual Education Act (1968). While the Civil Rights and the Voting Rights Acts had to do with the rights of the population, the Bilingual Education Act only provided funds for the development of a select few programmes to demonstrate the effectiveness and utility of using two languages for instruction to improve the academic achievement of language minorities.

The passage of the Bilingual Education Act, however, caused three things to happen: (1) it encouraged states to repeal the state laws that prohibited the use of the non-English language, or that mandated only English as the medium of instruction in public schools; (2) signalled that it was alright to use the non-English language to teach language minority students; and (3) made nationally visible the condition and problems of language minority students. California was one of the states which repealed its English-only policy in the public schools, and adopted a 'bilingual' approach as the media of instruction for language minority students. It took almost a decade for these programmes to be widely implemented, develop a theoretical and research base.

The earlier restrictive language policies started to give way to a broader, participatory set of language policies. These included:

- The 1974 *Lau v. Nichols* US Supreme Court decision which required school districts to provide language services for students who were not proficient in English in the public schools.
- The 1974 Equal Educational Opportunity Act, prohibiting language discrimination.
- The 1975 amendments to the Voting Rights Act of 1965, provided for bilingual ballots and electoral services for Latinos, American Indians and Asian language groups.

- The 1978 Court Interpreters Act providing interpreters for deaf, hard-of-hearing as well as language minority defendants in Federal Court who could not understand English well enough to participate in those proceedings, so as to meet their needs as well as the Court's needs.

By 1980, there were several laws that reflected the national linguistic diversity in national language policies. Many of the restrictive English language policies established at the beginning of the 20th century were eliminated in the name of an expanded understanding of civil rights. The Civil Rights movement itself in this country, however, had not paid much attention to language as a right or as an issue. With the exception of bilingual education, language policy was an intimate concern of language minority groups and their organizations. This is an important point for understanding how the language debate developed and changed between 1980 and 2000.

The language debates in the eighties and beyond

Three key points should be made about the language debates of the eighties: political organizations exclusively or primarily organized around language issues were created, reflecting the polarization of the debate and the refinement of the ideologies and polemics of the debate; there were changes in the official status of English; and the public policy debates on language broadened and took on a greater importance within the national body politic.

During the eighties, organizations were created on at least two sides of language policy issues: those promoting an official status for English and those opposed to it. Those promoting an official status came to be known as the English Only movement, while those that opposed an official status for English argued for English-plus goals. Specific goals for each side were identified and clearly centered on language. Unlike the seventies, language issues became part of the national policy debates because of these organizations.

In general, the goals of the English-only movement can be summarized as follows:

- Amend the US Constitution to designate English as the official language of the US.
- Raise public awareness of the threat that other languages pose to English by organizing local English Only groups and increasing the media attention on the issue.

- Reduce or eliminate language assistance and bilingual programmes and policies. The movement has advocated to eliminating services in non-English languages like 911 emergency services, bilingual materials regarding free pre- and post-natal care, and information on public health issues.
- Reduce funding for bilingual education and restrict those programmes to make minimal use of the non-English language.
- Make proficiency in English a precondition for citizens to exercise their right to vote by eliminating bilingual ballots and electoral services.
- Adopt stricter standards of English language proficiency in determining eligibility of citizens.
- Adopt measures penalizing government workers and other public employees who speak non-English languages and promote English only rules in the workplace.
- Monitor and discourage the use of non-English languages by businesses for advertising and other activities.

The English-plus movement that was a reaction to the English-only movement had its own goals:
- To block passage of the English language amendment at the federal, state and local level.
- To increase public awareness of the dangers to civil rights posed by English-only, nativist movements.
- Increase public awareness of the assimilation process among immigrants and other factors outlining valuable facts about bilingual ballots and bilingual education.
- Work for continued availability of bilingual education programmes for children and increased levels of funding for those programmes.
- Create new programmes and opportunities for adults to become proficient in English.

These organizations specifically created to oppose the English Only movement did not survive the eighties. The organizations that came together in these anti-English-only coalitions have continued to oppose the movement, reflecting the English-plus goals and strategies faithfully in the absence of an alternative strategy through most of the eighties and nineties. The changes in the official status of English came mainly in the second half of the eighties, and mainly at the state and local levels. Some of these changes were constitutional changes, others were programmatic changes. For example:

1981   Virginia adopted English as official language.

1984   Indiana, Kentucky, Tennessee adopted English as official language.

1984   English only 'Bilingual education' programmes were allowed in the Federal Bilingual Education Act reauthorization. These 'Special Alternative' programmes were part of a budget compromise that increased the amount authorized for the Act in exchange for a percentage of the new monies to be spent on programmes that used only English for instruction of Limited English Proficient students.

1986   California passed an initiative declaring English the official language of the state. This initiative became a bellwether for other states which allow for the creation or adoption of law through a popular initiative or referendum.

1986   The Immigration Reform and Control Act required English language and citizenship classes for those persons who wanted to regularize their immigration status within the US, through an 'amnesty' programme.

1987   Arkansas, Mississippi, North Carolina, North Dakota, South Carolina adopted English as official language.

1988   Arizona, Colorado, Florida adopted English as official language.

1990   Alabama adopted English as official language.

By 1990, 17 states had declared English as their official language through this process, nine between 1986 and 1988. Most of these laws were constitutional amendments, and had three parts: 1) declaration of English as the official language of the state; 2) a duty of the legislature to enforce this law; and 3) where allowed, a 'private right to action' to enforce the law (meaning that a private citizen has the right to bring suit or a legal case to require the legislature to enforce the law).

In addition to these changes in the status of English, an 'English-plus resolution', written to celebrate and support linguistic and cultural diversity was adopted by several major and medium size cities as well as the states of Louisiana (1987) and New Mexico (1989). Also, many professional organizations adopted resolutions opposing the English Only movement or specific changes in the official status of English, or in celebration of English-plus, multilingualism and multiculturalism:

1986   The National Association for Bilingual Education (NABE), Teachers of English to Speakers of Other Languages (TESOL), adopted resolutions against English-only.

1988   The National Council for Teachers of English adopted a resolution against English-only.

1988   The Mexican American Legal Defence and Education Fund adopted a resolution that outlined the following principles of its language rights programme: Be it further resolved that MALDEF confirms the following principles: 1) the individual has a right to be free from discrimination based on language; 2) language is a national origin characteristic; and 3) individuals have a right to learn English and their native language if it is other than English.

Many of these changes, especially the states' adoption of English as the official language, created a ripple effect of legally questionable actions regarding situational language policies: e.g. private employers requiring English oral language and literacy proficiency as a condition of employment; an excuse for the modification or elimination of bilingual education laws; and individuals acting like language police prohibiting the uses of non-English languages, writing and materials in public. This ripple effect is better understood within the broadening of the public policy debates on language during the decade.

California reflected these national debates. While the 1986 adoption of English as the official state language was declared 'symbolic' by the courts, the language debates swirled around bilingual education and the use of non-English languages in the schools. The state law on bilingual education was not renewed by the Republican Governor of the state in 1986, despite having been passed by the legislature. When Governor Pete Wilson, a Republican, was elected, he vetoed the bilingual education bill. In 1994, he also coopted the sponsorship of a popular referendum (Proposition 187), which prohibited undocumented immigrants from participating in social welfare programmes, medical aid or public schooling. This proposition was passed by the voters, but eventually most of its provisions were found unconstitutional by the federal courts. The debates around this proposition, however, polarized the state and the national body politic. Many of its provisions found their way into the 1996 immigration reforms adopted by the newly-elected, conservative, Republican-led Congress, and were often applied to both undocumented and legal immigrants.

This California proposition was followed with another in 1996, opposing programmes aimed at affirmatively redressing prior racial and sex discrimination (known popularly as Affirmative Action programmes). This proposition (numbered 209) was also passed by the voters, and remains legally viable. Again, the impact of this proposition was to divide the public along similar political lines, and was viewed by racial and language minorities, in general, as aimed at them, and as anti-immigrant. These two 'wedge issue' propositions were followed with a third in 1998, aimed at making English the official and almost exclusive language of instruction in the public schools, and at ending bilingual instruction. This proposition (numbered 227) also passed. It too was seen as a wedge issue referendum. Voting on these three propositions tended to be by party, by class and by race. It is important to note that the majority of voters who voted on these propositions represented a smaller proportion of the eligible electorate than their proponents or the media would have us believe. These propositions were passed with a far cry from a popular mandate (see Table 8). Their legacy, however, is that they changed the social and political climate in California and provided a momentum for conservative, nativist and xenophobic groups and social forces. While California became more like the rest of the world rather than the rest of the nation, cultural panic ruled the day.

Table 8   Voter eligibility and participation in California's propositions 187, 209 and 227 (Source: Huerta, 1999; Jones, 1998)

	1994	*1996*	*1998*
Propositions	187	209	227
Eligible voters	18,946,358	19,526,991	20,653,410
Registered voters	14,723,784	15,662,075	14,805,677
Actual voters	8,592,969	9,657,195	6,206,618
Voted in favour of propotision	5,063,537	5,268,462	3,582,423
% of registered voters	34.4	33.6	24.2

Outlook

The language politics in California in the last two decades has challenged and shifted some principles around which educational policy was built. California educational policy had a long-time tradition of providing schooling opportunity for all children regardless of residency or citizenship status. This was not a concern of the schools. The broader public good dictated that the education of all children in the state would benefit the state. This principle was challenged, unsuccessfully, by Proposition 187. But its after-taste lingers in the political elixir. A second principle of educational policy was that a student who was not proficient in English had a right to be taught in a language which (s)he could understand. While the implementation of this left much to be desired, it guided much of the educational policy, teacher education and programme standards for 25 years. This was challenged successfully by Proposition 227. The principle still lives, albeit in diminished capacity, in the persistence of bilingual instruction demanded by language minority parents, and executed by bilingual teachers and administrators.

There has been a definite cultural policy backlash against immigrants and language minorities during the last decade of the last millennium. It is not clear that this backlash has run its course, or that the above stated principles will not be re-affirmed. However, it may require a substantial shift in political representation by language minorities for these interests to be reflected in law and educational policies.

References

California Department of Education (1999) http://www.cde.ca.gov/demo-graphics/reports/statewide/course97.htm

Castro, R. (1977) The bilingual education act: A historical analysis of title VII. In R.F. Macías (ed) *Perspectivas en chicano studies I* (pp. 81-122).

Huerta, R. (1999) *California's initiative process: Tyranny of the majority or tyranny of the minority?* Santa Barbara, CA: University of California, Santa Barbara Center for Chicano Studies.

Jones, B. (1998) *Statement of the vote: Primary election, June 2, 1998.* Sacramento, CA: Secretary of State.

Leibowitz, A. (1969) English literacy: Legal sanction for discrimination. *Notre Dame Lawyer* 45 (7), 7-67.

Leibowitz, A. (1970) The imposition of English as the language of instruction in American schools. *Revista de derecho Puertorriqueño* 38 (10), 175-244.

Leibowitz, A. (1971) *Educational policy and political acceptance: The imposition of English as the language of instruction in American schools.* ERIC document no. ED 047321, (March).

Macías, R. (1993) Language and ethnic classification of language minorities: Chicano and Latino students in the 1990s. *Hispanic journal of behavioral sciences* 15 (2), 230-257.

Macías, R. (in press) Language politics and the sociolinguistic historiography of Spanish in the United States. In P. Griffin, J. Kreeft Peyton, W. Wolfram and R. Fasold (eds) *Language in action: New studies of language in society.* Cresskill, NJ: Hampton Press.

Macías, R. (in press) The flowering of America: Linguistic diversity in the United States. In S. McKay and S. Wong (eds) *New immigrants in the United States: Background for second language educators.* Cambridge: Cambridge University Press.

US Census Bureau (1993) *Language spoken at home and ability to speak English for the United States, regions and states: 1990.* (Special tabulation of the 1990 Census of Population). (1990 CPH-L-133). Washington, DC: US Census Bureau, Education and Social Stratification Branch.

US Census Bureau (1999) *Statistical abstract of the US: 1999.* Washington, DC: US Government Printing Office.

Wolf, E. (1966) *Sons of the shaking earth.* Chicago, IL: University of Chicago Press.

Majority and minority languages in South Africa

NEVILLE ALEXANDER

As an object of comparison concerning the challenge posed by language issues in the European Union, the post-apartheid Republic of South Africa is useful both because there are generic similarities between the language situation there and in Europe and because the two situations are so very different. Such a comparison can serve to highlight the differences and thus to clarify the strategic and policy implications of specific choices.

To begin with conceptual and terminological questions: in South Africa, for reasons that will become apparent presently, we prefer not to speak of majority and minority languages. We have constructed a simple typology consisting of a gradient of three categories, i.e. 'high-status', 'low-status', and 'endangered' languages. The main reason for this approach and for the explicit avoidance of the terminology of 'majority' and 'minority' languages is political and ideological. Because of the immediate apartheid past and the conscious strategy of promoting national unity ('nation building'), we are wary of giving or strengthening the impression that the present government operates from the premise that some languages are intrinsically more important or more valuable than others. The terminology we prefer indicates clearly that the languages are viewed within a historical perspective, one which involves centrally colonial conquest, racial and other forms of domination, including linguistic discrimination. In other words, we imply essentially that this is an inherited situation that must change in favour of what are loosely called 'marginalised' languages, including South African Sign Language (SASL).

A second reason why the terminology is different is that - as with so many other things - apartheid, specifically, and racism more generally, turned everything upside-down. Thus, even though Afrikaans and English are the languages of arithmetic minorities, they are the dominant languages and manifest all the features of what are generally referred to by sociolinguists and sociologists of language as 'majority' languages. And, conversely, the demographically strong indigenous African languages, especially isiXhosa and isiZulu, though, together, they are spoken as a first language by almost one-half of the population of South Africa and between 60% and 70% of all South Africans understand isiZulu, manifest all the features of 'minority' languages in the typical West European country. This is so because, for reasons of the peculiar history of South Africa, the speakers of the African languages have, until recently, constituted social minorities; they are at present undertaking the painful attempt to free themselves from this situation and from the stigma that goes with it.

The matter is further complicated by the fact that Afrikaner, i.e. white Afrikaans-speaking intellectuals who consider themselves to be part of an ethnic group, insist on using what for our purposes I refer to as the Eurocentric terminology. Consequently, they see Afrikaans as a 'minority' language but, curiously, do not seem to realise that they are treating English as a 'majority' language even though it is spoken as a first language by under 9% of the population of South Africa. This view at the very least implies a different (consociational) notion of democratic consensus from the majoritarian notion to which the present government is committed, in that the thinkers and strategists of the core Afrikaner community make it clear that their respect for and acceptance of the constitution is dependent on the extent to which it effectively assuages the fears of 'minorities' about language and culture. This is the main reason why the right wing under General Viljoen, the leader of the Freedom Front, during the last hours of the negotiations insisted on the establishment of an ethnically defined forum where such issues could be discussed and resolved. Whether this will happen in practice is indeed one of the crucial outstanding questions of contemporary South Africa.

Since 1994 especially, the question of immigrant minority languages, as understood in Europe, has been latent as a 'problem' since millions of people have been surging towards South Africa in search of better opportunities or because of the impossible conditions in their war-torn countries. Although it is still too early to speak of a consolidated or definitive policy in this regard, there is no doubt that the authorities in practice have tended towards a policy of neglect at best and, at worst, what one can only describe as a xenophobic policy (see Plueddemann, 1999). For those who are fortunate enough to speak one of the many cross-border languages that connect South Africa with its neighbours, there is in principle no problem since they can fit into existing schools in the townships and even in the rural areas.

These remarks are important for purposes of orientation since we will be appearing to be speaking generically of the same things whereas, in the South African situation, we have to bear in mind that we are looking at a mirror image of the typical West European country.

Demolinguistic profiles and their representation in the media

From Table 1, based on the 1996 census figures, we get an approximate idea of the relative order of numerical importance of each of the main home languages used in South Africa.

Table 1   Main home languages in South Africa (Source: Census 1996, http://www.stassa.gov.za/census96/HTML/CIB/Populstion)

	Numbers	As %
Zulu	9,200,144	22.9
Xhosa	7,196,118	17.9
Afrikaans	5,911,547	14.4
Pedi	3,695,846	9.2
English	3,457,467	8.6
Tswana	3,301,774	8.2
Sotho	3,104,197	7.7
Tsonga	1,756,105	4.4
Swati	1,013,193	2.5
Venda	876,409	2.2
Ndebele	586,961	1.5
Other	583,813	0.6
Total	40,583,573	100.0

Although English is spoken as a home language by less than 10% of the population of South Africa, the dominance of the English language becomes startlingly evident from an analysis of broadcast schedules of the South African Broadcasting Corporation for 1996. Table 2 gives an overview of the average and proportional language allocation from 6.00 - 24.00 o'clock at three SABC stations in 1996.

Table 2   Average and proportional language allocation at three SABC stations
in 1996

	SABC 1	SABC 2	SABC 3	*Average*
English	65.08	59.61	95.26	73.32
Zulu	4.64	0.62	0.00	1.75
Xhosa	4.57	0.14	0.00	1.57
Afrikaans	3.53	14.06	0.14	5.91
Sepedi	2.70	3.72	0.00	2.14
Setswana	3.46	3.38	0.00	2.28
Sesotho	3.12	3.72	0.00	2.28
Setsonga	0.00	0.21	0.00	0.07
Seswati	0.21	0.00	0.00	0.07
XhiVenda	0.00	0.21	0.00	0.07
SiNdebele	0.21	0.00	0.00	0.07
Multilingual	12.49	14.34	4.60	10.48

Except for the fact that, because of pressure from organized Afrikaans
groups and from the Freedom of Expression Institute, among others, the
rapid diminution of broadcast time in Afrikaans has been halted and
slightly reversed, the situation has remained much the same. There is no
doubt that a strong case can be made for Afrikaans, even though a
privately-funded Afrikaans TV channel will soon be operative as the
Afrikaans elite cease looking towards government as the sole source of
protection and promotion of the language. However, it is obvious that the
really marginalized languages are the indigenous African languages
taken together and Tshitsonga, Siswati, XiVenda and SiNdebele in
particular. South African Sign Language did not even feature in the
analysis at that time. In summary, almost three-quarters of all South
African television programmes are broadcast in English. In actual fact, the
proportion is much larger, since the rubric 'multilingual', which accounts
for another 10%, in fact refers to programmes that are largely in English.
Until dubbing and subtitling become feasible and economically possible
(in terms of the SABC's logic), South African TV will remain essentially
English, which is not to say that it is in any way 'good-quality' TV or that
it is even understood by most people who watch it. But that, as we know,
is a global problem.

These illustrations explain the situation on the ground better than any words could do. However, an even more telling datum is the fact that of all the complaints about alleged violations of language rights received by the Pan South African Language Board (PANSALB) between 1 July 1998 and 30 June 1999, more than 95% were complaints against central government, provincial government and parastatal institutions. The vast majority of these emanated from Afrikaans-speaking individuals or institutions, usually against the unconstitutional or 'illegal' sole use of English as a means of communication by the relevant body with the public. Besides revealing possible lack of organization and political will on the part of the government and quasi-government agencies concerned, this datum reflects the level of organization of language communities and the corollary degree of passionate commitment to the protection and promotion of their specific language(s). As a result, the PANSALB Report, from which these facts are taken, concludes that '... there is a need for the PANSALB to educate people about their rights and improve its system of monitoring and attending to issues of language rights violations ...' (PANSALB, 1999: 30).

By way of correcting the perspective, it should be pointed out that the PANSALB is a watchdog organization the main 'target' of which is precisely the new government. It would be able to assist a member of the public to bring a suit of linguistic discrimination against another member of the public or against a private-sector organization but would not itself have the right to institute such action. In regard to government, on the other hand, it has considerable clout.

Radio, which is still the most widespread and most popular electronic medium, is the domain in which the multilinguality of South Africa really comes into its own and where the potential of the indigenous languages can be gauged accurately. It is a critically important fact that the popular state and community radio stations broadcast largely in these languages and that English (and Afrikaans) radio listenership simply cannot be compared with, for example, Zulu or Southern Sotho or Xhosa listenerships. This fact might constitute the launching pad for the eventual establishment of the African languages as languages of power in South Africa.

Sociolinguistic status of South Africa's languages

This question has to be examined against the background of the consequences of colonial conquest, slavery, migrant labour and apartheid. It is a very large question and there is a wealth of sociolinguistic and historical literature in which the processes of linguistic discrimination and underdevelopment in the southern African region are described from diverse perspectives (see, among others, Hirson, 1981; Alexander, 1989, 1992; Du Plessis & Du Plessis, 1987; Mesthrie, 1995).

In a nutshell, the processes that shaped language policy and attitudes during the past 50 years or so can be summed up as follows: under the National Party's Christian National Education policy of the Afrikanerisation of South African society, the African languages were deliberately developed as *Ausbau*-languages, i.e. even where it was possible in linguistic and political terms to allow the varieties of a particular language cluster or sub-group, such as the 'Nguni' group, to converge into a more embracing standard written form, they were systematically kept separate through lexical and other corpus-planning manoeuvres. The languages concerned were, moreover, starved of the essential resources in such a way that they could not be used in contexts that implied or demonstrated real power. General social and political policies ensured throughout the era of high apartheid that the African languages remained languages of low status. The apartheid governments gave the impression that they were doing their best to develop and to modernize the African languages when in fact they were underdeveloping them quite deliberately. With utmost cynicism, a mere sense of social progress (like special language boards for each of the African languages) was given in order to impress 'the international community' which was under the spell of the movement for African independence and liberation from colonial rule at the time.

Tragically, the anglocentrism of the political, and to some extent of the cultural, leadership of the oppressed people in effect, if not in intention, ensured the predictable outcome of these policies. For it is a fact of historic significance that the African (or black) nationalist movement because of the salience of the racial question did not react to cultural oppression in a manner similar to that of the Afrikaner (or white) nationalists. At the critical time when Bantu education was being imposed on the black people from the fifties to the seventies, the leadership of the liberation movement across the board made a *de facto* decision to oppose Afrikaans in favour of English. The option of promoting the African languages while also ensuring as wide and as deep a knowledge of the English language was never considered seriously. In effect, therefore, the hegemony of English, its unassailable position - as Chinua Achebe calls it - became entrenched among black people. Because it was the only other language that could compete with Afrikaans as a means to power (jobs and status) and as the only means to international communication and world culture at the disposal of South Africa's elites, it became, as in other African countries, the 'language of liberation'.

The important point, however, is that because of the attitudes referred to and the lack of foresight on the part of the leadership, the resistance to the cultural-political policies of the National Party did not result in the kind of cultural movement for the development of the African languages which, in retrospect, was completely possible. Unlike the resistance manifested by the _Afrikaanse taalbewegings_ (Afrikaans language movements) in response to the cultural-imperialist policies of Lord Milner at the beginning of the 20th century, the even cruder Milnerist policies of Dr Verwoerd and his brothers merely gave rise to a middle-class strategy of convenience and evasion, namely, the strategy of promoting or tolerating the sole value of English. While there was no policy of actually denigrating the African languages, there was also no deliberate and systematic attempt to develop, modernize and spread the knowledge of the indigenous languages both for the intrinsic empowering value of such an exercise and as an explicit strategy of cultural-political resistance.

In actual practice, the vast majority of South Africans do not at present have a sufficient command of the high status languages (English and Afrikaans) so that they can compete for well paid jobs and prestigious career options on a basis of equality with the 20% of the population who do have the requisite language skills. On the other hand, the language resources that the majority do have (most of the metropolitan and urban population can speak with high proficiency at least two - often radically different - African languages), are not validated in the market place. In other words, the indigenous languages are not accorded a status such that knowing them is of material or social benefit to the speaker outside the relevant speech community itself. This situation is made a thousand times worse by the fact that in South Africa, language and colour (or 'race') coincide to a very large extent because of the peculiar historical development of the labour market. Because of the legacy of Bantu education specifically, a general 'semilingualism' prevails and most of the youth have been handicapped in the merciless race for power, position and individual progress in the very competitive society in which we live.

Most people, naturally, want to acquire the kind of proficiency in English (and to a lesser extent, in Afrikaans) which will enable them to compete for well-paying jobs. They have what Kellman (1975) calls an instrumental, not a sentimental, allegiance to the English language. They value their own languages as community and home languages and as bearers of cultural identity, in general terms (urbanization has inexorably brought about a questioning of traditional values and notions of identity). The question of 'survival' of these languages does not arise. Except for the endangered Khoisan languages, none of the indigenous languages display any sign of lack of vitality. Afrikaans strategists and intellectuals raise the issue in terms of 'survival' (not vitality) simply because they insist (correctly in my view) that the constitutional obligation of equal treatment is being openly and deliberately flouted by people in government.

Of course, in linguistic terms, the crisis which all African people face, i.e. the 'powerlessness' of their languages, is acutely experienced by black South Africans. One of the derivative elements of the crisis is the lack of confidence most people have in the value of their first language (mother- or father tongue) which the total situation under apartheid produced. This is a very important aspect of the syndrome of the colonized mind. Most people really believe, for example, that the African languages 'do not have the words' for most modern objects and scientific concepts. As a result, they have come to believe that it is essential that they learn the English language so that they can overcome this 'deficit' of their languages. The resultant loss of self esteem and of a dignifying self image is fatal.

Language in education

In line with the mind set described above, most educators in South Africa continue to think of the indigenous African languages in the same way as - according to Lord Acton - the European mariners during the 'voyages of discovery' thought of the African continent, i.e. as an obstruction on the way to India. The African languages are, in this paradigm, seen as impediments that have to be 'overcome' on the way to mastery of the English language. Or, to change the metaphor: English is seen by most black South Africans and by the educators of their children as the pot of gold at the end of the linguistic rainbow.

It is necessary to stress that this remains true today in spite of the progressive, even radical, changes in language policy in education which have been made in the wake of the democratic elections of 1994. After 1976, when the militant intervention of the school children of South Africa forced language policy changes on the apartheid state from below, the real situation in the classrooms of the majority of the people was that their own languages were either not used as languages of teaching at all or, in most cases, were used for the first three or four years of initial literacy and then either dropped abruptly or gradually. With a fair proportion of exceptions, most of the teachers who are expected to teach their subjects through the medium of the English language, through no fault of their own, are not proficient in that language. This subtractive bilingualism approach was (and continues to be) an unmitigated disaster. Hardly any materials in the African languages exist beyond the junior primary (first three years) phase, most of the rest are not only inadequate in quality but have to be shared; very often a single copy has to make do for a whole class of forty and more children.

One of the most disturbing consequences of this situation, inherited from the apartheid period, is the fact that children are unable to read and write their mother tongues and, worse, they cannot read and write English (or Afrikaans) with any confidence either. Given this *de facto* illiteracy - at best semi-literacy - with which children emerge from the primary school (and this is still more than 60% of black South African children), it is no wonder that what we refer to as a 'culture of reading' is non-existent. This factor, in turn, means that there is no market for books and other publications in the indigenous languages and consequently no motivation for publishers to produce reading matter in these languages on a large scale. The vicious circle that has been set up is one of the most difficult sociocultural phenomena with which South Africa's educators and intelligentsia are confronted. Plueddemann (1999: 334) cites the 1991 statistics for book titles published in South Africa. Despite the fact that three-quarters of the population have an African language as their home language, only 15.8% of all book titles published in that year were in one or other of the nine main African languages of South Africa. As against this, English titles comprised almost one-half of all books published in the country although native English speakers comprise only 8.7% of the population and, we ought to add, virtually all imported titles are in English. Afrikaans, whose speakers comprise 15.7% of the population, accounted for 33.8% of the local book market.

A core of language specialists have during the past 15 years or so been working consistently to break through this barrier. Together with many other African social scientists they have come round to understanding the importance of developing the indigenous languages of the continent and of not steering their resource-hungry countries in the direction of teaching only the former colonial languages instead of the peoples' first languages. They have come to identify the optimal situation as that in which additive bilingualism/multilingualism involving, where appropriate, the former colonial language as one of the package of languages to be learned can become state policy because of the availability of resources and of political/strategic foresight on the part of the leadership. What has become ever more obvious is that it is true that no nation has ever thrived or reached great heights of economic and cultural development if the vast majority of its people are compelled to communicate in a second or even a third language. Prah (1993: 72-73) in an important work, goes as far as maintaining that the educational policies of post-colonial African governments which neglected the modernization and development of the indigenous languages are one of the main reasons for the abysmal failure of all economic development programmes on the continent. The colonial heritage of which the use and high status of the languages of the colonial masters are an integral part sets up a vicious circle in which

> African languages are underrated as possible vehicles of science and technological development. Because they have for decades been underrated, this has led to a retardation in their development and meant in consequence a retrenchment of African languages and cultures in the effort to develop Africa. This retardation implies stagnation and the confirmation of the inferior status of African languages and cultures in the general discourse on development in Africa. (Prah, 1993: 46).

This position is equally true of South Africa, in spite of the superficial appearance of technological modernity. Besides everything else, the lack of creativity, spontaneity and initiative that comes with people having to use a second, and even a third, language for participation in all the most important public domains predisposes the situation to becoming one that is characterized by failure and mediocrity. This, more than anything else, explains why South African education, viewed in the mass, is so devastatingly bad. Because the link between language, culture, science and technology has not been explored in depth in regard to the indigenous languages, we are faced with a situation where our children have to acquire the concepts in this vital area almost entirely via what is in every respect a foreign language (usually English) for them. Since they do not live in an English environment normally, there is no spontaneous reinforcement of that which they learn (by rote) in their classrooms. Add to this the fact that their general environment is devoid of print stimuli and of a natural-science culture, and it becomes crystal clear why it is that despite millions of Rands of investment in second-language English programmes, progress in these fields is discouragingly slow.

Prospects

Although the processes by which we have arrived in the present period of transition are very important for the understanding of some of the contradictions and tensions that characterize the situation, we have to forego a discussion of these. Suffice it to say that South Africa is in the grip of a painful transition from an undemocratic and oppressive past to a more hopeful democratic dispensation. As in all other social domains, radical policy and practical interventions are being undertaken in the domain of language policy in order to smooth this transition. On paper, we have one the most progressive language dispensations in the world today. The constitution guarantees complete equality of rights for the 11 official languages and an independent statutory body, the Pan South African Language Board, and its affiliated structures have been established specifically to see to it that the constitutional and legislative provisions are adhered to by all organs of state. The Department of Arts, Culture, Science and Technology is the line function department for all matters pertaining to language and under it it has the National Language Services, which has to provide all services required by any department of state.

Without going into detail, it can be said that partly because of the Afrikaner obsession with the language question and because of the nature of the compromise that led to the negotiated settlement, the legal and institutional infrastructure exists in order to promote the development and 'equal usage' of the official languages and, in the educational sector, even of SASL. The reality is very different. With very few exceptions, the tendency towards (English) unilingual government has been strengthened and the Board finds itself fighting rearguard actions on behalf of a few individuals and groups. It keeps coming up against the argument of cost-effectiveness and does not have any legislative backing for insisting on alternative approaches. At this very moment, the PANSALB is getting ready to take the SABC to court for reducing even further the TV time for the marginalized languages, including Afrikaans. It has recently found that the Post Office is in breach of the Constitution because it has its signs in English only in most urban areas of the country. Moreover, the Board is in the process of setting up lexicographic units for each of the 11 official languages. These units have set themselves the task as a priority of developing comprehensive monolingual explanatory dictionaries and are being assisted and trained, paradoxically, by the Afrikaans lexicographic unit (the *Woordeboek van die Afrikaanse Taal*) which has a wealth of experience. Five of nine Provincial Language Committees are already functioning. Each of these has to see to it, among other things, that the relevant provincial government is carrying out the constitutional provisions relating to the official languages in the province. Legislation has been agreed to for the setting up of 'language bodies', each of which has the responsibility of inspiring the speakers/users of the language concerned to write and develop the language in all domains. These are, naturally, hopeful signs but they also indicate the nature of the struggles that lie ahead of the people who are trying to improve the status and functionality of the low-status languages.

In education specifically, the situation is equally desperate. Beyond the junior primary school, as indicated already, there is hardly any L1-medium education except for the plus-minus 20% who are either English- or Afrikaans-speaking at home. Even for Afrikaans speakers, the situation is becoming worse and many children tend to go to English-medium schools or classes. This tendency is the result of uninformed choices made by parents with extremely negative attitudes to African languages and because, hitherto, government has done very little in practice to promote L1-medium education. The new Minister of Education, however, has gone on record publicly in favour of L1-medium education and an additive (as opposed to the existing subtractive) approach to multilingual education. An important idea, raised by professor Keith Chick, that was canvassed at a conference in Durban in July 1999, is that we may have to look at the possibility of interpreting the constitutional provision in terms of which the individual parent (or learner) has the right to choose the language of learning and teaching in such a way that it does not imply necessarily the right to choose the technical didactic means by which that right is realized in practice. A few projects exist where the problems that come up in the implementation of such programmes are being studied and numerous interventions are being promoted in order to change the manner in which teachers are (not) being trained at colleges and in university faculties of education to deal with what is becoming the (typical, urban) multilingual classroom. The crucial step that has to be taken is for colleges and faculties to agree to implement what is there on paper already, i.e. to train prospective teachers to be able to teach in at least two languages. This will give the system a push in the direction of dual-medium education which, in the view of many of us, is a necessary transitional strategy in South African schools in respect of language medium policy for the simple reason that as long as English remains the language of power, people will and should want to have their children acquire proficiency in that language but, on the other side, given what we know about the history of language policy in the rest of Africa - and elsewhere - we ought to develop the indigenous languages as deeply and widely as possible to serve as languages of tuition at all levels of the educational system. This is the real test of empowerment and, therefore, one of the litmus tests of the democratization of the system. For, as long as people have to use a second, or even a foreign, language to access their most basic and routine daily requirements, democracy will remain an aspiration rather than a reality. The same holds true for the noble idea of the 'African Renaissance'. Without the full development of the African languages, this programme will remain foreign and elitist, at a great distance from ordinary African people.

Concluding remarks

In conclusion, it ought to be clear from what I have said hitherto that a series of language planning steps is necessary in order to ensure that the theoretically unchallengeable policy positions of the new South Africa are realized.

At the level of status planning, some of the steps that could be undertaken would include large-scale generalized critical language awareness campaigns which should be initiated over the next five to ten years, so that the black people in particular can begin to understand the linkages between language and power. Besides these campaigns, specific local and regional actions to enhance the value, visibility and status of the African languages are essential. For example, the use of multilingual (or bilingual) signposts and name boards for all government buildings, roads, etc. The requirement that knowledge of an African language would be a recommendation for a post in the civil service since a large proportion of the clientele prefer service in one or other African language, would do a great deal to empower these languages and their speakers. It is also a 'natural' affirmative action policy, one which avoids the unnecessary allegation of 'reverse racism'. Government and other dignitaries should be encouraged to use the African languages for high-profile announcements of national or international significance. Needless to say, there are many more initiatives which, at relatively little cost, would raise the status of the low-status languages of South Africa.

In regard to corpus planning, besides the usual technical initiatives around dictionaries, glossaries, technical registers, etc., it would be exceptionally important that interpreters, translators, journalists and media practitioners as well as teachers are trained on a large scale. Besides the job-creating potential of these processes, they will establish and consolidate the infrastructure, or the hardware, of a multilingual society and will enable smooth communication in all directions. Major translation programmes into the local languages of the most important works of world literature and science should be started. At the same time, ways and means have to be found to encourage the writing and publication of creative literature in the low-status languages. Initiatives being undertaken in this direction by the Department of Arts, Culture, Science and Technology are supported by all language practitioners and are bound to produce some positive results. In this connection, networks between writers, teachers, researchers and other language professionals with their counterparts in other African countries are essential and, of course, completely in line with the strategy of promoting the 'African Renaissance'. Existing networks, of which there are a few important ones, have to be strengthened systematically. Something like the European Bureau for Lesser Used Languages, adapted to African conditions and building on the existing facilities of the Organization of African Unity, would quickly give direction and momentum to the rehabilitation and promotion of the indigenous languages of the African continent.

Above all, the linkage between these languages and economic development have to be made in a systematically planned manner. Rewarding people for their knowledge of African languages, used as analytical instruments, will restore the balance nationally, continentally and eventually internationally, between the relevant local and the global languages. Research in this direction is being designed in South Africa and it is to be hoped that some far-seeing private-sector interests will help to ensure that it gets off the drawing board. Paradoxically, I expect that

Afrikaans business interests will seize the opportunity first. The languages of South Africa, with the exception of those we label 'endangered', will continue to display their vitality. The challenge we face is, clearly, to enhance their status and their functionality as integral elements of an ensemble of languages bound together in a single system of national communication which is itself linked into the global system by means of English mainly, the international language that has come to be hegemonic in southern Africa.

References

Alexander, N. (1989) *Language policy and national unity in South Africa/Azania*. Cape town: Buchu Books.

Alexander, N. (1992) South Africa: Harmonizing Nguni and Sotho. In N. Crawhall (ed) *Democratically speaking. International perspectives on language planning*. Cape Town: National Language Project.

Du Plessis, H. and Du Plessis, L. (eds) (1987) *Afrikaans en taalpolitiek: 15 Opstelle*. Pretoria: HAUM.

Hirson, B. (1981) Language in control and resistance in South Africa. *Journal of African affairs* 80, 219-237.

Kellman, H. (1975) Language as an aid and barrier to involvement in the national system. In J. Rubin and B. Jernudd (eds) *Can language be planned? Sociolinguistic theory and practice for developing nations*. East-West Center: The University Press of Hawaii.

Mesthrie, R. (1995) *Language and social history. Studies in South African sociolinguistics*. Cape Town and Johannesburg: David Philip.

PANSALB (1999) *Annual report June 1999*. Pretoria: Pan South African Language Board.

Plueddemann, P. (1999) Multilingualism and education in South Africa: one year on. *International journal of educational research* 3 (4), 327-340.

Prah, K. (1993) *Mother tongue for scientific and technological development in Africa*. Bonn: Zentralstelle für Erziehung, Wissenschaft und Dokumentation (ZED).

Immigration and language policy in Australia

ULDIS OZOLINS
MICHAEL CLYNE

There are very real similarities between Australia and many parts of Europe in the actual sociolinguistic situation, especially as it obtains in relation to immigrant languages in many cities. Quite simply, European cities and many districts are becoming as culturally and linguistically diverse as those of Australia or other New World countries, as revealed by several of the other studies in this volume. At the same time, there is a vast gulf in terms of policy response to this situation: acceptance of immigrant languages as part of European reality is far from being reached, or in some cases far from even being considered to be an issue.

The European Cultural Foundation amassed numerous published and unpublished statistical surveys and other data to give possibly the most comprehensive overview of languages and language use in Western Europe ever assembled (ECF, 2000; see also ECF, 1998; Broeder & Extra, 1998). Given the reluctance of many European countries to conduct a census, for various reasons, and given the lack of language questions in the censuses that do exist, language data needs to be built up through countless smaller surveys and must be approached with great caution. Yet curiously, the data presented by the ECF seem to reveal a most uncertain factual basis to much contemporary European discourse on language policy. In comparing the relative salience of regional minority languages as compared to immigrant minority languages in Western Europe, the relativities presented in Table 1 could be gleaned from the statistics.

Such a relative accounting of speakers of regional as against immigrant minority languages would strike many faced with the realities of linguistic diversity in Europe as absurd. Certainly these figures recognise the greater salience of immigrant language issues in Germany. Yet it is ludicrous to consider that regional minority languages in France have twice the number of speakers, or that policy issues of regional minority languages in France are twice as salient as those of immigrant

Table 1   Salience of regional vs. immigrant minority languages in Western
Europe ('?' indicates where the compilers of statistics have themselves
used estimates or expressed some reservations about numbers)

	Apparent regional minority language speakers		*Apparent immigrant minority language speakers*
Germany	1	<	27
France	2.3 ?	>	1
United Kingdom	2 ?	>	1
Italy	4	>	1
Spain	41	>	1
Netherlands	4 ?	>	1

minority languages. The small relative number of immigrants in Spain
again may be readily accepted, but the relativities for the UK and the
Netherlands (and probably Italy) must be seriously doubted. Indeed,
tracing back the sources of statistics (eg back from the ECF compilations
to the Home Page of the European Bureau of Lesser Used Languages)
reveal the extraordinary uncertainty of much of the language data - the
figures for France on regional minority languages coming all the way
from the 1952 French census.

It is our argument that such use of figures works against the interests
of both regional minority languages and immigrant languages: it gives a
false impression of the numbers speaking regional minority languages
(which are arguably strong in Catalonia and Wales but often struggling
and threatened elsewhere), leading to an exaggerated avowal of their
strength and an institutional apathy in terms of policy towards them; and
it undermines the salience of immigrant languages, which are relegated
to being of importance (outside of Germany) to only an insignificant
minority. Such a situation is not easily solved by calling for language
policy to be based on the facts of the situation. It should be noted that the
projected expansion of the EU into Eastern Europe will bring new issues
for the autochthonous languages there, especially where they are often
the languages of powerful neighbours. In positive contrast to Western
Europe, however, censuses in Eastern Europe are standard social policy
tools, and often contain language data. In Europe, the very recognition of
sociolinguistic facts is clearly intertwined with strong ideological
commitments to a particular representation of national culture and language. Advances in language policy must take note of these ideological

factors, as much as of any scientific basis of measuring languages and their use.

Surprisingly however, an examination of Australian language policy may still be of benefit, as we will see there too the important intertwining of both ideological and scientific concerns in addressing language policy: very often exactly the same ideological impediments to language policy have long since been encountered in New World countries. There are we believe at least five aspects of policy implementation that are revealed in the Australian situation that have relevance for Europe. We set them out briefly here, before examining in details the Australian experience.

Multiculturalism as a goal?
It is crucial to understand that no multicultural society has ever, initially, consciously *wanted* to become multicultural. This is as true for the immigrant countries of the New World as it is for present-day Europe. Many of the resistance to cultural diversity seen in Europe have their precedents in New World countries which at various times have stressed assimilation, cultural homogeneity, and checks to immigration. New World countries moved to a more accepting stance towards multilingualism in response to specific pressures and social forces, now becoming apparent in Europe as well. A series of stages in such responses, by no means automatic, can be identified.

Response to initial demographic pressure of immigration
In New World countries, an initial response to multilingualism has come when significant immigration begin to affect a state's demography, forcing the state to engage in some minimal language planning simply to ensure its own adequate functioning. Primitive language services (usually not professional) spring up for interpreting/translating for key institutions (police, health, administration). There may be some specific programmes to teach the host language to immigrant children to ensure access to education. At this stage, there is no wider acceptance of Immigrant Minority Languages (IMLs) in public life or social policy. The European version of this stage also saw some early programmes, now abandoned, which taught home languages to children in preparation for eventual return to their homelands.

Policy innovation, unevenness and drift
Policy starts to develop when one or more sectors, agencies, institutions or regions begin to accept language diversity as relatively permanent, and

take policy initiatives in addressing this, generating responses in other agencies as well. Such moves as introducing generic and professional language services, steps to teach some IMLs in schools, finding ethnic health workers or gathering initial data on immigrant background variables are signs of this more advanced stage.

Language initiatives across a spread of institutions
A crucial aspect of policy development is the growing awareness of language issues across a range of institutions. Beliefs that one institution (usually school) can 'solve' language issues are often entertained but are always transcended: language has relevance to many institutions and policy makers in broadcasting and media, social welfare, information services, commerce and other spheres find an increased salience of IMLs in their sphere (e.g. Fishman, 1991). Language policy can take advantage of enabling changes elsewhere, such as an increase in available broadcasting spectrum or new requirements for access and accountability, introduced as mainstream policies but providing important opportunities for linguistic minorities.

Ideological and institutional change
The most recent stage which has to some extent (but never completely) been reached in Australia, is to have an ideological shift of recognising the contribution of immigrants to the nation's culture, and indeed accepting the slow transformation of that culture through acceptance of cultural diversity and shift in identity. Such a recognition has come hand in hand with a new awareness of the contribution of the indigenous populations as well. In Australia also, this has come with a renewed interest in and promotion of the national language, Australian English, and a tying together of language interests in these various domains.

Demographic and linguistic background of Australian postwar immigration

Australia's present language policies in relation to immigrant languages need to be understood in the context of Australia's massive post-war immigration programme, which has led to more than doubling Australia's population in the last half-century, from just under 8 million to now over 18 million. Immigration to Australia has always been intended for permanent settlement and eventual citizenship: short-term migrant labour or *gastarbeiter* programmes have not existed in Australia. The post-war immigration programme was initiated for reasons of defence and national development, and started in the belief that migrants would come from the favoured source countries of Britain and Ireland, and that the White Australia Policy would be maintained. However, there were insufficient migrants from the British Isles, and Australia accepted large numbers of other European migrants. Paradoxically, while the post-war immigration programme sought to build and maintain a White Australia, the ultimate consequence of deliberately accepting an increasingly diverse range of migrants was to weaken and then overturn completely the White Australia Policy.

The first post World War II non-British groups were Eastern and Central European displaced persons, followed by Maltese, Dutch, Germans, and Austrians and Italians (fifties). As the supply of factory workers for Australia's secondary industry needed to be maintained, immigrants came from further field, such as Greeks (late fifties and sixties), Turks (late sixties and early seventies), and various groups from Yugoslavia and Lebanon (over a longer period). Many of the groups were refugees, including two waves each of Hungarians, Czechs, Poles and Chileans, as well as Timorese, Lebanese, ethnic Vietnamese, and Chinese from Vietnam and mainland Chinese. Gradually more emphasis was placed on the immigration of business people and those with professional qualifications as well as on family reunion. The business migrant category brought to Australia many Taiwanese and Hong Kong Chinese.

According to the 1996 Census, 14.6% of the Australian population used a language other than English (hereafter LOTE) in the home. The proportion was 26.4% in Sydney and 25.4% in Melbourne. The percentages would be higher still if they included those using LOTEs elsewhere; the Australian Census asks specifically for language spoken in the home. Table 2 shows the breakdown of home use of the most widely used LOTEs and the aggregate totals of Aboriginal languages, totals of English-only speakers and total population numbers in each State and Territory in 1996. It will be seen that the most widely used LOTEs are Italian and Greek nationwide, though Arabic and Cantonese occupy the top two places in New South Wales, especially Sydney which has attracted most of the recent migrants from outside Europe.

Language shift varies greatly between the ethnolinguistic groups (and between the States) in the first generation, from 3% shift to English as the only home language among people born in the former Yugoslav republic of Macedonia to 61.9% among those born in the Netherlands. Many of the

Table 2 Home users of community languages in Australia by state, 1996 (excluding overseas visitors)

	NSW	Vic	SA	QLD	WA	Tas	NT	ACT	Australia
Aboriginal languages	1,132	319	2,149	5,038	8,250	33	27,038	58	44,017
Arabic	125,698	39,478	3,607	3,474	3,786	375	71	1,110	177,599
Cantonese	107,259	53,887	6,593	15,964	14,542	800	822	2,403	202,270
Croatian	26,218	25,429	3,894	3,909	6,204	327	65	3,106	69,152
Dutch	9,804	11,346	4,077	7,703	5,591	1,323	235	651	40,766
German	29,372	27,460	11,851	16,441	8,553	1,935	877	2,319	98,808
Greek	92,990	124,671	28,086	11,319	5,782	1,318	2,715	2,889	269,770
Italian	102,773	160,061	43,356	24,732	38,609	1,634	844	3,743	375,752
Macedonian	29,941	32,978	923	879	5,995	39	20	572	71,347
Maltese	17,749	23,713	1,330	1,741	460	31	22	196	45,242
Mandarin	40,651	25,636	2,984	11,406	9,031	432	398	1,373	91,911
Polish	18,264	20,869	8,631	5,183	7,184	1,094	65	1,479	62,769
Spanish	48,577	22,648	3,143	8,468	5,088	523	317	2,490	91,254
Tagalog	38,401	16,035	2,705	8,712	2,767	359	1,139	866	70,444
Vietnamese	59,378	54,039	11,079	11,686	10,125	125	508	2,325	146,265
English only	4,721,807	3,357,652	1,213,908	2,988,652	1,467,703	430,085	133,572	249,933	14,564,924
Population	6,038,685	4,373,537	1,427,960	3,368,857	1,726,112	459,673	195,110	299,245	17,892,507

earlier immigrant groups (Germans, Austrians, Maltese, French, Hungarians) who arrived in the assimilationist era also have high shift rates while many of the more recent ones that are culturally more distant from the dominant group (e.g. Turks, Lebanese, Vietnamese, Taiwanese) and the Greeks experience low rates of shift. In the second generation, the rate of language shift is higher than that of the first but the rank ordering of shift rates is very similar. There are massive differences between second generation rates in exogamous and endogamous families (e.g. Japanese: endogamous 5.4%, exogamous 68.9% shift; Korean: endogamous 5.4%, exogamous 61.5% shift). The recent Census has demonstrated an unprecedented intergenerational shift (Italian 14% first to 57.9% second generation shift; Greek 6.4% to 28%). It remains to be seen whether the newer groups fall into the 'normal' pattern of shift within two or three generations, but there are indications that Cantonese and Mandarin will not survive as long as Macedonian, Turkish or Arabic (Clyne & Kipp, 1997).

Early postwar language policy

Australia did not set out in its post-war immigration scheme to foster multiculturalism or multilingualism. Quite the contrary. Australia at the end of World War II was an avowedly monolingual and monocultural country, with extremely rigid views on assimilation of non-Britishers into 'Australian norms', at best a neglect of the Aboriginal population and Aboriginal languages, strict regulation of the use of other languages in publications and public life, and little interest in the languages of the region around it. This was in spite of an earlier tradition of multilingualism in the 19th century as a result of substantial European immigration, when there were bilingual schools (for some time even funded by the State), public use of LOTEs in many churches and in the transactional domain (including the requirement that government tenders be advertised in German as well as English in South Australia), and language enclaves in some rural areas (Clyne, 1991a).

Ironically, both the strong assertion of Australian nationalism around federation in 1901, and the renewed strengthening of ties with Imperial Britain as a result of World War I, reinforced monolingual tendencies in Australia. With non-whites excluded from the country, other non-British groups fell under suspicion, particularly the Germans in and after World War I, but also the Italians. Immigration policy was strongly oriented to

British and Irish immigrants, and assimilation was stressed for non-British groups. In the thirties the long Depression cut immigration to a trickle and reinforced identification of Australian culture with mono-lingualism. In this respect, attitudes in Australia as a new world country were not essentially different to those prevailing towards linguistic and cultural diversity that have more recently obtained in some European countries.

Changes to the previous attitudes to other languages in Australia came pragmatically, and in the beginning were firmly predicated upon the notion of assimilation. Wary of possible negative attitudes towards arriving non-English speaking background (NESB) migrants, the Australian government from 1947 carefully initiated a programme of English teaching to immigrant adults (but not children), set up reception centres to provide short-term accommodation to newcomers, used interpreters where appropriate, and encouraged Australians to foster assimilation and good-neighbourliness.

The immigration programme thus demonstrated a crucial responsi-bility that was assumed by the government - if NESB migrants were to be brought to the country, it was the government's responsibility to help them linguistically; it was the government's responsibility to assist them to assimilate, rather than ignore their plight. This was not a programme of fostering cultural diversity, but rather one of submersion of other cultures and languages, in accord with the assimilationist assumptions of the day (Ozolins, 1993). However, this fundamental assertion of respon-sibility was to have profound consequences, and stands in sharp contrast to the position of some other governments in nations of immigration who assert that fitting into the society is the individual migrant's own responsibility.

Early post-war language policy was thus pragmatic and assimilation-oriented. There was no bilingual education, the main languages taught in schools were French and Latin, the holdings of public libraries were almost entirely English, there were severe limitations on the amount of radio broadcasting in LOTEs, no television programmes in LOTEs, and little provision of services in the languages of the immigrant groups (Ozolins, 1993).

It was a series of grass-roots initiatives both by immigrant groups and by individual Australian institutions that began to see changes to this approach over the fifties and sixties. This period saw:

- A growing confidence of migrants in asserting their needs and cultural interests, forcing the abandonment of previous restrictive regulations on foreign language publishing and radio broadcasting. Immigrant communities also established language maintenance institutions, particularly part-time self-funded language schools (known in Australia as 'ethnic schools'), as well as their own press and radio programmes.

- A growing awareness of social and economic complexities of immigration that began to raise doubts about a simple assimilation outcome. In education, for example, it had been assumed that migrant children needed no special treatment in terms of language learning at school, but that scattering them into overwhelmingly Anglo-Australian schools would lead to rapid language learning and assimilation. Yet as immigration increased, population concentrations resulted in numerous schools of overwhelmingly NESB intake. Similar needs to change previous practices arose in welfare, health systems and employment (Martin, 1978).

- Languages such as Italian, Russian, German and Dutch began to be slowly introduced into the school systems, taught both to background speakers and non-background speakers. However, this did not always proceed smoothly, as there were concerns of native speakers gaining an 'unfair' advantage over others, a persistent problem in attitude and examination formalities.

Multiculturalism and innovations in language policy in the sixties and seventies

The official discourse of assimilation slowly changed, giving way over the sixties to integration as the guiding principle for migrant settlement, but by the mid seventies this had changed to an emphasis on multi-culturalism. There were a number of factors motivating these changes: by the seventies there was a quest for a new national identity which differentiated Australia from Britain, following the latter's membership of the European Community and retreat from the South-East Asian region, and Australia was also redefining itself in relation to its region. Internally, there was a need for this search for identity to reflect the change in Australia's demography, as this period saw the rise of a new section of the Australian elite (in the judiciary, academia and the medical profession) which was not of British ancestry. More broadly, there was a new political situation with openly cosmopolitan elements starting to replace 'old guards' in both the major political parties; importantly, shifts in thinking on immigration and multiculturalism were generally bipartisan and not politically divisive. And more broadly still, the international climate favoured ethnic rights movements among a number of other social reform movements (Clyne, 1991b). As a result of these changes, the decade from the end of the sixties to the end of the seventies in Australia saw a remarkable string of initiatives in language policy through a combination of government interest and grass-roots activism. The list of innovations over this period includes the following domains.

Language education
- A rapid expansion of the range of languages taught in schools up to matriculation level; the total now is over 40 languages, representing every significant immigrant language. Only a fraction of these were taught in regular schools; for the smaller languages Education ministries established connections with ethnic schools, and set up examination boards that would ensure appropriate standards. In some states Saturday Schools of Languages coordinated this activity. Teachers in ethnic schools were also enabled to undergo teacher training and professional development alongside mainstream teachers. In the eighties small grants were made available by Federal and some State governments to ethnic schools for their programmes at lower levels as well. Tertiary level language teaching also diversified. Such initiatives were strongly influenced by increasingly vocal migrant education activist organisations prominent from the mid seventies (Clyne, 1991b; Welch, 1997).
- A growing recognition of the importance of supporting mother tongue development and literacy skills, most notably by beginning to teach languages in primary schools.
- The Child Migrant Education Programme was introduced in 1971 to complement long-established adult migrant teaching, providing for English as a Second Language (ESL) teachers and some intensive language centres for new arrivals.
- A series of initiatives in the neglected teaching of Asian languages and cultures in schools, which became a favoured policy area in the eighties and nineties. There were also attempts to improve the language capacity of departments such as Foreign Affairs, Trade and Defence through increased language training.

Language services
- Introduction of the Telephone Interpreter Service (TIS), an Australian invention, by the Department of Immigration in 1973, steadily aug-

mented by specialist on-site interpreting/translating (I/T) services in the health, education or legal fields. Following the principle of government responsibility for bringing NESB immigrants to Australia, it was specifically government agencies that developed major language services where need was identified either at the State or Federal level. Private sector services also operated in areas of civil law, private medicine and commerce.

- Professionalisation of I/T in immigrant languages through the establishment of the National Accreditation Authority for Translators and Interpreters (NAATI) in the late seventies, which set standards of accreditation and training programmes in a large number of languages (currently over 50), including indigenous languages and Auslan (Australian Sign Language). Uniquely in the world, the NAATI accreditation system covers the full gamut of bilingual and interpreting/translating work through a five-level structure from bilingual aide to international conference interpreter/translator. It accredits practitioners either through its own testing programme, or by approving courses at various levels, or by recognition of overseas qualifications. In the Australian view, those interpreters who work in the major immigrant languages in community settings are providing a professional service and need to be seen as professionals, with accreditation and status to match (Ozolins, 1991; 1998).

- Formal recognition of the language capacities of public servants through the Language Availability Performance Allowance, providing a small reward to those who used LOTEs in their contact with clients, and could pass a bilingual aide test.

Broadcasting
- Policy moved from a system of regulation of LOTEs in radio and television to actively supporting such broadcasting, resulting in ethnic radio being financed by the federal government from the mid-seventies, with immigrant programme committees eventually in around 65 languages. This was brought under the umbrella of a new public broadcasting body, the Special Broadcasting Service (SBS) in 1978. SBS also introduced multicultural television from 1980, which was not produced by ethnic communities but was a professional broadcasting enterprise charged with buying or producing quality programmes related to cultural diversity, not only in Australia but from a global perspective; about 50% of programmes are in LOTEs, and subtitled in English.

- Outside the government-funded ethnic radio, there was also increased broadcasting in LOTEs in community radio as access to the broadcasting spectrum diversified, and programmes in LOTEs also were part of the still few community television initiatives.

Census and information
- From 1976, language questions have been included in the five-yearly Australian Census. These questions have essentially been of two kinds: one about language use, usually languages spoken in the home, and a second question asking respondents who do speak LOTEs for a self-assessment of their level of English. Despite certain difficulties in the questions asked, these have since been a valuable source of information about LOTEs in Australia. Other questions on the Census also ask for respondents' country of birth, and country of birth of parents. One Census also asked a question on respondents' heritage. As well as the main Census, other institutions particularly Education ministries also regularly carry out an 'Ethnic census' of NESB schoolchildren, asking for languages used in various settings, and background information on children's families. At more specific institutional levels, recording background information including language to be used and need for an interpreter is part of hospital or social security records. What kind of information in the Census, surveys or institutional records can be of most use to language planners is an important issue (Clyne, 1982; Clyne & Kipp, 1997).

In many cases there was little prior local or overseas experience for such innovations, yet this spate of initiatives in quite distinct spheres fundamentally changed assumptions towards language issues in Australia. Significantly, these moves were not part of a national blueprint or centralised decision-making, but rather reflected a period of policy innovation, unevenness and some degree of policy drift, often at an individual enterprise or departmental level. Australian institutions found they could and did respond to issues of multilingualism in a variety of pragmatic ways, in some cases displaying considerable ingenuity and inventiveness (Kalantzis *et al.*, 1990; Romaine, 1991).

These innovations in LOTE policy also came in a context of growing interest in other language issues. Alongside the activism of multicultural groups came the final emancipation of Australian English from its previous status as an inferior version of British English. By the seventies, an increasingly nationalistic tide of sympathy supported the recognition of Australian English, and its codification through the publication of the Macquarie Dictionary in the early eighties (Lo Bianco, 1997).

The seventies also saw growing interest in Aboriginal language issues. The first bilingual education programmes in Australia were in Aboriginal languages in the Northern Territory in 1973. This has resulted since in greater control by some Aboriginal communities of their schools, including in some cases setting up completely independent schools teaching 'two way' or bilingual programmes (Australia, Senate Standing Committee on Education and the Arts, 1984; Walsh & Yallop, 1993).

Development of an explicit coherent national languages policy

While the policies described above were the actions of many different agencies, the need for coherence in language policy began to be identified as a major issue from the late seventies, as the various interest groups identified common threads of concern. One influential policy document was the Galbally Report in 1978, a landmark report in that it was tabled in federal parliament not only in English, but also in ten community languages. This report looked comprehensively at post-arrival services for migrants and recommended policies to improve settlement, communication and education, and detailed concrete policy steps to be adopted by all federal instrumentalities (Australia, Review of Post-Arrival Programmes and Services to Migrants, 1978). More broadly, this enquiry argued that multicultural perspectives should not be limited to considerations of how migrants were treated, but needed to infuse Australian institutions so that awareness of cultural diversity and of the way immigration had changed Australian society was spread throughout the population.

In the late seventies a broad coalition representing educators, diverse communities, government policy makers and language professionals came together to identify a number of national issues requiring coordination in language policy. The coalition brought together groups that had previously had little contact with each other, for example migrant education activists and the emerging profession of applied linguists, or groups that had seemingly been at loggerheads over priorities, such as those advocating migrant language teaching and those supporting traditional foreign language teaching. Importantly, the coalition was concerned to have language policy be relevant to the broadest range of population and linguistic groups, and in particular not to be seen as the advocacy of any one special interest (such as LOTE teaching in schools, or only being concerned with languages of ethnic communities). A critical move was to get a number of interests representing *English* to join this coalition, and include such issues as literacy for mother tongue English speakers, issues of Australian English, and issues of racism and sexism in language, as well as issues of teaching migrants English, thus establishing a complementarity between English and LOTE issues. Aboriginal language interests also joined the coalition, as did a number of other groups such as Deaf groups promoting a better understanding of Australian Sign Language (Ozolins, 1993).

As a result of this activism, the Senate Standing Committee on Education and the Arts took up a broad-ranging reference on developing a coordinated language policy in 1982. Their report, *A National Language Policy*, released in 1984, covered an extremely wide range of issues, but managed to subsume them under four guiding principles for language policy in Australia:

- Competence in English.
- Maintenance and development of languages other than English.
- Provision of services in languages other than English.
- Opportunities for learning second languages (Australia, Senate Standing Committee on Education and the Arts, 1984: 4).

The many recommendations of this report were fine tuned in a further report *National Policy on Languages* (Australia, Department of Education, Joe Lo Bianco, 1987), which gave a balanced rationale for multilingualism, and recommended several coordinating programmes in second language learning and intercultural communication, an adult literacy action campaign, an Asian Studies Programme and a National Aboriginal Language Programme. These were granted $28 million per year in new funding. The report also led to the eventual establishment of a National Languages Institute of Australia (NLIA) which was funded to conduct and disseminate results of applied linguistic research.

Equally important at this time of the late eighties were State initiatives, in both education and language services. In education, virtually all State and territory governments began to implement broad polices to stem the long-term decline in overall language learning and make it a part of the core curriculum, in some cases in secondary school only, but in several States in primary schools as well. Some States appointed teachers additional to normal school staffing establishments to teach languages. Increasing numbers of primary schools taught languages by the beginning of the nineties, with school of high migrant density leading the field, though many language programmes were not specifically targeted at the migrant groups in the school.

Shifts in policy in the nineties

Ideological shifts in the nineties were to put new pressures on maintaining effective language polices. Government policy orientations generally stressed neo-liberal economic principles, financial stringency, an end to large government projects, some degree of outsourcing and privatisation, and a reluctance to assume greater responsibility for social policy. In line with this, there were some specific retreats and changes of priority in language policy, for example by a Federal Education Minister John Dawkins who attempted to limit the previous generous contributions to language policy in favour of a single-minded stress on English literacy (Clyne, 1991a; Moore, 1991; Lo Bianco & Freebody, 1997). This policy line has been repeatedly pushed since, particularly in relation to literacy levels in schools and consequent links to unemployment issues. Championing of English literacy has led to the government recently abandoning programmes of bilingual education for Aborigines in Northern Territory government schools, as well as stressing English learning in the education of Deaf children. From some quarters also, LOTE programmes have been criticised for taking up valuable time that could be devoted to English literacy.

In relation to LOTEs, Dawkins in much of his rhetoric believed greater emphasis should be given to Asian languages alone, a policy orientation that resulted later in the adoption of a national programme for promoting four languages - Indonesian, Japanese, Korean and Mandarin - above others so that they become the languages studied by a majority of school students (Australia, Council of Australian Governments, 1994; Kirkpatrick, 1995). Several proponents of Asian language learning explicitly attacked programmes in other languages, particularly those aimed at language maintenance, unravelling the previous fairly united coalition of language interests. This line of policy has been generally followed by subsequent Federal governments, but the State systems have continued to support teaching in a wider range of languages outside the ones federally nominated as priorities, and devoted considerable resources for curriculum development and teacher training in a diversity of languages.

In other areas, too, federal governments signalled withdrawal, for example in some cases outsourcing or privatising language services, such as I/T or teaching ESL to new arrivals, and in some instances limiting access entitlements. Despite these vicissitudes, in other ways language policy found new ground in the nineties. The most significant shift in understanding here is the greater recognition of the language abilities of the population as a resource. Prime Minister Keating's government strongly promoted a policy of Productive Diversity, recognising the linguistic and cultural resources present in Australia, as have several State governments. One clear message from this is that the tiresome distinctions between community languages and trade and business languages are clearly breaking down: several languages of large migrant communities are global languages, and with shifts in international economies and the search for niche markets, a vast number of languages are used for business and international communication (Djité, 1994). For example, several international companies have recently established call centres in Australia to serve global or regional needs, because of the availability of competent speakers of a wide range of languages.

A crucial aspect here however is that language resources need to be developed, not merely taken as they are. Background speakers of other languages, unless they have already received a full education in that language, will need help to develop their skills to high levels of proficiency and, where appropriate, academic achievement. From time to time Australian education systems are still uneasy about 'background speakers', with confused categorisations of students for language teaching and examinations, thus in some cases frustrating both LOTE background speakers and those studying a language from scratch (Clyne, 1998). For language to be truly seen as a resource, this obstacle will still need to be overcome.

One further shock to immigration and related policies came in 1996 with the entry into Federal parliament of a populist independent member, Pauline Hanson, who criticised the abandonment of the White Australia Policy, attacked Asian immigration and condemned multiculturalism as weakening the nation. While previously a small number of politicians or public figures had expressed such views, there was an eruption of angry debate over these issues with Hanson's arrival, in ways perhaps familiar to many European countries. Hanson subsequently garnered most support in rural and provincial areas of a few States, particularly Queensland, reflecting the very differential impact of demographic changes and visibility of migrants, for most support for her came in those areas which had least migration. For a period this intervention seemed to bring significant disabling changes for languages, with policy makers downplaying multicultural issues in particular. But the upshot of this debate in Australia recently has been a very strong reaffirmation of principles of multiculturalism and the benefits of diversity, and Hanson lost her seat at the 1998 Federal elections.

Rather than sporadic outbreaks of racism or xenophobia, it is more general government ideologies and outlooks that now threaten many of the advances made in language policy and broader social policy (Gibbons, 1995). These include a general retreat from providing services, selling off of resources, user-pays, retreat from planning, continual change of direction and personnel and advisers, and weakening of the public service as a policy-advising force. The Australian experience has also been however that the pursuit of this ideological direction brings strong reactions, not only from victimised groups but from the wider community as well, demanding fairness and maintenance of public services.

What can Australian experience contribute to European aspirations?

While it would be presumptuous to advocate blueprints for other countries, certain principles of Australian approaches can be identified to show what is possible in detailed language policies, both in terms of pragmatic situational responses, and attempts to gain more comprehensive policy perspectives through such measures as a National Policy on Languages:

- A government that allows speakers of other languages to move to a country must take responsibility for their integration into the society, including paying attention to language issues.
- Acceptance that despite a large effort in teaching English to immigrants, other language needs will continue, such as the need for language services (Stevens, 1999). Moreover, cultural diversity in the population will create demand for and interest in use of other languages in many spheres including education and economic activity.
- Australia has not had primarily a rights-driven approach to policy, and there is no basis for extensive arguments over constitutional rights such as in the USA. Rather, Australia has had a policy-driven approach, employing an often-identified and useful language policy trichotomy of language needs, language rights and language as a

resource. An absence of an overt discourse of rights has also meant political reaction to language policy initiatives have been relatively rare and muted.

- Language policy is not coterminous with language education policy. Areas as diverse as language services, interpreting and translating, broadcasting, administrative and legal processes and wider issues of languages in public life are an indelible part of Australian language policy.

- Language policy has been aimed at institutions, public service, health and education systems etc rather than at political processes; rarely has language policy been the object of partisan political concern. Thus language policy is not seen as something for 'them' - for immigrants or outsiders - but for Australian institutions, and how they can adequately service all their clients.

- In education, there have been relatively positive attitudes towards the introduction of other languages and multicultural perspectives into school curriculum, but a diversity of actual institutional measures have been used to accomplish this, such as links between mainstream schools, ethnic schools and Saturday Schools of Languages. Priority languages can be identified for more systematic development, but Australian experience shows too narrow a focus on a small number of languages is unlikely to be successful. Messy as it seems, allowing a diversity of languages with flexibility in institutional arrangements is likely to be the more satisfying policy option.

- Inclusiveness on various levels has been a hallmark of Australian language policy, for example including English in overall policy formulations and in coalitions supporting broader approaches to language policy, and in other cases making links with indigenous or Auslan language issues; enabling a very large number of languages to be studied and recognised by the school system; in Interpreting/Translating, including all languages including indigenous and sign language into one accreditation system, and including all levels of I/T and bilingual work within that same system.

- There is an information base to make language policy decisions, not only through the nation-wide Census but also in institution-specific information recording.

- Timing and seizing opportunities in a wider policy context is important, as is awareness of enabling or disabling polices which may affect languages. For example, many changes in Australian broadcasting were not brought about primarily with ethnic communities in mind, but these communities were able to take advantage of the introduction of such broadcasting forums as access radio and community radio, and diversification of the broadcasting spectrum.

- Major policy documents have stressed comprehensiveness and coordination in language policy, underlining national directions and fostering grass-roots understanding of language issues. The building of coalitions is crucial, including parties concerned with the national language.

It can be seen from the Australian experience that collaboration on language issues between different language interests is a real possibility, rather than exacerbating divisions. Common interest in linguistic diversity has been broadly supported, despite a range of opposition to aspects of language policy from specifically anti-immigrant moves, to emphasis on literacy in the host language, to retreat from provision of government services for economic/ideological reasons. Significantly, most aspects of Australian language policy have survived these attacks, but at some cost. Even on the side of those defending say immigration policy, there is still a need to attend to the specifics of language policy: as political debate grows, detailed language policies can suffer as emphasis is put on seemingly more vital issues such as confronting racism or stopping victimisation.

References

Australia, Council of Australian Governments (1994) *Asian languages and Australia's economic future*. Brisbane: Queensland Government Printer.

Australia, Department of Education, Lo Bianco, J. (1987) *National policy on languages*. Canberra: Australian Government Publishing Service.

Australia, Review of Post-Arrival Programs and Services to Migrants (1978) *Migrant services and programs* (The 'Galbally Report'). Canberra: Australian Government Publishing Service.

Australia, Senate Standing Committee on Education and the Arts (1984) *A national language policy*. Canberra: Australian Government Publishing Service.

Broeder, P. and Extra, G. (1998) *Language, ethnicity and education. Case studies of immigrant minority groups and immigrant minority languages*. Clevedon: Multilingual Matters.

Clyne, M. (1982) *Multilingual Australia*. Melbourne: River Seine.

Clyne, M. (1991a) Language policy. Are we going backwards? *Current affairs bulletin* 68 (6).

Clyne, M. (1991b) *Community languages: The Australian experience.* Cambridge: Cambridge University Press.

Clyne, M. (1998) Managing language diversity and second language programmes in Australia. In S. Wright and H. Kelly-Holmes (eds) *Managing language diversity.* Clevedon: Multilingual Matters.

Clyne, M. and Kipp, S. (1997) Trends and changes in home language use and shift in Australia. *Journal of multilingual and multicultural development* 18 (6).

Djité, P. (1994) *From language policy to language planning.* Melbourne: National Languages and Literacy Institute of Australia.

European Cultural Foundation (1998) *Which languages for Europe?* Amsterdam: ECF.

European Cultural Foundation (2000) *Statistics and information on education of migrants' children in the EU.* Amsterdam: ECF

Fishman, J. (1991) *Reversing language shift: theoretical and empirical foundations of assistance to threatened languages.* Clevedon/Philadelphia: Multilingual Matters.

Gibbons, J. (1995) Multilingualism for Australians? In T. Skutnabb-Kangas (ed.) *Multilingualism for all.* Lisse: Swets & Zeitlinger.

Kalantzis, M. *et al.* (1990) *Cultures of schooling.* London: Falmer.

Kirkpatrick, A. (1995) The teaching and learning of the four priority Asian languages. *Australian review of applied linguistics,* Series S (12).

Lo Bianco, J. (1997) English and pluralistic policies: The case of Australia. In W. Eggington and H. Wren (eds) *Language policy: Dominant English, pluralist challenges.* Amsterdam: John Benjamins.

Lo Bianco, J. and Freebody, P. (1997) *Australian literacies. Informing national policy on literacy education.* Canberra: Language Australia.

Martin, J. (1978) *The migrant presence.* Sydney: Allen & Unwin.

Moore, H. (1991) Enchantments and displacements: multiculturalism, language policy and Dawkins-speak. *Melbourne studies in education.* Melbourne: Melbourne University Press.

Ozolins, U. (1991) *Interpreting translating and language policy.* Melbourne: National Languages Institute of Australia.

Ozolins, U. (1993) *The politics of language in Australia.* Cambridge: Cambridge University Press.

Ozolins, U. (1998) *Interpreting and translating in Australia. Current issues and international comparisons.* Melbourne: Language Australia.

Romaine, S. (1991) *Language in Australia.* Cambridge: Cambridge University Press.

Stevens, C.A. (1999) Selection and settlement of citizens: English language proficiency among immigrant groups in Australia. *Journal of multilingual and multicultural development* 20 (2).

Walsh, M. and Yallop, C. (1993) *Language and culture in Aboriginal Australia.* Canberra: Aboriginal Studies Press.

Welch, A. (1997) *Class, culture and the state in Australian education. Reform or crisis.* Frankfurt-am-Main: Peter Lang.

Linguistic minorities in India

AMITAV CHOUDHRY

If nationalisms in the rest of the world have to choose their imagined community from certain 'modular' forms already made available to them by Europe and the Americas, what do they have left to imagine? (Partha Chatterjee, 1993: 5)

With a population of approximately 1000 million people, who, together, represent four language families, i.e. Indo-Aryan and Dravidian, Austro-Asiatic and Sino-Tibetan, 1652 languages with 10 major writing systems, 18 scheduled languages and 418 listed languages, India is certainly one of the leading multilingual nations in the world today. India presents a unique example of ethnic, socio-cultural and religious diversity that has resulted in linguistic diversity. There are also 'other' privileged languages, which are included in the list of the Indian Literary Academy (22 languages). There are 34 languages (or more) in which newspapers are published; almost 67 languages are used in primary education; 80 languages are used for promoting literacy. Indian languages derive strongly from the ethnic community or the territory in which a particular language is used. In the numerous language contact situations, the incidence of bilingualism and multilingualism is very high. Many minority language users speak three or four languages; moreover, there is evidence of considerable linguistic heterogeneity even within communities. All the States and Union Territories of India are multilingual, despite the dominance in each of speakers of the scheduled languages. In fact, the language situation is extremely dynamic, with new languages evolving to serve as the *lingua franca* in several areas.

Historical background

In the years immediately after India attained Independence, there was great concern to protect and safeguard the interests of linguistic minorities in India. India's national leaders, the framers of the Constitution, and the Union and State Governments were fully aware of the problems as well as the aspirations and expectations of linguistic minorities. In view of the multilingual character of the Indian society, it was not desirable to ignore the sensitive issues concerning linguistic minorities in post-Independent India. In India's multilingual milieu, linguistic minorities are confronted with a wide range of language problems. The Indian Constitution provides necessary protection and safeguards to minority language speakers and guarantees equal treatment and full opportunities to them. The fundamental provisions in respect of linguistic minorities are contained in Articles 29 and 30 of the Constitution. Beg (1993) points out that the word 'minority', prior to occurring in Article 30, had appeared in the relevant Draft Article (corresponding to the present Article 30). Elucidating the word 'minority', B.R. Ambedkar, Chairman of the Drafting Committee of the Constituent Assembly, made the following remarks in the Constituent Assembly:

> The word is used not merely to indicate the minority in the technical sense of the word (as we have been accustomed to use it for the purpose of certain political safeguards, such as representation in the Legislature, representation in the Services and so on), it is also used to cover minorities which are not minorities in the technical sense, but which are nonetheless minorities in the cultural and linguistic sense. The Article intends to give protection in the matter of culture, language and script not only to a minority technically, but also to a minority in the wider sense of the term. (Quoted in Government of India, 1975: 24)

These Articles and the Articles 347, 350, 350-A and 350-B are meant to solve many of the problems of linguistic minorities relating to education, administration, mass communication, language use and language development. The Constitution was adopted on 26 November 1949, it came into effect on January 26, 1950, and was updated in 1996. The relevant Articles are mentioned below:

> *Article 347*: On a demand being made in that behalf the President may, if he is satisfied that a substantial proportion of the population of a state desire the use of any language spoken by them to be recognised by that state, direct that such language shall also be officially recognised throughout that state or any part thereof for such purpose as he may specify.

Article 350: Every person shall be entitled to submit a representation for the redress of any grievance to any officer or authority of the Union or a state in any of the languages used in the Union or in the state, as the case may be.

Article 350A: It shall be the endeavour of every state and of every local authority within the state to provide adequate facilities for instruction in the mother tongue at the primary stage of education to children belonging to linguistic minority groups, and the President may issue such directions to any state as he considers necessary or proper for securing the provision of such facilities.

Article 350B: There shall be a special officer for linguistic minorities to be appointed by the President. It shall be the duty of the special officer to investigate all matters relating to the safeguards provided for linguistic minorities under this Constitution and report to the President upon those matters at such intervals as the President may direct, and the President shall cause all such reports to be laid before each House of Parliament, and sent to the governments of the states concerned.

Prior to this, a Resolution was adopted by the Working Committee of the Indian National Congress on August 5, 1949 about the use of language for educational purposes. Its main features are briefly summarized below:

- At the primary stage a child shall get instruction in his mother tongue which will be according to the wishes of the guardian or parents of the child.
- In areas where different languages congregate, public primary schools giving instruction in the language of a minority will be opened or sections joined to other primary schools, if there is a reasonable number of pupils in a class demanding instruction in that language.
- Instruction at the secondary stage will ordinarily be given in the Provincial language but where a sufficiently large number of pupils demand it, schools may be run for sections attached to other schools in a minority language, provided that there is infrastructural support.

At a Conference of Provincial Education Ministers in August 1949, the 'first all-India level decisions' were taken. A Resolution was adopted which was approved by the Central Advisory Board of Education and the Government of India. These are the salient points:

- The medium of instruction and examination at the Junior Basic Stage must be the mother tongue of the child and where the mother tongue is different from the Regional or State language, arrangements must be made for instruction in the mother tongue by appointing at least one teacher, provided there are no less than 40 pupils speaking the language in the whole school or 10 such pupils in a class.
- The mother tongue will be the language declared by the parent or guardian to be the mother tongue; the Regional or State language, where it is different from the mother tongue, should be introduced not earlier than in class 3 and not later than at the end of the Junior Basic Stage.
- In order to facilitate the switching over to the Regional language as medium in the Secondary Stage, children should be given the option of answering questions in their mother tongue, for the first two years after the Junior Basic Stage.
- At the secondary stage, if the basic criteria of numerical strength of the minority language and infrastructural support exist, then schools thus established will be entitled to recognition and grant-in-aid from the government.
- The regional language will, however, be a compulsory subject throughout the secondary stage.

In the end, the Resolution clarified that 'the arrangements prescribed above will in particular be necessary in metropolitan cities or places where a large number of people speaking different languages live, or in areas with a floating population speaking different languages'.

Criteria for determining a linguistic minority

In the Indian context, Beg (1993) observes that a linguistic minority may be determined in terms of the numerical strength of speakers of a language located in a particular region in relation to the numerical strength of speakers of another language or languages in the same region. It is in this sense that India may be called 'a country of linguistic minorities'. Pattanayak (1973: vi) states that even the Hindi-Urdu language amalgam which is the majority language spoken by approximately 46% of the total population is a minority language in the context of the totality of speakers using non-Hindi languages. This situation is noticed for the macro-structure of the country. For its micro-structures, i.e. the constituent States, there are dominant languages, i.e. languages whose

speakers generally make up more than 50% of their respective populations. Khelkar (*op. cit.* Bandyopadhyay, 1999) proposes the concept of
Hirdu to refer to the Hindi-Urdu amalgam. It is very rarely found that the
speakers of a dominant language in a State make up less than 50% of the
total population of that State. The census reports also show that none of
the States and Union Territories are monolingual. In every State, there are
sizeable groups whose mother tongue does not happen to be the dominant or the majority language of the State. Along with the dominant
language, there will be a non-dominant or minority language (or
languages) whose speakers make up less than 50% of the total population.
Similarly, it is rarely found that the total of speakers of all minority
languages in a particular region make up more than 50% of the total
population of that region. The exceptions are Meghalaya (52.54%),
Nagaland (86.06%), Andaman and Nicobar Islands (75.32%) and
Arunachal Pradesh (76.61%), where the speakers of minority languages
make up groups which, in totality, comprise more than 50% of their
respective State populations.

If one looks at the distribution of the Scheduled languages in the
listing of the Indian Language Census (1991), the first aspect that needs to
be highlighted is the staggering 7,964,849 speakers listed under 'others'.
Though this is less than 1% of the total of Scheduled language speakers,
it reflects the amalgamation tendencies of the major languages. All the
unlisted languages whose numbers are less than 10,000 are listed under
'others'. More than 50% of the population listed under 'others' is
accounted for under Hindi. Table 1 gives a comparative picture.

Table 1 Figures derived from the Indian Language Censes (1991)

Combined figures for all Scheduled languages	Combined figures for languages listed under 'others'	Total Figures for Hindi	Figures for languages listed under 'others' accounted for under Hindi
807,441,662	7,964,849	337,272,114	4,642,954

Another astounding fact is that Hindi has 48 variants and there is a slot
for 'others' under each scheduled and non-scheduled language. Ironically, even a non-scheduled language like Bhili/Bhilodi has 14 variants.
Therefore, keeping a slot like 'others' facilitates hegemonic groups to

indulge in a numbers game, simultaneously succeeding in subjugating the 'listless' linguistic minorities to oblivion.

Crystallisation of minority linguistic groups

Choudhry (1998) states that the peaceful premise on the basis of which the States were reorganized as political and administrative units was to reduce conflict between the major minority language speakers of India and to imbibe a spirit of nationalism amongst its people. Going back a little into history, Bandyopadhyay (1998: 2) reports that 1) in 1837, it was decided by the British Government to introduce different vernacular tongues in the administration instead of Persian or Sanskrit; 2) at this time and for the first time in India, language-consciousness arose with the equation of land and language, both of which were to be well-defined, well-determined by erasing the indeterminacy or fuzziness of boundaries as it had been in existence before the introduction of the Nation State (Kaviraj, 1992; Chatterjee, 1993; Khubchandani, 1997); 3) the concept of the Nation State, as Benedict Anderson (1983) pointed out, is a result of print capitalistic imagination made available by Europe and the Americas; one had to choose and imagine one's community from certain modular forms like language or religion; 4) by this derivative imagination (Chatterjee, 1993), the linguistic-nation-state boundaries were solidified and scheduled in the Independent Indian constitution. In the process, it gave a new dimension to conflict and tension amongst different minority speech communities that, prior to such a situation, enjoyed an almost peaceful coexistence. The best example is found in the case of Punjab where, in the 1961 Census, Hindi speakers made up 55.6% of the total population. After the reorganization of the State in 1956, however, which led to the creation of Haryana, Hindi speakers in Punjab were reduced to a linguistic minority.

Beg (1993) argues that this is the process of changing a minority linguistic group into a majority group, but the fact remains the same. The reorganization of States on the basis of linguistic dominance could not solve the problems of linguistic minorities for various reasons. Instead it resulted in the creation of numerous linguistic minority groups. Pattanayak (1978: 176) very aptly remarks: 'Although linguistic states are formed on the basis of dominant languages, no state contains all the dominant language speakers within the state boundary... This results in a paradoxical situation where majority language speakers in one state become the minority in another'. As a consequence of the reorganization of States, the speakers of Hindi in Punjab, the speakers of Punjabi in Haryana, the speakers of Bengali in Mizoram, the speakers of Gujarati in Maharashtra, the speakers of Telugu in Karnataka, the speakers of Tamil in Kerala and the speakers of Kannada in Tamil Nadu were left in a minority status. Evidently, there is no solid and enumerated boundary; there is in fact a fuzzy boundary, and therefore any attempt to demarcate linguistic 'lines of control' becomes a self-defeating purpose. Well-defined economic modelling has permitted researchers to use the term 'poverty line', but the same kind of analogically modelled term 'minority line' cannot be used with predictable authority in the Indian plurilingual context.

The second reason according to Beg (1993) is social mobility. In a country like India, with a large proportion of the rural sector being under the poverty line, social mobility takes place as a consequence of urbanization and industrialization. The urban centres and industrial locales command socio-economic power. The speakers of one language migrate to the region of another language with a view to consolidating their position *vis-à-vis* socio-economic power. In the process, they form a linguistic minority group. The main attraction for concentrations in urban centres is employment and economic betterment. However, some other factors which play an important role in attracting minority groups and contributing to concentrations in urban centres are better education, better civic facilities, a higher standard of living and a mere sense of getting urbanised. Today, almost all cities in India are composed of a variety of linguistic minority groups, and India's metropolises such as Bombay, Calcutta, Delhi, Madras, and also Bangalore and Hyderabad, are no exceptions.

Non-state minority languages

Schedule VIII of the Constitution of India specifies 18 languages. Of these, Sanskrit, Sindhi and Urdu are so-called 'non-State' languages. The remaining 15 languages, viz. Assamese, Bengali, Gujarati, Hindi, Kannada, Kashmiri, Konkani, Malayam, Manipuri, Marathi, Nepali, Oriya, Punjabi, Tamil and Telugu are State languages, and they are spoken predominantly in their respective States. Sanskrit, the classical language, 'is the language of special status in India'. Its total number of speakers at the all-India level are a meagre 49,736 (Census, 1991), a very small minority indeed. Hence, Sanskrit has only a limited sociolinguistic function to perform. Sindhi has a substantial number of speakers. The number of speakers of Urdu is also large, but both Sindhi and Urdu are non-dominant languages. They are also known as 'non-territory specific' languages. These two languages are broken up by geopolitical discontinuity, as their speakers are spread over more than one State, totally separated from each other. Unlike the 15 scheduled languages mentioned above, Sindhi and Urdu are not spoken by the majority population in any State and Union Territory. Hence, they are at a greater disadvantage. Both languages are under the threat of assimilation and shift. Sindhi and Urdu in India, today, are languages with a limited functional value (Beg, 1993).

I would like to take this opportunity to interpret the concept of diaspora in terms of fluidity of languages. Khubchandani (1999) states that the groups maintaining primordial ties of language, caste and religion transcending the communitarianpolitico-physical space are here treated as diasporas. Historically, the stateless Jewish community, spread all over the globe (before the creation of Israel in 1948), is cited as a classic example of diaspora, signifying psychological/cultural bonds among its members. Very recently, the supporters of the Nepali language in the Darjeeling Hills of the State of West Bengal (majority language: Bengali) have risen in revolt against the State Government's continued apathy towards their language and have expressed their right to self-determination. A similar situation has emerged in the north-eastern State of Assam (majority language: Assamese) where Manipuri is the sufferant diasporic language.

Non-scheduled minority languages

Of the 96 non-scheduled languages identified by the Census authorities, only the following eight are spoken as majority languages: Ao (Nagaland), Bhili/Bhilodi (Dadra and Nagar Haveli), Gorkhali/Nepali (Sikkim), Khasi (Meghalaya), Konkani (Goa, Daman and Diu), Lushai/Mizo (Mizoram), Manipuri/Meitei (Manipur) and Nissi/Dafla (Arunachal Pradesh). Each of these majority languages is also spoken by a minority population in another State or States. The remaining 88 languages are spoken by a minority population in one or more than one State.

Most of the non-scheduled minority languages are spoken by tribal communities, a majority of whom still live in remote and inaccessible places. Most of the tribal languages have hitherto remained unwritten and have less than 1,000,000 native speakers each. None of the tribal languages account for even 1% of the total household population of India. These languages too have a limited sociolinguistic status and are largely used for intra-group communication. As the functional significance of the tribal minority languages is very restricted, there has been a tendency among tribals to interact in their respective dominant State languages. That is why bilingualism among tribals has been much higher (Ghosh, 1988: 137). Due to the sociolinguistic value, socio-economic power and multi-domain importance of the languages of the majority groups, there is a tendency of language shift among tribals in favour of the respective dominant State languages. To fulfil their educational needs as a socializing process, many of the tribal communities had their traditional institutions that prepared their young ones to take on roles as socially useful and productive members of the community. The protagonists of modern education in tribal societies immediately discarded these traditional institutions as they did not cater for literacy needs, without even examining the possibility of suitable mutual adoption of these institutions and the modern education system. Even today there has been hardly any progress in the direction of teaching tribal children through their mother tongue; the teachers themselves come from outside and do not know the mother tongue of the children; the books are written with an alien environmental background, and most books are translations from other tribal language books (see also Choudhry, 1998: 9).

Language problems of linguistic minorities

The threat to the survival of minority languages at the hands of regional, national, or colonial-international languages has urged linguists to propose various language policies by appropriate planning. Some are of the opinion that maintenance of minority languages can be ensured by the proper promotion of literature in the mother tongue. Subramonium (1997: 3) points out that the policy of having one administrative language is not suited to the multilingual, democratic Indian situation, and therefore a multilingual policy is suggested by him. In consideration of the promotion of minority languages, the very definition of a minority language creates the problem whether this concept refers to a linguistic, cultural, or numerically proportional minority.

Sreedhar (1995: 5) emphasizes that multi-lingualism, multi-ethnicity, and pluri-culturalism have been the strength of India and should continue to be so. Unfortunately, one also finds fissiparous trends, particularly in relation to linguistic minorities. Ordinarily, any number of linguistic groups can coexist in a pre-industrial, preliterate community, so long as the elite shares a lingua franca. The problem arises when one of these languages is recognised as the sole official language, resulting in members of that linguistic group benefiting at the expense of others.

Beg (1993) asserts that linguistic minorities have to face many problems of language use and language maintenance. They find difficulties in preserving their language in the process of change and modernization of society, and they are constantly under the threat of assimilation (Pattanayak, 1978: 174). As linguistic minorities lack numerical strength, they are 'totally engulfed in another language environment' (Mahapatra, 1992: 55). Some linguistic minorities suffer because they are 'broken up by geopolitical discontinuity'. The speakers of the majority language never bother to learn a minority language (with the exception of English, which is an internationally recognised language and has a different function in India). But for various functional reasons, linguistic minorities have to learn the language of the majority or the dominant group as a second or additional language.

The language problems of linguistic minorities relate to the domain of language use and language maintenance. The question of language use in the domains of education, administration and mass communication is very vital to linguistic minorities. With reference to minority multi-lingualism, Subramonium (1993: 5) observes that such a situation results in the emergence of a dominant minority, ensuring its preservation and loss of other minorities at the hands of this major minority. What is interesting is that if this major-minority language serves as a link language in centres of cultural and business activity and plays a secondary role in the domains of administration and education, even in an area dominated by a major language, it motivates the language to become a powerful force in language maintenance (e.g. Tamil of Palghat and Chittur functioning as the link language in Kerala). On the other hand, in States and Union Territories where there are no facilities to use the minority language in these domains, minority language maintenance becomes a very difficult and challenging task, and linguistic minorities are led to make a switch from their own language to the language of the majority group. Thus the process of language shift among linguistic minorities begins. Field work conducted by Panikkar (1985) to study the minority language situation in Kerala reveals that the minority language speakers who reside outside their language pocket areas generally show a tendency towards language shift, i.e. in Kerala from their mother-tongue to Malayam. This is applicable to all Tamil and Tulu communities who are scattered outside their pocket areas all over the State (Panikkar, 1985: 293-294).This study also shows that the desire of a minority language community to acquire social and political acceptability brings forth loss of their language and the acquisition of the State language. This is revealed in the tendency to shift from Tamil to Malayam amongst the Nadars of Trivandrum district.

Choudhry (1998) states that linguistic minorities fail to break through the narrow confines of the social and economic limits of the region to which they are restricted by the language they grow up speaking. The limit of their language is truly the limit of their world, which may lead to deprivation of considerable magnitude. Consequently, on the Indian scene we find an attempt being made by ethnolinguistic minorities to gain autonomy or to assert their ethnic identity through the revival of their language. Therefore, Singh (1987) predicts that all the deprived linguistic areas outside any of the list of Scheduled or Non-Scheduled languages (especially from the eighth schedule) are all movement-prone zones.

According to Misra (1979), different ethnic and language movements in India may be attributed to two main focuses: concern with the nature and form of the standard language and/or the language of written literature and concern with the political demands, involving the creation of separate State or administrative units based on linguistic and cultural considerations, granting of certain rights and privileges, including the use of language in education, administration and mass media. Movements of either or both kinds of concerns have developed and/or are still in progress in different parts of the country. In his analyses of handling language movements, Choudhry (1998) says that language planning and planning of linguistic identities for linguistic minorities in multilingual and pluricultural India is a convoluted undertaking in which policy decisions have to be made and policy implementations have to be executed with care and proper understanding of the vibrating ethno-linguistic currents in a given region.

Linguistic minorities and human rights education

In a report submitted by the Government of India to the UN Secretary General, on November 3, 1998, entitled *Comprehensive Implementation and Follow-up by India of the Vienna Declaration and Programme of Action*, the following points have been noted.

In India, human rights are taught as part of the school curriculum in all 18 official languages. The National Council for Education Research and Training (NCERT) has prepared a Source Book on Human Rights for the use of textbook writers. The Council is also preparing a Teachers' Handbook on human rights. School textbooks are being revised so as to incorporate learning capsules for promoting of human rights education. The National Council of Teachers Education (NCTE) has prepared modules on Human Rights for teacher-educators. These modules have already been translated into the national language (Hindi), and further translation into other regional languages is in progress. Schools have also been observing the 10th of December as Human Rights Day.

Ten universities have been identified for the introduction of courses in human rights education. The Indira Gandhi National Open University (IGNOU) has set up a special cell to promote human rights education using the distance education mode. Furthermore, since its inception, the National Human Rights Commission has made concerted efforts to focus attention on human rights education.

What is paradoxical here is that the Report talks about human rights but refers to human rights education in only the 18 official languages and 10 universities where the medium of instruction is obviously either English or one of the official Indian languages. Regional minority languages and other minor languages have been marginalised by not giving them access to this specialised source of information, thus denying them the right to be aware of their rights. The efficacy of some languages for educational purposes does not purport denouncement of other less efficacious languages for the same purpose. In reality, this does not seem to be true.

The fights of vulnerable groups have received special attention in India ever since independence, and the Constitution itself contains extensive provisions for the promotion and protection of the efforts of all minorities, including certain special groups of people unique to Indian society and known as the Scheduled Castes and Scheduled Tribes. These measures have been further strengthened through a recent amendment to the Constitution granting Scheduled Tribes local self-government and a high degree of autonomy in the management of their day-to-day affairs, control over natural resources and other developmental activities in the areas where they live. The Government has set up a National Commission for the Scheduled Castes and Scheduled Tribes and a National Commission for Minorities to promote and protect the rights of these vulnerable groups. Furthermore, a National Minorities Development and Financial Corporation promotes economic and developmental activities for minorities.

Obviously linguistic human rights is not within the purview of these points in the Report. Some State governments are optimistically hoping that minority languages within their jurisdiction will die out before they get a chance to be used in education (Choudhry, 1998: 7). The Commissioner for Linguistic Minorities has advisory powers only and cannot force the State governments to follow his recommendations. States are eager to implement policies that are a deliberate attempt at discouraging minorities to retain their language; instead, they encourage the acquisition and use of State languages. States having achieved linguistic autonomy are reluctant to grant it to any ethnic group within their States. Therefore, States have been more successful in attempts at creating regional nationalism than the federal government has been in their attempt to promote Hindi in support of nationalism in the country (Choudhry, 1981).

In response to their subordinate position, Singh (1993: 24) states that linguistic minorities may adopt two policies: integration or conflict. Under 'integration' we have *pluralism*, in which a minority group is allowed to retain its cultural and linguistic identity, giving rise to the situation of linguistic pluralism and *assimilationism*, in which a minority group is encouraged to lose its linguistic identity, thus creating a melting pot situation in which there is direct adoption of the language of the majority. Similarly 'conflict' can be divided into *secessionism*, based on the principle of antagonism, in which a minority group fans its passion of linguistic exclusiveness, and *militancy*, in which a minority group strives to gain control over the dominant majority and, in the process, tries to extend its linguistic sphere of influence.

'Planning' in a vibrant multilingual society

According to Pattanayak (1998: 139), India has an unbroken tradition of 3000 years of oral transmission of knowledge. In a multilingual and multi-ethnic country, this tradition ensured a) maintenance of group identity within an interdependent network of cultures; b) maintenance of small communication zones within a broad communicative matrix through a gradual merging of borders and a shared common core; c) maintenance of group autonomy and resistance against incursions by empire builders into the affairs of the people; and d) awareness of individuals and groups comprising the Indian cultural area, the various linkages and balances at the micro and macro levels, and participation in the maintenance and furtherance of tradition in the face of constant changes. Mother tongues held the key to this unique and delicate balance. With the professionals and decision-makers stepping in to impede the free transmission of knowledge through the imposition of artificial standards, certified education, print capitalism and uniform mass media, the large body of illiterates became 'uneducated'. The very foundation of diverse faiths, multiple ethnicities, hundreds of minority languages, and small communication zones is also threatened in the process. Today, radio (All India Radio covers 90% of the country, serving 97.3% of the people covering 24 languages and 146 dialects in its home service) holds the potential of carrying knowledge to the doorsteps of individuals and acting as an ally of diverse mother tongues, as much as it can become a powerful enemy hastening their destruction. Unless the large body of existing mother tongue teachers is oriented to an understanding of their role in furthering the speaking and understanding of mother tongues for the dissemination of information and knowledge and the building of communication networks, they would succeed in enervating the society they are pledged to build. Similarly, it is crucial that the bilingual elite in a linguistic minority initiates cultural projects to provide its mother tongue with the necessary linguistic equipment to enable it to become an adequate language for present-day culture. In accordance with Chatterjee's (1997) position on the importance of the bilingual elite, I wish to emphasize that the bilingual intelligentsia have to come to terms with their own language as belonging to the inner domain of cultural identity from which the neo-colonial intruder has to be kept out, to enable it to become a zone over which the nation first affirms faith in its functional efficacy and helps in its transformation, to make it adequate for the modern world.

The multilingual reality in India dictates that the country should aim at unity underlying diversity in its educational language planning rather than seek triumph over diversity through uniformising and stultifying constraints of a monistic policy (Choudhry, 1998: 14). Similarly, Singh

(1993: 35) suggests that in development planning one must take a pluralistic paradigm seriously, where identification and observation of language problems are essentially classificatory, and the description of language and education planning strategies are essentially based on our understanding of planning typology, whether they are comprehensive or partial, global or local, predictive or a combination of these strategies.

As capital-intensive planning, high technology and standardisation in a society divided among a few rich and a large number of poor accelerates the intrusion and control of smaller groups by the elite without providing safeguards, similarly a standard language with the active support of the State and with an endorsed education strategy infiltrates into the autonomy of small groups without providing them with protective devices for the maintenance of their culture. Given the context presented, linguistic minorities today are in urgent need of protective support.

References

Bandyopadhyay, D. (1998) *Erasing pluralingualism: Recovering pluralingualism.* Tech. Report: LRU/TR/12/99-2000. Calcutta: Indian Statistical Institute.

Bandyopadhyay, D. (1999, forthcoming) (M)other tongue syndrome: A switch-over from breast to bottle. In *South Asian language review* (Prof D.P. Pattanayak Felicitation Volume). Mysore.

Beg, M. (1993) Linguistic minorities in India. *IJDL* XXII (2), 1-33.

Chatterjee, P. (1997) *The nation and its fragments.* New Delhi: OUP.

Choudhry, A. (1981) Language attitudes of a linguistic minority in a regional area. *Osmania papers in linguistics* 7 (8), 116-130.

Choudhry, A. (1998) *Language policy and planning in a plural society: The Indian multilingual ethos.* Paper presented at the conference 'Which languages for Europe', organised by the European Cultural Foundation, Oegstgeest, The Netherlands, 9-11 October, 1998.

Ghosh, T. (1988) Tribal communities in India. In L. Khubchandani (ed.) *Language in a plural society.* Delhi: Shimla, Indian Institute of Advanced Study in association with Motilal Banarasidas.

Government of India (1950) *The constitution of India.* New Delhi: Ministry of Law.

Government of India (1975) *Report of the Committee for the promotion of Urdu.* Ministry of Education and Social Welfare.

Government of India (1991) *Census.* Language tables.

Government of India (1998) *Comprehensive implementation and follow-up by India of the Vienna declaration and programme of action.* Submission by Government of India for the Report of the UN Secretary General. Statement made at the

United Nations Third Committee (Social, Humanitarian and Cultural) on November 3, 1998, New York.

Khubchandani, L.M. (1999) Linguistic diasporas: Plurilingual Societies in the Context of Information Technology. *Linguistics today* III (1), 26-41.

Mahapatra, B.P. (1992) Nehru's approach to linguistic minorities. *South Asian language review* 2 (2), 50-57.

National Human Rights Commission of India (1999) *The Pune declaration on Eeucation for human rights in Asia*. Submitted at the Asia and Pacific Regional Conference on 'Education for Human Rights', organized in India by the World Peace Center of MAEER's MIT (Pune), the National Human Rights Commission of India and the Indian National Commission for Co-operation with UNESCO, at the initiative and with the support of UNESCO, to commemorate the fiftieth anniversary of the Universal Declaration of Human Rights and the United Nations, Decade for Human Rights Education (1995-2004). Pune: NHRCI.

Pattanayak, D.P. (1973) Preface. In *Distribution of LInguages in India, in states and union territories*. Mysore: Central Institute of Indian Languages.

Pattanayak, D.P. (1978) Education for the minority children. *Indian linguistics* 39 (1-4), 174-182.

Pattanayak, D.P. (1998) Mother tongue: An Indian context. In R. Singh (ed.) *The native speaker: Multilingual perspectives*. New Delhi: Sage Pub.

Singh, U.N. (1987) On some issues in Indian multilingualism. In U.N. Singh & R.N. Srivastava (eds) *Perspectives in Indian planning* (pp.153-165). Calcutta: Mithila Darsan.

Singh, U.N. (1993) Foreword. In *The otherness of English*. Delhi: Sage Publishers.

Sreedhar, M.V. (1995) Presidential address. *IJDL* XXIV (2), 1-7.

Subramonium, V.I. (1997) Exploring the cases for the preservation and loss of languages in India. *IJDL* XXVI (2), 1-104.

Languages in Turkey

KUTLAY YAĞMUR

Describing the sociolinguistic situation in the Republic of Turkey is not an easy enterprise. The reasons are manifold, but mainly the limited availability of academic resources and the non-availability of up-to-date information on ethnic groups in Turkey make the task hard. For a thorough understanding of the present sociolinguistic situation, it is necessary to provide a short account of Ottoman linguistic practices and the Turkish language reform. There will be three sections focusing on the sociolinguistic context, demographic characteristics and the present status of languages in education. In the first section, a brief account of the sociolinguistic situation during the Ottoman Empire and the Turkish language reform as part of a modernization movement is documented. In the second section, present demographic data of language groups in Turkey are examined. In the final section, language education practices and the status of minority languages in education are discussed.

The sociolinguistic situation in historical perspective

The account of Turkish language development throughout history is an intriguing one. The great empires of recent times, such as the Austro-Hungarian Empire in Europe, and the Spanish, British, French, Portuguese and Dutch colonies in other continents, have left their languages behind to a certain extent. However, the Turkish language was not always left in most of the countries the Ottomans ruled for 600 years. The reasons are numerous, but the political and ideological formation of the Ottoman Empire turns out to be the main reason (for a comprehensive account see Akşin, 1988; Lewis, 1974).

With the spread of Islam among the Turks from the 10th century onward, the Turkish language came under the heavy influence of Arabic and Persian cultures (contact with Persian dates back to much earlier times). Starting from the Seljuki period in the 10th century, Arabic was used for religious education, Persian for literature, and Turkish for daily communication. During the reign of the Ottoman Empire, the linguistic situation became even more complex, and the ratio of original Turkish within the Arabic-Persian dominated Ottoman language was reduced to a minimum. As a result, a synthetic language called *Osmanlıca* emerged. *Osmanlıca* was a synthetic blend of Arabic, Persian and Turkish, with linguistic features of each. This synthetic language was not only loaded with many Arabic and Persian words, but also with grammatical rules derived from these three languages. As a consequence, there were three types of rules for inflection, derivation, suffixation, compounding and concord (Başkan, 1986). *Osmanlıca* became the high-status language of religion, culture and administration. As a literary language, it was almost unintelligible to common people. Only the elite of the Empire spoke and mostly wrote this synthetic language. The Turkish language and the people who spoke it were undervalued and even looked down upon by the administrative classes.

Osmanlıca became increasingly the language of culture, art, science and technology in the Ottoman Empire. This linguistic situation is intriguingly similar to the linguistic climate in South Africa documented by Alexander (1999), with one very interesting difference. According to Ngugi (1994, cited in Alexander, 1999: 39), in the African continent, the colonizing powers systematically undervalued the indigenous 'people's culture, their art, dances, religions, history, geography, education, orature and literature' and they deliberately elevated the languages of the colonizers. In the Ottoman case, as far as the Turkish language and people were concerned, there were no colonizing powers from outside that imposed a foreign language upon them, but it was their own rulers and intelligentsia that did so. Because of the widespread use of the Ottoman language in administration and education, the Turkish language was limited to daily communication. Over time, there appeared a huge gap between common folk and ruling classes. Intellectuals used the synthetic amalgam of Ottoman, and they distanced (rather alienated) themselves from the majority of people who spoke Turkish. Since Turkish was underrated as a means of scholarly writing, people came to believe that Turkish did not have adequate means and words for scientific work. As Alexander (1999) points out, there can be nothing more devastating than the under-estimation of one's own mother tongue. In the case of Turkish, this wound was not inflicted by outside colonizing powers but by the Ottomans themselves.

On the other hand, the Ottomans never interfered with religious and linguistic practices of nations that lived under the Ottoman Empire.

Greeks, Armenians, Arabs and so on were all allowed to practice their religion and to maintain and develop their languages. Anyone who lived within the borders of the Ottoman territory was under the protection of the Sultan, irrespective of his/her ethnic or religious background. The basic distinction among inhabitants of the Empire was not made on the basis of language and ethnicity but on the basis of religion. The Ottoman Sultan was the defender of the faith and representative of Islam; and Ottoman was the language of religion, culture and the Caliphate. In short, Islam was the uniting factor between all different Islamic ethnic groups living within the Ottoman territory. Nevertheless, in the 19th century, a wave of nationalism affected first the various ethnic groups living within the Ottoman territory and afterwards the Turkish intellectuals. Influenced by the European Renaissance, the Ottomans themselves wanted to implement reform programmes, but they were rather unsuccessful.

Language reform in Turkey is mostly associated with Atatürk and the beginning of the Turkish Republic in 1923. Since the 1860's, however, Turks had been asking themselves what an authentic Turkish identity should look like. Also for the domain of language, intellectuals like Ziya Paşa and Namık Kemal realized that the Ottoman linguistic obscurantism was a barrier for reform movements (Gallagher, 1971). Since then, Turkish intellectuals have strived for the simplification of language and for the elimination of unnecessary borrowings from Arabic and Persian. Especially in the early 1900's, with the growing influence of the press and the rise of Turkish nationalism, the language reform movement was accelerated. The philosopher Ziya Gökalp is believed to be the father of Turkish nationalism and to be the mastermind behind Turkish language reform. (Ziya Gökalp had a Kurdish background, but he wrote the principles of Turkish nationalism. Mustafa Kemal Atatürk's reform movement, therefore, is broader and more advanced in vision than Gökalp's.)

Only after the war of independence was the language reform fully commenced. The Ottoman Empire had sided with Germany in the first World War; however, they lost the war and the allied forces (England, France, Greece and Italy) invaded the Empire. From 1920 to 1923, under the leadership of Mustafa Kemal Atatürk, the Turks were able to win the most difficult and devastating war of their history. Regaining independence for the Turks made Mustafa Kemal an unequalled hero, which, in a way, enabled him to carry out the most fundamental reforms of Turkish history. The Republic of Turkey was founded on the ashes of the Ottoman Empire in 1923. Believing in western civilization and modernization,

Atatürk and his followers implemented a series of reforms to catch up with the modern world. The reform movement was more than a language reform for the new Republic. The reform clearly aimed at the cultural and ideological transformation of the Turkish society from religious conservatism to western-oriented modernism and secularism.

The first step was achieving secularism, which meant that the theocratic way of life was abandoned. The Constitution was changed by deleting the clause that stated that the official religion of the Turkish State was Islam. Any allusion to religion or religious titles was amended. All religious schools were closed, and wearing religious garments outside places of worship was banned. In schools, Arabic instruction and Arabic-medium education were banned. Hence, the Latin alphabet replaced the Arabic script, which had always been a symbol of Islam among Muslims. All of these and many other reforms point to a fundamental ideological change from Oriental to Occidental civilization. It shows a clear move away from the Ottoman heritage; all members of the Ottoman ruling House were expelled from the Turkish land. By renouncing its Ottoman heritage, Atatürk wanted to make Turkey a full-fledged member of the modern world as represented by western civilization. However, Islam had been at the center of the Ottoman culture and world-view, and the demotion of Islamism and Ottomanism created a cultural void. What was going to replace the cultural, ideological and religious gap created by the act of *de-Ottomanism*? Embracing Turkish national identity and emphasizing Turkish-ness was the new alternative. During the Ottoman period, many different religious and ethnic groups had existed side by side for centuries. Ottoman identity was above ethnicity, which was why there had been no serious conflicts between people of different ethnic and religious origin. Nevertheless, many Turks wanted to reclaim their national identity. Mustafa Kemal and his ideology proclaimed Turkish nationalism and a democratic republic as alternatives to Islamic identity and monarchy.

The reform movement under the leadership of Mustafa Kemal was an act of modernization and nation building, and language planning was a fundamental and crucial component of that process. The Turkish language reform involved two different processes: the change from Arabic to Latin script and the renovation of the vocabulary. Since the rate of literacy in Turkey was extremely low, achieving the change of script was relatively easy as a symbolic act. However, the 'purification' and renovation of the vocabulary have been going on for the last 70 years. Without special study, no Turkish citizen is at present able to read or understand the Ottoman language. Even Atatürk's *Nutuk* (36 hour speech of Mustafa Kemal to the Republican People's Party congress in 1927) can not be understood by present generations without a gloss, which is why most of the books written in the early Republican period are rewritten in modern Turkish. When we look at present-day Turkish, the reform movement certainly has achieved most of its goals.

As briefly documented before, the Turkish nation-building process is rather recent, and language reform plays an important role in that process. At the formal, level Turkish is the official language of the Republic of Turkey, but in reality many languages other than Turkish are spoken throughout the country (details are presented below). Even though the Turkish language reform has largely been a successful enterprise, there are signs that the same type of 'self-inflicted wound' caused during the Ottoman period surfaces in different forms. There are fundamentalist (Islamist) groups who claim that Arabic should be the language of instruction in schools so that Turkish children can read their religious book (*Koran*) and be 'proper Muslims'. There are also groups who claim that Turkish is not fit for scientific study, which is why English should be the medium of instruction in schools so that full integration with the modern world can be achieved. As a matter of fact, there are a considerable number of private and state schools where the medium of instruction is English. The symbolic value attached to English-medium instruction among the general public is very high indeed, and concepts like globalization, westernization and modernization, contribute to the spread of English in Turkey.

During the Ottoman Empire, borrowings were made from Persian and Arabic. Nowadays, the borrowings are mainly made from Western languages, in particular from English (Boeschoten, 1997). The spread of English in Turkish life is noteworthy, but it is in no way comparable to the Ottoman period. Some aspects of the Turkish linguistic context are intriguingly similar to the South African context described by Neville Alexander in this Volume. Some groups in Turkey also claim that, since Turkish lacks many words and concepts, it is not suitable as a full-fledged medium of instruction. The intriguing difference, however, is that colonizing powers in South Africa spread the idea that local languages were not suitable for instruction, but in Turkey there have been no such colonizing powers.

Demographic data

In the previous section, a brief account of the socio-historical status of Turkish was presented. It was shown that the Ottoman Empire was a multi-ethnic and multilingual state. In spite of ethnic, linguistic, racial and religious differences, people co-existed more or less in harmony. In today's Turkey, there are also many different linguistic groups. In this section, information concerning their numbers will be presented. The numbers come basically from three main different sources (Andrews, 1989; Dündar, 1999; Grimes, 1996).

Andrews (1989) presents a well-documented account of linguistic groups in Turkey. In documenting the complicated intergroup setting in Turkey, he shows that not only religious conviction but also religious denomination is crucial in understanding the setting. Andrews (1989: 17) provides the following working definition of ethnicity in the Turkish context:

> By ethnicity we understand the concepts, sentiments and actions, which characterize ethnic groups. They define these in contra-distinction to other, comparable groups within a state. Ethnic groups are generally endogamous groups, whose criteria for cultural self-definition are common traditions selected from the past.

For the maintenance of cultural and linguistic characteristics in a group, endogamous marriage seems to be most decisive in Andrews' definition. However, when we closely examine language maintenance patterns and marriage patterns of persons from different linguistic groups, it is intriguing to see that intergroup marriages are quite common provided that both persons belong to the same religious denomination. An ethnic Sunni-Kurd can marry a Sunni-Turk, but a Sunni-Kurd cannot easily marry an Alevi-Kurd because of strict religious sanctions (like the religious restrictions imposed on the marriages between Protestants and Catholics). In other words, not ethnicity but religious denomination of the person to be married is the most decisive factor. Tribal organization is another prevailing force that affects intergroup relations and in-group norms. Turkomans and *Yörüks* (nomads) in Anatolia are good examples. In some cases, linguistic groups maintain their group identity because of a sense of exile or expulsion from their homeland. The immigrants from Crimea, Russian Altays or the Caucasus are perfect examples. As a matter of fact, various factors of language, religion (denomination), organization, occupation, exile and material culture (sometimes in isolation or in combination) make up group characteristics and group identity. As pointed out by Andrews (1989), multiple ethnicity is an inherent characteristic of Turkey. The Ottomans were able to achieve unity in spite of this diversity through Islam and through semi-autonomous bodies of religious minorities, but the prevailing present-day Turkish ideology aims at forming 'one nation-one language' through the principle of *linguistic unitarianism*, as seen in the case of France.

The history of censuses goes back to the Ottoman Empire in Turkey. The first two censuses were taken in the periods of 1326-1360 and 1360-1389 for the purpose of gathering information about the farming land and the population that worked on the land. Until the 19th century, the censuses were done with the purpose of identifying cultivation areas and the population associated with the land so that an estimation of revenues could be made. It was especially important to gather information about farming practices of local populations. Every thirty years, the Ottomans registered the farming land and the population on it. Also in the lands conquered, they used to make a profile of the land and of the population on it, which involved population movements if this was required for an effective use of the farming land. In these censuses, only the heads of families and unmarried sons were to be registered. These practices of gathering information about land and about the male population (also for military drafting purposes) cannot be considered as 'censuses' in its modern sense. The first comprehensive census during the Ottoman period was done in 1844. In this census, all people, both male and female, were registered. In 1891, the first Central Statistics Bureau was established, and activities of this institution were defined by legislation. This system continued until the republican period.

In the republican period, the first census was done in 1927 for the purpose of documenting the characteristics of all people residing in the country. This census is considered to be the first statistically reliable and comprehensive census in Turkish history. In this census, age, gender, marital status, education, languages spoken, religion and occupation of the population were documented. The results were made public. The second census was carried out in 1935. Afterwards, a census has been taken every five years, and this practice still goes on. Beginning with the 1927 census, there were questions on the first and second language spoken at home and on religious conviction. The results were published in tables documenting the distribution of the population along the criteria of age, gender, first and second language spoken at home, religious

Table 1   Distribution of languages and estimated number of speakers per language in the Republic of Turkey (– stands for no information given).

Language	Dündar (1999)	Andrews (1989)	Grimes (1996)
Abaza (Abazintsy)	12,399	–	10,000
Abkhaz (Abxazo)	–	–	35,000
Adyghe (Circassian/Cherkes)	106,960	1,100,000	1,000,000
Albanian, Tosk	53,520	53,520	65,000
Arabic (North Mesopotamian)	533,264	569,058	400,000
Armenian	55,354	69,526	70,000
Avar (Daghistan)	–	5,223	–
Balkan Gagauz Turkish	–	–	327,000
Balkar and Karaçay	–	3,917	–
Bulgarian (Pomak)	57,372	101,328	270,000
Chechen & Ingush	–	8,998	8,000
Crimean Tatar	–	–	300,000
Domari (Romani)	–	–	20,000
Estonian	–	300	–
Georgian	79,234	83,306	91,000
Greek (Christians)	127,037	10,000	4,000
Greek (Muslims)	–	4,535	–
Hebrew	13,491	25,000	–
Hemshinli	–	44,000	–
Hertevin	–	–	300
Kaldani (East Syrians/Asuri)	–	7,000	–
Kabardian	–	–	202,000
Karapapah	68,000	106,000	–
Kazak	–	5,000	600
Kirghiz	–	1,137	1,137
Kumyk	–	1,703	not known
Kurmanji (Northern Kurdic)	2,817,313	6,200,000	6,500,000
Ladino (Judaeo-Spanish)	–	7,226	20,000
Laz	81,165	115,000	92,000

Language	Dündar (1999)	Andrews (1989)	Grimes (1996)
Molokans (Russians)	–	1,600	–
Osetin (Ossete)	8,943	8,943	588,000
Polish	–	501	–
Romani (Kiptice/Gypsy)	4,656	10,633	40,000
Serbo-Croatian (Bosnian)	57,209	–	61,000
Sudanese	–	5,000	–
Syriac (Assyrians/Arameans)	–	40,000	–
Tatar	12,302	–	Not known
Turkish (Anatolian Turkish)	28,289,680	28,289,680	46,278,000
Turkmen	–	–	925
Turoyo	–	–	3,000
Uyghur	–	700	500
Uzbek	–	5,051	1,981
Zaza	–	2,000,000	1,000,000

Some notes on Table 1: *Gagauz Turks* commonly practice Christianity. *Bulgarian Turks*: according to Mango (cited in Andrews, 1989: 93), between 1923 and 1980, 488,000 people from Bulgaria either immigrated or were deported to Turkey. Also Balim (1996: 103) reports that around 300,000 Turks were expelled to Turkey in 1989. There are still 1.5 million ethnic Turks in Bulgaria. The number above for *Bulgarian-Pomak* excludes ethnic Turks. *Tatar*: This is an approximate number for all Tatar speakers in all countries. The exact number of Tatar speakers in Turkey is not definite (Grimes, 1996). *Zaza* is confused mostly with Kurmanji (Kurdish) but Zaza and Kurdish are not mutually comprehensible (Andrews, 1989: 122). *Greek*: in the 1965 census, the number of Greek speakers was reported to be 130,240, but according to Andrews (1989: 143), after the split-up of Cyprus there was considerable emigration to Greece and elsewhere. *Muslim Armenians*: 24,000 Armenian speaking and 20,000 Turkish speaking. *Ladino*: 2791 persons speaking Spanish as mother tongue and 4435 speaking Spanish as a second language. *Gypsy*: according to Andrews (1989: 139), some provincial statistics are unclear, and Istanbul, which has a large gypsy population, is omitted. *Serbo-Croatian*: the number is estimated to be much larger after the conflict in Bosnia in the early nineties. *Turkish*: the numbers from Dündar (1999, based on 1965 census) and Andrews (1989) come from the 1965 census and the figures indicate persons speaking Turkish as mother tongue in 1965; more recent statistics on people speaking Turkish as mother tongue are not available.

denomination, literacy, occupation and marital status for all cities and geographic regions. Until 1965, the findings on first and second language spoken at home and religion were published, but the findings on these data were not made public between 1965-1985. After the 1985 census, the questions on first and second languages and religion were completely excluded from the list of census questions.

As pointed out earlier, due to the non-availability of up-to-date information on linguistic groups in Turkey, it is very hard to give a comprehensive account of the topic. Nevertheless, in this section, on the basis of the information obtained in the 1965 census (cf. Dündar, 1999), Andrews (1989) and Grimes (1996), the estimated number and distribution of linguistic groups in Turkey are presented. It is necessary to point out that the linguistic groups and the numbers of speakers for each language are inconsistent in different sources, which is why figures from three different sources are presented here. These sources were chosen because they are well documented and most comprehensive. According to Andrews (1989: 53), the official census figures in most cases are under-counts because 'in many cases members of ethnic groups have preferred to give their mother tongue as Turkish, while reserving their own as second-language.' Andrews also points out incorrect classifications of languages in some cases. In the 1965 census, 34 languages were reported to be spoken in Turkey. According to Grimes (1996), this number is 42. Details are presented in Table 1.

Turkic languages

Grimes (1996) reports that Turkish is spoken by the largest group in the country (about 90% of the total population). Turkish is the official language of Turkey. It is an agglutinative language and belongs to the Altaic group of languages. The Turkic group includes languages like Altay, Azerbaijani, Balkar, Bashkurt, Kazakh, Karaçay, Kirghiz, Kumuk, Tatar, Turkmen, Uyghur, Uzbek and Yakut. The majority of Turks practices Sunni-Islam, and endogamy is very strong among them. However, endogamy rules are not determined by ethnic or linguistic criteria but by religious denomination criteria. A Sunni-Turk cannot easily marry an Alevi-Turk under normal circumstances; even though they have the same ethnicity and language, different religious denominations makes it hard. There are strong familial, social and religious sanctions against such mixed marriages. In this way, denominational endogamy ensures the maintenance of religious separation. Nevertheless, especially in urban areas, this practice is gradually becoming obsolete. As opposed to Sunni-

Turks, most Alevi-Turks are rather liberal and support the Turkish Republic's modernization and westernization principles.

Group identity of Turks is based on language and nationality (*Turkishness*), and partly on religion. Recently, some religious groups have tried to bring forward religious identity as a unifying factor among all ethnic groups (as was common in the Ottoman period), but Mustafa Kemal's ideology introduced a new sense of identity based on the Turkish language and history. This ideology has been shaped and transmitted by the State through education with the purpose of unifying the population. According to the official discourse, anyone who lives within the borders of Turkey is a Turk, irrespective of his or her ethnic, linguistic or religious background. In this reasoning, citizenship is taken to be the unifying factor between people of diverse linguistic and religious backgrounds.

Even though other Turkic-speaking groups were grouped differently in the 1965 census, generally all Turkic speaking populations are treated as Turkish. Turkic languages belong to the Altaic group, but they are not always mutually comprehensible. Most of these groups assimilated into the mainstream community much faster than other groups, but they still speak their own language varieties (for details of their numbers, see Table 1).

Kurdic languages

Kurdic languages are spoken by a large group of people in Turkey. Kurmanji, Sorani, Gorani, Behdini, Herki, Kurdi, Shikaki, Surchi (and also various dialects such as Guwii, Hakkâri, Jezine, Urfi, Bâyazidi, Qochani, Birjandi, Alburz, Sanjâri and Judikâni) belong to the Kurdic language group (Grimes, 1996). Zaza is mostly associated with Kurdish but it is a different language. The main Kurdic language spoken in Turkey is Kurmanji, which is a branch of the Iranic languages, with extensive Arabic and Turkish loans. Due to the long-standing language contact between Kurmanji and Turkish, there are many loan words in Kurmanji, which is why some Turkish scholars mistakenly claimed that Kurdish is a Turkic language. Due to the same reasoning and to political reasons, some politicians identified Kurdish as a language spoken by 'mountain-Turks'. The total number of Kurmanji speakers in Turkey is highly controversial because of the political concerns of all parties involved. If we take Grimes (1996) as the most representative and well-documented source, the total number of Kurmanji speakers in Turkey is about 6,500,000. Because of Turkish-medium instruction in schools, Turkish is the dominant language among most Kurdish speakers, but in rural areas and among less educated people, Kurdish is more dominant. According to Dorleijn (1996), Kurdish is the *lingua franca* even for native speakers of Turkish in some southeastern rural towns. One can also hear Kurdish spoken in major cities such as Istanbul, Ankara and Izmir. Nevertheless, Kurdish is not taught in schools, and there are no cultural centers for the development of Kurdic languages and cultures.

Just as in the case of Turkish speakers, religious denomination carries more weight than ethnicity for Kurdish speakers. Group identity is formed primarily by religion, then language and tribal organization (Andrews, 1989). Especially among Alevi-Kurds, intergroup marriages with other Alevi-Turks and Alevi-Zazas are more frequent than with Sunni-Kurds. Also for Kurdic people, endogamy is based on religious denomination and not on ethnicity. Like Alevi-Turks, Alevi-Kurds support the principles of modernization and westernization in Turkey.

Zaza

Like Kurmanji and Gorani, Zaza is also an Iranic language, but it is different from Kurdic languages. Zaza and Kurdic languages are not mutually comprehensible (Andrews, 1989). Different from Kurdic people, Zaza identity is effectively based firstly on language, and then on religion. There are two main groups of Zaza's based on religious denomination, i.e. Sunni and Alevi. The total population of Zaza speakers is estimated at 2 million. Zaza is mostly spoken in east and southeast Anatolia.

Arabic

Arabic speaking people belong to one of the largest linguistic minority groups in Turkey. They mostly live in the southeast of Turkey, in the provinces of Mardin, Urfa, Siirt, Hatay and Adana. There are smaller groups in the provinces of Muş, Bitlis, Diyarbakır and Gaziantep. The use of the Arabic language differs from region to region. In Mardin and Hatay, Arabic is spoken dominantly by local people but in towns like Siirt, Konya-Ereğli, Tarsus and Adana, it is replaced by Turkish.

Immigrant languages from the Balkans

After the first world war, a number of Islamic groups from Balkan countries were exchanged with Christian populations living on Turkish territory. Greeks, Bulgarian Pomaks, Bosnians, Croatians, Serbians and Rumanians are some of them. These groups were ethnically different, but because of their Islamic belief they were deported or transferred to Turkey. There are only estimations of their numbers, and figures vary from source to source. According to Mango (1981) (cited in Andrews, 1989), between 1923 and 1980, 488,000 Bulgarian immigrants settled in Turkey. Also 303,000 inhabitants of Yugoslavia and 122,000 of Rumania settled in Turkey in the given period. These groups have not always assimilated into the mainstream society. This might be due to the fact that they are still identified as *muhacir* or *göçmen* (both meaning immigrants) by local people. In some rural areas, local people avoid contact with these 'immigrants'. Different physical characteristics of these groups also differentiate them from the majority. Nevertheless, being from the same religious background, intergroup marriages between these immigrant groups and local populations have been increasing, especially in the urban areas. Another major group from the Balkan are the Albanians. Most of them are fully Turkicised, and they speak mostly Turkish. Intergroup marriages between mainstream community members and Albanians are very common.

Immigrant languages from the Caucasus

Like the immigrants from the Balkans, many linguistic groups from the Caucasus were either expelled, fled away, or immigrated to Turkey. Almost all linguistic groups from the Caucasus share a common history of expulsion from their lawful lands to Turkey. All of these *Circassian, Chechen-Ingush, Daghistanis, Georgian* and *Hemshin* groups are predominantly Islamic. Circassians are the largest among the Caucasian groups (1,150,000). They are mostly concentrated in certain provinces and live in closed communities, especially in rural areas. Most of them are bilingual, but in urban areas many of the younger generations are monolingual in Turkish. *Adighes* and *Abhazas* are the two major sub-groups of Circassians. There are further sub-divisions among them based on tribal organization or dialect differences. As opposed to Circassians, *Chechens* and *Ingush* people do not have certain concentration areas. They are dispersed around Istanbul and Kocaeli. According to Bennigsen (cited in Andrews, 1989), around 40,000 Chechens emigrated to the Ottoman Empire in 1865 and 20,000 were deported by Russians in the same year, but many of those 'were destined to die out'. Present figures show around 10,000 Chechens and Ingush in Turkey but recent conflicts in Chechnya resulted in forced emigration of many Chechens to Turkey again. Apparently, Chechens and other Caucasian groups see Turkey as a safe-haven to escape oppression. *Avar, Lak* and *Lezghian* sub-groups constitute the main *Daghistani* group. Like other Caucasian groups, their group identity is based on a common sense of exile from their homeland.

Daghistanis are famous for their strong language maintenance and material culture, but in recent times, as for all other linguistic groups, this has been changing. Younger generations move to bigger cities for better opportunities and education, and Turkish becomes the main vehicle of communication. The Hemshin group is different from the other Caucasian groups in terms of self-identification. They are originally Armenian speaking but do not always accept Armenian origin (Andrews, 1989). The fact that they were converted to Islam might play a role in their self-definition. The eastern Hemshin group (around Artvin, Hopa and Kemalpasa) speaks a dialect of Armenian origin, but western Hemshin people (around Rize province) are strongly Turkicised. Nevertheless, they are still referred to as Armenian by the neighbouring Laz group. The Hemshin group is not mentioned in successive censuses, but, according to local population indications, there are about 40,000 Hemshin people living in Turkey. After the Circassians, the largest Caucasian group are the Georgians. According to Grimes (1996), about 91,000 Muslim Georgians live in Turkey. As a result of the increase of out-group marriages, first-language maintenance has been weakened amongst them. Georgian still seems to be widely used in the domestic domain, while Turkish is used in contacts with the outside world and for schooling. Nevertheless, younger generations are more assimilated into the main-stream community.

Non-Muslim linguistic groups

Apart from local populations of Armenians and Greeks, there are other Christian groups who were either deported from their homeland or came at their own will to Turkey. There are small groups of Estonians, Germans, Poles, Cossacks, Arameans and Christian Arabs. There are around 4000 Greeks mainly concentrated in Istanbul. Like the Greeks, the 20,000 *Ladinos* (Judea-Spanish) live mainly in Istanbul. Christian groups have their own schools and places of worship. The Greek Orthodox Church contributes to the strong linguistic and cultural maintenance of Greek people. In the same vein, the Armenian Apostolic Church promotes the linguistic and cultural development of Armenians. They have special schools, trusts for welfare and opportunities to use and print the Armenian language. Like Jews and Greeks, Armenians enjoy the privilege of an officially recognized minority status. As opposed to Armenians outside Turkey, Turkish-Armenians are more interested in peaceful co-existence with the Muslim majority in Turkey (Andrews, 1989).

Language maintenance and shift

As pointed out in the first section, Atatürk's principle of nationalism assumes that anyone who is a citizen of the Republic of Turkey is Turkish. According to the official discourse, this does not suggest any allusion to ethnic identity. Apart from the official view, the popular view in Turkey is actually rather realistic. Many people recognize and accept the ethnic and linguistic differences amongst them. Most of all, a sense of a common homeland and a common destiny unites all Armenians, Greeks, Kurds, Tatars, Turks and so on, irrespective of their ethnic or religious background. Ethnic differences are more prevalent among rural populations but much less so among urban populations. With the strong effect of Turkish media and educational institutions, the rate of assimilation to Turkish among all groups in urban areas is very high, with the exception of some southeastern towns, where Kurdish (mainly Kurmanji), Zaza and Arabic are the main languages of communication.

There are some factors that accelerate the pace of linguistic assimilation of various linguistic groups into the mainstream society. The main agent of assimilation is education. The principle of nationalism aims at linguistic absorption of all people into Turkish. This policy has been supported and promoted by the educational system. No language other than Turkish can be taught at schools or at cultural centers. Only Armenian, Greek and Hebrew are exceptions to this constitutional rule. Secondly, domestic migration from rural to urban areas speeds up the assimilation of younger generations of all linguistic groups. The rate and speed of linguistic assimilation in urban areas among all groups is much bigger than in rural areas. Mass media are other strong agents of linguistic absorption. All information and news is transmitted in Turkish. There are more than 30 national television stations, both private and public, and also local TV stations, which only broadcast in Turkish. Apart from domestic migration, education and media, military service is another agent of linguistic integration. In remote parts of the country, especially in the mountainous east and northeast, not everyone receives adequate schooling. Those who could not learn Turkish in schools are destined to do so during their military service when they are 20 years old. Every male citizen of Turkey is required to do the military service, and if someone who joins the army is illiterate, he receives literacy training in Turkish. There were special classes for this purpose, but because the rate of literacy has become much higher, these classes are not prevalent anymore. Finally, socio-economic upward mobility and job opportunities require a good command of Turkish. Families want a good education and good jobs for their children, and a good command of Turkish is essential to achieve that goal.

Due to the above-mentioned factors, most of the linguistic minority groups in Turkey integrated into the mainstream community, with the exception of some Kurdic speaking groups. Even though the Kurds, like the Circassians, Arabs or Laz, have an Islamic background, they partly avoided the linguistic shift. Oran (2000) has discussed the reasons why some Kurdic groups maintained their languages. According to Oran:

- Kurdic groups have always maintained their unique identities throughout history.
- They have mostly been concentrated in large numbers in the same region for centuries.
- Their integration into the economic structure of the country was not easy due to their geographic remoteness.
- Because of this geographic remoteness, they maintained a traditional, tribal and conservative way of life.
- As opposed to many other ethnic groups in Turkey, they are an indigenous group.

As a matter of fact, the number of speakers per language group, and the language use and choice patterns of these groups are not known. As long as there are no sophisticated sociolinguistic and ethnolinguistic investigations on language maintenance and shift patterns of linguistic groups in Turkey, not much can be said about these patterns. Turkish policies concerning linguistic groups are absorption-oriented. The *unitarian* or 'melting pot' approach as practised in some other countries is also the approach taken by Turkish policy makers. Like the concept and practice of *laicism*, the *unitarian* approach was also borrowed from France. Language policies, westernization, de-Ottomanism, de-Islamitism and all other concepts of shift from Islamic civilization to western civilization reflect the historical dilemma experienced by Turkish people. Atatürk not only embraced westernization and modernization of the nation against religious conservatism, but he also reformed all institutions in the country. In doing so, his models were Western European institutions. What he achieved in the early twenties is a 'revolution' for many foreign and Turkish historians but a 'tragedy' for many others. To be fair, however, Turkish reforms should be evaluated with respect to the circumstances and options available in the period immediately after the first World War.

Languages in education

'Mother tongue' education is mostly limited to Turkish teaching in Turkey. No other language can be taught as a mother tongue other than Armenian, Greek and Hebrew, as agreed in the Lausanne Treaty, see below. According to the Turkish Constitution (Chapter 3, Section 2, Article-42):

> No language other than Turkish shall be taught as a mother tongue to Turkish citizens at any institutions of training or education. Foreign languages to be taught in institutions of training and education and the rules to be followed by schools conducting training and education in a foreign language shall be determined by law. The provisions of international treaties are reserved.

As is clear from Article 42, the Turkish constitution does not allow mother tongue education in languages other than Turkish in public and private schools. However, education can be conducted in so-called modern foreign languages (such as English, French and German) in both public and private schools. Throughout the country, there are English, French and German medium schools, where the main subjects (like physical sciences, math and so on) are taught in these languages. It is generally claimed that education in these languages contributes to modernization and westernization in Turkey.

In order to understand the status of minority languages in Turkey, we need to take a look at the situation after the war of independence. The Treaty of Lausanne, signed between the Republic of Turkey and the allied forces (the British Empire, France, Italy, Japan, Greece, Romania and the Serb-Croat-Slovene State) on July 24, 1923, marks the beginning of the Turkish Republic. In this treaty, there was a special section (III) on the protection of minorities in the Republic of Turkey. Articles 38-44 regulate the rights of religious minorities in Turkey. In the Treaty of Lausanne, the classification of inhabitants of Turkey was made on the basis of religious conviction as 'Muslims' and 'non-Muslims'. The emphasis on religious identity in those times was so profound that population exchanges between Turkey and Greece were compelled not on the basis of ethnic or linguistic criteria but on the basis of religious criteria only. Greek-speaking Muslim populations were exchanged with Turkish-speaking Greek Orthodox and Turkish Christians. The allied forces, however, did not accept the population exchanges of Istanbul-Greeks with Salonica

Turks in Greece. About 900,000 Greek Orthodox Christians were ex-changed against 400,000 Muslims from Greece (Zürcher, 1995). In order to guarantee civic, religious, educational, commercial, judicial and political rights of Armenian, Greek and Jewish people living in Turkey, clear-cut and strict stipulations were made in the Treaty of Lausanne. The clause concerning language and education (Article 41, Section 1) reads as follows:

> As regards public instruction, the Turkish government will grant in those towns and districts, where a considerable proportion of non-Moslem nationals are resident, adequate facilities for ensuring that in the primary schools the instruction shall be given to the children of such Turkish nationals through the medium of their own language. This provision will not prevent the Turkish Government from making the teaching of the Turkish language obligatory in the said schools.

As a result of clauses 38-44, Christian and Jewish minorities in Turkey established their own schools and enjoyed a number of special rights bestowed by the Treaty of Lausanne. However, no minority groups other than those based on religious criteria, were mentioned in the Treaty of Lausanne. None of the Islamic groups such as the Bulgarian Pomaks, Circassians, Arabs, Kurds or Bosnians were mentioned in the Treaty because these groups were all considered to be Islamic. Even though the new Turkish Republic's official ideology was against religious allusions, the allied countries insisted that religious minorities' rights be stated explicitly in the Treaty of Lausanne. In order to promote national unity, successive Turkish governments have emphasized the equality of rights and responsibilities before the law of all inhabitants of the Turkish Republic, irrespective of ethnic, religious, or linguistic differences. Turkish official discourse claims that discriminating between citizens of a country on the basis of ethnic, religious or linguistic grounds is not in harmony with the principles of a Unitarian state structure. This type of reasoning is very similar to the French official discourse on the nation-state.

Conclusion

In line the themes of this Volume, demographic, sociolinguistic and educational perspectives on the Turkish context have been presented.

Ethnolinguistic and religious diversity had always been there during the Ottoman Empire, and they are still there at present. In spite of large diversity, the Ottomans achieved unity through their religious commitment to *oneness* (all Muslims belong to same large united whole). Mustafa Kemal Atatürk rejected the concepts of Ottomanism, Islamism, and their associated institutions. He strived to establish a democratic, westernized and modern industrial society after Western European countries. Atatürk's language reform needs to be evaluated in the historical context as presented above.

When we closely examine the linguistic policies in multicultural societies like Australia or Canada, it is easy to see that these countries' growth and wealth depend on the successful integration of various ethnolinguistic groups. These groups participate in the same culture of a modern-industrial society (Kalantzis *et al.*, 1989). Industrialism and globalization have created new norms and perspectives. Industrial and urban cultures put more emphasis on individual values than rural cultures do. Urban culture requires cultural and linguistic integration of individuals into the mainstream society, or good education, social mobility, goods and services will remain beyond reach. In rural areas, however, a more traditional cultural value system remains dominant. This in a way explains the language maintenance of some groups in rural areas of Turkey. Irrespective of generation, gender and social class, people in rural areas have more or less the same social and linguistic identification. In-group norms are stronger, and there are relatively strong sanctions for those group members who do not comply with these norms. However, the same ethnic groups behave differently in open industrialized contexts. Both traditional and modern values can co-exist in urban areas, where individuals can belong to multiple groups. In urban contexts, exogamous marriages among various ethnic groups are very common, and even the taboo of marrying someone with a different religious denomination is broken among younger generations. However, endogamous marriages are maintained in rural areas. The same endogamous marriage pattern is observed among Turkish immigrants in Western Europe. They display the same sociocultural characteristics as their counterparts in Turkey. In modernizing countries like Turkey, the push towards assimilation into the mainstream society comes more from industrialism. Moreover, linguistic minority groups that do not receive institutional support in education, media and political institutions have difficulties maintaining their linguistic and cultural values because most languages are limited to the domestic domain. Even in pluralist-multicultural societies like Australia and Canada, the dominant language serves as *lingua franca* in the culture of industrialism. Industrializing Turkey is no exception to this general rule. Turkish is the *lingua franca* in public life, but there are many other languages that are acquired and used as first or second languages.

Acknowledgements

I owe many thanks to Hendrik Boeschoten and Guus Extra for reading and making valuable comments on an earlier version of this chapter.

References

Akşin, S. (1988) *Türkiye Tarihi 3: Osmanlı devleti 1600-1908* [History of Turkey 3: The Ottoman State 1600-1908]. İstanbul: Cem Yayınevi.

Alexander, N. (1999) Multilingualism and education in the new South Africa. In G. Extra (ed.) *Over Babylon gesproken* (pp. 33-53). Tilburg: Babylon.

Andrews, P.A. (1989) *Ethnic groups in the Republic of Turkey*. Wiesbaden: Dr Ludwig Reihart Verlag.

Balım, Ç. (1996) Turkish as a symbol of survival and identity in Bulgaria and Turkey. In Y. Suleiman (ed.) *Language and identity in the Middle East and North Africa*. Surrey: Curzon Press.

Başkan, Ö. (1986) Turkish language reform. In R. Günsel and C.M. Kortepeter (eds.) *The transformation of Turkish culture: The Atatürk legacy*. Princeton, N.J.: The Kingston Press, Inc.

Boeschoten, H. (1997) The Turkish language reform forced into stagnation. In M. Clyne (ed.) *Undoing and redoing of corpus planning* (pp. 357-383). Berlin/New York: Mouton de Gruyter.

Dorleijn, M. (1996) *The decay of ergativity in Kurmanci*. Tilburg: Tilburg University Press.

Dündar, F. (1999) *Türkiye nüfus sayımlarında azınlıklar*. [Minorities in Turkish Censuses]. İstanbul: Doz Yayıncılık.

Gallagher, C.F. (1971) Language reform and social modernization in Turkey. In J. Rubin and B.H. Jernudd (eds) *Can language be planned?: Sociolinguistic theory and practice for developing nations* (pp. 159-178). Honolulu, Hawaii: University Press Hawaii.

Grimes, B.F. (ed.) (1996) *Ethnologue: Languages of the world*. (Internet edition: http://www.sil.org/ethnologue/).

Kalantzis, M., Cope, B. and Slade, D. (1989) *Minority languages and dominant culture: Issues of education, assessment and social equity*. London: Falmer Press.

Lewis, G. (1974) *Modern Turkey*. London: Ernest Benn.

Oran, B. (2000) *Küreselleşme ve azınlıklar* [Globalization and Minorities], 3rd edition. Ankara: Imaj Yayınevi.

Zürcher, E.J. (1995) *Turkey: A modern history.* London: Tauris.

Berber and Arabic in Morocco

JILALI SAÏB

The present chapter aims to provide an overview of the sociolinguistic status of Berber and Moroccan Arabic in Morocco. This restriction in the list of languages which constitute the linguistic repertoire of Moroccan speakers is motivated by the fact that Berber and Moroccan Arabic are the only varieties that are spoken natively, i.e. they are mother tongues and hence those of Moroccan immigrant minorities in Europe. Another motivation is that ongoing policy-making discussions and debates about issues raised by the question as to what is the most pedagogically and socio-psychologically suitable and efficient medium of instruction for the Moroccan educational system have all pitted standard French against standard Arabic. The latest evidence of this is provided by the Royal Commission on the Reform of Education (set up in 1998). They have not considered the use of the mother tongues (i.e. Berber, Arabic and Moroccan Arabic), which have remained until recently (1998) excluded from such discussions (cf. Saïb, 1995 [1991]; 1996 and the references therein cited).

The overview will be both retrospective and prospective, and it will be carried out within a language planning perspective. We will try to provide information about the Moroccan language profile and language policy, and to highlight the points of similarity and difference between Berber and Moroccan Arabic and indigenous regional minority languages in Europe, as concerns their distribution and vitality in the public domain. The insights to be gained from it may be of some interest and help for European academics and policy-makers, especially in view of the perspective that immigrant minority languages may be accorded the same status as that awarded to European regional minority languages. For reasons that will become apparent below, we feel that Berber and Moroccan Arabic should be awarded such a status.

The language situation in Morocco

The language situation in Morocco has been discussed in a number of studies on bilingualism (e.g. Abbassi, 1977; Boukous, 1979a/b; 1995; Gravel, 1979; Bentahila, 1983; Ennaji, 1991), on 'Arabization' (e.g. Hammoud, 1982; Grandguillaume, 1983; Elbiad, 1991; Moatassime, 1984; 1992) in Morocco, and on language loss and shift in both the Moroccan and immigrant contexts (El Aissati, 1996). The resulting language profiles and language ranking in terms of functions, status and prestige basically agree. Before we present the repertoire of languages available to Moroccans, some demographic facts are deemed necessary.

Demographic data

Ever since the independence of Morocco in 1956, figures for Arabs and Berbers have been conspicuously absent from the various censuses that were taken. The reason was clearly political: the ethnocentric pan-Arabist political establishment, which has been repeating *ad nauseam* that 'Morocco is an Arab country' and that 'all Moroccans are Arabs', obviously does not want Berbers to know how many of them there are, what their demographic weight is, for fear that they may demand corresponding political power. Even though, under some pressure from Human Rights organizations, the latest census questionnaire included a question on mother tongues added at the last minute, the results for this item have been withheld - it is said again for political reasons. Yet, in many predominantly Berber regions (e.g. Azilal, Beni Mellal), some anti-Berber census takers have deliberately ignored the question altogether and have not collected facts about people's mother tongues. Therefore, it has not been possible up to now to give actual figures on the Arab and Berber segments of the population. Those that were given (e.g. between 40% and 60% for the Berbers) were characterized as being just estimates. The same holds true for the figures quoted in the 13th Edition of *Ethnologue* (Grimes, 1996), upon which Berber scholars (e.g. Moatassime, cf. below) would have strong reservations.

According to the latest census (2 September 1994), the total population of Morocco is 26,073,717 inhabitants, of which 26,023,536 are Moroccans and 50,181 are non-nationals. Compared to the 1982 census, the population has increased by 5,654,162 people (or 27.7%). The number of urban dwellers has increased by 4,677,436 people (or 3.6%) over the number mentioned in the 1982 census. Thus, urbanization has reached 51.4% in 1994 (as opposed to 42.7% in 1982 and 35% in 1971). The relevance of the urbanization figures for our subject lies in the fact that this creates the conditions first for Berber-Moroccan Arabic bilingualism, and then for language shift from Berber to Arabic (cf. El Aissati, op. cit.; El Kirat, in progress).

By adding the figures provided by the *Centre d'Études et de Recherches Démographiques* for areas that are indisputably predominantly Berber-speaking, we believe that a good indication of the demographic weight of Berbers can be obtained. When applied to the numbers provided in the 1994 census, this operation has yielded a figure a little over 10 million (exactly 10,05549) or 38.6%. Of course, this is not counting the millions of Berbers who live in large cities that are predominantly Arabic-speaking (e.g. Casablanca, Rabat, Salé, Fès, Tangier and Tetouan) and the hundreds of thousands of emigrants who live abroad. Adding these numbers would most likely bring the percentage to the 60% estimate given by some Berber scholars who have examined this issue (e.g. Moatassime, 1992: 22). If this percentage turns out to be correct, this would explain why the Berber language has been minorized even though it is a majority language.

The language profile of Morocco

Morocco is a fairly simplex multilingual country with four languages which coexist with one another, albeit in some kind of competition. The linguistic repertoire available to Moroccan speakers comprises two kinds of languages: national languages and foreign ones. To the first kind belong two main typologically different languages: Berber, with its three macro-dialects (Tashelhiyt, Tamazight and Tarifiyt) (Saïb, 1991); Arabic, with its standard varieties (Classical Arabic and Modern Standard Arabic); and dialectical varieties (regional and ethnic). The second kind is made up of two former colonial languages, French and Spanish. More recently, English - which has no colonial links with Morocco - has been spreading rapidly (Sadiqi, 1990), owing to the international status that it attained in various fields (notably science, technology, media and business). As was stated in the introduction to this chapter, only two language varieties (Berber and Moroccan Arabic) are spoken natively, all the others are learned at school. Some geographically remote monolingual Berber areas excepted, Moroccan Arabic is spoken throughout the country because most Berbers (especially the men and the young) are bilingual.

In terms of geographical distribution, the Berber macro-dialects are used predominantly in specific regions of the country: Tashelhiyt in the south-west, Tamazight in the central and south-eastern parts, and Tarifiyt in the northern ones. However, transitional varieties exist between dialectical areas, which makes the passage from one area to a neighbouring one fairly smooth. They are thus regional lects or geolects. The linguistic differences between the Berber dialects have to do mostly with phonology and the lexicon (cf. Saîb, 1976; 1991; Boukous, 1985). The geographical distances between them and the lack of prolonged social interaction between their speakers have led to a low degree of mutual intelligibility between speakers belonging to extreme parts of the Berber domain (e.g. Tashelhiyt and Tarifiyt speakers). According to Laghouat (1995), a geographer, the three macro-dialects have a different weight linguistically. Basing himself on the census of 1982, he estimates that Tashelhiyt is used by 50% of the Berber population, Tamazight by 29% and Tarifiyt by 21%. It would be interesting to find out whether there have been any changes based on the figures of the 1994 census. Thus, taken singly, the Berber macro-dialects are minority regional 'lects', but when grouped together, they represent a numerically important linguistic community.

Moroccan Arabic also subdivides into varieties (cf. Abbassi, 1977; Boukous, 1979a/b): urban (Ar. *mdini*) varieties (originally spoken by people of Andalusian origin); rural (Ar. *rubi*) varieties (spoken by former bedouin tribes which have become sedentary); mountain (Ar. *jebli*) varieties (spoken by actually Arabized mountainous Berber tribes); bedouin (Ar. *badwi*) varieties (spoken by semi-nomads in the eastern highlands); and hassani (Ar. *hassani* or *ribi*) varieties. The geographical locations of the five types of varieties are old cities such as Fès, Rabat, Salé, Tangier and Tetouan (for the first type); the Atlantic plains and adjacent highlands (for the second type); the south-western and south-eastern slopes of the Rif mountains (for the third type); the lower Moulouya river basin and adjacent highlands in the north-east (for the fourth type); and the western Sahara (for the fifth type). Thus we have both ethnic (Andalusian) and regional varieties (the other varieties). As is the case for Berber, Moroccan Arabic varieties exhibit linguistic differences at the levels of phonology and the lexicon. However, if the recently introduced Hassani variety is not included, there is a fairly good level of mutual intelligibility between the dialects. Moreover, a sort of 'Common' Moroccan Arabic - a comprisal of the dialects of Fès, Meknès and Rabat - has emerged as a *lingua franca* for regional dialect speakers and even for Berber speakers belonging to different and geographically distant dialect areas. Not unlike Berber dialects, Moroccan Arabic dialects have different demographic weight: according to Laghouat (op. cit.), the users of the *rubi* dialect represent three quarters of the rural Arabic-speaking population, those of the *jebli* 17%, the *bedoui* 7% and the *hassani* 1% (based on the 1982 census figures). Unfortunately, no figures are given for the urban speakers; therefore the powerful Andalusians' number continues to be a mystery.

Sociolinguistic attributes and functions

As is the case in other multilingual contexts, the languages which make up the linguistic repertoire of Moroccans can be ranked on the basis of the sociolinguistic attributes assigned to them, explicitly or implicitly. These attributes, in turn, influence the social attitude towards them and determine the kind of social function that they are permitted to perform. An examination of these attributes and functions was conducted by Boukous (1979a/b; 1995), using the Stewart's 1968 model, built upon four parameters: standardization, vitality, historicity and autonomy. These parameters were proposed in order to find answers to a set of questions crucial for the establishment of language planning policies. According to Bell (1976), 'standardization' is concerned with the question of whether or not a language possesses an agreed set of codified norms accepted by the speech community and used in the formal teaching of the language. 'Vitality' addresses the question of whether or not the language possesses a living community of native speakers. 'Historicity' has to do with whether or not the language has grown up or grew up through use by some ethnic or social group. 'Autonomy' concerns the question of whether or not the language is accepted as being distinct from other languages or varieties (Bell, op. cit.).

The results of Boukous' application of Stewart's typological model to the national languages of Morocco (hence excluding French and Spanish) are as follows (Boukous, 1995: 28). Standard Arabic possesses standardization, historicity, autonomy and even vitality since, although it does not have native speakers, an enormous amount of literature is written in it. Moroccan Arabic does not have the attributes of standardization and autonomy, but does possess those of historicity and vitality. Berber possesses the attributes of historicity, autonomy and vitality, but not that of standardization. Even so, concerning the two varieties that are the focus of this chapter, he concludes that Moroccan Arabic is a 'geolect' of Arabic, and that Berber is a 'vernacular' in the sense of the Unesco definition (1953). This definition, it shall be recalled, characterizes a vernacular as 'a language which is the mother tongue of a group which is socially or politically dominated by another group speaking a different language'. Given the political and social systems that have prevailed in Morocco until very recently, we can only agree with Boukous' assessment.

In terms of sociolinguistic functions, it has been established that Standard Arabic fulfils that of the language of religious and public institutions, Moroccan Arabic that of a vernacular, and Berber that of a vernacular for intra-group communication and of medium for the support of Berber identity. Because Standard Arabic is a) the only national language that has benefited from centuries of codification; b) the language of the Holy Quran and a highly esteemed culture; and c) the official language of the Arab world, it is accorded a high status. As non-codified, non-liturgical and territorially confined lects, Moroccan Arabic and Berber could be assigned only a lower status than that attributed to Standard Arabic. However, we feel that this should not be used as an excuse to ban them from the educational system. Yet, this is exactly what was done, not because of Moroccan Arabic but because of Berber, a language which the politically dominant elite would like to ban (for an explanation, see next section). One surprising thing about these results, though, which militate in favour of the upgrading of the status of Berber, is that this latter variety fares better than Moroccan Arabic in terms of number of attributes.

The present status of Berber and Moroccan Arabic

The sociolinguistic status of Berber and Moroccan Arabic ought to have been determined on the basis of objective facts drawn from the language situation of Morocco presented above where: a) they are the only mother tongues; b) their combined demographic weight is close to 100%; c) they are the languages of communication in daily interpersonal exchanges; and d) they could have posed stiff competition for the two prestigious non-mother tongues and school languages, had they benefited from corpus planning and teaching. These latter languages are Standard Arabic, with its two varieties (see above) and the former colonial languages French and Spanish. As will be discussed below, this has not been the case. Status has been determined on purely ideological grounds (cf. e.g. Grandguillaume, 1983; Moatassime, 1992; Boukous, 1995).

The main point to be made about the accorded sociolinguistic status of Berber and Moroccan Arabic in independent Morocco is that it was the work of members of the pro-Arabization nationalist elite of the Istiqlal Party who, as officials of the first national government, gave themselves the absolute right to establish the language policy of the country. They simply viewed Berber and Moroccan Arabic as vernaculars to be used in non-formal domains (e.g. the home or the street). In other words, the two real mother tongue varieties were accorded, by this elite and their followers, a low status in the market of symbolic goods (*le marché des biens symboliques*, cf. Bourdieu, 1980; 1982, quoted in Boukous, 1995). Moreover, they have been subjected to a consciously planned process of minorization and excluded from the school domain. While Moroccan Arabic can be said to be represented in the educational system via its more prestigious relative (Standard Arabic), this can not be said for Berber. As has been incontrovertibly established, Berber is a Hamitic and not a Semitic language (as Arabic is), hence linguistically a completely different language altogether.

In absence of any legislative text spelling out the principles and criteria on the basis of which the official language policy in Morocco was - and still is - established, we can only view this status as being a *de facto* one. This is in striking contrast with the status accorded to Standard Arabic which is, *de iure*, the official language of the State (cf. the Constitution's preamble which, moreover, recognizes it as the sole 'national' language). This state of affairs begs the question as to how this surprising minorization of a numerically majority group of languages (see above) has come about? The answer to the above question comes directly from the language policy based on Arabization in Standard Arabic that was initiated by the Istiqlal-led first national government (1955-1956) and that was established on strictly political and ideological grounds (centred around Islam and the Nation), and not educational ones. The ideological grounds had to do with the following questions (cf. Grandguillaume, 1983: 37): the role that Standard Arabic is destined to play as a 'unifying agent', its role as 'guarantor' of national identity, and the relationship between language and the law *dans la mesure où la langue est toujours l'imposition d'une loi*. A number of arguments have been developed, which Boukous (1996: 76-77) grouped into four types: a) religious arguments based on the fact that Classical Arabic is the language in which the Holy Quran was revealed; b) historical arguments claiming that 'Arabic has been the language of the Moroccan State ever since the introduction of Islam into the country'; c) cultural arguments highlighting the role of Standard Arabic as the crucible for Arabo-Islamic linguistic and cultural heritage; and d) pan-Arabist ideological arguments emphasizing the function of Standard Arabic as *le ciment qui solidifie les liens entre les différentes régions de la Nation Arabe*. In fact, the very well-informed and sharp analyst Grandguillaume (1983: 35) goes as far as viewing the conflicts around the imposition of the language policy of Arabization as a class struggle.

Returning to the question as to what should have been done prior to the taking of that very important decision, it can be noted that no socio-linguistic survey was conducted to elicit the opinions of the Moroccan people concerning the language of instruction retained or to establish the bases upon which a language planning policy had to be devised. Yet, it was a decision that committed the educational future and career of generations. Such a survey would have revealed the exact number of literate people in standard Arabic, the number of Berber and dialectical Arabic speakers, and the logistical needs in terms of trained and operational staff and teaching materials. It would have led to devising a well thought out policy of Arabization and would have spared the nation the catastrophic consequences of the attempt by the first Istiqlalian minister of education to just implement a largely improvised and hastily devised policy of Arabization in the first grade of primary school (in 1956-1957). The periodical running of this kind of surveys later on would also have spared the nation the catastrophic scholastic results achieved by pupils (see below). These results have now been admitted by educational and non-educational officials, including some champions of total Arabization. Though it has gone through ups and downs, periods of acceleration and periods of stagnation, and has led to a dramatic lowering of educational standards, Arabization has been retained as the sole official language policy of the country. Its continuation comes from the fact that all the successful Royal Commissions set up to reform the Moroccan educational system were made up mainly of representatives of political parties among whom the staunch supporters of total Arabization have always held sway. The latest Royal Commission, set up in 1998, was no exception.

One thing that should have argued against considering Standard Arabic as the native language for Moroccans has to do with the results of its imposition as a language of instruction in Morocco. As has been amply documented, the results of the imposition of Arabization policy in the Moroccan educational system have been, by the educational authorities' own admission, quite dismal (cf. Jarousse & Mingat, 1992; Radi, 1995). In particular, the scholastic achievements of pupils in rural and mountain-ous areas, from which most Moroccan immigrants to Europe come, have been very low for quite some time. This has resulted in a high drop-out rate, especially for monolingual Berbers (cf. Saîb, 1995 [1991]); 1996; and the references therein cited), forced to undertake their schooling in two non-mother tongues, i.e. Standard Arabic and French. According to Radi (1995: 68) in 1983, of the total pupil population of primary school (5 grades), 54.6% passed, 32% repeated the year, and 13.4% dropped out altogether. In a World Bank commissioned report (1992), Jarousse and Mingat give the following figures: 63.8% of the school age population attended the first grade, and of these only 49.5% reached the fifth grade (figures for the school years 1987/1988 and 1989/1990), hence a survival rate of 77.6%. While some improvements in comparison with the pre-reform period before 1985 have been achieved, the drop-out rate (22.4%) is still quite high overall and in fact very high in rural areas. As for the success rate at the *baccalaureat* exam (end of high school), it was only 11.2% for the period investigated. By contrast, the children of the well-to-do socio-economic and political elites (including those of the champions of total Arabization) are made to escape this fate through attending foreign mission schools, e.g. *la mission culturelle française*. To crown all, the freshmen with 'Arabized' training in scientific institutions (Faculties of Sciences, Medical schools, Engineering schools, etc.), had to drop out and enroll in Faculties of Law or Letters, because they were unable to pursue their studies in French. This would not have happened if we had kept a balanced bilingual system of education. In fact, the results in the latest census (2 September 1994) for the question about knowledge of foreign languages show a clear preference for French-Arabic bilingualism among literate people.

To sum up, then, the low status of Berber and Moroccan Arabic has been - and continues to be to this date - determined by a policy of political, administrative and socio-economic dominance, exercised by the adherents to a pan-Arabist ideology among the political establishment, and led by the *Istiqlal* and *Union Socialiste de Forces Populaires* parties. This also follows logically from the fact that most of the first ideologues of the Istiqlal party were graduates of totally Arabized traditional schools or the 'free schools' (where Arabic was dominant), set up by the Nationalists. Standard Arabic having been chosen, by fiat, as the national and school language in 1956, and later on promoted as the sole official language of the country (cf. Constitution of 1962), no other national language variety - Berber nor Moroccan Arabic - was deemed worthy of any consideration, let alone official recognition and promotion. In fact a campaign of disparagement targeted Moroccan Arabic and Berber. The former was considered a 'corrupt version' of standard Arabic spoken by illiterates; the latter was thought to be a disturbing 'remnant of the past and a dangerous threat to national unity'. As we have seen above, the two mother tongues lack two (Moroccan Arabic) and one (Berber) socio-linguistic attributes, respectively. Drawing on a study by Laghaout (op. cit.), Boukous (1996: 74) quotes the following indicative figures for the degree of use of Moroccan Arabic, Berber and Standard Arabic: they are between 70 and 80%, between 45 and 55% and between 10 and 20%, respectively.

By contrast, Standard Arabic, which in Fergusonian terminology is a High Variety in all respects, was deemed the only language capable of unifying the country and providing it with an authentic Arab-Islamic identity marker, and replacing the colonial languages (French and Spanish), which were imposed, each in their respective zone of influence, as the languages of school and administration in Morocco. This stance has continued to be taken to this day by the Istiqlal party, the top leadership of which comes from the descendants of the ethnic Andalusian minority refugees living in Fès. These are known for their *salafism* (resuscitation of the glorious Islamic past with cautious acceptance of some aspects of modernism), their unquestioning adherence to the pan-Arabist ideology (notably that of the *baath* parties of Syria and Iraq), and their suspicion (if not hostility) towards Moroccans of non-Andalusian origin (notably Berbers, but also Arabs of Bedouin origin). The other political parties, with the exception of the *Mouvement National Populaire* and to a certain extent the *Parti du Progrès et du Socialisme*, have adopted the same stance as the Istiqlal Party as concerns Arabization in Standard Arabic. Moreover, they distinguished themselves for their silence and indifferent attitude concerning the promotion of Berber (to be at least the subject matter of a language course), a taboo subject until the Royal speech of 20 August 1994.

The future status of Berber and Moroccan Arabic

Given the fact that the past and current 'statuses' of Berber and Moroccan Arabic have been determined on strictly ideological grounds, and that the policy of Arabization, on the altar of which they were sacrificed, has failed, one can hope for a somewhat brighter future (hence a better status) for our two mother tongues. A number of incontrovertible demographic, sociolinguistic, psychological, and pedagogical arguments can be advanced for their promotion and, in the case of Berber, their inclusion in the educational system, at least as the subject of a language course (cf.

Saíb, 1995 [1991]; 1996, for the presentation and support of these arguments). They run contrary to the old language policy used up to now and the 'new-old' one recommended in the educational charter project worked out by the 1998 Royal Commission on Educational Reform. This charter largely ignores Moroccan Arabic, which could have been promoted at least as the language of informal education in terms of basic and functional literacy. Yet, this is what politically neutral Unesco experts suggested way back in 1953 (cf. Saíb, 1995 [1991]; 1996). As for Berber, it makes its teaching transitional and geared solely toward supporting a better learning of Standard Arabic, still the only national language of instruction. It is not aimed at maintaining and promoting Berber, the language of the group that Berber activists for linguistic rights call a 'minorized majority'. Moreover, it recommends that its teaching be: a) a regional affair and done in terms of individual dialects (each for the specific area where it is spoken); b) optional and not obligatory; and c) left at the discretion of regional and local school authorities. Be this as it may, there are a number of positive developments, some of which have come naturally owing to demographic and sociolinguistic pressures, that will keep Moroccan Arabic and Berber alive and well. We discuss them in turn.

One such development has come from the fact that Standard Arabic has not acquired any native speakers, and especially not from the children of the pan-Arabist champions of Arabization. This is in spite of 43 years of its imposition as the only national school language, billions of centimes spent in promoting it (*Institut d'Arabization* budgets, materials development, costs of seminars and conferences galore). As stated above, the children of the elite (among whom we find Istiqlalians) are made to escape the negative effects of the policy through having them attend French or Spanish foreign missions schools, or the American school, where the language of instruction is surely not Standard Arabic. It is clear, therefore, that Arabization is only for the populace, not for the elite.

Another development concerns the degree of use of the two mother tongues as language varieties for intra- and intergroup communication. It has increased because of: a) galloping demography; b) a high illiteracy rate (officially set at 65%); c) the low percentage of Standard Arabic users in all sociolinguistic domains (which Laghouat, op. cit., puts somewhere between 10 and 20%); and d) the awkwardness felt when using Standard Arabic in interpersonal communication. Moroccan Arabic, in particular, has invaded many domains of use. Thus, in spite of the government's requirement that Standard Arabic be made the language of official business communication, Moroccan Arabic and Berber are used in oral exchanges in many domains, such as administration, teaching, public lectures and speeches, the media, entertainment fields (theatre, cinema, video, music), banking and advertising. By and large, Standard Arabic is excluded from oral exchanges, either because it is not well mastered or because people feel that its use is pedantic. Moreover, this exclusion is helped by the emergence and development of a third variety, middle Arabic, linguistically lying between Moroccan Arabic and Standard Arabic. As observed by linguists (cf. Youssi, 1989), this variety of Arabic gets its phonology, morphology, and syntax from Moroccan Arabic, and a great deal of its learned lexicon from Standard Arabic. The educated elite, who are its users, prefer it to this latter variety. Our observations about the development of this middle variety make us think that, when full literacy is achieved, it will replace Moroccan Arabic. Meanwhile, it is helping it to thrive.

Though the two mother tongues are mostly oral, a respectable amount of literature has been created in them. The same applies to artistic productions, such as musical works and movies. Many Berber literary works have been published in Arabic, Tifinagh (the old Berber alphabet) and Latin scripts. Some Berber activists have engaged in translating international literary works and international declarations on human rights, such as charters and other documents. They have also produced works detailing the reasons as to why Berber should be recognized as the second national language, i.e. after Standard Arabic. Thus, the Berberist cultural movement's demands have to do with establishing social justice, equity, and equal linguistic and cultural rights, not the replacement of Standard Arabic by Berber. Over fifty registered Berber cultural associations concerned with the official recognition by the State of Berber as the second national language, and with its maintenance and promotion, exist in Morocco. A very informative doctoral dissertation (Aourid, 1999) was devoted to the cultural substratum in the protest movements in Morocco, with a focus on Islamic and Berber discourses. The latter can be found in a number of periodicals concerned with the promotion and maintenance of Berber which are published by these associations. However, due to lack of State financial support, which is accorded to the organs of political parties irrespective of their political leaning, some periodicals have stopped appearing. There is some hope that the projected governmental Media Charter will make up for this exclusion. In the domain of corpus language planning for Berber, a number of general and specialized grammars, dictionaries, and course books have been published in both

Latin and Arabic scripts. Their authors are, for the most part, academics. This is in addition to ongoing research in terms of e.g. dissertations and conference proceedings.

Concerning the teaching of Berber, a number of experimental schools have been created through the initiative of individuals or cultural associations. Examples of these are a school in Temara, two schools in Rabat, a school in Khemisset, and another one in Agadir. There are undoubtedly others. Both Moroccan Arabic and Berber are taught at the American Peace Corps and at a recently created independent Language Institute in Fès, run by an American. Moroccan Arabic has been the object of a course at the French Cultural Center for years. The last years have seen the teaching of Berber at the French _Lycée Descartes_ in Rabat, within the 'Home Language Teaching' scheme. Berber has also been taught within the Moroccan Dialectology course offered by the Archaeological Institute in Rabat for the last five years. Official sanction has been given to the teaching of Berber at the Al Akhawayn University. Both a language course and a literature course are given. The former started in 1999, the latter in 1998. The manual for Level 1 of the language course was asked to be written in Arabic script. However, a version in French is being prepared. Accompanying audio materials have also been created. Reliable sources (from the university and the Palace) have said that the new king has been shown the manual and that he liked the work. This augurs well for the long-awaited implementation of the late king's instructions concerning the teaching of Berber dialects, at least at the pre-school and primary levels (cf. Speech of 20 August 1994).

As Morocco is trying hard under international pressure to establish a Human Rights culture, the Berber activists have made of the maintenance and teaching of their language a Human Rights issue. The contemplated upgrading of the status of real Moroccan mother tongues by European Union countries will put the Moroccan authorities under a great deal of pressure to do likewise. This will help the cause of their defenders. This is in addition to sociolinguistic and pedagogical arguments for the use of mother tongues in education that can be found in the 1953 Unesco report and other subsequent studies (cf. Saïb, 1996, for a full discussion). In the Unesco report, we can read: 'It is axiomatic that the best medium for teaching a child is his mother tongue ... In particular, pupils should begin their schooling through the medium of the mother tongue, because they understand it best ... Educationally, they learn more quickly through it than through an unfamiliar linguistic medium'.

Conclusion

The main objective of this chapter was to present an overview of the sociolinguistic status of the 'minorized' and neglected mother tongues of Morocco, i.e. Berber and Moroccan Arabic. This low status was made to 'emigrate' to Europe due to Moroccan officials imposing Standard Arabic as a 'native language' in intergovernment conventions on the teaching of 'Home language and culture'. In these conventions, Standard Arabic was put forward by the officials as *the native language* of *all* Moroccans (sic), which has prevented the European countries from according Berber and Moroccan Arabic a proper status in their educational systems.

This chapter sought to demonstrate that the low status that Moroccan Arabic and Berber have was accorded to them on political and ideological grounds, and not sociolinguistic and pedagogical ones. Implicit in the discussion of issues in this chapter is the suggestion that the status in question ought to be accorded on the latter grounds. In this way we can ensure that language planning policy is determined by objective facts drawn from sociolinguistic realities of the country.

This is the lesson that can be drawn from what has been done in Morocco. The fact that, judging from the proposed Educational Charter of 1999, the ruling elite in this country has failed - deliberately and for reasons spelled out by Grandguillaume way back in the early eighties - to draw it, should not discourage nor prevent us from doing what would be scientifically and not politically correct. Future generations of Moroccan pupils (residents and immigrants) may stand the chance to benefit from this. The multilingual repertoire of Moroccans is a great resource, which should rationally be exploited to its fullest potential. Hopefully the upgrading of Berber and Moroccan Arabic in the European context of immigrant minority languages will lead to a similar upgrading in their country of origin.

References

Abbassi, A. (1977) *A sociolinguistic analysis of multilingualism in Morocco.* PhD dissertation, University of Texas at Austin

Aourid, H. (1999) *Le substrat culturel des mouvements de contestation au Maroc: Analyse du discours islamiste et amazighe.* Thèse de Doctorat, Université Mohamed V-Agdal.

Bell, R.T. (1976) *Sociolinguistics: goals, approaches and problems.* London: Batsford Ltd.

Appendices

Declaration of Oegstgeest (the Netherlands): moving away from a monolingual habitus

Approved on 30 January 2000 at the international conference on regional, minority and immigrant languages in multicultural Europe, convened by the European Cultural Foundation (established in Amsterdam)

Art. 1 Taking into account:
- The intrinsic relation between multiculturalism and multilingualism in Europe, as expressed in the vitality of regional, minority and immigrant languages.
- The (outdated) Directive 77.486 of the Council of the European Communities on the schooling of children of migrant workers (1977).
- The Charter on Regional or Minority Languages of the Council of Europe (1992).
- The Framework Convention on National Minorities of the Council of Europe (1995).
- The Universal Declaration of Linguistic Rights (1996).
- The current support program of the European Commission for measures to promote and safeguard regional or minority languages.
- The aims(*) of the European Year of Languages (2001), prepared by the Council of Europe.

Affirmative conventions and action programmes on regional, minority and immigrant languages within the context of multicultural Europe should be based on a non-exclusive acknowledgement of the existence of all of these languages as sources of linguistic diversity and cultural enrichment.

Art. 2 The development of new programmes for regional, minority and immigrant languages should further enhance and strengthen the positive developments of principles and action programmes as referred to in Article 1.

Art. 3   European, national, regional and local action programmes should
         be set up to upgrade the status of regional, minority and
         immigrant languages in public domains, in particular the
         domains of:
         • Education.
         • Audiovisual media and the written press.
         • Public libraries and information/Internet services.
         • Translation and interpretation services.
         • Books and translations.
         • Occupational requirements.

Art. 4   Statistics on language use and language abilities offer highly
         relevant evidence on the degree to which languages function as
         core values of cultures, and should be considered as long-term
         complements to nationality and/or birth-country based statistics
         on the multicultural composition of (school) populations.

Art. 5   Language statistics on multicultural (school) populations should
         be considered as important tools for language planning in
         general, for educational planning in the domains of the learning
         and teaching of languages, and for sociolinguistic research.

Art. 6   Education in regional, minority and immigrant languages should
         be offered, supervised, and evaluated as part of the regular
         curriculum in preschool, primary and secondary education.

Art. 7   The range of regional, minority and immigrant languages to be
         offered in preschool, primary and secondary education should be
         based on the demographic composition of the school population
         and the expressed desire of parents and pupils.

Art. 8   Both primary and secondary school reports should contain
         information on the pupil's proficiency in regional, minority and
         immigrant languages, thus demonstrating that progress in these
         languages is conceived as part of school success.

Art. 9   European, national, regional and local action programmes should
         be set up for regional, minority and immigrant languages with a
         focus on:

- The ·development of curricula, learning methods and evaluation tools.
- The initial and post-initial training of teachers.
- The cross-national exchange of methods, tests and teachers.

Art. 10 Information on the rationale and contents of the provisions mentioned under Articles 6 through 9 should be made available in the range of languages under Article 7.

Art. 11 European, national, regional and local research programs on regional, minority and immigrant languages should be promoted, in order to contribute to our awareness and understanding of language diversity in multicultural Europe. The following priorities should be considered for such research programmes:
- Municipal or larger-scale surveys on language use of multicultural school populations.
- Macro and micro studies on regional, minority and immigrant languages in education.
- The status of regional, minority and immigrant languages in other public domains.

Art. 12 This declaration should be made public and brought to the attention of those European, national, regional and local institutions and agencies that play an important role in the development of language policies.

(*) The European Year of Languages 2001 has three major aims:
- To increase awareness and appreciation among young people and adults, including parents, policy deciders and those responsible for language teaching, of the richness of Europe's linguistic heritage.
- To celebrate linguistic diversity and to promote it by motivating European citizens to develop plurilingualism, that is, to diversify their learning of languages including less widely used and taught languages, whilst also protecting and encouraging multilingualism in European societies.
- To encourage language learning on a lifelong basis, not only by creating awareness of its necessity, but also by providing sufficient information concerning ways and possibilities of learning, depending on regional and national situations and possibilities.

List of contributors and affiliations

ALEXANDER, Neville
PRAESA, University of Cape Town, South Africa
e-mail: nalexand@education.uct.ac.za

BAKKER, Peter
Institute for Linguistics, Åarhus University, Denmark
e-mail: linpb@hum.au.dk

BOYD, Sally
Department of Linguistics, University of Göteborg, Sweden
e-mail: sally@ling.gu.se

BROEDER, Peter
Babylon, Tilburg University, the Netherlands
e-mail: peter.broeder@kub.nl

BUSCH, Brigitta
Centre for Intercultural Studies, Klagenfurt University, Austria
e-mail: brigitta.busch@uni-klu.ac.at

CAUBET, Dominique
Institut National des Langues et Civilisations Orientales, Paris, France
e-mail: caubet@ext.jussieu.fr

CENOZ, Jasone
Department of English, University of the Basque Country,
Vitoria-Gasteiz, Spain
e-mail: fipceirj@vc.ehu.es

CHOUDHRY, Amitav
Linguistic Research Unit, Indian Statistical Institute, Calcutta, India
e-mail: chou@isical.ac.in

CLYNE, Michael
Department of Linguistics and Applied Linguistics, University of
Melbourne, Australia
e-mail: m.clyne@linguistics.unimelb.edu.au

EDWARDS, John
Department of Psychology, St. Francis Xavier University, Antigonish,
Canada
e-mail: jedwards@stfx.ca

EDWARDS, Vivian
Reading & Language Information Centre, University of Reading,
United Kingdom
e-mail: v.k.edwards@reading.ac.uk

EXTRA, Guus
Babylon, Tilburg University, the Netherlands
e-mail: guus.extra@kub.nl

GOGOLIN, Ingrid
Institut für Schulpädagogik, University of Hamburg, Germany
e-mial: gogolin@erzwiss.uni-hamburg.de

GORTER, Durk
Fryske Akademy, Leeuwarden, the Netherlands
e-mail: dgorter@fa.knaw.nl

HUSS, Leena
Centre for Multi-ethnic Research, Uppsala University, Sweden
e-mail: leena.huss@multietn.uu.se

LOPEZ GARCIA, Bernabé
Taller de Estudios Internacionales Mediterráneos,
Autonomous University of Madrid, Spain
e-mail: teim.uam@uam.es

MACÍAS, Reynaldo
University of California at Los Angeles, USA
e-mail: reynaldo@csrc.ucla.edu

MIJARES MOLINA, Laura
Taller de Estudios Internacionales Mediterráneos,
Autonomous University of Madrid, Spain
e-mail: laura.mijares@uam.es

ØSTERN, Anna
Department of Dramapedagogy, University of Jyväskylä, Finland
e-mail: alostern@edu.jyu.fi

OZOLINS, Uldis
Politics Department, La Trobe University, Bundoora, Australia
e-mail: u.ozolins@latrobe.edu.au

REICH, Hans
Institut für Interkulturelle Bildung, University of Koblenz-Landau,
Germany
e-mail: iku@uni-landau.de

RIEMERSMA, Alex
European Bureau for Lesser Used Languages, Leeuwarden,
the Netherlands
e-mail: berie.frysk@fryslan.nl

ROBERTSON, Boyd
Department of Gaelic, University of Strathclyde, Glasgow, Scotland
e-mail: a.g.b.robertson@strath.ac.uk

SAÍB, Jilali
Department of Enlgish, University Mohamed V, Rabat, Morocco
e-mail: jsaib@caramail.com

STEPHAN, Rüdiger
European Cultural Foundation, Amsterdam, the Netherlands
e-mail: rstephan@eurocult.org

VAN DER AVOIRD, Tim
Babylon, Tilburg University, the Netherlands
e-mail: tim.vdravoird@kub.nl

WILLIAMS, Colin
Department of Welsh, Cardiff University, United Kingdom
e-mail:	williamsch@cf.ac.uk

YAĞMUR, Kutlay
Babylon, Tilburg University, the Netherlands
e-mail:	k.yagmur@kub.nl

YTSMA, Jehannes
Fryske Akademy, Leeuwarden, the Netherlands
e-mail:	jytsma@fa.knaw.nl